WRITING

STEP BY STEP

Tenth Edition

Randy DeVillez

Moraine Valley Community College

KENDALL/HUNT PUBLISHING COMPANY
4050 Westmark Drive   Dubuque, Iowa 52002

Book Team

Chairman and Chief Executive Officer   Mark C. Falb
Vice President, Director of National Book Program   Alfred C. Grisanti
Editorial Development Manager   Georgia Botsford
Senior Developmental Editor   Angela Willenbring
Prepress Project Coordinator   Sheri Hosek
Senior Prepress Editor   Angela Shaffer
Permissions Editor   Colleen Zelinsky
Design Manager   Jodi Splinter
Designer   Suzanne Millius

Illustrations by Eric DeVillez
Cover photo by Eric DeVillez

For Sue

> classic love
>
> isn't it
> ironic
>
> that I
> so empty
> can fill you up
>
> that you
> so broken
> can make me whole
>
> coming together
> we prove again
> the paradox of love:
>
> > one plus one
> > is
> > one
>
> (1985)

For Beth and Eric:

Hi neighbors! Only you two could make an entire country move on your honeymoon. "Shark Attack!! Outta the water."

For Christine and Mike (& Pepper):

Thanks to you (& Robert) for carrying our junque. And for all those wonderful hugs, dinners, desserts, & good times.

For Rich and Valerie:

With you, whether it's Wal-Mart or Kiawah, life's a beach! "Mrs. Henning, I smell. . . ." Habana Cohiba, Jr.? "Oat Man!!"

For Stephanie, Brian, Miranda, and Sierra:

My Pi pizza, Cuban cigars, Sue @ The Field, pre-wedding moons, big-girl boas & Princess Angelina Ballerina. Oh, my!

To the memory of my friends and co-workers:

Alice Allen and Larry Keogh

To the memory of my friend and office mate:

Mike Goodstein. . . . if heaven exists, you have earned a new Vette every day of eternity. Run a tollbooth for me. . . .

"I have often thought how interesting a magazine paper might be written by an author who would—that is to say who could—detail, step-by-step, the processes by which any one of his compositions attained its ultimate point of completion."

Edgar Allan Poe
The Philosophy of Composition
Graham's Magazine (April, 1846)

Contents

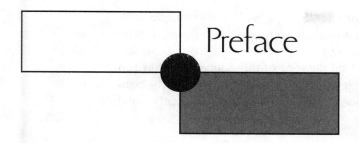

Preface

Before you read this book, I think you should know something about its writer:

For the past thirty years (give or take), I have had the yearly pleasure of reading the private thoughts and feelings of several hundred student writers. If you think about it, this is rather remarkable. While I was walking the other day, I focused on what this has meant in my life. I came to several conclusions:

For one, I have learned a great deal. I have learned of the practical (such as how to make dog stew, from a paper by one of my international students; I read it to our dog Troubles, but he seemed offended); I have learned of the difficult (such as how to say goodbye to an aging father that one student was reluctantly placing into hospice care); I have learned of the illegal and immoral (such as how to run a credit card scam or how to have an affair and not get caught); I have learned of the tragic (such as having to deal with the death of a friend killed by a drunk driver); I have learned of the most-private (such as how it feels to have an abortion and to have to live with the lingering feelings); I have learned of the humorous (such as why it is not a good idea to wear a two-piece swim suit on a jet ski); I have learned of the all-too-familiar (such as you think you know who your real friends are, but . . .); I have learned of the truly determined (such as even though I am blind, I am going to become an auto mechanic. Bart did become one, by the way).

Two, although these student authors have ranged from mid-teens to mid-eighties, they share a trait. If I can meet the challenge and help each find his or her voice, that voice has much to say. I am not Superman; I cannot always find the way to help the student find the way. But there are more victories than defeats. The role of midwife is interesting. I help and I coach and I nurture. When one of my students wins a prize in a writing contest, I feel true joy. When one of my students fails, I feel like a failure. When a student offers a handshake and a sincere thanks, I find that those cliches about the joys of teaching have become truths. Although my colleagues think me mad when I say it, I just love teaching writing, so much so in fact, that I have quit teaching most other courses. I derive much satisfaction from being a literary midwife.

Three, writing and the teaching of writing have an impact which goes beyond the class and the classroom. On one level, this is practical: if you can communicate more clearly you might end up with a better job or a higher grade or a bigger paycheck. On another level, it transcends the practical. Writing is thinking. It is a way of focusing, of reaching decisions, of making choices, of reaffirming values and beliefs, of rekindling one's own imaginative fires. This is education in the truest sense.

Before you read this book, I think you should know something about its approach:

In its basic approach to writing, this book is a traditional rhetoric. It is unique, however, because all of the examples for study (writing teachers call this "a models approach") are student-written; the writing has not been edited or altered. This book is also unique in its style. Most of the writing books I sort of read as a student were written by people who seemed to have no personality. My editors have graciously allowed me to be myself. Since I am more of a jeans and vest kind of guy, you'll not find the tone of this educational tome to be bow-tie and tweed-jacket, if you know what I mean. My textbook has frequently been referred to as either a student-friendly book or a book appreciated by most students—and some teachers. I take both to be compliments.

Each chapter presents clear steps (step-by-step, get it?!), directions, and explanations. There are also suggested topics and approaches. Tucked at the end of most chapters, you'll also find student examples, plan sheets, and evaluation forms for you and for a classmate.

Although designed primarily for classroom use, *Writing Step by Step* is a practical guide for any individual who wants to learn or review the basics of written communication.

The Tenth Edition

I trust that the following features of this new tenth edition will help you to improve your writing.

- New sample essays are included because I believe that students learn by studying and analyzing the work of other students.

- Examples of directed-audience writing help students avoid the dreaded "Burger-Weenie" syndrome. (See Chapter One.)

- Tearout sheets are included for self-evaluation and peer-evaluation.

- Brainstorming examples and invention strategies help to create subjects and topics.

- New illustrations are sprinkled throughout the book. (Thanks again to my son, Eric.) The illustrations in Chapter Two emphasize why "Close doesn't count" in communication.

- Chapter Sixteen reflects technological changes in research and documenting electronic sources.

- An index has been added.

This edition has an updated interior format to aid students in locating important features and concepts. The student examples are screened for easy identification as in past editions. Various icons have been added to the presentation of the content to highlight concepts with a similar theme.

 ASK YOURSELF . . . helpful hints to evaluate and plan a strategy for various writing components.

 SUGGESTIONS . . . provide tips to help improve writing skills.

 STRATEGIES . . . highlight methods for achieving writing goals.

 HEADS UP . . . alerts you to potentially troublesome areas in the writing process.

 CHECKLISTS . . . provide an opportunity to do a final analysis of your writing by double checking that the important elements of the writing assignment have been covered.

THUMBS UP . . . identifies the correct manner of presenting ideas.

 THUMBS DOWN . . . identifies the incorrect manner of presenting ideas.

 OUTLINE . . . indicates examples of outlining.

 CAVEAT . . . warnings regarding writing strategies.

FINAL NOTE . . . This year as I revised this text, I worked hard at improving my writing. I hope that you are ready to work on improving your writing. If you are ready, let's turn the page and begin. . . .

When he is surprised, he always screams out "Cowadunga!"

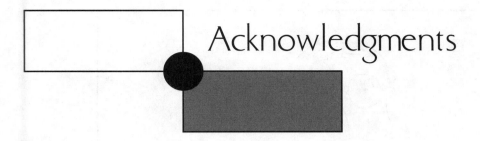

Acknowledgments

By the time a textbook has reached its tenth edition (this book, in fact, is older than most of the students I teach), its writer has become indebted to many persons in many ways.

At this moment, I feel somewhat like the Academy Award recipient who stumbles through names and then ends by saying, "I know I have probably forgotten people who are important." Therefore, I hesitate to begin a litany of names. However, there are thanks to be dispersed, folks to be granted gratitude.

I want to thank all of my colleagues, both part-time and full-time. You probably don't realize just how encouraging it truly is when you take the time to deliver a positive comment about a new edition or a new feature. These comments—usually delivered as we gather around the departmental coffee pot seeking a caffeine fix between classes—motivate me not to murder my editors whenever they mention the subject of a new edition (translation: give up another year of nights and weekends to rewrite this baby).

And speaking of editors—and the entire staff of Kendall/Hunt Publishing—we have been friends and family as well as business partners for a long time. (Honest! I didn't really mean that "murder" comment in the last paragraph. . . .) I sincerely thank you for the professional relationship we have shared over the years.

I want to thank all of my students for all of the lessons you have taught me; I especially want to thank those of you who have consented to the publication of your writing. I thank you for the gift of sharing your thoughts, feelings, and voices.

I want to thank my family. As one of my editors at K/H once said to me at lunch, "I know a lot of people smart enough to write a textbook. I just don't know many of them dumb enough to give up all their time to do it." He was, of course, a prophet. So, pretty please accept the dedication of this manuscript in place of the few letters I didn't have time to write, for the times I asked you to walk the dog when it was really my turn, and for the most-unforgivable offense of letting you talk to the answering machine (only once or twice, honest) instead of me when I was in the middle of typing one of the rare intelligent thoughts I've had in this lifetime. You are all loved.

Randy DeVillez
Grayslake, IL

My uncle feels me with joy.

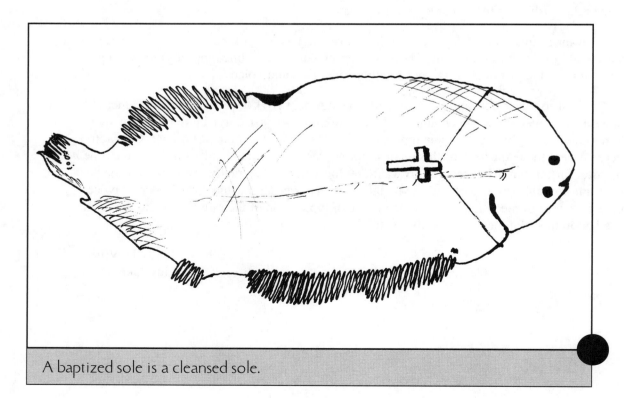

A baptized sole is a cleansed sole.

To the Student

PLEASE READ THIS—EVEN IF YOU DO NOT READ THE REST OF THE BOOK

Although it was over thirty years ago, I remember vividly my first day as a student in a college writing class. I was experiencing all kinds of sensations, but more than anything, I was worried about the teacher who was soon to enter the room. I wasn't sure why exactly, because my high school English teacher (God bless Mary DeWitz) had prepared me well. Part of my insecurity was attributable to the overall newness of the college experience. Part was attributable to the fact that I was sitting in a writing class. I felt vulnerable; I felt like I was going to be judged . . . not only on my control of verbs and commas and other grammatical gizmos, but also judged on my thoughts and feelings. Eventually, as I gained confidence, these insecurities vanished, but it was a long time before I felt comfortable with my writing teacher and with my writing.

Now, as a teacher of writing, I have a ritual I perform whenever I am about to meet a class for the first time. As I walk down the hall toward the classroom, I stop just before I reach the door. I close my eyes briefly (not wanting anyone to begin CPR or anything drastic), and I reflect upon that rainy August morning when I was a college freshman sitting on the other side of the lectern in Ms. Carlson's English 101 class. My act of recalling those memories shapes my approach to the teaching of writing. I don't ever want to forget how I felt that morning.

Once I enter the room and begin an overview of the course, I try to convince my students that I am like any other professional whose help they might seek. Similar to the allergist, the wedding coordinator, the veterinarian, the lawyer, or the auto technician, I am but another professional trying to offer assistance in some aspect of their lives. Rendering this assistance, however, is not always easy. Most people who hire a wedding coordinator or seek the help of a mechanic are very direct and honest about why they want that person's assistance. When seeking the help of a writing professional, however, lots of folks react differently. Instead of candidly saying, "I know what I want to say, but. . . ." or, "I'll be damned if I can figure out how to paragraph an essay except to just divide it into hunks to create the illusion of paragraphs . . . Help me now, quick!", most students try to "hide" their writing problems and anxieties. Imagine visiting the doctor because you're ill. When she enters the examining room, you are most-likely prepared with a litany of symptoms and complaints which you quickly rattle off. You want a quick diagnosis, a prescription, and a start toward better health. Most people don't go to the doctor and say, "I'm not going to tell you why I'm here. You figure it out, give me a prescription, and then I'll probably get better. If I don't, I'll blame you." Consider your attitude about writing; if you are honest with yourself—and your writing teacher—you might get a bigger return for your tuition.

Since you're reading this, I have also entered your life. Like your classroom teacher, I am a consultant, a coach, a drill instructor, a midwife (pick your favorite metaphor)—anything but the grammar cop, the G.P.A. assassin, the enemy. As students, you don't really hire us, and we don't guarantee you an A or three credit hours in exchange for your tuition. The good news is we are here to help you. The bad news is you will have some work to do. How much work depends upon your level of writing competency, your motivation, and your commitment to becoming a better writer.

Perhaps all this seems obvious to you, but after my thirty years in the teaching trenches, I am absolutely convinced that many students don't consciously perceive the student-professor relationship in this way. If you can engage in some honest self-evaluation and some appropriate attitude adjustment before beginning your writing course, you might gain more from it. The following suggestions are offered to help you in this process:

❖ **First:** I suggest—for the most part—you study the chapters in the order they appear. As this text's title implies, each chapter builds upon the concepts and skills developed in the previous chapters. Although many classes which study this text will not use all of the chapters, you probably will use most. (Keep in mind it is not illegal to read those chapters and sections which your professor chooses to omit.)

❖ **Second:** This text uses a models approach; that is, you are shown examples of writing which are models of what your teacher expects. All of the models in this textbook are student-authored, and they reflect the variety of human voices which the planet offers: long and short, formal and informal, tragic and humorous, serious and whimsical, etc. They are all presented to give you an idea of what is expected of you. Don't regard them as perfect models to mimic or copy. Like my writing (and yours) they are not perfect. Each example, however, represents a genuine attempt to communicate. I think they all succeed; I am proud of each entry.

❖ **Third:** Be yourself. Believe in yourself. Be willing to stretch yourself. Whether you have come to college as a mid-year high school graduate or after a forty year "vacation" from school, you are a person with thoughts and feelings to communicate. Inside of you are several voices waiting to be given the opportunity to present themselves on paper.

❖ **Fourth:** If you are given the opportunity, choose subject matter that is of interest to you. Chapter One presents some techniques for brainstorming and inventing. If "what to write about" is your biggest fear/problem, some of those techniques might make your life easier.

❖ **Fifth:** Ask for help when you need it. Don't wait. Asking for help means, "I want to improve; I care about what I am doing." Asking for help does not mean, "Geez, am I stupid, or what." Also, be selective in whose help you seek. Trained tutors and teachers and peer tutors will help you understand what you are struggling with. They lead you to answers instead of providing them. Friends, classmates, parents, main squeezes, and the family dog (if you are really desperate) don't always teach. They just make corrections. Some day, some time, that unlearned lesson will come back to haunt you when the person who corrected "things" for you is no longer around.

❖ **Sixth:** Writing is important. Many people with writing problems try to convince themselves otherwise, but most adults realize that the ability to communicate effectively is a necessity. Success in writing depends, in part, upon being able to spell, punctuate, and properly use grammar. If you need help with these skills, ask your teacher for assistance.

❖ **Seventh:** Learn to assess your strengths and weaknesses as a writer. Be realistic in the process and in the goals you set for improving your writing. Your instructor's job—in addition to teaching the mechanics and techniques of writing—is to give you a fair and honest evaluation of your writing skills. Your job is to take that feedback, study and analyze it, formulate some plans for the next assignment, and—if necessary—ask your instructor how to improve those areas where you are weak. This process is called learning how to write.

Once, at the end of a semester, a departing student told me that I had done a good job, but there was one area where my teaching needed improvement: every paper I evaluated and returned to him nagged him about the same problems. He said I should have used more variety in my comments! It never occurred to him that I "nagged" him each time because he repeated the same mistakes each time. That student taught me something about the process of writing (and giving feedback to students).

Now I require students to do a self-evaluation of each writing assignment they hand me to critique. I ask them to write what they perceive as the strengths and weaknesses of their performance. If it is a few weeks into the course, I ask them to "flashback" to the last assignment. What were its strong points? How were they carried over to this assignment? What were the weak points? (What caused the grade to go down?) How does this current assignment reflect an attempt to eliminate those weaknesses or problem areas? Then comes "the killer": What have you done to improve your writing skills in this assignment? Although this process of self-evaluation is not always accepted with great joy, my students admit that it does help them improve and learn. And, that, of course, is why most of us get up and go to college several days a week.

If you would like to try this evaluation process (joyfully, of course), you will find Self-Evaluation Sheets to assist you in evaluating your writing.

If you are feeling very ambitious and very brave, you will also find Peer-Evaluation Sheets which you might ask a classmate to fill out—after reading your writing. For many student writers, this is anxiety producing. Choose wisely. Look for that student—like yourself—who always attends, who turns papers in on time, owns a textbook with frayed pages, knows the teacher's name, and carries around the handbook which the teacher suggested, not required. If you see high-lighting in the textbook and paper clips in the grammar book, you know you've chosen the right peer critic. This critic, like your teacher, can help you understand the strong and weak points of your writing, the effectiveness of your communication skills.

❖ **Eighth:** Do not give up; don't expect everything to happen at once. Writing, like most other skills, takes time, effort, and work to develop. If you strive to improve, you will. Many people become discouraged when miracles don't occur overnight. Not all students will become A writers, but all students who try to improve will finish the course writing at a more-competent level than when they began the course.

Good luck with your course and with your writing!

My neighbor has one saab story after another it seems.

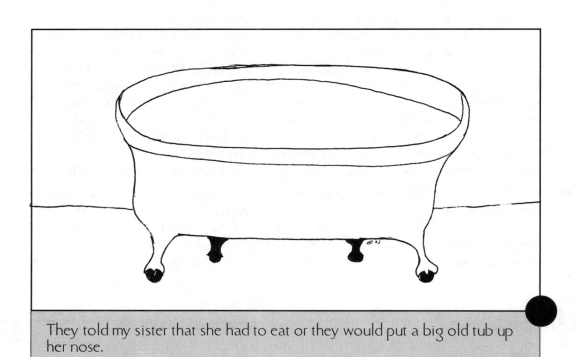

They told my sister that she had to eat or they would put a big old tub up her nose.

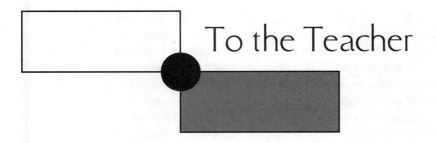

To the Teacher

AND ANYONE ELSE INTERESTED . . . .

As I begin the tenth edition of this text and my thirtieth plus year of teaching writing to college and university students, I cannot help becoming somewhat philosophical—attributable to several factors, I'm certain, including senility: becoming a grandfather, inhaling chalk dust for thirty years, having read hundreds of thousands of student papers, and having endured an existential number of meaningless committee meetings. From the depths of my shadow self, however, comes a nagging voice proclaiming, "Now that you are becoming senile, you have finally figured out what you are doing; pass it on." So, if you will indulge me while I wax poetic, I would like to share a few conclusions I have reached about this profession of ours:

❖ **One:** I think we (as teachers of writing) have to distinguish between what we do to help our students and what we do to help ourselves. To impress our peers, we have to use all the correct and latest jargon—even if we don't have a clue to its meaning. (Let me be the first to plead guilty.) We also have to adopt all the proper stances, approaches, and pedagogies: writing across the curriculum, writing as process, critical thinking, multi-cultural diversity, journaling, using the personal computer—you name it, in thirty years I've been there and done that—sometimes more than once! And to some extent, all of this is important and vital—but perhaps more so to us than to our students. I have observed that whether I am teaching the student who uses a half-chewed #2 pencil with no eraser or working with the student in one of our sparkling new IBM micro labs, my students learn best and most when I give them lots of practice, lots of room to experiment, and lots of honest and immediate feedback.

❖ **Two:** Feedback to students must be just that: honest. This is not always easy. It isn't easy in these student-as-consumer and grade-conscious times to look a student in the eyes and say, "I am sorry. I know you worked hard on this paper. I know you tried. But the grade still isn't where you and I would like for it to be— yet." It sometimes helps if the "bad news" comes in private conferences, especially if there is time to discuss *why* the grade is a reflection of the student's writing skills. This is why I feel it is so important to teach our students to analyze the strong and weak points of their writing; then they realize that they *earn* grades, that we don't *give* grades.

❖ **Three:** I feel it is important that we role model writing. We are not just teachers of writing; we are writers. All of us, of course, have the great American novel started in manuscript form. Every summer and Christmas break, we add a few more pages or chapters. Soon, however, we go back to teaching and the endless correcting of papers; eventually, the manuscript gets buried. But we don't stop writing. We write letters of recommendation. We write memos, budget reports, committee documents, etc. I feel we should share some of this writing with our students—not just the results, but the process. Last semester, for example, I was one of several people asked by one of the deans to evaluate some software that he would be purchasing for one of our computer labs. Since I teach my classes in that lab, his choice of software would have a major impact on my teaching, my students, and my day-to-day life at the college. I wrote a report which compared and contrasted the two software packages under consideration; I wanted my voice heard on this issue. (It was, by the way.) While this was occurring, I was also teaching my students about comparison-contrast. In class, I referred to my experience with the software purchase to illustrate how a writer uses comparison-contrast as a method of communicating to a specific audience (in this case, my boss). I asked my students to attempt something similar, to write a directed-audience essay using comparison-contrast; I encouraged them to write about an issue that was real, a decision they were attempting to make or justify, or a recommendation they were proposing to someone specific in their lives. Their papers reflected an understanding that comparison-contrast wasn't the end (or goal) of this process, but rather the means. Most of my students had something to say to someone. Their papers had a personal investment which transcended "doing homework." I feel it is our responsibility to tear down those imaginary barriers between the classroom and the "real" world, between ourselves as teachers and ourselves as writers who teach writing.

❖ **Four:** If you are reading this, you must be somewhat like me in terms of your philosophy about the teaching of writing (or you teach under a sadistic department chair who forced my book upon you). If we are soul mates, I'd like to tell you that I worry about our profession. Some of us have lost sight of what we are after. For me, the "bottom line" is pretty clear: I want my students to write better when we part company than when we met. I want them to have their own voice (not mine—which is probably good). I want them to have confidence in their writing. I want them to be competent and confident with the grammar, punctuation and mechanics of their own writing (not exercises in a workbook). I want them to say to another teacher or a boss or a prospective employer, "Let me at that keyboard; I can express myself, in a couple of different styles, in fact." I want them to enjoy writing as much as I do, as much as they did when they wrote on walls with crayons. I want them to write appropriate to audience and purpose. . . . Or as one of my students once said, "You know, this writing stuff doesn't have to be so difficult."

For the past three semesters, meeting individually with my students, I have been asking them non-scientific, open-ended questions (no grant money backing this undertaking), such as, "If you could tell your last writing teacher to change one thing about how you were taught, what would it be?" or, "What could your last writing teacher have done differently that would have helped you to become a better writer?".

Their answers impress me. Students want to be held accountable for grammatical errors, but they want explanations, not marginal hieroglyphics. They want freedom in choosing topics. They want to be given more writing (not one student has requested less writing). They want to be able to write in more than one voice or style. So on and so forth, but the reality is: students know. They know when they are being taught. They also know when they aren't.

Their answers also worried me. Here are some "writing guidelines" my students have been previously taught: All paragraphs must have nine sentences. You can only have twenty-five commas on a page. You can't use contractions. You cannot use any single-syllable words. Sentences must alternate between periodic and loose. All nouns must be preceded by three adjectives. (Wouldn't you love to read six pages of this kind of description?) I repeat: Some of us have lost sight of what we are after.

We have produced a generation (or more) of student writers who can write several pages without an **is** or a **was** or an **I** or a **you** or a contraction. They count their commas and their sentences, and they measure their margins. But they do not see themselves as having something to say. They lack confidence. They worry that they and their writing are boring. And they don't seem to be very interested in their own writing. . . . I sincerely believe that they can do better if we do better.

❖ **Five:** The computer is not going to be the savior of our students. Before you label me a Luddite, I am writing this (composing, in fact) on a computer. I require my students to use a computer. I do most of my teaching in a computer lab. In fact, I spend most of my on-campus time in a computer lab where I observe my own students and other teachers' students who use the lab to "write" their papers. Most students—the vast majority, in fact—use the computer as a typewriter; the backspace key is faster than waiting for the White Out to dry. And the spell check genie brings higher grades—if you use it. I see few students who compose at the keyboard (even though I show them how); most type from written copy. I also discover more errors in diction and usage since most students have become spell check dependent. Students who rely upon grammar checkers tend to have a "wooden" style. I think we need to teach our students word processing software; we also need to teach them to use and trust their own brains.

Well, I am wise enough to know there are as many philosophies of teaching writing as there are teachers of writing, that there are as many truths as there are truth sayers. So, I'll shut up now. Whatever your philosophy and/or approach to our craft, I wish you well, and I thank you for adopting (or at least teaching) my book. In closing, I share with you my fortune from yesterday's lunch at the Hunan Inn: "One learns most when teaching others." Amen.

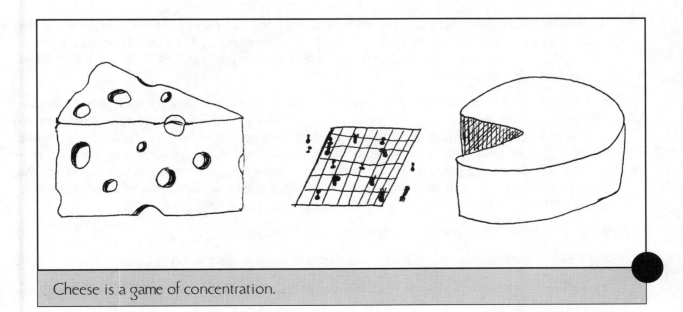

Cheese is a game of concentration.

A WORD ABOUT EVALUATION

SELF-EVALUATION:

Some suggestions and advice:

- Your perceptions of your writing and your writing process help your instructor understand you as a writer. By listing your perceived weaknesses, for example, you are not providing your instructor with ammunition to lower your grade. Nor are you bragging by listing your perceived strengths. Rather, if you listed structure as a strength, but you turned in a five page paper written in one huge paragraph, your instructor knows it is time for the two of you to chat about the concept of structure.

- Analyze your writing using the terminology of writing: unity, coherence, development, structure, organization, transition, etc. Use the language of the discipline.

- Think back: what was your grade on your previous writing assignment—and why? If you can't remember, look. Grades are a symbol of your writing skills and grammar skills. What did you do well? What did you need to improve? What concrete steps have you taken to improve?

- Think current: what makes this most-recent piece of writing a good effort for what was assigned?

PEER-EVALUATION:

Some suggestions and advice:

- You are evaluating another student's writing. You are **not** editing; you are **not** making corrections. Do **not** write on the paper. Rather, read it. Then write comments and suggestions on the peer-evaluation form. If you have questions about something you read, ask the writer.

- Analyze your peer's writing (as you did your own) using the terminology of writing.

- Be positive. Rather than writing, "Your punctuation stinks," phrase the comment, "I think maybe you need to check your commas."

- Review what the teacher assigned and make certain that the paper fits the requirements. If the assignment was to write a directed-audience persuasion paper, is that what the peer gave you to read? If not, he or she will be grateful to be told. (You might hold out for a free lunch if you save someone's grade!)

- Don't hesitate to compliment the writer. Here are some comments written on peer-evaluation forms currently on my desk: "Your opening story is a great hook. It really made me want to continue reading your paper," "This paper really made me think about this issue," "I really like how you expressed your ideas through the examples," and "I felt the same way when my parents said they were going to get divorced. Your essay gives me hope." Imagine you are the writer getting back your peer-evaluation form and reading these comments. What would they do to your desire to write?

- Tell the writer what makes him/her an effective communicator.

- What, in your opinion, might have been added, deleted, or done differently?

Although they might seem awkward—and definitely difficult at first—both types of evaluation will benefit you as a writer.

Getting Ready to Write

Let's be honest. For a lot of people, preliminaries are not important. To these people, spring training lacks the excitement of opening day; preseason just doesn't compare to the excitement generated between the coin toss and the opening kick-off of the home opener; qualifying laps and time-trials just don't pump up the adrenalin like the echoed sound of, "Gentlemen, start your engines!"; and in no way does watching the previews at the beginning of the video cassette focus the attention as does the beginning of the movie that the video store finally got in. . . .

Well, I've never been one of "those" people. I like preliminaries. (Sometimes, if you know what I mean, the previews are better than the movie.) In preliminaries I find meaning and enrichment. For example, my memories of pre-school are much more precious to me than my memories of graduate school. I enjoy Christmas shopping just as much as I do unwrapping presents; in some ways, the innocence and mystery of puppy love was much sweeter than the realities of married life (at this point, Sue, I would remind you of your numerous, dreamy eyed stories of Chip and Peter!); and I know with firm conviction that watching and coaching T-Ball was fun—Little League was hell.

So. Maybe Section One of this text does have something important to offer you. Best not skip it. Who knows? Might be something in Section One to make writing easier. Or maybe to make it more challenging. Who knows? So, tell me: what kind of person are you? How do you feel about preliminaries?

Our grandmother received her last rights.

I love giving friends warm barehugs.

The Process of Writing

OVERVIEW

One of the more-interesting students I've taught was a young man who was also a painter—a watercolorist. He appeared in my course, having twice been unsuccessful at passing introductory composition: to state it briefly, he was full of frustration and hollow of esteem. After I worked with him a few weeks, I discovered his "process of writing." He carefully took pen and paper (and a supply of White Out) and sat and stared at the paper for the longest time. Then, after a dozen or more sighs, he began to (slowly) move pen across paper. From time-to-time, he would place the pen aside and grab a handbook to check on punctuation or usage, or he would grab his dictionary to check spelling. Then, the book would close, the sighs would flow, and the pen would again begin to move. After an hour or so, he would hand me the "finished" product. As I observed his approach to writing, one I have seen frequently, I asked him about his area of expertise—watercolor.

I asked him if he would show me how he painted, and he agreed. As we entered the art room on campus, he began to explain how he came up with material to paint. He showed me sketches done in pencil. He showed me various "trial" paintings based on the sketches. He eventually showed me his portfolio and many of his finished paintings. He gave me one of his small watercolors, a treasure that I placed in my office.

Then we began to chat about the process he used to paint—and the process he used to write. He was bright and didn't waste time looking for the message I was trying to give him. When he applied the same process to writing as he did to painting, he found less frustration, better results, and more esteem. Somewhere, there is a message for you here, too.

My watercolorist discovered that writing was not just writing; it was, in fact, a *process* that involved writing. He found it easier to write when he began to record ideas that interested him and drew from his list when he needed subject matter. He also discovered it was easier and more time efficient to write a rough draft (and sometimes two) and then revise; this process took no more time than slowly writing one draft. He found he caught more of his mechanical errors if he put the "finished" product away and returned to it later for proofreading. The lesson he learned was an old one: writing doesn't really begin, and it doesn't really end. Writing is never truly finished nor is it ever perfect. Like any of the other processes we attempt over a lifetime, writing grows with us and our effort. Several years later, the student returned and asked for the watercolor he had given me. After starting art school, he had learned new techniques using salt added to the paints. What was a beautiful watercolor painting became even more beautiful after he "revised" it using his newly learned techniques.

If you approach writing from a process perspective, you, too, might find more success and less frustration. This first chapter really deals with your attitude about writing and your philosophy of writing; the skills and techniques of writing will come in later chapters. Whether you communicate with pen and paper, acrylics and canvas, or word processor and printer, the philosophy and process you use will determine your success as much as—if not more than—the skills and techniques you will learn in later chapters.

PART ONE: PRE-WRITING

PRE-WRITING: ATTITUDE

Pre-writing is what it sounds like: the process of getting ready to write, the process of choosing subject matter and focusing on what you want to say about that subject—and to whom and how. Much of the pre-writing process is mental. There are several steps that might help you focus and start writing.

- **First:** Give yourself "permission" to write about what you really want to write about. Although some teachers assign topics to their students, many do not. This means that you are free to communicate the ideas that you really want to share. This, of course, may not be easy for you to do. It is one of the most-difficult aspects of communication for many people—and writing *is* communication. Putting yourself down on paper is taking a risk that the person who reads what you write might not like what you write and/or how you write about it. Keep in mind that not everyone who reads what you write will like it. Also keep in mind that a lot of what you write and how you write it *will* gain acceptance. Generally speaking, if *you* don't like what you write, most readers won't either. When you write about what really interests you, however, you will have a stronger desire to do a better job. You will put forth greater effort, and you might find yourself engaging in bizarre acts: checking spelling a second time, consulting a handbook to check on comma placement, reading a rough draft to a friend to get a feel for audience reaction. In short, because your interest will be invested in the writing, you will more likely do a better job. To do this, you must free yourself of notions such as, "If I write about this, someone will think I am dumb or crazy or too sentimental." For example, I once had a male student hand me an excellent definition essay on the word *love*. When he handed me the paper he said, "I don't think you are going to like this one or give it a high grade." "Why?" I asked. "Because it is on love . . . and I am a guy," he replied. At the time, I was writing the draft of a book of love poetry. When I communicated that information to him, he smiled and walked off, content that his ideas would be accepted. I don't think he was seeking my permission to write about love; he was seeking his own. Somewhere or somehow, he got the idea that a man is not supposed to write on such a subject. I am glad that he gave himself permission to write about what was on his mind. He wrote an excellent essay which I had the pleasure to read.

- **Second:** Realize that writing—like any other skill—can have "on" and "off" days. It might bother you that your tennis game or your golf game is "off" on any given day, but that doesn't drive you to take up skeetshooting and never touch a tennis racket or a golf club again. In fact, a few days later, when your game is "on" again, you have no fear of that tennis racket or golf club. But have a bad day or two with the pencil or the computer, and it may mean FREEZE the next time you hear the dirty word *write*. Realize that there will be days when the desire is there but the words aren't. There also will be days when the words flow so freely they seem to be writing themselves. Because writing is such a personal and subjective act, it is affected by our moods, our health, and our environment. On any given day, give time to your writing; if it doesn't work out on that day, try the next day.

- **Third:** Pay attention to time and setting. These factors are significant but often overlooked. When do you do your best writing? Morning? Afternoon? Evening? Night? Middle of the night? Setting is also important. Where do you do your best writing? In your room? In the sun at the beach? At a table in the student lounge? On the family room floor? Certain other environmental factors are important in that they can help you or distract you: music, lighting, temperature, etc. For example, I work best in two places: (1) sitting at my desk surrounded by my favorite possessions and stereo speakers and (2) sitting near water, such as at a beach, a pool, a lake, or a river bank. Although I can write almost anywhere, these two locations seem most conducive. Locate a spot that seems to suit you and go there when you need to write.

- **Fourth:** Try to spend a few minutes writing every day. You don't have to write just to complete assignments for school or work. Writing, like other skills, generally "comes easier" when it is practiced regularly. Writing is communicating; as such, writing is one of the human urges that wants to be satisfied. Watch a young child. He or she will "write" before writing skills are truly developed. If the child is denied crayon and paper, any wall will do just fine. You, too, at one stage in your life felt this urge to put part of yourself on paper (or walls) for someone else to share. Why not get back in the habit? Then, when you "have" to write, the process of writing feels more comfortable and more natural. Writing is not just something that is connected with classrooms; it is a part of your life.

- **Fifth:** Give yourself an honest evaluation of your writing skills and of how important you think writing skills are to your college education, your career, and your life. Your writing teacher's job is to evaluate your writing honestly and objectively. Ask him or her for a list of the strengths and weaknesses in your writing. Study the list and understand each item on it; then, when you write, make an effort to play upon your strengths and to eliminate and/or correct your weaknesses. Obviously, writing requires work, attention, and discipline; it is not a mystical or magical process—at least for most of us. In addition to discussing writing skills with your writing teacher, discuss them with teachers of other courses, particularly those in your major field of study. What kind of writing skills should you have to get the degree or certificate or education that you desire? How much will you have to write to get the job you want? You can also gain insights into these requirements by reading the want ads in the Sunday paper or in the trade journals and magazines. What do the ads in your field say about writing or communication requirements? Another valuable source of information is someone who works in the field you hope to enter. Ask the traffic officer if he or she writes on the job. Or talk to the social worker about writing case studies. Or ask the research scientist about the role of writing in his or her job. Seek the truth about your writing skills and honestly evaluate how they may help (or hinder) you in your education and your career. If you learn that you have work to do (and all of us do), accept that knowledge and use your writing course to begin that task.

- **Sixth:** When writing for a particular assignment, focus on what you are trying to accomplish, on what your purpose is for writing. Believe it or not, your purpose is not (or should not be) to earn a good grade, to show the teacher you understand the assignment, or to "hop another hurdle in your race for a diploma." Remember: writing is a means to an end: communication. Let me illustrate. Several years ago, one of my students encountered a lot of frustration when writing a process paper (a "how to do something" paper). Her topic? Splitting the atom. Upon reading several pages of her drafts (and there were several), I asked her why a returning student in her 40's was writing on this topic. Her answer was predictable: atom splitting is a college topic, especially for an adult student. I risked a smile and a question: "Did you have any other topics in mind?" "Oh, yes," she replied. "I had a really good paper started—but I gave up on it." That paper was on how to pick out a good puppy to take home to love and spoil. After the student and I reviewed the "puppy" paper, we agreed that it really was good. As her teacher, I wanted her to demonstrate mastery of writing concepts and techniques. The paper that she really wanted to write revealed that mastery; the paper she was *just* writing lacked that mastery. Why? The atom paper was written not to say anything except "Look. I listened. I did my homework. *Give* me an A." The puppy paper was written for a purpose; it communicated ideas that were important to the writer. The paper was the means, not the end. It *earned* an A.

Pre-Writing: Audience Analysis
Avoiding the Burger-Weenie Syndrome

Analyze your audience before you begin to write. This is one of the most important steps to take before you begin the actual writing. Although many students think the audience is obvious, it is not. Your audience is almost never your teacher. Your teacher is your advisor, your critic, and your evaluator, but not your audience.

Your audience is that focal point you envision as you write. Although this may sound a bit confusing, it is a concept with which you are familiar. You are already accustomed to tailoring your writing to an audience. You know, for example, that the letter you write to your lover would be very different from the letter you write to the customer service representative of a company that sold you a bad product. The love letter would probably be very informal; it might be written in incomplete sentences, and paragraphing might be the farthest thing from your mind. Since you are most likely writing to convey deep feelings, your main interest will be in content and in language. The letter of complaint, on the other hand, would most likely be formal and very "correct." It would be to the point and well-written. The tone of the love letter would be warm and soft; the tone of the complaint letter might be firm, angry, demanding, and sarcastic. If you wrote a third letter—say to the director of personnel at a company where you would like to become employed—the writing would be different yet. Obviously the answer to "Who is my audience?" will affect your topic and how you work with that topic when you begin to write.

When it is up to you to determine the audience you're writing for, you are writing for what is referred to as a *general audience*. This is the term for that nondescript, faceless reader you envision when you write. Most teachers give this audience a visible form by telling their students to imagine they are writing for their classmates. Although this is much-less specific than saying to write for the president of the college, it does provide some insight into the nature of the audience with which you are to communicate. Many of the assignments you are given as a college student—especially in a writing course—are geared for a general audience. The following questions should assist you in analyzing the nature of your audience before you begin to write.

 ## ASK YOURSELF

1. If I am not writing for a specific audience, what are some of the characteristics and traits of the audience I am writing for?
2. How much—or how little—does this reader know about my topic?
3. What is the reader's attitude toward this subject?
4. Why does the reader feel this way?
5. What is my purpose in writing to this reader?
6. How much information do I need to present for this reader?
7. How can I be consistent in presenting this information to the reader in order to prevent a shift in my concept of who this reader is?

Keep in mind that not all of these questions are answerable, but those that are should assist you.

Another way to solve the audience analysis problem is to write directed-audience essays. That is, write to a very real, very specific audience. When writing directed-audience essays, you will usually have one of two types of audience.

- **One:** A very specific person or persons:
  - ❑ Dear Sierra
  - ❑ Dear Elvis
  - ❑ To the woman who broke my heart
  - ❑ A message for the neighbor who always parks in front of my drive

- **Two:** A very specific group of people who have something in common:
  - ❑ Dear potential steroid users
  - ❑ To all non-handicapped users of handicapped parking
  - ❑ To all rude people who hang up on me, your friendly phone solicitor, when I'm trying to make a living
  - ❑ Dear three-pack a day smokers who say the patch doesn't work
  - ❑ So. You're one of the fortunate about to buy those hard-to-get Bulls tickets from a scalper; be careful

When doing directed-audience writing, you have two methods for setting it up.

- **One:** Mention the audience, identify the audience in the opening section of your essay:
  - ❑ For all of you body builders who are tempted to use steroids, let me share with you some insights from one who learned the hard way
  - ❑ If you are just beginning a shrunken head collection, I would like to suggest that you limit your collecting—at first, anyway—to one or two very focused areas
  - ❑ If you are one of those persons who thinks that it can't happen to you, that the suffering from drinking and driving will happen only to someone else, allow me to share what happens when you receive a DUI. Take it from one who knows, your whole life changes

- **Two:** Write the essay in letter form; use an opening (greeting) and a closing. Mention the audience as you write; personalize it:
  - ❑ Dear football fanatic
  - ❑ Dear jock who thinks that cheerleading is not a sport
  - ❑ Dear two-timing scuz
  - ❑ Dear blue-eyed hunk who sits in front of me in psych
  - ❑ Dear child I saw being spanked in K-Mart by your mom

Directed-audience writing is real because it is based upon some idea or feeling which the writer truly wishes to communicate. Directed-audience writing removes writing from the realm of just doing homework and places it in the realm of communicating. The student writer is no longer writing to please his teacher but is writing to please himself or herself. Directed-audience writing also helps the writer avoid the most dreaded . . . **Burger-Weenie Syndrome.**

I know. I know. You want to know. Just what is this Burger-Weenie Syndrome? Well, for starters, if you are a student in my class, it is a ticket to failure. It means the student writes without a purpose, writes for no other reason than to turn in a paper which says he or she understood what I assigned. Allow me to share the genesis of the Burger-Weenie Syndrome.

Several years ago, on a beautiful spring day (these are scarce in Chicagoland), I was sitting at my roll-top desk reading student essays. I had the mini-blinds closed and had myself convinced it was snowing, raining, and sleeting. I reached for the top paper and glanced at the title page: Burgers and Weenies. I was apprehensive, but I turned the page and began to read. If you will allow me to paraphrase, this is how my middle-aged brain remembers the opening:

Burgers & Weenies

Burgers and weenies have much in common. For starters, they are both food. Meat, in fact. They are both meat. Round meat. But they are different kinds of round. Burgers are flat round and weenies are tubular round. This difference in roundness is important because of preparation. You can boil your weenie, but you can't boil your burger. It will fall apart. But you can fry both. . . .

At this point (and this is, I'll admit, as far as I read), I began to make primal noises and began to drool and foam into my rapidly graying beard. My wife called the paramedics who revived me. Once revived, I began to think.

"Why," I asked myself, "would a twenty-year-old college student write this? Why would a forty-five-year-old college professor read this? What, in fact, are we both doing?!?"

Well, I am prepared to answer those questions. I had asked the student to write a comparison-contrast paper. And that he did! However, he was writing for only one purpose: to prove to me he could write a comparison-contrast paper (ironically, he proved just the opposite). "Who," I ask, "was his reader? Who did he envision as his audience? What does this reader know or not know about burgers and weenies? Or about anything?!"

Now, let's not despair. In fact, let's take the topic of burgers and weenies and approach it from a directed-audience perspective. For example, let's write to the international student in our class who has only been in the United States for a few weeks. She is not accustomed to American food. We could write to her to inform her about the good ol' American junk foot diet of burgers and weenies. We could probably say something important to her about the topic. We would not, however, just be rambling on without purpose about burgers and weenies. Or, we could write a letter to the young latch-key kid who lives in the townhouse next to ours. We could inform him that there are a few easy ways to make an after-school snack using the microwave and the all-American burger and/or weenie. He doesn't have to eat peanut butter and jelly every day until his folks arrive home to prepare the evening meal. Again, we would be writing about the same topic (burgers and weenies), but the situation and the audience would lend the paper more meaning, more purpose.

 **Note:** A lack of meaning and purpose usually leads to a bad grade. In one of the pigeon holes of my roll-top desk are sheets of stickers, burger and weenie stickers to be precise. If I return a paper to one of my students and the paper sports one of these little culinary gems, I have told the student that the paper lacks purpose. That is to say, the student has succumbed to the dreaded Burger-Weenie Syndrome.

If you skim through the example, student-authored essays included in each chapter, you will find that many of them are written in directed-audience form: that is, the writer has addressed a specific person and written to communicate very specific feelings and/or ideas. If you have never written this way, you might want to try it. Generally, my students find that writing is much easier when it is done for a purpose. Most writing does not occur in "a vacuum." I don't think, for example, that you will one day find yourself employed as an accountant (diploma on the wall, neatly framed) and have your boss say, "Hey! Write a cause-effect memo for me." However, I can envision your boss saying, "You know, this year has seen real changes in capital gains laws. Put together a one-page mailer for our clients who might be affected by this and let them know how we can help them with the changes and some investment strategies." What your boss wants is communication. By focusing on your audience and purpose, you should find that communication easier.

An example might help convince you of how you can improve your writing by focusing your writing. Last summer two of my students wrote persuasion essays against cigarette smoking. One essay was good. The writer had a sound grasp of why smoking was a bad habit. She went through many of the arguments against smoking: it is bad for the smoker's health, it is expensive, it is not acceptable to some segments of society, etc. Her essay, however, lacked energy; it was like "all the other essays" against smoking. It was competent but lacked ooomph. The second essay was excellent. Even though in terms of content, this second essay paralleled the first, there was one critical difference: this student wrote her persuasion paper to her father who happened to be a lifelong heavy smoker. She wanted her father to stop smoking. Throughout her essay, she addressed him by name, told him of the dangers to his health, told him of her love for him and how she wanted him to be around for a great many more of her accomplishments. This essay had energy; it had ooomph. I believe this occurred because she had a specific purpose—a real purpose—for writing. She wrote that essay for herself and her father, not for me as her writing teacher.

I would urge you to avoid writing in a vacuum. Don't write to show your teacher you know how. Don't write to get a grade, to get a credit hour, to get a diploma, to get a job. Write because you are a person with thoughts and feelings to share with someone. Your voice matters.

PRE-WRITING: BRAINSTORMING AND INVENTING

Once other pre-writing steps are completed, you might want to focus on another area of the getting-ready-to-write process: brainstorming or inventing. Although this coming-up-with-subject-matter step should be the most-creative and exciting part of the composing process, unfortunately for many students, it is the most frustrating part. My experiences as a writing teacher convince me that this is the biggest problem for the majority of student writers. Time after time, students drop by my office or stop me after class to tell me that they have no ideas to write about.

When students say they can't find a topic for an assignment, what they are probably feeling is a lack of self-confidence. All college students have many ideas and interests, but many students hesitate to write about those interests because of imagined embarrassment or a lack of confidence. Oftentimes the person who can't find a topic is just too close, too involved, to see how interesting a paper dealing with his personal interests, experiences, ideas, etc., might be. There is an old saying that very aptly describes this condition: "You can't see the forest for the trees." Sometimes the writer is just "too close" to recognize a good topic. A true story illustrates this.

Several years ago, a student walked into my office and told me he was going to have to drop his writing class. He was unable to think of a topic for a process paper, and, since it was the first assignment, he knew he would never be able to come up with enough topics for the entire course. Besides, he told me, he couldn't write a process paper, because he didn't know how to do anything. I didn't believe him and tried to steer the conversation into a different direction to try to help him find a topic. (See, teachers *are* sneaky!)

As we talked, the student told me that if I happened to be going into the city over the weekend I should stop at a certain art gallery and view an exhibit of his photography. He continued telling me about his interest in photography, including how he had built his own darkroom and did his own developing and enlarging, how he came across the ideas for certain projects, that some of his photos had been published—all this from a person who five minutes earlier had told me he didn't know how to do anything! He just didn't think that anyone—especially his writing teacher—would find his interests worth reading about.

If at this point you are thinking, "Yes, but that guy is a photographer and I don't know how to do anything like that; what do I know?", maybe you need to examine your own self-confidence.

To gain the self-confidence that you need to choose topics, there are several steps you might want to follow. If you are given a topic by your instructor, a lot of the "What-do-I-write-about?" problem is eliminated. Even within these assigned restrictions, however, you will have some freedom. If the topic you are assigned is broad or general, such as *entertainment*, you are free to narrow or restrict it to suit your personal tastes. The broad subject of entertainment could be approached in any number of personal, specific ways, for example, how you began your hobby of collecting shrunken skulls, why highly paid entertainers should be required to give concerts to benefit charity, the effects of TV commercials on the American intellect, or a comparison-contrast of your favorite actress in two very different leading roles. Although a very general topic was assigned, you would have ample freedom to select an individual, specific topic. No teacher except a very masochistic one wants to read a hundred or more essays on the same specific topic.

If the assignment is open (that is, not assigned or "given"), then the subject matter has to come from you. You will have to "invent" your topic. Many students make the assumption that these "topics" are *outside* of themselves, that these topics are floating around the universe like shooting stars. If luck prevails, one of these stars shoots into the mind of the student writer: inspiration! In truth, the good topics—the genuine topics—are *inside* the student writer. He or she just has to "look" inside, select a topic, and begin writing some thoughts on paper. In the following section of this text, you will find some invention strategies (or methods) to help you "look inside" yourself to discover what topics are waiting to be born.

Strategies *for* Inventing *Writing Subjects*

1. Topics/student examples in the textbook
2. Pay attention to yourself
3. Topics/subjects that you have written about previously
4. Pay attention to the world around you
5. Free writing or spontaneous writing
6. Write a letter
7. Journaling
8. Networking
9. Branching or clustering
10. Dreams
11. Make and use your own list of favorite writing topics

1. **Topics in the textbook/student examples in the textbook.** Skimming the list of topics later in this chapter and at the end of each chapter might help you find your own topics. So, too, might skimming some of the many student examples in the chapters. You will soon discover that you are not so different from your peers or their topics. Perhaps some of those topics that you gave up on a short while ago might seem less "dumb" or "embarrassing" or "trivial." Students who wait for topics that have never been written about before have a very long wait ahead of them.

2. **Pay attention to yourself.** That's right! That's what you read: pay attention to yourself. The next time you find yourself daydreaming or interrupt your own doodling during your prof's lecture on the semicolon, ask yourself an important question: "Where was my mind just then?" "Has it been 'sidetracked' there before? Often?" If so, perhaps there is a topic lurking nearby. If your thoughts are preoccupied, in fact, writing might be useful in thinking through those thoughts. Last semester, one of my students found it hard to complete an assigned cause-effect paper. Every time she sat down to write, she found herself thinking about the possibility of having to put an elderly relative in a nursing home. After I suggested she explore the effects of such an action, she not only found the paper easier to write, she found her personal decision easier to make. You no doubt have heard the rumor that writing is thinking; if you pay attention to what you are thinking about, you might also find many topics to explore on paper.

3. **Topics/subjects that you have written about previously.** I'm not suggesting that you recycle old papers or old ideas. Rather, think back to the persuasive speech you gave last semester. Could you return to that topic, add to it the further thoughts you have had on the topic, enhance it with your newly acquired writing skills? If so, there is nothing academically dishonest about returning to a topic. This is the tenth edition of this textbook; as times and people change, so do ideas about certain subjects. Besides, different approaches to the same topic result in very different kinds of writing. One of my former students was a journalism major who wanted to be a sports reporter. Most of the papers he wrote for our class were on sports, but each was different. The process paper on how to choose a set of golf clubs was very different from the persuasion paper against the use of steroids in body building.

4. **Pay attention to the world around you.** Sometimes it is useful to skim the daily newspaper or a recent weekly news magazine. Listening to the radio and TV can also spark your imagination. I

know this contradicts current educational theory. TV, however, inspired one of my students to write a classic comparison-contrast essay on her father and Homer Simpson. Another student discovered that watching a fund-raising auction on PBS gave her a topic for persuasion: people who watch public television should contribute their share of programming costs. So, paying attention to the world can put you in touch with all kinds of ideas, from current events to creative concepts.

5. **Free writing or spontaneous writing.** All this means is grabbing pen and paper (or whatever media you prefer) and just writing. Write what comes to mind. Scribble thoughts. Doodle. Cross out. Turn the page. BUT keep writing. Don't be overly concerned with paragraphing or spelling or the mechanics of writing. Instead, concentrate on writing thoughts. Explore your mind. You—like many of my own students—might be surprised at how much writing you can do in a short period of time. If you would practice this technique several times a day for a few minutes, you would find that you become much more adept at transferring information from gray cells to paper.

Obviously, this technique is for freeing creativity and the thought processes. (It probably is not a good technique to use for your term paper for History 311.) After you complete an "exercise" of freewriting, reread it. Circle or underline any ideas that you feel you could expand upon the next time you do the exercise—or when you have a paper to write and "can't find a topic." Maybe the topic was found the last time you did some freewriting. This technique only takes a few minutes at a time; most of us can "waste" that amount of time in many less-productive ways. Some of my students tell me that they do freewriting between classes when they have a few minutes to pass.

Here is a sample of free writing one of my students did in class. After two minutes of free writing, she listed some topics which the exercise had helped her "invent."

9 o'clock   9 o'clock   9 o'clock
nine   nine   nine
nine lives .... why cats, not dogs ??
dog dogs my dog: Trix
good sleep buddy, walk buddy
good friend
He's good to me. Knows my mood for
the day: {sad
        happy
        blue 😟
        crabby

Always glad to see me.
Had him 9 (☺) years   (nine/nine/nine)
He's funny at times
　　　　- runs & slides on rugs on floor
　　　　- takes "sun baths" and follows the
　　sunlight as it moves across the floor
　　　　- goes to bed at night when he hears
　　　the theme music to end the
　　　10:00 news....
　　　　-lk —— TIME'S UP ——

Possible Topics:
①　Explore myth/folklore of the #9. What's
　　it mean?
②　Dog as true companion.
③　Funny things dogs do to entertain
　　us.
④　How do dogs sense what owners
　　are feeling?

Here is a second example of free writing, this one composed at the keyboard:

```
sun's out & I'm in
not fair
go to the fair: ferris wheel (fair-us wheel)
                roller coaster
                arcade games (not fair at all)
                long lines
                water rides (definitely wet rides)

go to the beach: fair-skinned
                 sun burn
                 scoping the scenery
                 watching the kids

go to the zoo: watch the animals
               dolphin show
               jerks who feed the animals
               watch the people
```

```
possible writing topics:

1. how smart are the engineers (I hope) who design
   roller coasters and other amusement park rides.
2. safety issues.
3. what are/how are arcade games set up as scams.
4. narrate the summer beach trip when I got severe
   sun burn and sun poisoning.
5. classify the kinds of people at the beach.
6. explain my love of dolphins.
7. describe some of the disgusting human behavior
   I've seen at the zoo.
```

6. **Write a letter.** Maybe it is a letter that you will mail. Tell your boss why you deserve a raise or a paid vacation. Tell your pastor what should be on the menu for next year's mother-daughter banquet. Tell your senator what's wrong with the last piece of legislation he or she helped pass. Maybe it is a letter that you will never (never!) mail. Tell the hunk you shared Bio station with last semester what you would really like to do with him on Tuesday afternoons. Tell your best friend what you really think of his latest attempt to grow a beard. Tell your neighbor your real impressions of his cute little puppy.

   As with any invention strategy, letters are to help you discover what is really going on inside your brain. Reread your letters. Are there any ideas that could be "pulled" and shaped into a well-developed paper? Maybe the letter to the hunk could inspire an essay on fantasies, or on daydreams, or on things we feel or think but never say. Maybe the letter to the friend could lead to an essay on honesty in friendships.

7. **Journaling.** I find that many of my students keep a journal or an idea diary. Almost every day they record ideas that cross their minds, situations they find themselves in, conversations they overhear, and/or events that shape their lives. Sometimes these entries can be good sources of ideas and topics for assigned papers. They can also provide important links in the process of self-discovery or self-awareness.

   Let me use one of my students as an example. One young man in my class had always been a journal writer. For a few weeks, he had been exploring some thoughts about what it meant to work as a bagger in a grocery store. This process began one day when a customer said something less than gracious about the intelligence it took to bag groceries. So, he worked through a few thoughts in his journal. A few weeks later, I asked the class he was in to write an extended definition essay. His topic and much of the writing were already done in his journal: "what is a bagger?". His essay and definition were excellent.

8. **Networking.** This is an exercise that many writing teachers show their students; it has a variety of names or labels but only one purpose: to help students find a topic. Networking is also very helpful to writers who need to narrow a topic. Writing on scrap paper, place at the top—and center—the general or broad topic you have "invented." Under it, list some of the more-specific subtopics. Choose one of those you have listed and write it in the center of the page. Break this subtopic into still more-specific subtopics. Continue this process until you have arrived at a narrow, specific topic that interests you and meets your needs for a particular assignment.

Here is a networking sample from one of my students:

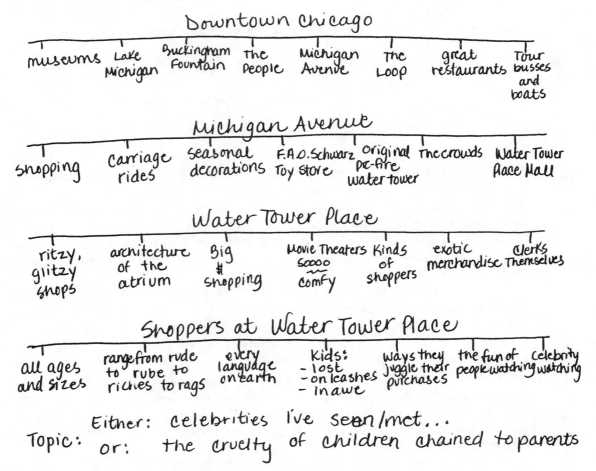

Downtown Chicago

museums　Lake Michigan　Buckingham Fountain　The People　Michigan Avenue　The Loop　great restaurants　Tour busses and boats

Michigan Avenue

shopping　Carriage rides　Seasonal decorations　F.A.O. Schwarz Toy store　Original pre-fire water tower　The crowds　Water Tower Place Mall

Water Tower Place

ritzy, glitzy shops　architecture of the atrium　Big # shopping　Movie Theaters soooo comfy　Kinds of shoppers　exotic merchandise　Clerks Themselves

Shoppers at Water Tower Place

all ages and sizes　range from rude to rude to riches to rags　every language on earth　Kids: - lost - on leashes - in awe　ways they juggle their purchases　the fun of people watching　celebrity watching

Topic:　Either: celebrities I've seen/met...
or: the cruelty of children chained to parents

The single minute spent by this student in narrowing her topic is far less than the amount of time most students spend trying to come up with an idea for a theme. When you have trouble selecting a topic, begin pushing the pencil across the paper. Simply thinking about the broad topic will more likely lead to frustration and wasted time. Writing your ideas will give you a sense of direction and purpose.

Most bug universities have orientation days.

Here is another example of networking for you to study:

Entertainment

| Sports | dancing | parties | malls | movies | flea markets |

flea markets

| indoor | outdoor | craft fairs | junk swaps | fund raisers |

outdoor flea markets

| fun way to spend nice day | types of sellers | types of buyers | merchandise / bargains | food-vendors |

Sellers themselves

| local | professional | low-lifes I don't trust | vagabonds | stories to tell | the hagglers |

Sellers' stories

| tales of cross-country adventures | "story" behind the wares (value, $) | "story" behind the wares (origin, history) | stories about their lives | eavesdropping on stories between sellers & buyers |

Topic: The next time you want to hear stories with human drama, go to a flea market -- not a movie theater.

9. Branching or clustering. This is another of those techniques that goes by several names. This strategy is very similar to networking, but with one major change. Clustering begins in the center of the page and grows outward, adding to ideas all around the center. Clustering permits free association of thoughts in many directions. Here is an example done by one of my students:

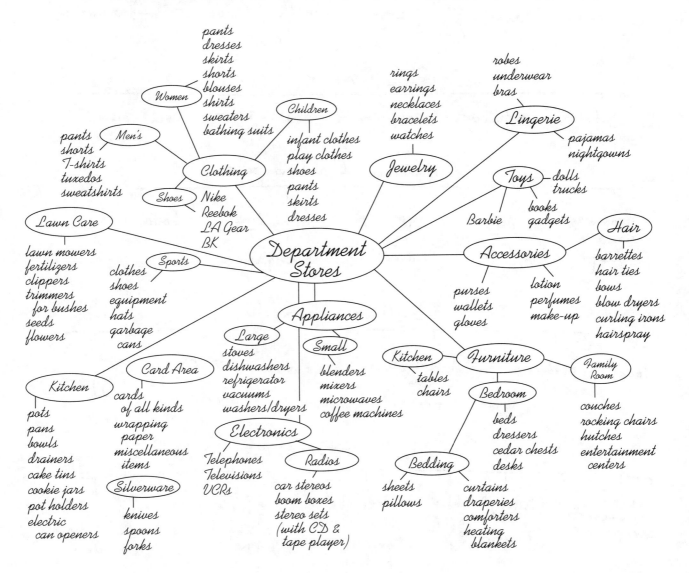

Melissa Decker

Because I have found many of my students like the clustering exercise, and because they tell me it helps them find topics, I have included other samples:

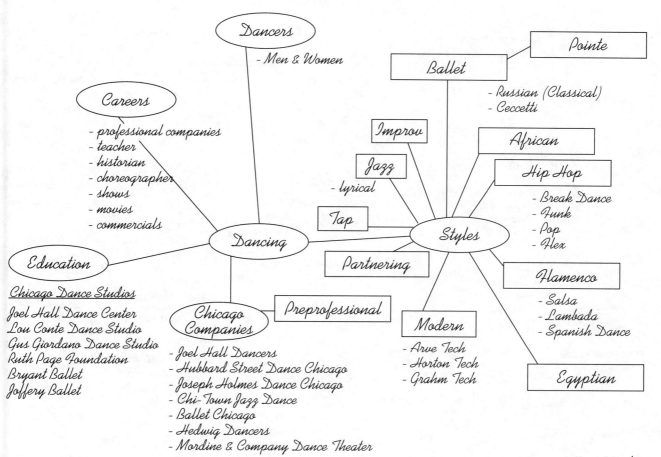

Dancers
- Men & Women

Ballet
Pointe
- Russian (Classical)
- Ceccetti

Improv

Jazz
- lyrical

African

Hip Hop
- Break Dance
- Funk
- Pop
- Flex

Careers
- professional companies
- teacher
- historian
- choreographer
- shows
- movies
- commercials

Tap

Styles

Partnering

Flamenco
- Salsa
- Lambada
- Spanish Dance

Dancing

Education

Chicago Dance Studios

Joel Hall Dance Center
Lou Conte Dance Studio
Gus Giordano Dance Studio
Ruth Page Foundation
Bryant Ballet
Joffery Ballet

Chicago Companies

Preprofessional

Modern
- Arve Tech
- Horton Tech
- Grahm Tech

Egyptian

- Joel Hall Dancers
- Hubbard Street Dance Chicago
- Joseph Holmes Dance Chicago
- Chi-Town Jazz Dance
- Ballet Chicago
- Hedwig Dancers
- Mordine & Company Dance Theater

Kari Nealis

To perform the Heimlick manure, locate the victim's diagram.

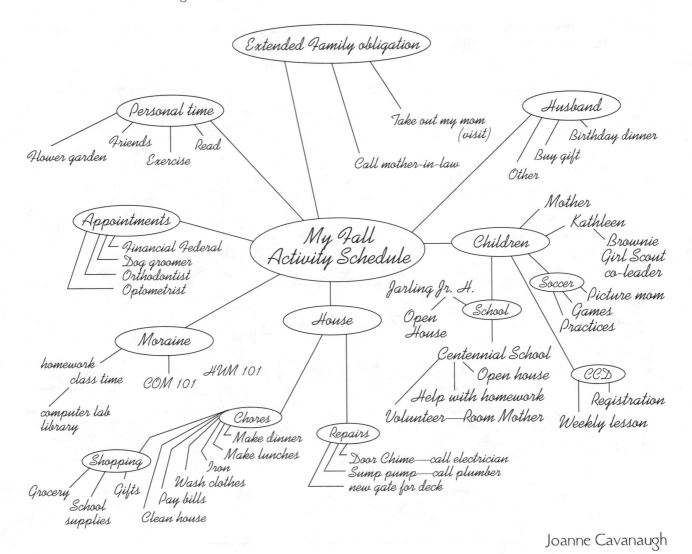

Joanne Cavanaugh

10. Dreams. If writing is nothing more than our thoughts and feelings on paper, then dreams—which are representations of our feelings—should be a valuable resource for inventing ideas for writing. Although this sometimes seems to surprise students—and even teachers—it shouldn't. Some of the world's most creative pieces of literature have had their roots in the dreams of their creators. Robert Louis Stevenson dreamt *Dr. Jekyll and Mr. Hyde,* poet and mystic William Blake dreamt much of his work, and Steven Spielburg dreamt much of the beloved *E. T.* Keep in mind that invention strategies are meant to put you in touch with where your thoughts and feelings are channeling your natural energies. Your dreams—including daydreams—do just that; they are a natural invention strategy—if you can tap them.

   One of my students wrote a very creative essay called *Running.* Its title and main idea (always being "on the run") were inspired by a series of dreams she had experienced prior to writing the essay. In her dreams, she had found herself always running but never catching up with her boyfriend, her teachers, her boss and co-workers, her parents, her friends, her softball coach, and—in one dream—even herself. These various dreams and dream images became the support for her paper. Like many of us she found herself always running to meet the expectations of everyone in her life—and she felt she was always running late, or slow, or out of synch. Her dreams—because she was able to use them—helped her invent a good topic and write a very insightful and interesting essay.

11. Make and use your own list of favorite writing topics. Someday when you have a few minutes to kill between classes or before the dentist attacks your wisdom teeth, jot down a few of the subjects that you always seem interested in. At the end of this section, you will find a space to record them so you won't forget them. When you are given an open assignment for a paper, look over your list of interests and choose one to write about. If you have difficulty in generating such a list (or "seeing the forest for the trees"), listen to your conversations or your thoughts. What makes you angry? happy? intrigued? amused? depressed? hopeful? hopeless? joyful? Write down these ideas for future use. As stated previously, you do have interests. Look for them.

■ my favorite topics are:

_____

_____

_____

_____

_____

_____

_____

_____

_____

_____

■ if all else fails: how I spent my _____ vacation

PRE-WRITING: DRAFTING AN OUTLINE

Some teachers view outlining as a part of the pre-writing process; some teachers do not (I find most students have the same value system). I think outlining can help a writer focus and order his thoughts and ideas and feelings. I therefore recommend the use of a "grocery list" outline or a "scratch" outline (see page 91). A scratch outline is just a "scratched out" list of ideas a writer wants to include (or thinks he or she might want to include) in a piece of writing. Like a grocery list, this type of outline serves as an organizer, a reminder. Here is a sample from one of my students:

Why I decided to attend a community college

- talked with friends away at college
- costs lots of bucks to go away
- not sure of major or career
- community college a lot cheaper
- closer to home
- I'm last to leave home
- father's retirement
- mom's illness
- I can help out & stuff at home
- really the two 'big' reasons (↑) but there was a third (less important)
- some of my old buddies staying here
- miss old friends

The above outline lists some of the ideas the student wants to include in the paragraph when he writes it. Although nothing holds him to what he has written, he has a good outline for his ideas. He has focused his thoughts to write an assigned paragraph.

For some teachers and students, this outline gives them enough direction to begin the actual writing process. Some teachers and writers, however, like to do more-involved outlines, more-formal outlines (see pages 93–96). Here is how the student shaped his ideas into a more-formal outline:

Why I decided to attend a community college

  I. Personal reasons were one factor
    A. I wanted to remain close to my family
    B. I am the last kid to "leave the nest"
    C. I want to give my parents some help
      1. My dad is near retirement age
      2. My mother has been quite ill

 II. Educational reasons were another factor
    A. I was not sure of a major
      1. Friends away at school told me of the expense of switching majors and trying courses
      2. Community colleges offer lots of classes to try and lots of majors

B. Community college seemed less expensive than a resident college
  1. Tuition is considerably less
  2. Commuting costs are less than costs for room and board

This second outline reveals that the student has put more organization and more development into the ideas he originally expressed in the scratch outline. When asked why he reversed the order of the two ideas when he went from scratch outline to formal outline, the student replied that since he wanted to emphasize his personal reasons he placed them first. He also decided to concentrate on the two primary reasons he listed in the scratch outline; he omitted the third. As you can tell from examining the student's formal outline, much of the composing process is completed before the writer transfers information from the formal outline to paragraph form.

By the time you have reached this stage in the writing process, you are through with the pre-writing part of the process and ready to get down to the serious business of part two: writing.

PART TWO: WRITING

WRITING: FIRST DRAFT

The first draft—as its name implies—is the writer's first attempt at putting the ideas and words into paragraph (or essay) form. The main concern should be the development of the ideas: that is, making sure that what needs to be said gets said. The writer should also pay attention to the structure and the organization, especially if writing an essay. Following the formal outline (if there is one) usually makes this job a little easier. Although the writer should always be mindful of sentence structure, punctuation, spelling, and grammar, these areas are not of primary importance in a rough or first draft. Here is the student's first draft of his paragraph:

> As a senior last year, one of my decisions to make was to decide between going to the local community college near the house or a university away. For sure, one thing, was that I wanted to remain near my family. Dad is close to retirement age. Mom hasn't been in good health. As I am the youngest in the family and the last to leave. I thought I could be of some use to them for awhile. I could help out. And repay them for all of their help. I had a second reason, also, I talked with a lot of my friends who had gone away to school from the year before me in school. They were paying a good sum of money, but were undecided about majors and so forth. They found it expensive to shop around for courses. Likewise I am similarly unsure of a major or a career. The community college seemed a wiser choice to shop around. The community college offers a great many areas of study and courses. The community college is also a lot less expensive. The tuition, for example, is about half. I do pay for commuting, but that is less than my friends were paying for room and board. These were the main things in my choosing a community college.

Although this paragraph in rough draft form contains a few awkward sentences and some ungrammatical sentences—and even some awkward choices of wording—it still does a good job of expressing the ideas. By following the formal outline, the student has written a draft which has good structure and good organization. The main idea of the paragraph also comes through clearly. The next job is to revise some of the sentence and wording problems (called *diction*) and prepare the second (and perhaps final) draft.

WRITING: SECOND DRAFT

To prepare his second draft of the paragraph, the student did two things. First, he revised the first draft by going over it with a pen and writing in some corrections he wanted to make. Second, when he was typing the second draft, he made still more changes. Here is his first draft again; this time it shows his handwritten changes:

~~As a senior~~ last year, *when I was a h.s. sr.,* ~~one of my decisions to make was to~~ decide *I d* ~~between going~~ to *go to* the local community college near ~~the~~ *my* house. ~~or a university away. For sure, one thing,~~ *One of the deciding factors* was that I wanted to remain near my family. Dad is close to retirement age, *and* Mom hasn't been in good health. ~~As~~ *Since* I am the youngest in the family and the last to leave. I thought I could be of ~~some use to them for awhile. I could~~ help *to them,* ~~out.~~ ~~And~~ repay them for all of their help. I had a second reason, also, I talked ~~with a lot of my friends~~ *also* *to people* who had gone away to school ~~from the year before me in school. They~~ *and* were paying a good sum of money, but were undecided about majors. ~~and so forth.~~ They found it expensive to shop around for courses. Likewise I am ~~similarly~~ unsure of a major or a career. The community college seemed a wiser ~~choice to shop around.~~ *place to sample courses.* The community college offers a great many areas of study and courses. The community college is also a lot less expensive. The tuition, for example, is about half. I do ~~pay for~~ *have* commuting, but that is less than my *expenses* friends were paying for room and board. *at a univ.* These were the main ~~things~~ *factors* in my ~~choosing a~~ *decision to attend* community college.

WRITING: THE FINAL DRAFT

Here is the student's final typed draft; as stated, it contains the handwritten corrections plus those corrections he made at the keyboard:

Last year, when I was a senior in high school, I decided to attend a community college near my home instead of going to a university. One of the factors in my decision was that I wanted to remain close to my family. I am the youngest in my family and the last child to leave. My father is near retirement and my mother is not in good health. I thought that I would repay them for all they have done for me by staying closer to home for another year or two and helping out. I also spoke with people I knew who were going away to school and paying a lot of money for their education, but they weren't sure what they wanted to do. I'm not sure of a career yet, either, and I felt that the local community college was a good place to take a sampling of courses and find out what I want to major in. This sampling of courses led me to another conclusion; it was a lot cheaper to attend the community college. The tuition was less than half that at a university, and, although I had to pay for commuting expenses, those costs were less than room and board at a university. My reasons might not be beneficial to everyone who is considering college, but they helped me make my decision.

Bob Poole

Revising is the process of rewriting what you have written in order to improve it. The extent of the revision depends upon the quality of what you have previously written. It might be necessary to revise only a sentence or two, or it might be necessary to rewrite a paragraph or a portion of a paragraph. Sometimes it is necessary to do extensive revising, even rewriting an entire essay or an entire section of a long essay. All this revision requires work and time. It also requires taking pride in the quality of the finished written product. This effort and pride are best summarized in an old adage: anyone can write, but only real writers rewrite. Only very rarely will you do your best job of writing the first time you sit down to place words and ideas on paper. Rather, writing is an ongoing process, a process of writing, reading to evaluate, and then rewriting based upon the evaluation. In truth, most writing is never finished; instead the writer reaches a point of personal satisfaction and accomplishment with it. (For example, I have written this paragraph two times; although a second rewrite might improve it, it will have to do until the next edition in a few years.)

As you learned in the last section, and as you will learn in the following chapters, writing begins with the pre-writing and the invention processes, including audience analysis. What usually follows is a series of steps: scratch outline, formal outline, first draft, second draft based upon evaluation of the first draft, polished copy, and evaluation of the final copy. Not all writers use all of these steps, of course, but the more methodical you are in writing and revising and proofreading, the more satisfied you will be with the final product (and its grade). You must find a method of writing that best suits your needs and talents. If you work on a computer or word processor, for example, your process of writing will be very different from the process of a person who types or who writes in longhand using fountain pen and tablet.

PART THREE: POST-WRITING

 ## POST-WRITING: PROOFREADING

One of the most-important steps in writing is proofreading. It is also one of the most-ignored aspects of writing, especially student writing. Many times students and I sit in my office and review their writing. Frequently a student will look at mistakes and say, "I can't believe I did that!" What the student really is saying is, "I should have caught that error before I handed this in for grading." Sometimes the mistakes constitute the difference between an A and a B, between passing and failing. Proofreading can make the difference between finishing a writing assignment and finishing a writing assignment with pride. I strongly suggest that you take the time to proofread anything you write, be it a sentence, a paragraph, or an essay.

Naturally, my first suggestion is that you do take the time to proofread. Secondly, almost too obvious to mention, is make sure you do it at the correct time, or more correctly, at the time best for you.

Too many writers do their proofreading immediately after they finish writing or recopying. This makes it difficult to proofread accurately because of fatigue, a desire to "get it over with," and a familiarity with the writing—perhaps including some memorization. This results in a reading of what the writer *thinks* he has written—not what he *has* written. Sometimes there is a difference.

At the other extreme is the student who waits until the last minute and skims over the paper while slowly walking toward the instructor. Any mistakes discovered at this point are probably a lost cause.

Somewhere between these two extremes is a better time. I always suggest a "cooling off" period between the writing and rewriting and the proofreading. A day or two will create a certain distance between the writer and what he has written. This distance will help the writer be more objective; it especially will reduce the memory of the writing and permit a more accurate reading of what actually appears on paper.

Proofreading will require more than one reading. Maybe one reading is necessary to check the organization and to check the content to insure that all ideas have been structured effectively, explained fully, and expressed clearly. A second reading might be used to concentrate on the style, the sound, the smoothness. A third reading might be used to look over the mechanical aspects of the writing—grammar, spelling, punctuation, sentence structure, etc. Needless to say, trying to find mistakes in all of these areas in one reading would be difficult.

How, when, where, why, whether you proofread—the choices are yours. You'll have to decide upon a method which works for you. I recommend writing at the top of the first page a list of mistakes you know you have a tendency to make. Then use that as a checklist for errors to avoid. Most writers tend to repeat the same types of errors; even as writers, we are creatures of habit.

Another suggestion is to begin proofreading at the end of your essay, working your way to the beginning of the essay by reading one sentence at a time. This method forces you to concentrate on each individual sentence; it enables you to criticize the sentence, its content, its style, and its grammar. Unfortunately, it won't help you assess the content of entire paragraphs or of the entire essay; that will require a beginning-to-end reading.

I suggest that you proofread in a quiet area; the silence naturally helps you to concentrate. Try to read slowly and aloud, forcing your eyes, mouth, and ears to work together. Listen for clear, precise sentences; listen and look for pauses and for correct and incorrect sentences; try to listen to the style of your writing, including your favorite but too-often-used words, phrases, and sentence patterns. Accurate proofreading is work; it requires patience, practice, discipline, and concentration. None of these is an easy trait to master. Just remember, your grade might be at stake!

There is probably no such thing as perfect writing. However, anyone who writes can take the time to rewrite what he writes in order to make it as good as possible. Years ago, it was a popular notion that a writer sat down, allowed the pen to kiss the paper, and due to some type of chemistry, words flowed from the writer's brain, through the arm, out the pen's tip to reside on paper. Nothing else needed doing, especially proofreading or polishing. Of course, it took a "special" individual to perform this task; this excused the common person from being a good writer.

Well, most of us will probably never experience this type of intellectual chemistry, and most of us will never write "the great American novel," but then we aren't really expected to either. The courses we take and the careers we choose will require that we write clearly and express ourselves well in order to communicate with our readers. An important part of that communication process is proofreading.

Proofreading (similar to revising) is much easier when the writer works using a computer. Moving or changing words or sentences, deleting phrases, correcting punctuation errors, correcting spelling, or even adding a brilliant thought or two—all of these changes are relatively simple when using a computer. I used to accuse students of not wanting to find errors because discovery led to correction—which meant work! On the computer, such work can almost seem like play; poor spellers, for example, smile when they watch a spell check system "magically" erase the thought of red circles all over a completed essay! If you have never written at the computer, you should try it. You might rediscover some of the joy that left your writing process when you abandoned walls and crayons.

PROOFREADING: A CHECKLIST

Most of the writing concepts mentioned in the following checklist appear in various chapters throughout the text. The most important information is assembled here for you to use to proofread any writing assignments you'll be doing.

PROOFREADING CHECKLIST

✓ If required, the coversheet should include title, name, date, course, section number, instructor's name, and specific assignment. Additional information and a specific format might be required. Check with the instructor or with the college's style manual.

✓ The introduction should contain a thesis statement announcing the topic, narrowing the topic, and perhaps explaining what points will be covered and in what order. Try to interest the reader.

✓ Body paragraphs should be unified and coherent and sufficiently developed to communicate the limiting idea of the topic sentence. Avoid writing paragraphs that are "choppy" or too lengthy.

✓ The conclusion should call attention to itself as the conclusion of the essay, as the final statement or summarization of the thesis. Be certain it is coherent and consistent with the overall tone and style of the essay.

✓ Check the coherence, unity, and development of the entire essay. Be certain that you have not strayed from the original thesis and that you have presented the information clearly and in sufficient depth.

✓ Check the essay for errors in the mechanical aspects of writing: grammar, spelling, punctuation, sentence structure, etc. Make a list of punctuation errors or spelling errors that you have a tendency to make. Use your list to "weed out" these errors.

✓ If you have borrowed ideas, words, sentences, or paragraphs from another person, writer, book, etc., you must include documentation. Failure to do so is plagiarism, a serious moral and legal offense.

✓ Make certain that you have not overlooked any obvious requirements dictated by common sense or by your instructor: your name, all pages included and in proper order, avoiding chartreuse ink on violet paper, etc. Individual instructors, departments, and colleges may have different requirements concerning type of paper, typing, ink, margins, font size, etc. When in doubt, ask.

POST-WRITING: EVALUATION

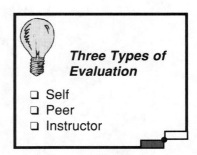

Three Types of Evaluation

❑ Self
❑ Peer
❑ Instructor

The process of evaluation occurs in three ways. **First** is *self-evaluation*. That is, before you pronounce your work finished and ready for submission to the instructor, evaluate your performance. Think back to the last graded paper returned to you by that instructor. What were its strong points? How have you worked to incorporate those strong points into this newest piece of writing? For example, if your teacher told you that you were quite good at detailing, how have you tried to add that same level of detailing (or even more, if appropriate) to the current assignment? Then, do the same with the weaknesses. What was weak in your last effort? What have you done to correct those weaknesses in the current assignment? Be realistic if it is a grammar or punctuation problem. Reducing the number of errors each time is more realistic than shooting for perfection. To assist you in this self-evaluation process, you will find sheets at the end of each chapter that requires you to write.

Second is *peer-evaluation*. Search your writing class for a warm smile. Behind it is probably a person like yourself who inwardly trembles at the thought of having another student read his/her writing. Once you get by the anxiety, however, you will find that it helps to have another person give you feedback about your communication skills. If you choose to work with the same peer tutor for the duration of the course (I recommend this), that person will also become familiar with your strong and weak points and become a helpful, trusted advisor. That person might even become your friend. To assist in this process of peer-evaluation, you will find sheets at the end of each chapter that asks you to write.

Third is *instructor-evaluation*. Meet with your instructor to review his or her comments. Before the meeting, do your work. Go over the paper and try to understand the comments and corrections. Consult a handbook or textbook if you don't understand something. Ask your peer tutor if he or she understands. Then, you are ready to work with your instructor. Ask questions. Be honest. Ask for explanations. Ask for references to sources for additional information. Don't apologize for "bothering" your teacher. We like it (even love it) when students want to improve. I tell my students, "You are not bothering me. Your questions are part of the reason I come to work. What bothers me are the students who just note the grade, snarl at me, say something bad about my mother, trash the paper, and then walk off! That's a bother. People who really want my knowledge and advice and help are true students."

Evaluation—like all the other steps in the process of writing—is important and deserves attention.

The Process of Writing: An Example of the Complete Process

Here is an example of one student's paper which was written to meet the requirements of a directed-audience comparison-contrast essay. Note how she went from outline to first draft (there was a second draft which is omitted here) to final word-processed copy. You will also find evaluation sheets attached after the manuscript.

Draft Materials

Dear Diary,
    Today, I realized that all the running around I've been doing lately has caused me to lose sight of the two most important things in my life. I was reminded of those things when:

A   Sunset as intro

B   Daughter   1. Looks
                2. Things she learns
                3. Things she says to communicate

C   Son   1. Looks
          2. Things he learns
          3. Things he says to communicate

D   Mikey + Aria together - my learning
Closing   compare sunset to Mikey + Aria

Dear Diary   Draft

As I drove home during rush hour Friday
evening, something caught my eye. ~~In~~ During all the
hustle and bustle of a Friday evening rush hour
drive something made ~~everything~~ all the commotion around me come
to a complete halt. There before ~~my eyes~~ me was the
most heartstopping sunset I've ever seen. The sun
was such a hot pink ~~it burned my eyes with~~ the
color became etched into my eyes. ~~The~~ Some Clouds
formed
~~were~~ grey clustered strings hanging from the
heavens. ~~Other The other clouds, above the~~

like a
balloon ~~Above the strings, were~~ Connected to the strings
~~were~~ brilliant
~~were flashing~~ white puffy clouds. As the sun
it's
sunk into the horizon, ~~the~~ color faded into a fiery
orange. ~~The That sunset~~
    I've been divorced for a year now. And all I do is run
around like the Energizer Bunny. I am a ~~mother of two~~ working, ~~a mother,~~
a college student and a ~~mother~~ of two.
    That sunset reminds me of ~~what the word~~
beauty really means. ~~I can see beautiful things
all around my if I would just take the time and
then once and awhile.~~

    ~~That sunset reminds me of
My children and drawing~~ are the two passions
of my life. ~~and sometimes~~ Lately I need a sunset or two
to remind me once in a while ~~to stop and recogni
enjoy their~~ "take a time out!" ~~myself and appreciate
their beautiful qualities~~ Slow down, relax and
open your eyes."

On weekends I do just that. ~~Then I open my eyes on~~ ⟨Draft⟩
Saturday mornings, I wake to my 18 mo. old daughter Aria, calling
~~my name~~ "more." ~~When~~ I walk in her room I see her standing in her crib with
the most beautiful and happy smile. She gleems with joy.
　　My daughter, who is eighteen months old, is
a character. She's just learning to talk. ~~which is~~
and the little things she picks up are just so amazing
to me. She'll pinch my cheeks and say, "gheek," as
she smiles. Her eyes sparkle with pride. She knows
she's communicating ~~in~~ on a level ~~ste~~ in which she
didn't know how to before. ~~Then~~ she ^gives hugs, ~~you its~~
~~like~~ she cuddles so close ~~to you~~ that its like she
wants to become one with me. ~~She knows~~ I
know she is communicating love.
As we leave the room, my three year old son ^Mikey wakes up. It's so funny
to see him in the morning. His hair sticks out all over like a porcupine.
With his eyes half shut he cries "Mommy, I want milk." No good mornings, just
"I wants."
　　My son, who is three years old, ~~is~~ also amazes
me. He comes home from preschool, singing songs that
I have never heard before. He doesn't forget that song;
he'll sing it for days on end. He recognizes not only
letters and numbers, but even movie titles and
commercial ads. Sometimes I think he can read.
　　~~While~~ we are singing, Aria grabs Mikey's hand &
　　~~Then~~ my daughter and son play ~~together,~~ ^their ~~you~~
interaction is ~~very~~ a learning experience for me.
They have their time of ~~brother~~ sibling rivalry, but
most of the time they enjoy each other's company. My
son puts puzzles together and my daughter watches
with intrege. She tries to mimic every move he

Draft

makes. ~~It~~ While he ~~is playing~~ plays with his blocks,
she ~~sits~~ sits ~~with~~ next to him. As he picks up two blocks,
she does the same. It's like an instant replay.!

Watching them play is like watching that
sunset. The world around me ~~is~~ doesn't exist.
I am overwhelmed with all they know and
have learned in such a short time. ~~I~~ To be able
to appreciate their accomplishments, even
though they are so small, is ~~beauty to me~~. best
relaxation.

As Saturday comes to an end, I remember
that sunset. ~~The world around me~~ For a short
time the world around me didn't ~~exit~~ exist. I
was able to, slow down, relax, and appreciate ~~my children~~
the loves of my life.

FINAL DRAFT

RACHAEL DRESDEN
COMP. 101/19
#4

"TIME OUT"

FRIDAY
3/14/97
8:30 PM

Dear Diary,

    During all the hustle and bustle of a Friday evening rush-hour drive, something made all the commotion around me come to a complete halt. There before me was the most heart-stopping sunset I have ever seen. The sun was such a hot pink, the color became etched into my eyes. Hanging from the heavens were clouds that formed grey clustered strings. Connected to the strings like balloons were brilliant, white, puffy clouds. As the sun sunk into the horizon, its color faded into a firey orange.

    Having been divorced for a year now, all I do is run and run like the Energizer Bunny. I am a mother of two, who works, and goes to college full time. When there's time to catch my breath, I grab a bite to eat or take a cat nap here and there. I'm so busy that the two most important things in my life seem to be trapped within a Monet painting. They have become just a blur of reality.

    That sunset reminded me of the two passions of my life. Lately, I need a sunset or two to scream out to me, **"Take a time out! Slow down, relax and open your eyes!"** This weekend I'm going to do just that.

On the run,
Rachael

SUNDAY
3/16/97
8:40 AM

Dear Diary,

It's me again. Today was such a wonderfully relaxing day. I woke to my eighteen month old daughter, Aria, calling, "Maie!" When I walked into her room, I saw her standing in her crib with the most beautiful and happy smile across her face. She was gleaming with joy. Her crystal blue eyes shimmered in the morning light. Her golden brown hair reflected the light in such a way that it formed a shining halo around her head. Aria saw me and said, "Hi Maie," in her raspy Liza Minelli like voice. Her arms sprung forward as her fingers flexed back and forth.

When I picked her up, she cuddled so close to me that her head fit between my neck and shoulder like a puzzle piece. Then, she lifted her head up, pinched my cheeks, and said, "gheek." She continued by pointing to my eye; she said, "eyeee." Then she grabbed my hair and said, "prity," (pretty). Her eyes sparkled with pride because she knew she was communicating on a level in which she never knew how to before. I put her down, so that we could walk into the family room together.

As we left the room, my three year old son, Mikey, woke up. He came running out of the bedroom looking for Aria. In a whining voice he cried, "Mommy, what's wrong Aria?" I couldn't answer his question because I was too busy staring at him. What a funny sight he is in the morning! His hair was sticking out all over like the quills of an angry porcupine. With his eyes half shut, he came straggling toward me, scratching his head like a lost little old man. Right away he said, "Mommy, I want milk!" He couldn't say, "Good morning," or "Hi," just, "I want."

As Saturday came to an end, that sunset came to mind. That day, for a short time, the world around me didn't exist. I was able to slow down, relax, and watch my children with an appreciation that will stay fresh in my memory like that sunset. From now on, Saturdays are my **"time out"** days.

Winding down,
Rachael

This was based on the gallop pole, I think.

I hate when my chick is having her mens trial cycle.

Name **Rachael Dresden** Section **101-19** Date **3/26/98**

SELF-EVALUATION SHEET: PART ONE

Assignment: {Comparison - Contrast
{Cause - Effect

Strong points of this assignment:

I feel my strongest point on this assignment is the direct-audience: me!

Creative, different.
Writing skills (organization, structure, & development) are under my control.

Weak points of this assignment:

I don't think I had any weak points...
maybe some commas.
It really helps to have real life, every day examples.
Without real life instances, I'd be lost.

General comments:

I feel I'm repeating myself by saying I enjoyed this assignment, but it's true.
I love to write!

(over)

SELF-EVALUATION SHEET: PART TWO

What were the strong points of your last writing assignment?

My strongest point was bringing my daughter's characteristics to life through description... and, in turn, bringing a new word/definition to life.

What were the weak points of your last writing assignment?

I had a few modification errors.
I also had some punctuation errors (commas) as well.

What have you done to correct those weaknesses in this assignment?

Read my handbook on commas.
Talked to the teacher.
Read, read, and reread my paper!

Evaluator's Name _Roy Roberts_ Section _Com 101-19_ Date _3-26-98_

PEER-EVALUATION SHEET: PEER-EVALUATOR #1

Writer's Name _R. Dresden_ Essay's Title _"Time Out"_

> **Directions:** (1) Remember not to write on another student's paper. Instead, use this form. (2) Offer concrete, specific comments using the terminology of writing (e.g., "The development in paragraph four might be improved by adding a brief example." or, "Check structure on page 3.")

What do you see as the strong points of this writing assignment: _Very "different" approach. Creative. I liked use of diary entries to establish audience. Writing skills look good: organized, structured, nicely detailed._

What areas do you feel might need additional work: _check a few commas_

Do you see any areas of grammar/mechanics (e.g. usage, spelling, fragments) that might need attention: _No — but I'm not the greatest at such matters._

General comments: _I wonder if she'll really "read" it !?!_

Good essay with a message almost all of us can identify with. I enjoyed reading Rachael's essay.

Dr. Jack Kevorkian used an ivy bag to administer the fatal dose.

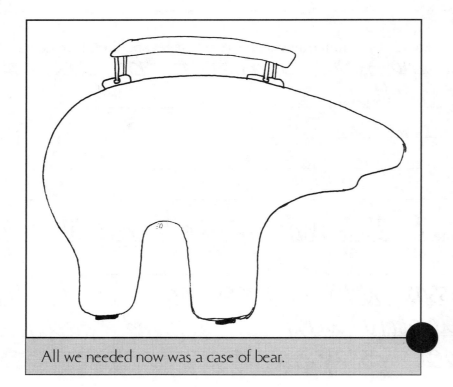

All we needed now was a case of bear.

Close Doesn't Count

OVERVIEW

I'm certain that you have often heard the old adage, "Close doesn't count except in horse-shoes, hand grenades, and sex." Although I am not certain about those three particular "arenas for closeness," I can guarantee you that when it comes to written communication skills and abilities, coming close definitely does not count. In fact, a "near miss" is sometimes just as confusing as being "way off the mark." Hitting a bullseye with words (that is, clearly communicating exactly what we mean and/or feel) is not easy. A direct hit requires a writer with a clear mind, a clear purpose, and an ability to be exact with words. A reader who is thinking clearly also assists in the communication process. Often, however, writers are not clear, and communication does not take place efficiently and effectively. The results are varied: frustration, confusion, humor, anger, disappointment, dejection, jealousy, sadness, broken hearts, etc. All of us have been affected by a breakdown in the communication process. Because this breakdown is so common, this chapter is simply a plea for you to think about one area of your communication, particularly your written communication: be very clear and precise with words and how you connect words. Although words aren't always the best means to communicate, they are the building blocks for most of our communication efforts. Make certain that the words you write convey exactly what you mean, not close to what you mean. There is usually a significant difference. It is the writer's responsibility to be clear and exact; it is not the reader's responsibility to translate. Sometimes, as writers, we get rushed or careless or even downright sloppy; we say to ourselves, "Oh well. My reader will know what I mean." Maybe. Maybe not. What is your personal goal as a writer? Bullseye? Near miss? Way off the mark? Am I anywhere in the neighborhood? How important to you are the feelings and the ideas which you place on paper?

A WORD ABOUT THE ILLUSTRATIONS IN THIS CHAPTER (AND THE REST OF THE BOOK . . .)

In my thirty years in the classroom, I have learned that the message of this chapter (write what you mean; don't be satisfied with being close) is an extremely important one. I have also learned that humor is an effective means of helping my students remember this lesson. Frequently, when words miss their target, the results are humorous, and because I am blessed with a warped personality (my wife is a psychotherapist, so I can make this claim with authoritative support) and because I am also blessed with a good memory, I have a knack for recalling the many miscues with words which I have encountered in student writing (and in my own prose). I am indeed a lucky man, for I am also blessed with an artistic and warped son (in fact, my other two sons and my daughter are also warped). When I began to brainstorm this chapter, I asked my son Eric to engage in a father-son bonding experience and help me with illustrations. Down through the years and editions, he has always been my illustrator, even now beginning his own career.

Another important point needs to be made here. A serious point. We are all human. We will make mistakes, including with language. All of us will write miscues from time to time. That is why we have to work at eliminating them. My written humor in this chapter and the humor inherent in the drawings are meant as a reminder of our foibles in attempting to communicate. Our humor is not meant to ridicule. Rather, by laughing at ourselves we might thereby remind ourselves that if we are not careful, our miscues might make the next edition of this text! (Actually, my miscues have been in all ten editions.) None of us will become perfect writers. But if we carefully select words and carefully construct sentences, if we concentrate, practice, revise, polish, and maybe get lucky, we can become better writers, better communicators.

WORDS GONE WRONG

Not too long ago, I was reading a young man's paper about his girlfriend who had "inherited" an older brother's beater. In essence, her hand-me-down car was a way to school and a big, frustrating drain on her paycheck. One sentence in his paper, however, was most memorable: *Even after she invested several hundred dollars in it, her rear end still wasn't right.* Now, I have had enough experience with cars and car problems to know what he meant. He meant (I think) that the car's rear end was malfunctioning. I don't know if it was a gear ratio problem, a differential problem, or a grease leak. I do know, however, that what his sentence says has nothing to do with what he meant, has nothing to do with his girlfriend's car. The way his sentence is written, it discloses a problem that requires a proctologist, not a mechanic or auto technician!

The following sentences are close to alike, but they are not the same; they communicate different concepts: *Even after she invested several hundred dollars in it, her rear end still wasn't right. Even though she has spent several hundred dollars for differential repairs, my girlfriend finds her car still doesn't run correctly.* Although my comments probably bordered on sexual harassment (not to mention political incorrectness), I had to point out to the young scholar the difference between writing about his girlfriend's rear end and her car's rear end.

Sometimes, a simple typing error (such as a careless space between letters) can drastically alter the meaning of a sentence (as shown on the right):

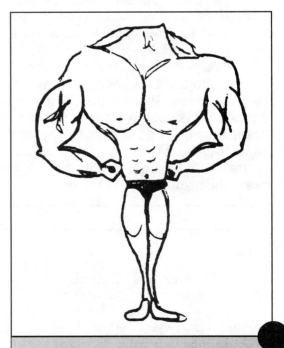

Every day, my brother works out and conditions himself in order to get a head.

One student wrote a very touching description of her grandfather. When she described his facial features, however, I was left to ponder the possibility of a family genetic disorder:

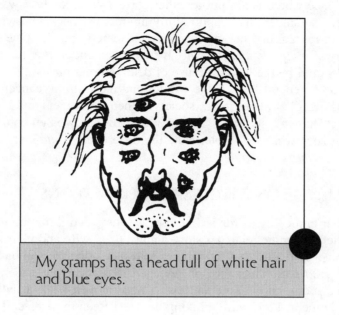

My gramps has a head full of white hair and blue eyes.

My gramps has a head full of white hair and blue eyes does not mean the same thing as *My gramps has blue eyes and a head full of white hair*. Sure. I know what she meant. But what she meant isn't what she wrote.

If you work on a word processor, then you know what a grade-saver the spell check software can be, but be careful with the suggested spellings it offers. Just because a word is spelled correctly doesn't mean it is the correct word to convey your ideas:

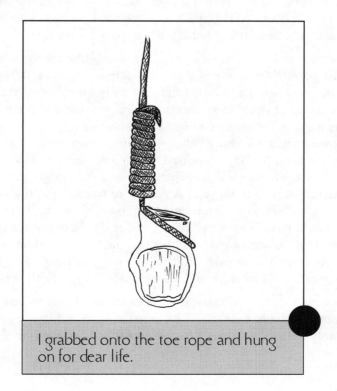

I grabbed onto the toe rope and hung on for dear life.

Although *toe* is spelled correctly, I think it was a *tow* rope he was hanging onto. I think. I hope.

Sometimes, our miscues occur because we have written without thinking about what we really wanted to say or we write a sentence which is not put together correctly. Recently, I was reading a student's paper on the subject of suicide. The student had captured my interest with her own writing and thinking, and she had also done a nice job of researching her paper to provide expert opinion. One sentence, however, seemed not to be true: *A majority of males commit suicide.* If this statement is true, males die of suicide more than any other cause; suicide would be the leading cause of death among males; the majority of males would be killing themselves. My own general knowledge would lead me to think cancer, heart disease, and violent crimes would be major "killers" of males in our society. When the student and I reviewed her paper, I asked her about this "statistic." "Oh yea," she said, "many more men than women commit suicide." This is what I thought she meant, but it isn't what she wrote. Note the difference: *A majority of males commit suicide. A majority of suicides are committed by males.*

AVOIDING COMMUNICATION MISCUES: SIX SUGGESTIONS

One. Sometimes our choice of words is fine, but we just need a few more words to clarify what we mean. For example, a friend of mine related a story about his ex-wife and their son. The sixteen-year-old's weekend curfew had been 12:30 a.m., but his mother said that since the son had been punctual, she would extend the curfew until 1:00 a.m. Then the son engaged in some typical teen behavior which led to an alteration in curfew. The mom said, "Your curfew is now moved back a half hour." So, the following Saturday, the teen came home at 12:15 a.m. thinking he was fifteen minutes early. According to his reasoning, if the curfew was moved back a half hour from 1:00 a.m., curfew would be 12:30 a.m. Arriving home at 12:15 a.m. would be good for a few brownie points with his mother. The mother was angry, however, because she thought the son was fifteen minutes late. After all, from her point of view, moving curfew back a half hour from 12:30 a.m. would make curfew at 12:00 midnight. Both felt treated unfairly by the other. It was a classic case of a failure to communicate/understand such simple words: *Your curfew is now moved back a half hour.* But moved back a half hour from which time? The original 12:30 curfew or the extended 1:00 curfew? Big difference to a pacing mother and to a teen on the prowl. A few more words would have truly clarified the situation: "Your curfew is now moved back a half hour from its original time. Be home at midnight. When we re-establish trust, we'll go back to 12:30, and eventually to 1:00, and then to your being responsible for yourself and your health. Get home and get your proper rest."

This incident reminded me of my own teen years. (If my children are reading this book for some god-knows-why reason, at this point I'd like for you guys to skip a few paragraphs. This is just one of those boring stories you have probably heard a million times at family dinner or on the way to Wally World. . . .) The day I got my drivers license, I decided to buckle to peer pressure and drive my friends to the weekend orgy at the lake. As I was leaving my parents' house on Friday evening, an experienced and licensed driver for all of forty minutes, I yelled and asked my father when he wanted me home. "Early," was his reply. So I came home in time for church on Sunday morning—seven a.m. service, in fact—the early service as the local parish priest referred to it. My dad was less-than joyous. I did not get much driving experience in the next few months, and I rediscovered my bicycle. A few more words from my father would have given me reason to ponder my actions and their consequences: "Be home early—no later than 1:00 tomorrow morning." Then, his meaning would have been very clear. I still might have chosen to ignore his words, but his words and their intent would have been clear. And because he was my father and I did know his values, I really did know what he meant when he said, "Early." Although it really didn't make much difference to him at that time, what he meant isn't what he said. (See, kids. You just can't reason with some parents. . . .)

Two. Sometimes communication miscues occur because the words we use are not appropriate for the audience we address them toward. For example, if I wanted to share with a colleague that a common student does not always act maturely in the classroom, I might (actually, I wouldn't) use educational jargon and say,

"Her behavior in the affective domain is somewhat juvenile and lacking impulse control." If this student is talking to the student next to her and bothering me in the middle of my orgasmic lecture on the semicolon, however, and I addressed her directly with this statement, I don't think she would understand: "Please desist. Your lack of impulse control in the area of affective behaviors is disrupting my cognitive processes." But I bet she would understand this statement: "Shut up!! I can't think with your constant babbling to your friend!" If I added the body language of a sneer, a growl, and a little drooling into my beard, I'll wager she would know exactly what I meant (and probably just stare at me and then go back to talking anyway. . .).

Language shared with co-workers in a professional setting falls into the same miscue category. I'll illustrate with a true story, one with serious repercussions. Many years ago, my father underwent cancer surgery. I lived in another state and had plane reservations for an early morning flight; I should have arrived in plenty of time before his scheduled surgery. When I arrived at O'Hare Airport that February morning, I was greeted by heavy fog. No flights departed (or landed) for five hours. By the time I finally reached my destination, I was mentally and physically exhausted.

Because I had been in contact with my family just before my flight had finally left O'Hare, I knew that my father had survived his surgery but was in serious condition. Once my plane had landed and I had made my way to the hospital, I raced up to the hospital information desk. I got my father's room number, boarded an elevator, and took a few deep breaths. As the doors finally swooshed open, I hurried down the hallway to room number 311 (I remember it to this day). As I entered the room, I was greeted by an empty room, the bed clothes in a pile on the floor, and a smiling hospital employee removing my father's name from above what I assumed to have been his bed. "Do you know where the man is who was assigned to this room?" I asked. She looked at me and calmly replied, "Oh. We lost him about an hour ago." I thought my father had died, and I unleashed the frustrations of the day by driving my fist into the wall and chanting some four-letter words. "Yes," she continued "We lost him about an hour ago. They moved him up to intensive care. He's on four now. You can go see him." At that point, I realized that her words, "We lost him. . ." meant that my father was not "their" patient any longer, that they had "lost" him to another ward, that he had been assigned to another floor, another nurses' station. Her common expression, "We lost him." brought a great deal of stress and anxiety into my life. I am convinced that a person with a "bad heart" might hear those words, misunderstand, and literally die from the shock of the experience. In the right context, those words might be life-threatening. We must be careful with our words. They carry significant meaning and great power.

Three. Sometimes the communication miscue takes place because of incorrect, awkward, or ungrammatical sentence structure. The examples referred to earlier (males and suicide, gramps and many eyes) illustrate this type of error. Other examples are not hard to locate. Just the other day, I was reading a paper written by one of my students who is in charge of training new employees at the bank where she works. My student wrote a letter to new employees to classify the kinds of customers a new teller might encounter during the first day on the job. The following sentence appeared at the beginning of the letter: *Being the new employee, I thought I'd better tell you about the types of customers you might encounter here at the bank.* The way this sentence is constructed, the writer is identified as the new employee. Correctly written to indicate the relationship between the writer of the letter (who has experience working at the bank) and the reader of the letter (who is the new kid on the block), the sentence might read like this: *Since you are the new employee here at the bank, I thought I would share from my experiences as a teller and inform you about some of the types of customers you might encounter.* This sentence clearly identifies the writer, the reader, and the purpose for the letter.

As I wrote earlier, such examples are not uncommon; read the several hundred pages of prose I've written in this edition, and I am sure you will locate a few of my twisted sentences. Here is one of my favorite twisted sentences from student writing:

More students, I feel, should expose themselves to the computer.

I'll be honest. During some of my frustrating moments at the keyboard, I have felt exactly like the guy in the drawing! However, I don't believe that Eric's depiction of exposing oneself to the computer is what the writer really had in mind; I think she meant that more students should take advantage of the opportunity to learn computer skills while in college. The sentences *More students, I feel, should expose themselves to the computer.* and *I believe more college students should learn computer skills while they have the opportunity.* don't communicate the same message; there is a difference. That difference should come to you in a flash (sorry!).

If you are like me, you catch the Christmas spirit and love to decorate your home for the holidays. However, I hope my wife doesn't adopt the decorating approach advocated by one of my students:

At Christmas time, I like to decorate the house with my husband. and *My husband and I like to decorate the house at Christmas time.* do not communicate the same ideas. I am certain that some of my family members would get very merry from hanging me on the gable end of our home with holly berries and blinking lights in my beard and pony tail. No thanks. I'll stay in front of the fireplace and sip Wild-Turkey-laced eggnog.

At Christmas time, I like to decorate the house with my husband.

Four. Our slip-ups in communication can occur because we spell a word incorrectly. The misspelling might drastically alter the meaning of our words (or the intent of our words). Students who spell words by how they sound, for example, are courting red ink:

I love to watch squirrels collect eggcorns.

Sometimes the word we spell incorrectly becomes another word which is spelled correctly. When this happens, the meaning of our ideas becomes drastically altered, as illustrated in this classic blunder from a student's essay:

The constitution was written by our four fathers.

Keep in mind, computer hackers and addicts, your spell check software most likely will not detect this type of error. *Four fathers* is spelled correctly. However, *four fathers* isn't *forefathers*—the correct spelling for the word the writer wanted. The best proofreading software you own is your own brain.

Five. Let's talk some more about that word processor and its spell check capabilities. Since these electronic wonders have worked their way into our lives and curriculum, students have discovered and created a new type of error that I never saw when students used "regular" typewriters. We have discovered a new way to say something other than what we meant. As you probably know, when a spell checker stops on a word it finds "suspect" or not in its dictionary, it offers a list of suggested spellings or suggested words. At this time, the student writer can select from the suggested list, insert the "corrected" spelling, and continue writing/proofreading. (Alternatives are to leave the original word and risk red ink or to haul out a paper dictionary and begin thumbing through it.)

Some of the words which I have seen students select from the suggested list and then "plug" into their papers—well, I've got to tell you, the word is spelled correctly but it can take your breath away because of the shock factor! (In case you're wondering, I have asked students, "Why did you use this word?". I just had to know. And the answer almost always is, "It was on the spell checker.") Allow me to illustrate:

My new guy is truly a deer.

Deer. Dear. Trust me, we are talking significant difference here.

One of my students confided that he had typed his paper rather quickly. Proofreading and spell checking were given even less time. In his haste, he mistyped the word *My*. Thankfully, the spell checker did catch the error; however, in his frenzied state, the student highlighted the wrong suggested spelling, and he turned in his paper with this sentence:

Moo uncle served in the Korean War.

The student was embarrassed, as you might imagine. Just to remind him that we are all human and prone to mistakes—especially when we rush—I inked a little note in the margin of his paper: Holy Cow!!

Six. Another easy way to write something other than what you mean is to make a mistake in usage. Usage, as you will discover in Chapter Three, is an area of diction consisting of words that sound alike but are spelled differently. The bad news is that they also convey different meanings. And the bad news gets worse. If you work on a computer, most spell check programs will not pick up errors in usage; the word is spelled correctly, but it is the wrong word. And the really super bad news is that the English language contains lots and lots of these kinds of words just waiting to work *their* (or is that *there* or *they're??*) way into your writing. Here are a few examples to illustrate how errors in usage can cause you to mean one thing and communicate another:

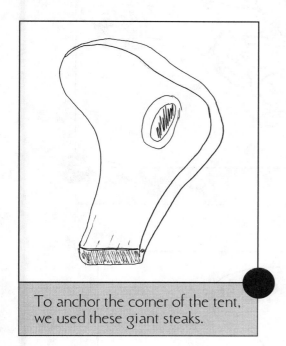

To anchor the corner of the tent, we used these giant steaks.

In olden times, witches were berried alive.

Well, whether (weather?) you're (your?) writing (righting?) a lot (allot?) of words or (are? our?) just a few, there (their? they're?) will always (all ways?) exist the possibility of an error in usage. I repeat: your brain is the best spell checker you have if you use it correctly.

A Few Parting Comments

This is one of the other lessons I have learned in my quarter century of teaching in the college classroom: material which is taught early in a course, even if mastered by the student, tends to be forgotten as the semester winds its way toward finals week. The same is true of textbook chapters. This chapter's lesson, taught early, might be forgotten by the time you reach Chapter Sixteen and begin concentrating on research documentation skills. So, to keep your memory and your interest focused on the important lesson taught in this chapter, you will find a few illustrations of miscues sprinkled throughout this text. Enjoy them—but don't forget their message: **close does not count** in communication; be precise and exact with your words.

Suggestions for Avoiding Communications Miscues

1. Use more words to clarify
2. Use words appropriate for the audience
3. Use proper grammatical structure
4. Spell words correctly
5. Monitor electronic spell checkers
6. Be aware of usage

After we left the restaurant, we got gas.

My closet friends threw me a great surprise party.

The Word

Although many writers devote a lot of time and energy to the larger elements of writing—the paragraph and the essay, for example—they sometimes neglect the equally important smaller element of the individual word. The truly effective writer is one who carefully chooses words which are not only grammatically correct and correctly spelled, but are also the precise and exact words to communicate the writer's ideas and/or feelings.

Section Two of this text will focus on two areas of the word: Diction and Usage. The section on diction should help you choose those words which most accurately communicate your thoughts and feelings. The section on usage should help you find your way through that maze of words which look alike and sound alike, but differ in spelling and meaning.

As you become more aware of words and their importance, you should find your writing more-polished, more-precise, and more-meaningful.

To disagree with him would be otter folly.

Drinking can weaken heart mussels.

Diction

OVERVIEW

Diction is word choice and word use. The writer who masters diction has control of the most fundamental element in the writing process and is able to communicate his or her feelings and ideas by the deliberate, precise, and correct use of words.

Frequently, diction is controlled by rules. For example, one rule states that writers should avoid nonstandard words such as *ain't* or *hisself.* Some areas of diction are controlled by guidelines instead of rules. For example, writing is considered polished and effective if it does not contain cliches such as *Helen was as cool as a cucumber* or *Mary was as white as a sheet.* Although cliches are not technically "wrong," writing that is fresh and original communicates more effectively. Still other areas of diction are controlled by personal preference. One person might prefer to write *I have always taken part in winter sports,* while a second writer might prefer *Participating in sports has always been one of mv favorite winter activities.*

The sections in this chapter should make you more aware of the words you use and the rules, guidelines, and choices you have in selecting those words.

PART ONE: IDIOM

Idioms are expressions in a language: *to lose one's head, to give someone a hand, to make off with* the loot, *to take a stand on* an issue, *to be angry with* a person, *to correspond with* someone. As each of the preceding examples illustrates, an idiom cannot be understood by a word-for-word translation. Rather, as native speakers of a language, we learn the meaning of each idiom by hearing it, reading it, speaking it, and writing it. Sometimes, especially if an idiom includes a preposition, it is not easy to be idiomatic; sometimes there are very subtle differences between idiomatic and unidiomatic expression: *superior to,* not *superior than; intend to do,* not *intend on doing;* and *prior to,* not *prior than.* Idioms which contain a preposition often confuse writers and speakers: *agree to* (a proposal), *agree with* (a person), *agree on* (a procedure), *agree in* (principle), and *agree about* (an issue). To be certain that writing is idiomatic, the writer should consult a dictionary; most dictionaries contain idiomatic expressions near the end of each word entry.

IDIOMS MOST FREQUENTLY CONFUSED BY WRITERS

accompanied by: Sharon was accompanied by Sharla.
accompanied with: His request was accompanied with a smile.

agree on: I am glad we agree on a plan of balancing the budget.
agree to: I agree to your proposal.
agree with: I agree with Betty on her suggestion for a bake sale.

angry at/about: Maryann was angry at the treatment she received.
angry with: Tom was angry with his brother.

argue about/for: Ned argued for passage of the censorship law.
argue with: Regina argued with Ned about his prudish attitude.

charge for: He knew he would be charged for his purchases.
charge with: Our neighbor was charged with forgery.

concerned for: I'm concerned for her health.
concerned with: Harvey is concerned with child abuse legislation.

concur in: I concur in your opinion of our new secretary.
concur with: I concur with Valerie in her decision.

differ from: In hair color, I differ from my brother.
differ with: I differ with Allan; he's wrong on the gun control legislation.

impatient at: I'm impatient at her talking during my lectures.
impatient for: Jon is impatient for Christmas morning to arrive.
impatient with: Ida is impatient with her husband when he snores.

interfere in: Don't interfere in my financial business!
interfere with: The noise interferes with my concentration.

join in: Come on, join in the fun!
join to: Where he joined wood to metal, the contrast was striking.
join with: Join with the others and worship the god of your choice.

occupied by: The seat was occupied by an old shopping bag lady.
occupied in: Jerry was occupied in study for finals.
occupied with: Selma was occupied with the puzzle.

part from: I cry at the part where the hero and the heroine are made to part from each other.
part with: I cannot stand to part with old clothes.

stand by: He promised to stand by her in difficult times.
stand for: I stand for humane treatment of all living things.
stand on: The candidate decided to take a stand on the abortion issue.

wait at: Wait at the drug store for me.
wait by: I will wait by the hour for you if it becomes necessary.
wait for: Let's wait for Billy before we board the bus.
wait in: Did you really wait in the rain?
wait on: I hate to wait on customers; otherwise the job isn't bad!

PART TWO: CLICHE

Cliches are those phrases that all of us rely upon when we don't want to be original in our speech or our writing. Once original and imaginative, cliches have become trite, overused, and ineffective: *all work and no play, the bitter end, hotter than hell,* and *nip it in the bud.* Such phrases tell the reader that the writer has nothing original to say, or nothing to say in an original style. To understand the staleness and predictability of writing which contains cliches, read the following passage and complete each phrase:

Although he tried to avoid it like __ _____, Ernest sometimes had to get up at the crack __ _____. Then he would work all day in his fields. Ernie was known to take a day off once in awhile, but they were few __ __ _____. Ernie even had to work at night, doing paper work and ordering supplies. Many nights he burned__ _____ __. I have always admired people such as Ernie; he holds a special _____ __ __ _____.

CLICHES FREQUENTLY FOUND IN STUDENT WRITING	
add insult to injury	*green with envy*
after all is said and done	*happy as a lark*
all boils down to	*hard as a rock*
beating around the bush	*other side of the coin*
better late than never	*selling like hot cakes*
in our world today	*sink or swim*
ladder of success	*in one ear and out the other*
last but not least	*water under the bridge/over the dam*
more than meets the eye	*in the final analysis*
needle in a haystack	*wise as an owl*
no sooner said than done	*cold as ice*
busy as a bee	*for all intents and purposes*
thin as a rail	*get down to brass tacks*
slow but sure	*couldn't care less*
young in spirit	*gentle as a lamb*
in this day and age	*easier said than done*
hit the nail on the head	*few and far between*
strong as an ox	*straight from the shoulder/hip*
face the music	*strike while the iron is hot*
worth its weight in gold	*wouldn't touch it with a ten-foot pole*

PART THREE: EUPHEMISM

Euphemisms are words or phrases that we use to conceal the truth or to sidestep the sometimes-objectionable or unpleasant aspects of existence: instead of saying someone has died, we say *he or she has gone to meet his/her Maker;* instead of saying someone is pregnant, we say *she is in a family way;* instead of saying someone is sweating because he was drunk the night before, we say *someone is perspiring because he overindulged in alcoholic beverages.* Because euphemisms use pleasant or somewhat acceptable words to express unpleasant concepts, they are sometimes referred to as circumlocutions or the more blunt "weasel words." When euphemisms are used to deceive, they become dangerous and dishonest: bombing missions become *strategic protective reaction strikes;* the ghetto becomes *the inner city* or *an economically depressed area;* a lie becomes *the politician's inoperative statement;* house insurance goes up in price and becomes *the home owner's protection policy.*

As a writer, be honest with your language; as a reader, be alert to the dishonesty in the language of other writers, especially those who are trying to win your vote or solicit your money. Sometimes, however, tact and respect dictate the need for euphemism; you might sustain a friendship by referring to your friend as *stout* or *burly* or *heavy-set* instead of *fat.* The fact is, however, that language, including euphemism, does not alter truth, even if it misleads us from it: *sanitary engineers* still mop floors and empty garbage cans; *terminated employees* are still fired; *ladies of the night* charge the same as whores and prostitutes; *passing away* is the same as dying.

COMMON EUPHEMISMS	
■ *caught in the act*	
visual surveillance	(spying)
creating a civil disturbance	(rioting)
laying to rest	(burying)
encountering strained financial circumstances	(bankrupt)
economically impoverished	(being poor)
driving under the influence	(driving drunk)
■ *in the market place*	
previously owned automobile	(used car)
airline boarding pass	(ticket)
mobile home	(trailer)
deluxe full wheel cover	(hubcap)
reconstituted fibers	(used wool)
preferred customer	(a person who pays his bills on time)
■ *in the halls of higher education*	
learning resources center	(library)
educational facilitator	(aide)
floor to ceiling portable room divider	(movable wall)
non-stationary educational station	(desk)
educationally disadvantaged	(dumb/uneducated)
■ *in the real world*	
halitosis	(bad breath)
dentures	(false teeth)
decorator bathroom tissue	(toilet paper)

going to powder one's nose	(going to the toilet)
receding hair line	(bald)
losing a step	(getting older)
senior citizen	(old person)

■ *on death and dying*

pass on/away	(die)
bodily remains	(corpse)
memorial service	(funeral)
dearly departed	(dead person)

■ *on the job*

custodial engineer	(janitor)
funeral director	(undertaker)
used car broker	(used car salesman)
professional educator	(teacher)
sanitary engineer	(plumber)
language facilitator	(translator)
corrections officer	(prison guard)

PART FOUR: REDUNDANCY

Redundancy, a form of wordiness, is saying the same thing twice; it is the unnecessary duplication of ideas: *free gift* (if it is a gift, it should be free); *basic fundamental* (*basic* and *fundamental* are very similar in meaning); *blue in color* (*blue* is a color).

REDUNDANT PHRASES AND EXPRESSIONS THAT APPEAR FREQUENTLY IN WRITING

at this point in time
six A.M. this morning
seven P.M. this evening
autobiography of his own life
habitual custom
cooperate together
repeat again
square in shape

attractive in appearance
expert in the area of
several in number
the reason because
seems apparent
advance forward
continue on
combine together

PART FIVE: WORDINESS (VERBOSITY)

Wordiness, sometimes referred to as verbosity, is using too many words to express an idea. Wordiness can occur in four ways: (1) using several words when one or two would suffice, (2) using unnecessary words and phrases, (3) using unnecessary repetition of words and/or phrases, and (4) using too many short and choppy sentences.

Avoid wordiness that is caused by using several words when one or two should suffice:

in this modern day and age	today
at this point in time	now
bring all this to a conclusion/end	conclude/end
during the same time that	while
in a great many instances	often/frequently
on account of the fact that	because
located in the neighborhood of	near
at all times	always
for the purpose of	for
in order to	to
until it becomes time to	until
in the event that	if
in the final analysis	finally
in a similar or like manner	similarly
in the neighborhood of	about/approximate
on a daily basis	daily
a large number of	many

Avoid wordiness that is caused by unnecessary words and phrases:

WORDY: Ron has decided on a career major in the field of accounting.

CONCISE: Ron has decided to major in accounting.

CONCISE: Ron is studying to become an accountant.

Avoid wordiness that is caused by the unnecessary repetition of words and/or phrases:

WORDY: In the poem, "After Apple Picking," which is about life, poet Robert Frost uses the symbol of apples to symbolize life's tasks.

CONCISE: In "After Apple Picking," Robert Frost uses apples to symbolize life's tasks.

Avoid wordiness that is caused by numerous, short, choppy sentences:

WORDY: The new soccer field was finished. It would be open for the first day of the new season. The field was covered with grass. The grass was green. It was also very thick. It looked like a carpet.

CONCISE: Ready for the first game of the season, the new soccer field resembled a carpet of thick, green grass.

PART SIX: DENOTATION AND CONNOTATION

The denotation of a word is what the word literally means. For example, in the dictionary, the word *cheap* means "low in cost, inexpensive." The connotation of a word is what the word implies or suggests. The word *cheap*, for example, could imply that something is less than high class or that something is not well made. Notice the differences in the meanings of the following sentences: (1) *I bought a cheap watch to leave in the gear in the fishing boat.* (2) *Hannah's dress looks cheap.* (3) *Although her dress must have been expensive, she certainly cheapens it.* (4) *She is a cheap date.* (5) *She is an inexpensive date.* (6) *She is cheap.* The differences in meaning are due to denotation-connotation.

When writing, pay attention to both the denotative and connotative meanings of words. Any of the following words could be used in a sentence describing a stabbing, yet each word would carry a unique connotative meaning: *knife, switchblade, sword, dagger, stiletto*. A *knife* suggests an implement used to peel potatoes, cut steak, or accidentally cut a finger. A *switchblade* connotes a threatening, secret weapon; even its name connotes the clicking sound of the opening blade. A *sword* connotes dueling royalty. A *dagger* suggests a planned, bloody murder. A *stiletto* suggests secrecy, conspiracy, and perhaps espionage or undercover agents. Obviously, using the "wrong" word in the "wrong" context could alter the meaning of a passage or of the reader's reaction to it. A gangbanger on a dark street corner would not carry a *sword*, nor would a double agent conceal a *switchblade* in a false-bottomed attache case.

Most words have a positive or negative connotation; although there are neutral words, writers tend to choose words that reveal feelings and/or attitudes toward a topic:

POSITIVE (favorable)	NEUTRAL	NEGATIVE (unfavorable)
professor	teacher	pedagogue
famous	well-known	notorious
cottage	summer home	shack
aroma	smell	stench
debated	discussed	argued
statesman	office holder	politician
term project	homework	busy work
limo	car	beater
exam	test	pop quiz
penal institution	corrections facility	jail

PART SEVEN: LEVELS OF DICTION

Anyone who has written a letter to an old friend and a letter applying for a job knows that each of us has several levels of diction we use to communicate our ideas and our feelings. Although we might use "Hello! How the hell are ya?!" for the opening sentence in a letter to a friend, it would not be a good opening sentence in a job-application letter. When we write or speak, we must decide which of the various levels of diction to use.

LEVELS OF DICTION: SLANG

The most informal level of diction—in fact, the opposite of all that makes language formal and elegant—is slang. Slang is considered to be extremely informal, racy, nonstandard, disrespectful, and—in some cases—crude: *the slammer, the fuzz, psych-out, burn-out, upper, kinky, blow it out your ear, cop a feel, take a hike*. Slang comes and goes in popular language and popular culture; it is, in fact, created by the various subgroups within our culture. The drug culture, for example, has given us slang expressions such as *roach, toke, nickel bag, bong, freak, horse, buy some shit*, and *take a hit*. The rock culture has given us slang expressions such as *groupie, on the road, gig, get off, roadie, jam*, and *heavy metal*. Some slang expressions come from other languages. *Schlemiel* (a loser) and *schlimazel* (a luckless person), for example, come from Yiddish.

Slang is generally to be avoided in formal writing. Contrast the levels of diction in the following examples:

  👎 SLANG: I dropped by to rap with my prof, but he was on such a downer that I decided to split and rap with my chick.

  👍 MORE FORMAL: I stopped to talk with my professor, but he was so depressed that I decided instead to spend the time talking with my girlfriend.

LEVELS OF DICTION: REGIONAL EXPRESSIONS AND WORDS

If you have travelled from one section of the country to another, you have no doubt noticed that there are expressions and words native to certain regions: *woods pussy* for *skunk, bubbler* for *water cooler, tote* for *carry, reckon* for *suppose, hale* for *healthy*. The danger in using regionalisms is that the reader will not know the word and its meaning; if you are writing for a general audience, avoid regional expressions. If you are trying to add local color to your writing, or if you are writing for a specific audience, however, the use of regionalisms could be quite effective. The following sentences illustrate the difference:

  👎 LOCAL: We decided to barbecue on the platform; Marge placed the roasting ears in a spider on top of the fire while I began to baste the bird.

  👍 MORE FORMAL: We decided to cook out on the porch; Marge placed the corn on the cob in a skillet while I began to baste the chicken.

LEVELS OF DICTION: JARGON

There are two types of jargon. One type is the specialized, technical language of specific professions. If a lawyer is writing for a lawyer, a physician for a physician, a teacher for a teacher, or an engineer for an engineer, then the use of jargon is acceptable because both the writer and the reader "speak the same language." A psychoanalyst, for example, would understand the following sentence: *Jane's issues are around individuation and separation. (Jane is afraid to leave home and go to college.)*

A second type of jargon is considered unacceptable in college writing. Unlike the jargon intended for a professional audience, this second type appears in writing intended for a general audience. This jargon obscures ideas and tries to impress the reader with the writer's words. This jargon attempts to sound highbrow, intellectual, and impressive. Instead of writing *"Let's see how this tax increase affects the small businessman."*, the jargon addict would write, *"Our committee will investigate the possible ramifications of increased revenue assumption, particularly as it impacts the lesser-stature corporations in the private sector."* A want-ad written in plain English might ask for *an employee who can get along with co-workers;* in jargon, *the employee should be able to interface with other corporate personnel.* As the following example sentences illustrate, jargon-free writing is much clearer:

  👎 JARGON: Those professional educators who exhibit a tendency toward jocularity and witicisms tend to have a low attrition rate.

  👍 PLAIN ENGLISH: Teachers who have a sense of humor tend to keep their students.

LEVELS OF DICTION: NONSTANDARD WORDS

Nonstandard words are those associated with the illiterate and the uneducated; nonstandard words are not acceptable in college writing. Examples of nonstandard words include double negatives such as *don't have no* and *can't never*. Other examples of nonstandard words include the following: *ain't, nowheres, nohow, anywheres, could of, should of, gonna, wanna, hisn, hern, hisself, theirselves, this here, that there,* and *hadn't ought*. In most dictionaries, such words are usually labeled as nonstandard or illiterate. Except for writing dialogue to indicate a person of little formal education or of low social stature, a writer should avoid nonstandard usage.

The following sentences illustrate the difference between nonstandard and standard words:

☞ NONSTANDARD: Ain't it a shame that he failed out of college; he would of done better if he'd applied hisself.

☝ STANDARD: It's too bad that he failed in his attempt at college; if he had applied himself, he might have been more successful.

LEVELS OF DICTION: ARCHAIC AND OBSOLETE WORDS

Archaic words are those words (or their meanings) that appear rarely in general use. Obsolete words are those words (or their meanings) that no longer appear in general use. Although these words are listed and defined in modern dictionaries to assist modern readers of older literature, archaic words and obsolete words should be avoided in college writing.

ARCHAIC AND OBSOLETE WORDS	
Archaic:	***Obsolete:***
prithee: I pray thee; please	*wan:* dark, gloomy
anon: immediately	*amaze:* to bewilder
kine: cows, cattle	*curious:* fastidious
methinks: it seems to me	*coy:* disdainfully aloof
unhelm: to remove the helm or helmet (of)	*coy:* to pet or to caress
betimes: promptly; quickly	*nice:* foolish

The following sentences illustrate the ineffectiveness of archaic and obsolete language in college writing.

☞ ARCHAIC/OBSOLETE: Methinks it behooves you to be more curious in preparing your final written draughts.

☝ MODERN: You should pay more attention to detail when you prepare your final draft.

LEVELS OF DICTION: PRETENTIOUS DICTION

Pretentious diction is also said to be ornate, artificial, fine, and/or flowery. Regardless of its label, it is to be avoided. Pretentiousness in diction occurs when the writer chooses words that sound phony, stiff, and pompous. The writer chooses to use flowery and polysyllabic words instead of simple, direct ones: the word *house* becomes *abode* or *domicile;* the word *begin* becomes *commence;* the word *college* becomes *institution of higher learning;* the word *party* becomes *festive social gathering.* Note that the words themselves are not pretentious or ornate; it is in the context of using elaborate words to convey simple ideas that the writing becomes flowery—if not boring and comical:

> ☞ PRETENTIOUS: While negotiating her evening promenade, Mrs. Jessup encountered a vicious and unfamiliar canine.
>
> 👍 SIMPLE/DIRECT: On her evening walk, Mrs. Jessup met a mean, stray dog.

PART EIGHT: GENERAL WORDS AND SPECIFIC WORDS CONCRETE WORDS AND ABSTRACT WORDS

Concrete words refer to those things that can be experienced, usually by means of the senses; they refer to tangible and material things: *banana, bucket seat, hot sand, totem pole.* Abstract words refer to those things that are qualities and ideas; they refer to intangible and nonmaterial things: truth, beauty, liberalism, culture. General words name classes or groups: *professions.* Specific words restrict a general class; *lawyers, doctors, teachers, dentists* are specific words based on the general class *professions.*

Effective writing avoids vagueness and communicates most effectively when it is composed of concrete and specific language. General words and abstract words are useful in stating main ideas (topic sentences and thesis statements): *When I partake in sports, I become accident prone. . . . Smoking is harmful to health. . . . Being perpetually late can strain a friendship. . . . Studying theory and practice make learning to write easy.*

Specific words and concrete words are used to explain and illustrate these ideas; specific and concrete words are used to develop the writer's ideas and feelings: *Last winter I fell and broke my arm when I was cross country skiing. . . . Cigarette smoking can cause lung cancer. . . . My friend, Bob, was forty-five minutes late picking me up today; he was twenty minutes late yesterday. . . . Learning to write scratch outlines helped me earn an A in my English literature class; I no longer fear in-class essay exams.*

PART NINE: USAGE

Another of the areas of diction is usage; usage means that the writer uses the correct and appropriate word when necessary. Writers frequently confuse words in the English language that are similar in spelling, meaning, and pronunciation. There are many such words in our language; become familiar with those you confuse. Most college dictionaries and handbooks have a usage section.

THE MOST COMMON TROUBLE AREAS IN USAGE

accept	knew	quiet
except	new	quit
expect		quite
	know	
affect	no	than
effect	now	then
a lot	later	their
allot	latter	there
		they're
all ready	lead	
already	led	threw
		through
all together	lessen	thorough
altogether	lesson	
		to
altar	loose	too
alter	lose	two
brake	may be	wear
break	maybe	were
breath	passed	we're
breathe	past	where
coarse	peace	weather
course	piece	whether
complement	personal	which
compliment	personnel	witch
conscience	plain	who's
conscious	plane	whose
desert	pray	your
dessert	prey	you're
hole	precede	
whole	proceed	
its	principal	
it's	principle	

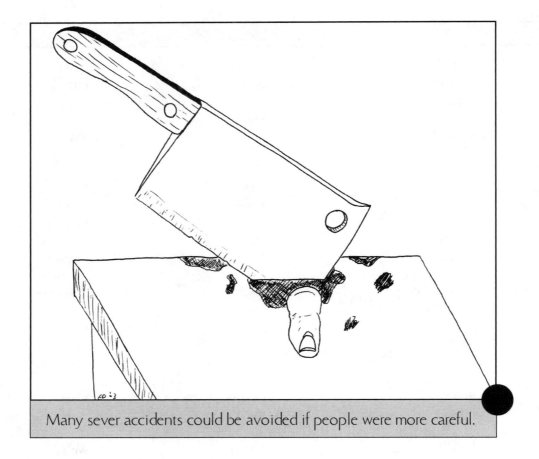

Many sever accidents could be avoided if people were more careful.

My boss is a big lyre.

The Paragraph

A paragraph, by itself, is an important method of communicating very focused ideas and feelings. A paragraph is also the basic building block of essay writing. Defined as a brief passage of writing, let's say somewhere between a half dozen and two dozen sentences, the paragraph communicates a single idea or several very focused and related ideas.

In Section Three, you will find information about the basic concepts of paragraphing: unity, coherence, structure, organization, development, and transitions. If you understand and practice these concepts when writing paragraphs, later, when we move into essay writing, you should find that writing papers is a little easier.

I am completing my final curses before applying to the nursing program.

At American weddings, the groom has a taxi.

The Paragraph

OVERVIEW

The paragraph—after the word and the sentence—is the smallest building block of writing. Mastering the art of paragraph writing will help you in many ways. Many essay exam questions, for example, require a paragraph-length answer. And just yesterday, a former student of mine stopped by to say hello and to ask me to look over an application she was submitting to a senior college. On the application, she had to respond to several questions about her intended major, career choice, etc. The directions on the form were quite clear: answer each question in a paragraph. Mastering the paragraph will also help you write papers. Longer pieces of writing, ranging from the traditional five-paragraph essay to the book-length tome you are currently reading, are "built" upon the mastery of piecing together individual paragraphs. So, for the moment, let's concentrate on learning or reviewing about writing a paragraph.

DOWN TO BASICS: PARAGRAPH WRITING

A paragraph is a very focused piece of short writing. Let's not get caught up on counting here. Usually, a paragraph has between two dozen and a half-dozen sentences. Flip to the student examples in this chapter and look at them. You'll notice that most of them probably fall within this range. I have never bothered to count the number of sentences in any of them. I hope you don't either.

Instead of focusing on the number of sentences, let's set up some more-important ways to define a well-written paragraph.

First, a paragraph must possess **unity**. That is, the paragraph is focused on one idea. A good paragraph must have this oneness of thought, this singleness of purpose. I know you have heard this before, but you are about to read it again: if you change ideas, change paragraphs.

Second, a paragraph should be **coherent**. That is, the paragraph is clear, logical, orderly—it makes sense after a single reading. All of the sentences tie together. Coherence is like glue adding cohesiveness to the ideas and sentences within the paragraph.

Third, a paragraph has **structure**. That is, the paragraph's first line is indented five spaces and all of the other lines are marginal (to the left). Again, simply look at the examples at the end of this chapter and notice how they conform to this structure.

Fourth, a paragraph has **organization**. That is, the paragraph's information is arranged in some type of order for a reason or reasons. (There is an entire section on this concept later in this chapter. I'll bet you can't wait, eh!)

Generally—but not always—a paragraph begins with a general statement. This general statement is called a **topic sentence**. The topic sentence, as the term implies, is the sentence which announces or contains the topic (subject) to be explained or discussed in the paragraph. The remainder of the paragraph is composed of specific sentences which support the topic sentence. Although a topic sentence can appear anywhere in a paragraph, placing it at the beginning just makes writing the paragraph in support of the topic sentence a little easier. Also, some writers find that placing the topic sentence at the beginning helps them stay focused, unified, and coherent.

Basic structure and organization of a generic paragraph:

I. Beginning   introduction   (topic sentence)
II. Middle   body   (support)
III. End   conclusion   (closing statement)

Let's look at an example and analyze it according to what we have learned so far:

> Contrary to popular opinion, some old is far better than new. Just think about that old comfortable pair of black pumps in your closet. You could pound the pavement all day long and then dance all night in those shoes. How could you ever replace them? You can't possibly part with your favorite old, tattered robe, the one you wouldn't dare wear when your mother-in-law stays over, but cuddled up under an afghan on the couch, you know that robe is the perfect thing to wear. Or think about old songs, the ones you know all the words to and boy can you belt those tunes out, especially while driving in the car! Along with those old songs are the old dances: twist, hitchhiker, swim, boogaloo, mashed potatoes—and those line dances! Funny how you never forget the moves. Old friends come to mind; you know, the ones you haven't seen in years but suddenly run into in the grocery store. You end up blocking aisle three for hours just reminiscing. It never seems to be a problem picking up right where you left off like it was yesterday. Those old songs inevitably remind you of old loves. You wonder what ever happened to so-and-so, that hunk. By the way, what did go wrong in your relationship? And you wonder what he's doing now and just how often he must still think of you. Old is what friends and memories are made of. Somehow, old does win over new.
>
> Pamela La Coy Krause

Let's study the paragraph. Notice that the paragraph begins with a general statement, a generalization that needs further explanation or illustration: Contrary to popular opinion, some old is far better than new. All other statements in that paragraph must develop, support, and illustrate what Pam meant by that thought. If the paragraph is written in just that way, then it will be unified and coherent. Let's break Pam's paragraph down into the format we used earlier:

I. Introduction
Contrary to popular opinion, some old is far better than new.

II. Body
The old pumps in the closet
The old, tattered robe
The old songs

    The old dances
    The old friends
    The old loves
    The old memories
   III. Conclusion
    Somehow, old does win over new.

From a structural point of view, it is obviously an excellent paragraph. As far as content is concerned, it is also excellent, for it is both unified and coherent. The paragraph sticks to one topic, and the thoughts are presented clearly. The paragraph has lots of detail, lots of specific examples to communicate Pam's thoughts.

THE TOPIC AND THE LIMITING IDEA

Read the two paragraphs which follow and decide for yourself which seems to be the more-effective:

A.   I really enjoy W. C. Fields' movies. Fields, a comedian known for his bulbous nose and whiney voice, made many movies in the early days of Hollywood. Some of his films, although lost to the public, were silent. He died on Christmas Day in 1946. Fields never did like Christmas, just like he did not appreciate kids or dogs. He was fond of Charles Dickens' novels, women, and booze. My favorite Fields movie is <u>Never Give a Sucker an Even Break.</u>

B.   The source of W. C. Fields' humor was often his own physical features. Mention the name Fields and most likely people will visualize that scarred, red, light-bulb shaped nose. Or, perhaps it is the whiney, controlled voice, Fields's vehicle for cynicism, that first comes to mind. Even the shape of his body added to the comedic effect: the spindley legs, the protruding belly, and the bowling-ball head. The finishing touch was Fields' agility, his ability to mold and maneuver his body into positions that were guaranteed to produce laughter. Fields was far from handsome, but his appearance was definitely an asset to his career.

Which paragraph is more-effective? I vote for B. Before I explain why I think B is a much better paragraph, let's take a look at A.

It is true that paragraph A does possess unity and coherence. It also follows the basic paragraph structure we have discussed. The problem is that the generalization is a bit too broad, and this affects the coherence. The paragraph has unity, but only in the broadest sense. Everything in the paragraph pertains to W. C. Fields, but other than this, the thoughts have nothing in common. The paragraph attempts too much; the focus of the paragraph is too broad. What, other than the fact that they are about Fields, do the day Fields died and the writer's favorite movie have in common?

Paragraph B, on the other hand, is more focused. The unity is unquestionably there, and the coherence is much stronger than in paragraph A.

Compare the topic sentences from paragraphs A and B.

A. I really enjoy W. C. Fields' movies.

B. The source of W. C. Fields' humor was often his own physical features.

Notice the structure of the second topic sentence as compared to the first. The writer of paragraph A fell into a trap that a lot of writers do. It is not enough to have a general topic or subject to write about, in this case, W. C. Fields. You need to narrow this. Finding the topic is only the first step. Narrowing or limiting the topic is the second. Writing is the third.

The topic sentence for paragraph A, for example, states that the topic of the paragraph is W. C. Fields. Paragraph B's topic sentence, however, states that the topic is W. C. Fields *and* that the source of his humor was his physical features. The rest of the paragraph supports only this one aspect of Fields. All other information, even though it might be about Fields, is left out.

A topic sentence can be broken down into two distinct sections: (1) the topic, and (2) the limiting idea. (These terms have no connection or relation to grammar.) The topic is what the term implies—it is the general topic or subject with which the paragraph will deal. The limiting idea limits, or narrows, that topic. This concept is exceedingly important, because it is actually the limiting idea which is the heart of the paragraph; it is the limiting idea that the rest of the paragraph develops.

To fully appreciate the function of the limiting idea, you need only to think of the various alternatives a writer faces before beginning to write. For example, consider a topic such as having a garage sale. This is a good topic to write about, but it is a very broad one. Any of the topic sentences below could generate a good paragraph, and each would be on the general topic of having a garage sale:

1. <u>Having a garage sale</u> is <u>a lot of work</u>.
         topic   limiting idea

2. <u>Having a garage sale</u> is <u>a good way to meet your neighbors</u>.
         topic   limiting idea

3. <u>Having a garage sale</u> <u>means cleaning out the attic, basement, and closets</u>.
         topic   limiting idea

4. <u>Having a garage sale</u> <u>requires a permit in certain suburban locations</u>.
         topic   limiting idea

5. <u>Having a garage sale</u> <u>brings you in contact with some very interesting bargain hunters</u>.
         topic   limiting idea

The student who did this exercise finally selected one of the five topic sentences and used it to write the following paragraph:

Having a garage sale is a lot of work. The first step is to set the dates and hours of your garage sale and to arrange for help from your friends and neighbors. Once that is taken care of, the real work begins. You must find enough tables or anything with a flat surface to arrange the items on. Book shelves could be an alternative if you run out of tables. Next, gather all the items you wish to sell. Then price these items (I find using labels easiest) according to value. Or you can "lump together" different items on one table and have a set price for that table. For example, you can have a $3.00 table meaning everything on that particular table costs $3.00. Be sure to have plenty of newspapers ready to wrap breakables in and have bags and boxes for people to carry out their purchases. After all, one man's junk is another man's treasure! Also have $40.00 to $50.00 in small bills and change in order to break big bills if necessary. A small box to keep the money in is also a good idea. About one week before the sale, if you want to reach a broader spectrum of people, place an ad in the local newspaper. On the eve of your sale, string signs announcing the sale around the lightpoles on the different corners of your neighborhood. Flags strung from your house to the curb generate more curiosity. Now, picture it: The day of the sale has finally arrived. Hordes of people are descending upon you. Relax! The hard work is over. Happy saling!

Celine McGinnis

PARAGRAPHS: TRANSITIONS ADD TO COHERENCE

Transitions are words and phrases that a writer uses deliberately to connect one idea to another, to connect one sentence to another, and even to connect one paragraph to another (or one part of an essay to another part). There are words that are "natural" transitional words within our language.

COMMON TRANSITIONAL WORDS/PHRASES

To provide examples: for example, for instance, specifically, to illustrate, an example of, indeed

To add: first, second, third, fourth, in the first place, in the second place, finally, further, furthermore, moreover, again, also, too, in addition, next, and, and then, besides, equally important

To compare: likewise, similarly, also, too, in a similar manner (fashion), in like manner

To contrast: but, yet, and yet, however, though, although, on the other hand, on the contrary, despite this, in contrast to this, otherwise, but at the same time, even so, even though, regardless, nevertheless

To indicate time: since, then, soon, until, now, until now, until then, when, whenever, later, lately, after, after a while, afterward, as, as long as, as soon as, at last, at that time, meanwhile, before, until then, during

To show a relationship: consequently, therefore, as a result, accordingly, thus, because, hence, otherwise, since, then, thereupon

To summarize, repeat, or conclude: to summarize, to sum up, in sum, all in all, altogether, as has been said, in conclusion, in other words, as stated, to repeat

To indicate place: above, below, next to, adjacent to, elsewhere, here, near, nearby, on the other side, there, to the north, to the left, opposite to, to the rear of, to the front of

Another way to add transitions to your paragraphs is to "create" your own transitional words and phrases; that is, as you are writing (or more precisely, perhaps, polishing), look for words that you can "plant" at the end (or near the end) of a sentence and then deliberately repeat at the beginning (or near the beginning) of the following sentence. This act of "planting and repeating" will link the sentences. If this all sounds very complex, it isn't. The following student paragraphs illustrate how the use of transitions adds polish and coherence to writing:

Doing ceramics can be a time-consuming task. The first task is to buy your unfired piece. This piece then needs to be cleaned of any and all seams. Once this cleaning has been done, you then need to fire the piece in a kiln. This firing process takes approximately six hours. Afterwards, the fired piece needs to cool completely. After the piece has cooled, you can start to paint it. The size and detail of the piece determine how long the painting will take. The painting of the piece can take an hour or could even turn into an all-day affair. When the painting is done and the paint has dried, you can then spray the piece with a matte coating. Once this coating has dried, you have your finished piece. If you think back over this entire process, you will realize a lot of time was invested to complete the ceramic piece.

Shirlee Hagen

The following paragraph lacks coherence. As you read it, notice how some sentences seem not to tie in with the ones surrounding them.

[1]Ken Kesey's novel, <u>One Flew Over the Cuckoo's Nest</u>, introduces the reader to some mental patients who are interesting characters. [2]Chief Bromden is a huge American Indian who finds it easier to fake deafness and dumbness than to deal with people. [3]Billy Bibbitt is a young man who stutters until he sleeps with a prostitute and loses his speech problem when he loses his virginity. [4]Always screaming and yelling Cheswick learns independence. [5]McMurphy is a prisoner who had himself committed to a mental institution because he thought it would be better than prison. [6]He is a gambler and a hell-raising con man. [7]Big Nurse is an ex-Army nurse who runs the ward in military fashion. [8]These characters are fascinating.

A reader does gain some information from the preceding paragraph; however, the writer failed to make the writing as coherent as possible. For example, sentences #2 and #3 just seem to be jammed together; although they are related thoughts, there is nothing written to emphasize the relationship. There is an even-more-abrupt shift in thought between sentences #3 and #4. Read the following revised version of the paragraph on Kesey's novel; pay particular attention to the italicized transitional words. When you have finished studying this version, contrast it to the original. Notice how coherence adds polish and precision to the writing.

[1]Ken Kesey's novel, <u>One Flew Over the Cuckoo's Nest</u>, introduces the reader to some mental patients who are *interesting characters.* [2]*One of these interesting characters* is Chief Bromden, a huge American Indian who finds it easier to fake deafness and dumbness than to deal with *the other inmates.* [3]One of *the other inmates* is *Billy Bibbitt.* [4]*Billy* is a young man who stutters until he sleeps with a prostitute. [5]*This incident* causes Billy to lose his speech problems as well as his virginity! [6]*Unlike Billy,* who is quiet, Cheswick is the complainer and the one who demands changes in unfair rules. [7]*This fighting spirit* in Cheswick is brought about by an inmate named *McMurphy.* [8]*McMurphy* is a prisoner who had himself committed to a mental institution to escape *prison life.* [9]*Life* in the mental institution allows him to pursue his favorite *activities:* gambling, hell-raising, and conning. [10]These *activities* do not endear him to *Big Nurse.* [11]*Big Nurse* is an ex-Army nurse who runs her ward in military fashion. [12]*These characters* are only a few of the interesting ones Kesey creates in <u>Cuckoo's Nest</u>.

Most of the transitional words in this particular paragraph are "created." That is, they are words that are not normally transitional words: names such as *Billy* or *Big Nurse* and words such as *activities* and *inmates*. However, the repetition of these words in key places makes them transitional.

METHODS OF PARAGRAPH ORGANIZATION

The organization of a paragraph determines the way in which the writer places his or her thoughts on paper. It is the plan used to present the ideas to the reader. There are many patterns that can be used to organize a paragraph. Usually, paragraphs are organized by a single method, but several methods might be combined also. What follow are examples of some of the most-common methods or patterns of organization. Each is briefly explained here; more-thorough explanations appear in the following chapters.

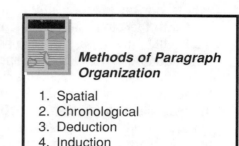

Methods of Paragraph Organization

1. Spatial
2. Chronological
3. Deduction
4. Induction
5. Order of importance

METHOD ONE: SPATIAL

Spatial organization is based upon space, physical arrangement, or physical layout. A paragraph which is arranged spatially presents its support while "moving" through "space." The writer "pans" with a pen or pencil or keyboard in much the same manner that you would pan with a movie camera.

> Most of my lunch hours are spent at my desk or in the cafeteria, but one day a few weeks ago, instead of looking at the same four walls, I had a chance to gaze out at our beautiful city. As a small bonus for the successful completion of a project, my Manager suggested I go out to lunch "on him." I decided to take a friend to Cite, the restaurant at the top of Lake Point Tower. When we arrived at the 70th floor, we were escorted along a wall of windows to our table. Our window faced north, providing us with a view of the city and lake that was breathtaking. Before us, billowy white clouds moved across a sky so blue I don't even know how to describe it. Below, dark green waves washed far enough on shore to keep all but the bravest joggers away. A small colorful garden peaked out between the base of the building and the lake. The buildings around us, all shapes and sizes, were lit by the sun. Their intricate architecture, hidden from view at ground level, was visible to us now. Our eyes traveled north along the shoreline, past North Avenue Beach and its sun worshipers, to the lush green of Lincoln Park. We could even see the lagoon, calm and empty at this time of day. To the right was Belmont Harbor where dozens of boats, sails flying, dotted the water. Finally, we came to one of my favorite landmarks: the old Edgewater Beach Hotel, still visible at such a great distance because of her pink facade. All of these beautiful sites reminded me of why I love Chicago—and of why I should get out more at lunch.
>
> Eileen Langan

METHOD TWO: CHRONOLOGICAL

Chronological organization is organization according to the passage of time. As the writer of such a paragraph, you will be "moving" the reader either backward or forward through time.

Working as an Audit Secretary is very boring. As an Audit Secretary, I have quite a bit of downtime. I have perfected filling up my day with several activities. When I arrive at work, I turn on my computer and head for the lunch room. At 8:30 a.m., we call this room the "Breakfast Room." I eat a bagel, greet everyone who comes to get coffee, and then talk with the people who are not ready to start their day. Once we all decide to make our way to our desks, it is 9:00 a.m. Walking to the mail room to pick up the mail, I stop to chat with the other secretaries. I walk back to my desk, where I sort the mail and distribute it within my department. Wishing my boss would give me something to do, I turn to my trusty computer for comfort. Should I pay some personal bills or play computer games? First, I choose to pay bills; this takes about a half hour. Needing a walk, I ride the elevator to the top floor and visit the Receptionist for a few minutes. After chatting with her, I make my way back to my desk, happy to see some paper on it. Yes, I have a whole twenty minutes of work to do! Well, it is almost eleven o'clock. I think I will play computer games until lunchtime. Taking a break from a strenuous game of Free Cell, I decide to go to the restroom, where I find some more people to talk to. On my way back to my desk, I stop to ask my fellow coworker and lunch buddy what she is having for lunch. We plan to go out and get something to bring back to the office. At 11:45 a.m. we head out to get our lunch. Lunchtime is great because I have a whole hour taken out of my day. After lunch, sometimes I will take a walk along the river. When I get back to the office, off I go to the restroom again. For the final stretch of my day, I do some homework, read a couple of chapters from my book, and end the day with a couple more rounds of Free Cell. I would not recommend that anyone work as an Audit Secretary, because, in my experience, it is boring.

Justine Atkocaitis

METHOD THREE: DEDUCTION

The thought process which progresses from general to specific is called deduction. It, too, is an effective method of paragraph organization. Many teachers refer to this as "funnel" organization; that is, the paragraph begins broadly and narrows gradually.

Walking at night is a wonderful way to end the day. By then, the major part of the day with all its attendant activities, its focus on schedules, and its particular stresses, has passed. The rest of the family is home and either getting ready for bed or already asleep. The dishes are washed, the laundry is in the dryer, the television has hopefully ceased its loud domination over the household, and the seemingly constant teenage telephone conversations have reluctantly ended. Ideally, homework assignments have miraculously been completed, bills have been paid, and another day is coming to a close. It is at this point that I particularly enjoy going out for a brisk walk under the night sky. I find this to be perhaps the best way to achieve relaxation and to guarantee a good night's sleep. I am fortunate to live in a place where it is relatively safe to walk after dark. The weather does not always permit these nocturnal outings, of course; there may be many frigid and iced-over winter evenings when it would be hazardous to step outside the door. At other times of the year, thunderstorms or excessive heat can prevent walking. On a clear, starlit night, however, especially when the moon is full, it is difficult to resist the urge to walk. Without the usual visual distractions of daytime, it seems more possible to meditate, to focus one's thoughts, and perhaps most of all, to relax. Maybe because the air is cooler at night, it also seems much easier to walk then; time and distance pass quickly. When the moon is full, it is amazing how light it can be outdoors—light enough, in fact, to cast a clear shadow. Sounds, especially, take on a new importance. In the summer there is a veritable chorus of the night noises, a constant, surprisingly, loud, all-pervasive, multi-layered drone. As the weather begins to cool in the fall, the noise subsides, and the prevailing sounds become those of wind-strewn, rustling leaves. Winter is characterized by its stillness, and I am struck not by the noise but by the quiet, interrupted only by the sound of creaking branches and the soft crunch of snow underfoot. Perhaps the most exciting time comes with the arrival of spring and the reawakening of the "spring peep-ers," which seem to be announcing joyfully that once again we have all survived the rigors of winter. Night walking provides a readily available escape into an unstructured world of peace and silence; it offers a way to keep life in perspective.

Nina Thorp

METHOD FOUR: INDUCTION

Induction is the thought process which is the opposite of deduction; induction moves from the specific to the general.

Eight hours of school has ended with the ringing of a bell and a grumble in my stomach. I run through the front door and notice nothing except the entrance to the kitchen and the smell of sauce cooking on the stove next to the espresso cafeteria. Uncle Tony stands dunking bread into the sauce pan and devouring it like it was his last meal. I look to my right; over the sink hangs a large ball of provolone cheese and a bunch of red peppers. The table is set for the usual six people. Glasses of melon and wine are care-fully set before each place setting; in the center of the table is a platter of supersod, cheese, and dried olives. Bottles of olive oil stand near the freshly baked bread that is in the bread basket that Great-Grandma Martha made. As steaming bowls of hot, freshly drained pasta covered in mounds of sauce are brought to the table, everyone spontane-ously reaches for the grated cheese, and Papa starts to say Grace. I love my Grandma's kitchen!

Martha Porzio DeMarco

METHOD FIVE: ORDER OF IMPORTANCE

The ideas in a paragraph may be organized according to their importance in relation to the main idea expressed in the topic sentence. Usually, the main idea is placed in one of two positions: (1) either it appears first and is followed by subordinate ideas, or (2) it appears last and is preceded by subordinate ideas.

There are several reasons why I decided to learn to swim at the age of fifty. One reason was that I wanted the exercise. I always knew I should be more active, but I never got around to being active; I just thought about it a lot. I knew that if I signed up for swimming lessons I would stick with them and force myself to get in shape—or in better shape. A second reason was a bit more practical. My husband and I just recently purchased lakefront property in Wisconsin. That means a lot of trips to the lake for boating and swimming and other activities. I wanted to be able to join in the fun, so swimming lessons seemed a wise choice. The third—and probably the most meaningful reason—was that I wanted to be able to swim in order to save my life in the event of an accident at the lake. Or, more importantly, I wanted to be able to save the life of loved ones. Knowing how to swim would give me a "stay-alive" factor that I thought important. Learning to swim at my age was one of the wisest things I ever did—next to talking my husband into buying a cottage on the lake.

Paula McCorrey

METHODS OF PARAGRAPH DEVELOPMENT

Development refers to the extent to which the writer explains his or her ideas on paper. A well-developed paragraph explains the main idea or ideas in sufficient depth so as to communicate them. There are many methods of development you can use when writing a paragraph. Not all paragraphs are developed by a single method; some paragraphs, in fact, might combine several. Following are examples of some of the most-common methods of development. Each is explained briefly here; more-thorough explanations appear in the following chapters.

Methods of Paragraph Development

1. Process
2. Example/Illustration
3. Comparison-Contrast
4. Classification
5. Cause-Effect
6. Definition
7. Description
8. Narration

METHOD ONE: PROCESS

When you explain how to do something or provide a set of instructions to be followed, you are developing your thoughts by *process*.

Working at a health care facility dedicated to preserving and saving lives makes death difficult to deal with for all employees. To find a patient in the process of dying is enough to send the adrenalin pumping as your only thought is "Live. Dammit. Breathe!" Quickly and efficiently a "Code Blue" is called, CPR is begun, and the room fills with professionals from ICU, CCU, Nursing, Respiratory Therapy, and Venoclysis. All are well-trained and immediately begin the job at hand: getting that patient to live. Often, success is at hand, and often, failure reigns. When it comes to human life, failure is frustrating and painful. Dealing with this is a common occurrence and the worst part of the job. Once the staff doctor has pronounced the patient dead, the last steps of patient care begin. First, the family must be informed. Often, in order to lessen this heart-rendering blow, a call is made telling them their family member has taken a "turn for the worse," then a second call is made minutes later informing them of the demise. The person making the calls must be calm, efficient, and understanding on the phone. Before the family arrives, the body must be cleaned because all the muscles relax during death, and then the body must be dressed in a fresh hospital gown, be groomed, and have all tubes and lines removed so the last sight of the loved one is peaceful. The belongings are then packed for the family to eliminate heartache and trouble at a time when most people are not thinking clearly. After the viewing, after coffee and sympathy have been dished out to the best of everyone's ability, the family departs to make their own arrangements for their loved one. The staff then begins the last steps in patient care that will ever be done for this person. A morgue sheet is brought in, and the body is bound and wrapped naked to send to the funeral home. The body is then placed on a morgue cart and taken to the morgue, a large, walk-in refrigerator, to be kept cool until the funeral parlor picks it up. Often, this is the staff's last chance to say goodbye to a familiar, respected patient. Most handle it best with humor, because it makes most negative emotions bearable. The most difficult experience in this for me was when I "lost" a forty year old diabetic during a Code Blue. He was a partial amputee, on kidney dialysis, blind . . . and his heart just gave out. To go through these steps on one so young, no matter the medical condition, is heart-breaking. This is why, of all the patient care duties, death and morgue care are the most difficult to make yourself do.

Joanne Ahmad

METHOD TWO: EXAMPLE/ILLUSTRATION

An easy and effective method of paragraph development is *example*. By using one or two related examples to support the topic sentence, the writer can very graphically and concretely illustrate her limiting idea. Notice the effective illustration through example in the following paragraph.

Historical romance novels almost always have the same pattern. How do I know this? I read at least one historical romance novel a week. There is the heroine. She is always very young, beautiful, petite, intelligent as any man, a virgin and one of her parents is dead or dreadfully mean. Then there is the hero. He is most-definitely deadly gorgeous, tall, muscular, a rogue, rich, intelligent and usually a duke or an earl. The forces of the world usually drive this virgin and rogue together. The force that brings the two together is usually a tragedy (falling off a horse, or crashing into each other at a party where the virgin is injured). The rogue will eventually fall in love with the virgin after he has rescued and taken care of her after the tragedy. The rogue will make love to the virgin either before they are married and he then has ruined her and they must marry, or he takes his virgin to the marriage bed. After the rogue has made love to his virgin bride, he is no longer a rogue and becomes a faithful husband. He only lusts after his wife. The rest of the historical romance novel involves the wife and now faithful husband in conflict. The husband usually does something dastardly (stays out all night gambling, is in a compromising position with a scarlet woman or loses all his money). The wife usually leaves her husband at this point, but in the end there is always a reasonable explanation for the dastardly deeds. The wife understands and forgives the husband. The couple have two to fifteen children, and everyone knows the last sentence of the novel: They live happily ever after.

Kathleen Malas

METHOD THREE: COMPARISON-CONTRAST

Comparison-contrast development is effective for pointing out differences (contrast) or similarities (comparison) or both (comparison-contrast).

Before I step out the door, I look for my purse. After I find my purse, I look inside to see if I have everything I need for the day. Sometimes, I name the items aloud as my fingers muddle through this mess. This could take a few minutes. I rummage through make-up, comb, brush, hand lotion, lists of people I have to call, hair spray, receipts, loose currency, loose change, sunglasses, Kleenex, envelopes, pencil, pen, calendar, tape measure, tiny cracker packages, credit cards that I haven't returned to my wallet, house keys, mace, wallet, cough drops, empty prescription bottle for my dog's medicine (which needs to be refilled), address book, etc., making sure everything is there before walking out the door. I usually have to look somewhere other than my purse for my car keys. For some reason I just put them down anywhere when I come in, so I have to find them when I go out. Before my husband steps out the door, he reaches for his wallet, comb, and keys. That's it. This is very simple. Not much thought or planning goes into this. He knows where these items are every morning. He is very organized and very matter-of-fact. I, on the other hand, need to take a good part of my life with me when I leave the house. My husband does not. If my purse is cluttered, so is my life. There is not much clutter in a wallet, comb, and keys. There's a lesson here somewhere, if only I could find it!

Clare Gornick

METHOD FOUR: CLASSIFICATION

Classification is the division of a group into subgroups based upon the uniform application of one or more principles. In the following paragraph, the writer classified during-movie talkers. He analyzed who talks, why, and to whom.

I am a movie fan; my hobby leads me to several movies a week. Lately, I have noticed that I am sharing the theater with a lot of talkers. From my study of this creature, I have determined that there are several categories of during-movie talkers. One category is the young child. This person obviously doesn't know better or does know better but lacks the social graces to discipline himself or herself to shut up. This usually results in a loud "Sssshhh" from the parent, which is sometimes more distracting than the kid. A second category is the less-than-intelligent moviegoer. This person is either too dumb to understand the plot of a suspense movie or detective thriller (or the person was in the bathroom or lobby at the wrong time). This person constantly asks questions about the plot, the characters, even the music. Usually, the person being asked the question replies, which means there are two people talking. A third category of talkers is the bored person. For whatever reason, this person just doesn't like what is happening on the silver screen and prefers to entertain himself or herself instead of just leaving. If two bored people find each other, I find a new seat. A fourth category of talker is the scared talker.

This is usually during a horror movie. The purpose of talking in this case is to maintain human contact. Also, while talking, the person is "allowed" to turn away from the screen and look at the person in the next chair. What is said doesn't matter, as long as eye contact with the screen is broken. The final category of talker is the obnoxious person. This person knows that he is funnier or scarier than the Hollywood writers and tries to improve upon the scripts for the benefit of the rest of the audience. His comments are loud at a time when the movie is soft, funny when the movie is sad, and obscene when the movie is tender. Thanks to these fellow moviegoers, I'm considering the purchase of cable television.

Arthur K. Caprio

METHOD FIVE: CAUSE-EFFECT

Cause-effect, sometimes referred to as causal (not casual) analysis, is another method of development. Using this pattern, the writer describes or explains a cause or a series of causes which brought (or may bring) about a given situation, or examines the effect or the series of effects which a given situation might (or did) produce. It is also possible that a paragraph could examine both cause(s) and effect(s).

Last semester, I learned the cliched "hard way" that I could not work forty hours a week and carry fifteen credit hours. Trying to be both a full-time worker and a full-time student had several effects on my life. For one, I was always tired. I would get off work early in the morning and then try to either do a little homework or grab some sleep before going off to campus. If I slept, I felt guilty for not studying; if I did homework, I felt guilty for stressing my body and not resting it properly. Once I got to school I could not concentrate; trying to participate was not possible. I felt bad that I would find myself nodding off in classes. A second effect, as you probably have guessed, was a less than respectable grade point average. Well, not quite. My grade (note: singular) was good, in the one class that I did not drop. I had no choice but to withdraw from the majority of my classes. My grades reflected my whacked-out priorities, not my intelligence. A third effect, I'm trying school full-time again this semester, but I have cut work back to part-time. Ironically, all the extra money I earned by working full-time or over-time went to pay this semester's tuition for the same classes I paid for last semester! I feel that I did not give myself and my studies a fair chance last term. I suppose I did learn something from the experience, but it was an expensive lesson.

Bob Bradley

METHOD SIX: DEFINITION

Definition, or more correctly, *extended definition,* is a method of development that provides an explanation or a clarification of the meaning of a word, a phrase, or a concept. Extended definitions are frequently personal or subjective; they may disagree with the dictionary definition or the accepted definition, or they may simply extend the definition.

My definition of fantasy is something that can exist only in your imagination, but can't really happen. When I was very young (four years old), I imagined a place I called my secret hiding place. My sister was six, and I told her about all the toys, games, rides, and homemade cookies I had hidden there. Karen believed every word of it. To get to my secret hiding place you had to follow me and do everything I did. Crawl under the table, snap your fingers twice, hop on one foot, do a somersault, whistle, turn around three times, etc. After taking her on a crazy trip for about an hour, I would hear Karen say she didn't want to go, or Mom would say, "Time for supper" or "Time for bed." Mom usually came to my rescue just minutes before we would have arrived at my wonderful secret hiding place. Almost every day for a year I would put my poor sister through these antics, but she never was able to visit my secret hiding place in person. Sometimes I would hide in the closet when she came home from school, and when she couldn't find me, she thought I was at my secret hiding place. She was a believer! Fantasy really hasn't changed much for me since I was four. I still have my secret hiding place in my mind. The toys and games are gone, but I've replaced them with other dreams and illusions. The function all this plays in my life is an escape from reality. There are no problems, unhappiness, loneliness, bills, or pressures at my secret hiding place. Do you want to go with me? First, you take two scissors steps, then sing "Jingle bells. . . ."

Kolleen Getridge

METHOD SEVEN: DESCRIPTION

Description, one of the four basic types of writing, is another excellent way to develop thoughts within a paragraph. Description helps the reader see what the writer sees, whether it is a person, a place, an object, etc. (You will find much more information about description in Chapter Seven.) As you describe in the paragraph you are writing, try to avoid piling up adjectives or taking inventory. Instead, concentrate on focusing concrete and specific detail; concentrate on communicating the feelings and the thoughts you have about your subject matter.

The room was dimly lit by one small bedside lamp which gave off just enough light for me to see what the room contained. At one time, this room was filled with hopes and dreams as the couple who occupied it anticipated the rest of their lives together. Their only son had been conceived here, a new life for them to share. But now this square area resembled a hospital room. The tops of the two dressers held all that was needed to care for him. The taller dresser held medications, saline solution, alcohol wipes, syringes, and a needle disposal container. This dresser was chosen for these items because of its height, for the safety of their two-year old. The lower and longer dresser held a box of tissue, lip balm, a stethoscope, a blood pressure cuff, and a watch with a second hand. The bedside table held his pitcher of water, cups, straws, emesis and wash basin, mouth swabs, and baby wipes. Below the bedside table was his bed pan and blue pads, used to protect the bed. The laundry basket lay next to these items filled with clean towels. The rocker in the corner, next to the bedside table, had a worn cushion on the seat and a pillow against its back. Taped on the wall opposite the bed were three charts which held information regarding when and what medication had been given and when the next dose was due. Above the head of the bed, the shades and curtains had been drawn across the windows. He lay in the king size bed covered with a rumpled navy blue sheet. The comforter lay across his feet, which slightly hung over the end of the bed. His once-two-hundred-plus pounds body was now hairless and reduced to skin and bones as a result of the chemotherapy. His eyes were only half open, and he drooled uncontrollably. The door, usually kept closed, now opened, and his son, in clean pajamas, blond hair still damp from his bath, entered the room and rushed past me to kiss him good-night. Little did he know, he was kissing his daddy good-bye.

Cheryl Kaner

METHOD EIGHT: NARRATION

Narration, also one of the four basic types of writing, is a natural way for writers, especially student writers, to develop ideas more fully and completely. Narration is story telling. Since birth, we have all been story tellers and have spent our lives honing our story telling skills. If you don't believe this, hide by my desk the day after a big assignment is due and listen to the tales of woe about late papers. Or listen to the tales of response to questions such as, "Where were you last night?" or, "What time did you get in this morning?" or, "Has anyone seen the last piece of French Silk that I left in the refrigerator?". Indeed, most of us are very good story tellers!

You will find a thorough treatment of narration in Chapter Eight, but for now keep in mind a few suggestions. The most important concept is to focus the story you are going to use, especially when you are writing a paragraph. Secondly, use the story to communicate the ideas and/or feelings that you wish to express in the paragraph. Select a specific incident, narrate it precisely and crisply, and use it to show or to communicate. Generally, the story will involve a conflict of some type; in fact, the story generally has to do with the resolution of that conflict.

My boyfriend Phil had the full weight of his body over my arms and upper body, as if I were about to throw him off at any second. All I remember was the intense heat and the sensation of a cigarette being extinguished between my legs. I heard the word "anaesthesia" and refused it. The doctor seemed a bit panicked at my loss of blood; I was not aware of it at the time. Phil talked to me the whole time, and I locked onto his voice to keep me conscious. I did not move a muscle for fear the doctor would accidentally cut me deeper. My legs were shaking badly, and my muscles started twitching uncontrollably. The doctor was agitated and had two other nurses helping Phil hold me down. I am usually apologetic with doctors and professionals, even when I am in pain, but that day, a different voice came out of me. This was my third visit to this particular surgeon to have my cervix cauterized to stop excessive bleeding from a LEEP procedure. This type of procedure is done when abnormalities are found on the cervix by a gynecologist. Phil had come with me at the doctor's request because she knew I would be difficult. The voice came out of nowhere when this particular surgeon joked about the "gusher" she was trying to "burn." "You had better fucking know what you're doing, lady, because I will kick your ass if I am on this table one more time." The funny thing was I said it very calmly and without anaesthesia. I have a very high threshold for pain. The nurses do not like this since it means the patient will be alert and possibly difficult. Besides, the conscious patient is more apt to sue than the unconscious one. Poor Phil just tried to talk me through it, and I kept talking over him calmly. The doctor insisted everything was fine; I just had to cooperate. By this time my team effort was greatly lacking. My sarcastic Irish temper shot out a few expletives about the doctor and her whole family and how I would not be paying the bill for her mistake. She assured me not to worry and hurriedly packed me full of so much gauze down there I could not breathe. Now, looking back on the experience, I know the procedure was necessary. Ever since the first day I spoke with her about my condition, I knew it would be a worse-case scenario. She did not whisper my diagnosis like I thought many doctors would have. She was very matter-of-fact and straight-to-the-point about all aspects of the disease, the possible causes, and the cure rate. My mind could not accept the chance I might have what she said. I took the approach that I would not have it, and that was all there was to it. This doctor caught me in the first stages of cervical cancer. In reality, this doctor saved my life.

Michelle M. Greaney

A Few More Examples

Here are a few more examples of paragraphs written by my students. I have tried to select a variety of topics, approaches, and styles for you to study.

A.   Driving along the road to my house conjures up many memories. I live at the end of a long, narrow road, more of a country lane really, peaceful in its tree-lined tranquility. Along the winding road, houses nestle quietly in the sun-dappled shade of towering oak trees. I have lived in this place for many years, and although there have been a lot of changes in the area and much new development is taking place all around us, this particular road has changed very little with the passage of time. As I returned home the other day, I thought of all my experiences on this road and realized how strongly it connects me to the past. I remember the long walks with our dogs, as they eagerly explored hidden scents in the overgrown brush along the road, panting, and tails wagging in anticipation. Later, there were walks with children in strollers, then toddling along, and finally off to school. I remember all the neighborhood children getting off the school bus and walking home, sometimes in small groups, jostling, playing; other times alone, trudging along solemnly with heavy book bags. I remember the many friends and neighbors who have driven on this road, the sound of voices, laughter, music, the crunching of tires on gravel as the cars pass. Many of my former neighbors have moved away, but they somehow remain connected to this place and unforgotten. I especially remember the many walks I have taken on this road and the wonderful timelessness of it. For years I have walked here in all seasons and at all hours of the day and night. I have experienced moments of pure joy in observing the natural beauty along the road, totally different in each season, at each moment. Here I have experienced times of peace and calm, quiet reflection and renewal, as the rest of life has surged, uncontrolled, around me. For me the road has been a wonderful gift, and its message is the connectedness of past, present, and future.

Nina Thorp

B.   There are several reasons why it is important to check and maintain proper tire pressure in the winter time. First, it is best for the tire to keep it inflated to manufacturer's specifications so that the tire is not damaged by either underinflation or overinflation. Both are harmful to the tire's performance and durability. Second, proper tire inflation is important to good traction at any time, but particularly so in the winter time when driving is sometimes done on hazardous road surfaces. Proper inflation guarantees maximum contact between the tire and the road surface, which means maximum traction efficiency. Third, driving in the winter time is a matter of thinking about personal safety. The chance of an accident in the winter is much greater because it is much easier to lose control of the car. This involves not only the proper traction, as previously explained, but also protecting the tire from the hazards of temperature extremes, salt and other chemicals applied to road surfaces, and road hazards hidden in snow. Proper inflation of the tires is a guarantee of personal safety. Every year, people die in auto accidents that might have been prevented with the proper maintenance of automobiles, including tire pressure.

Allen Colley

C.   There are many ways to teach a successful dance class to three and four year olds. What works best for me is attempting to think like a kid. One of the very first steps is making the children feel comfortable with me and with other classmates. This is often achieved by engaging in a five-minute discussion, or what I like to call "share time." This allows each child to sort of brag on himself or herself a bit. After "share time," each student finds a spot on the floor and we do Mousercise. This generally gets their adrenaline going so they are ready to go. Next comes a series of stretches which always involves goofy actions in order to keep them interested. For example, I often play a game called "Hello, Toes." The purpose of this game is to get the children familiar with their body parts. So I might say (in a deep voice while flexing), "Say hello, muscles." The kids answer with, "Hello, muscles!" (while flexing, grunting, and making a tough and mean face). We continue with the game until we have recognized some of the major parts in the body, parts which are used in dance. Now that the dancers are properly warmed up, it is time to work on ballet skills. First we start with our "Five Positions" song which demonstrates each ballet foot placement. We then continue with tendus, piques and ron de jambes. It is essential at this time that the children are given a five minute break. Next, the children put on their tap shoes, and we march in a circle for about five minutes to upbeat music, such as "Mickey Mouse Unrapped." Next, I give the children several basic steps, such as toe taps, heel steps, shuffles and marching to different songs. Finally, we end with a little game such as playing with hula hoops or bean bags. The children take off their shoes, give me a hug good-bye and go on their merry little ways. Getting into a routine like this enables the children to improve their dance skills each week.

Jennifer L. Keener

D.   My fantasy bed would be luxurious as well as elegant. As I gaze upon my bed, I admire its stone gray iron frame. It would have to be strong and sturdy to withstand even the most rambunctious of physical entanglements. The frame has a hollow rectangular canopy with a chain-designed border. Laced through the links is an off-white sheer cloth that drapes all four thin pillars. The mattress is a Sealy king-sized pillow top which measures 10 inches thick, so I don't only sink into this ever-so-soft feather-filled mattress, but I have plenty of room to stretch or even try new enticing positions. The sheets are eggshell in color and made of silk to wrap my body in smooth softness just as an egg encloses a chick for protection and comfort. Over these pleasurable sheets lays a gray goosedown extra thick comforter to keep even the coldest of toes warm. These items are necessities for a cold night or tender interlude. To top these essentials are four billowy pillows that cover the head of my bed as if they are a cluster of clouds. At the base hangs a stone gray dust ruffle to hide all the exotic and erotic delights. This is my ideal haven or refuge from all the hassles of my day.

Amy Pindel

E.   I wandered the quiet, brightly lit, sterile hallways. My mind was swirling, my heart was pounding, and my throat was dry. My body was weak, and my face paled with horror. My children's voices haunted my thoughts. I didn't know where I was heading but felt the urgent need to keep moving. I felt my eyes welling up with tears and my stomach rising to my throat. I came across a pay phone and abruptly stopped! I rummaged through my purse for change while controlling my urge to scream for help; I took the receiver in my hand, inserted the change, and dialed by complete instinct. I heard the voice from the other line, "Hello . . . Hello . . . "? I recognized my mom's voice. My voice cracked as I replied, "Hello, mom. . . . " With my next breath, I screamed from the bottom of my soul, "My husband has leukemia! Lord, God please help us!!"

Cindy Alarcon

F.   After a morning of skiing and sledding, it was time to eat. We decided on our usual spot; everyone agreed on the Restaurant Uhr, a quaint, family run restaurant in a small ski resort tucked away in the valley of Glarnerland. It is located in the heart of Switzerland, about thirty-five miles north of Zurich, which was our home for two years. Two years of beauty and mountains and outside dining. Yes, outside. The Swiss people love to be outdoors no matter what time of year. As we trudged up the old wooden stairs to the upper deck, we noted the smell of cheese fondue. We sat down in the warm sun; it felt good to rest our feet. As I looked around, I still could not believe my family and I were here, surrounded by the Swiss Alps. The sky was clear, not a cloud in sight. To my left I could hear cowbells and the sound of hooves coming up the road. It was a huge sleigh with two long seats facing each other; the people sat inside all covered with a bright plaid blanket. I watched them laughing and singing as they trotted down the narrow road. Directly below the deck was a small, brown, snow-covered cabin. It was a warming center for the ski instructors; the one o'clock lesson was about to begin. One by one, each instructor greeted his or her students with a warm smile and a hearty handshake. Just beyond my favorite ski run, which was wide and not very steep, the chair lifts sailed by. Together with the powdered blue sky, and the majestic Alps as the backdrop, it was a site I wanted etched in my mind forever. I took a deep breath of that clean, crisp mountain air, looked around the table at my family, and I thought, "This is the life for me. . . ."

Sheila Keating

G.   Sometimes, when I see eggs, I think of an event from my childhood, and I call my sister on the phone, and we laugh until we cry. In 1967, Chicago had its worst snowstorm in its recorded history. People became "snowed in," schools and stores were closed, and streets were impassable. The city came to a standstill. Days after the initial snowfall, people were finally beginning to shovel out. At our house, food was running low. My mom decided to send my sister and me on a "mission." We were to walk eight blocks for some groceries, including eggs. Like mountaineers conquering the Alps, we made our way through the towering mounds of snow. Once we had completed our shopping, we left the store. My sister carried the necessities; I carried the eggs. We trudged our way back. With "control center" in sight, mission accomplished, chest swelling with pride, I slipped on some ice. The bag of eggs landed in front of me, I landed on top of the bag, and the rest, as the saying goes, was history. I could have died right there on the spot, looking like a human omelette. When we arrived home, we related our story. With their renowned, dry sense of humor, the remaining—not to mention warm and clean—members of our family said, "Well, the yolk's on you." Since that day, a simple egg conjures up memories of childhood.

Joan Pierczynski

H.   The date was September 25, 1989. I was at my mother's house. The phone rang, and my sister answered it. Her expression told me the news wasn't good. "That was the hospital." She paused to gather herself, to prevent breaking down. "The doctor said she won't make it through the night. We are supposed to go to the hospital right away to say good-bye." As soon as she finished, I ran to be alone. I felt all the blood drain from my body. I sobbed and asked why. About an hour later, I was at her bedside. The nurse asked us to leave the room so she could remove all life support. When I returned, I held her hand and stroked it gently. Looking at her, I thought of all the moments I would miss. Just the two of us, sitting in church, teaching vacation Bible school, her trying to teach me how to make pie dough from scratch, no more Christmas Eves . . . I can still hear the heart monitor playing the sound of her heart . . . the pastor reciting the Twenty-Third Psalm . . . the urgency in her voice when she asked to get out of bed. Then, a sudden peace came over her and the rest of the room. The monitor played its last beat. My grandmother was dead.

Barb Chin

I.   The vacation my wife and I took to Mackinac Island last year taught us the meaning of relaxation. We both work full time and, like many, suffer greatly from the rigors and stress of our everyday lives. Having never spent much time away from home, we nervously packed the car and began our journey. Not more than fifteen minutes after leaving home, we experienced a rain storm that made us both wonder what we might be getting into. But soon after, the weather cooperated, and we were calmed by the beauty offered by a tree-lined route along the eastern shores of Lake Michigan. Arriving at our destination, we were introduced to the serenity of the island itself. Use of motor driven vehicles on the island was prohibited, so horse drawn carriages, bicycles, or walking were the only means of visiting the quaint shops, restaurants, and many houses dating back to the early 1800's. The pace was slow, the air clear, and after a day of strolling the island's mile-long main street, we rested in adirondack-style chairs found along the lake's shore. Later, we would find ourselves gazing up at the thousands of stars never visible in the Chicago night sky. Nearing the end of our trip, we felt none of the anxieties that one might normally expect when faced with the thought of returning home and resuming a "normal" lifestyle. Instead we talked of how wonderful it had been, awaking each morning and not being required to do anything but explore the day without any urgency, the calm of the water, or the sense of a vast universe beyond the confines of our own planet. This small island's "life" had forced us to slow down and experience a peace that we never knew existed. Excitedly, we planned this year's vacation, longer and more ambitious, during the ten hour ride back home.

Richard Donnellan

PARAGRAPHS—YOUR TURN

1 Choose a topic.

2 Think of all the various ways you could discuss or develop the topic you have chosen. Then decide which of these various ideas might be easiest for you to write a paragraph about.

3 Construct a topic sentence. Be certain that it is in ideal form: topic and limiting idea.

4 Rough out an outline of the paragraph. Try to jot down three or four specific ideas that will support or clarify the limiting idea.

5 Write a rough draft of your paragraph.

TOPIC SENTENCE—PARAGRAPH PLAN SHEET

EXERCISE ONE

Part One: Think of a subject or topic for a paragraph and write it in the blank provided. Then try to construct four or five topic sentences dealing with that topic.

Topic: _____

1. _____
             topic   limiting idea

2. _____
             topic   limiting idea

3. _____
             topic   limiting idea

4. _____
             topic   limiting idea

5. _____
             topic   limiting idea

Part Two: In the space below, try to rough out an outline for a paragraph that would develop one of the topic sentences you constructed above. Jot down three or four specific ideas to support, clarify, or explain the limiting idea.

_____

_____

_____

_____

_____

_____

_____

_____

_____

Part Three: Using the outline you made in Part Two, write the rough draft of the paragraph.

TOPIC SENTENCE—PARAGRAPH PLAN SHEET

EXERCISE TWO

Part One: Think of a subject or topic for a paragraph and write it in the blank provided. Then try to construct four or five topic sentences dealing with that topic.

Topic: _____

1. _____

topic   limiting idea

2. _____

topic   limiting idea

3. _____

topic   limiting idea

4. _____

topic   limiting idea

5. _____

topic   limiting idea

Part Two: In the space below, try to rough out an outline for a paragraph that would develop one of the topic sentences you constructed above. Jot down three or four specific ideas to support, clarify, or explain the limiting idea.

_____

_____

_____

_____

_____

_____

_____

_____

Part Three: Using the outline you made in Part Two, write the rough draft of the paragraph.

_____

_____

_____

_____

_____

_____

_____

_____

_____

_____

_____

_____

_____

_____

_____

_____

_____

_____

_____

_____

_____

_____

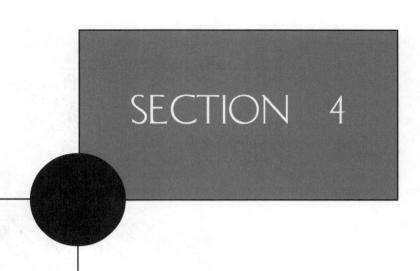

The Essay

Although some of the writing done at the college level is brief and done in paragraph form, most assignments require the student to write in-depth and at-length. The writing form that is longer than the paragraph is the essay.

An essay is composed of several paragraphs, as few as two or as many as necessary, all in support of an idea or a series of related ideas. Because of its length, the essay gives the writer an opportunity to explore a topic fully and to express ideas and feelings completely.

Section Four will give you information about the four basic types of essays.

FOUR BASIC TYPES OF ESSAYS
Narration tells a story or uses a story to communicate.
Description shows the reader an object, a place, a person, or an event.
Exposition explains the writer's views to the reader.
Persuasion convinces the reader to accept the writer's ideas.

In addition to learning the four basic types of writing, you will learn more about the various methods of structure, organization, and development.

Section Four also presents six rhetorical patterns of development: **process, example, comparison-contrast, classification, definition,** and **cause-effect.** They are representative of a classic approach to the teaching of composition, and they are the foundation of much essay writing. You will find that many of the writing assignments you are called upon to complete in your other classes and/or in your career might make use of one of these rhetorical patterns. These six patterns will give you a lot of flexibility as a writer, especially when you begin to combine the patterns. As you continue to study and practice writing, you will learn—increasingly—that there are few neat, non-overlapping categories of "how" something is to be written. Rather, when you write, concentrate on and rely on your writing skills to communicate your thoughts and feelings; communication is the end (or aim) of writing. The various patterns and techniques are simply the means of writing.

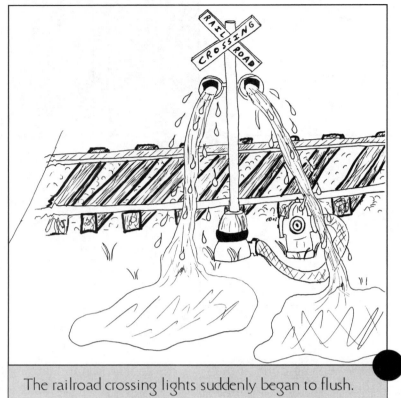

The railroad crossing lights suddenly began to flush.

My boyfriend's car has a fowl smell to it.

The Thesis Statement, the Outline and the Title

PART ONE: THE THESIS STATEMENT

The thesis statement (sometimes simply referred to as *the thesis*) is the generalization which an essay supports, develops, clarifies, illustrates, and/or explains. Every word, sentence, paragraph, and idea in the essay, regardless of the essay's length, must support the thesis statement. In short, the thesis of an essay is its focus, its main point or series of related points. It is the purpose for writing.

Perhaps the easiest way to understand the concept of the thesis statement and how it functions within the essay is to think in terms of what you know about topic sentences and their relation to paragraph structure and organization. Basically, the thesis statement serves the same purpose, functions in the same manner within the essay as does the topic sentence within the paragraph. The thesis statement is to the essay what the topic sentence is to the paragraph.

TOPIC AND LIMITING IDEA

Like the topic sentence, the thesis statement can be divided into two distinct parts: the topic and the limiting idea. The topic states the general topic or subject to be covered; the limiting idea narrows the topic to one specific aspect to be developed in the paper. It is the limiting idea which the remainder of the essay supports, develops, illustrates, and explains.

Here are some thesis statements from essays written by my students; study them, noting the structure of each:

1. <u>Roller skating in the park</u> is a <u>good way to gain a tan, a healthy body, and a few new friends</u>.
     topic   limiting idea

2. <u>My friend Trish</u> is a <u>disaster waiting to happen</u>.
     topic   limiting idea

3. <u>Coaching soccer</u> encourages <u>a person to want to kill some kids' parents</u>.
     topic   limiting idea

4. <u>Working in a fast food restaurant</u> lets me <u>observe the types of eaters in the world</u>.
     topic   limiting idea

5. <u>Water skiing</u> is <u>easy if you follow these seven simple steps and suggestions</u>.
     topic   limiting idea

Note that the placement of the limiting idea at the end of the thesis statement helps the writer give the essay a clear focus, gives the reader a clear idea of what is to come. It is important for a writer to have a clear focus or purpose; it is not enough for the writer to have a topic or a subject. Rather, what specifically about this topic does the writer want to communicate?

Let's assume, for example, that as your instructor, I ask you to write an essay. You decide to write about this new adventure in your life: attending college. But, what is your paper on college going to be about? What are you wanting to say about attending college? What do you want your reader to gain from reading your essay? Well, there are many possible avenues to meander in a topic as broad as attending college. I would suggest jotting down a few of those possibilities. Try to construct various thesis statements that could generate or focus an essay on the broad topic of attending college, such as those printed below:

Possible Thesis Statements

1. Going to college helps you meet many new people.
2. Going to college is terribly expensive.
3. Going to college helps you secure a future profession.
4. Going to college is a waste of time and money.
5. Going to college teaches the student responsibility.
6. Going to college while working full-time makes life almost too exciting.
7. Attending college taught me that living alone is saner than living in a dorm.
8. Attending college convinced me that all professors can be classified into one of four groups.
9. My two years of college convinced me that education is not defined as just classroom learning.
10. There are basically three reasons why I decided to quit college after my first semester.

All of the thesis statements deal with the topic of going to college. Further, each statement has a limiting idea that narrows the topic. It is entirely possible that all ten essays could be written with virtually little or no overlap of thoughts, examples, or details.

Remember: you are not ready to write when you think of a topic; you must first think of a limiting idea.

THESIS STATEMENT: SOME PRACTICAL APPLICATIONS

My students frequently ask me how long a paper should be. Ideally, it is the student, not the teacher, who determines the length of a paper. A paper should be long enough to adequately communicate the thesis statement. When the student writes the thesis statement, he is saying, "My paper will be of sufficient length to explain and clarify this idea or series of ideas."

Most teachers inform students as to the expected length of papers. Generally speaking, the teacher is giving an estimate, or a "rule of thumb," so that students have an idea of what is expected. There are teachers, however, who are quite strict as to specified length, and it would be advisable to meet their expectations. If your teacher tells you a paper should be of a particular length, ask whether that length is a guideline or a requirement.

Regardless of who or what determines the length of the paper, it is necessary that the paper be developed fully; there should be no unsupported or undeveloped generalizations. This is why the limiting idea of the thesis statement is very important. If you know your essay must be of a certain length, you must be certain that you have narrowed the topic properly so as to allow for full development of all ideas. If your topic is too broad, you might be forced to reduce the paper to nothing but generalizations in order to hold the paper to its required length. If your topic is too narrow, you might find yourself having addressed the topic satisfactorily and then having to stretch the ideas or "b.s." in order to have the specified number of pages.

These problems are some of the reasons many teachers who assign papers require students to hand in preliminary outlines and/or statements of thesis. By checking these, a teacher can usually tell if students have satisfactorily limited the topics for their papers. This can save a student a lot of unnecessary work, not to mention a potentially bad grade. When you are assigned a paper, don't hesitate to do this on your own. Ask the instructor if he or she would be willing to look over a thesis statement or an outline before you continue with the writing. Most instructors are willing to do this.

PART TWO: THE OUTLINE

THE OUTLINE

Before starting the actual writing of an essay, it is wise to make certain your thoughts are as organized as you think they are. Why not try an outline to be certain?

"Ah, outlining!" you say. "Learned that in junior high and said 'no thanks,' at least not in college." Lots of student writers feel that way. If you really feel outlining is a waste of time, look at it this way. If you outline before you write, you spend an additional few minutes to insure that your thoughts are organized. If they are, then the outline provides a blueprint or a road map to follow as you write—which minimizes your chances of getting lost or becoming unorganized. If, on the other hand, you try to outline and discover your thoughts are not quite organized or structured, then you've saved yourself a lot of time and headache.

Many of my students outline their papers, although I never require them to. (This saves them the trouble of having to write an outline after they have written the paper!) If you have problems with structure or organization, I really recommend it to you. It's another good technique to help you improve your writing.

Four Types of Outlines

1. Scratch
2. Topic Sentence
3. Topic
4. Sentence

■ The Outline: the scratch outline/the grocery list outline

This is the most informal method of outlining; like a grocery list, this outline is a simple listing of the ideas to be included. Here is a sample scratch outline:

Like the old song says, best things in life are free

- sunsets and sunrises
- a walk in the rain
- the smell of fall leaves (sound of them, too)
- rainbows
- shooting stars
- watching birds build a nest
- listening to waves come up on shore
- gathering sea shells
- listening to the quiet of early morning
- sound of snow falling in the deep woods

Here is a second example of a scratch outline:

As an experienced Picture Lady in the school system, I would like to give you some suggestions as to how to go about doing your first presentation on art to school children :

do your research
gather your materials and supplies
evaluate the "scary" events/ times you anticipate
make contact with the teacher
make contact with the students

Sandra Schmidt

■ The Outline: the topic sentence outline

This is another informal-yet-easy way to organize and gather thoughts before writing. This type of outline is a listing of the topic sentences that would appear in the body of the essay. Here is a sample topic sentence outline:

1. Locating an animal shelter near your home can be accomplished in several ways.
2. Selecting the right pet for you and your family is easy, but you do have to keep in mind several factors.
3. Filling out the paper work and paying fees is the next step in the process of animal adoption.
4. Before you can take home your pet, there are medical procedures and exams that must be implemented.
5. Preparation of your house for the arrival of the new family member also requires some planning.
6. Picking up the pet after surgery and bringing it home is the next item on the agenda.
7. Maintaining the health of your pet is important.
8. Helping the pet to blend in with the family requires every family member's help.
9. Maintaining good relations and providing continued financial support for the shelter must continue after you have settled in with your pet.

The essay which this outline would produce would have nine body paragraphs, one written in support of each of the topic sentences.

Here is a second topic sentence outline for you to study:

1. Censorship of reading materials is still a very controversial issue in many high school districts in the United States.
2. Mark Twain's <u>Huck Finn</u> has been banned in many schools because it is considered to be racist.
3. Studs Terkle's book <u>Working</u> has been the center of controversy because of its language.
4. Bernard Malamud's Pulitzer-winner <u>The Fixer</u> has been removed from school reading lists because of its language and its violence.

5. Some of William Shakespeare's plays have been taken off reading lists because they are considered to be too difficult for many students to read and understand.

Maria Cavelle

The Outline: the topic outline

The topic outline differs from the topic sentence outline in at least two important ways. One, it is not written in complete sentences; rather, it presents its information in words and phrases. Two, it has a formal method of structuring information in parallel categories by the use of letters and numbers. Roman numerals are used for main categories of information. Capital letters are used for subdivisions. Information within these categories is broken down by the use of Arabic numerals and lower case letters. Roman numerals are all equally indented as are all the capital letters, the Arabic numerals, and the lower case letters:

Statement of Purpose

I.
    A.
    B.
        1.
        2.
            a.
            b.
    C.
        1.
        2.
II.
    A.
        1.
            a.
            b.
            c.
        2.
    B.
III.

Here is an example of a topic outline:

Thesis: Buying a beach house changed my lifestyle by adding work.

I. Paper work
    A. Long-term
        1. Insurance
        2. Mortgage
    B. Short-term
        1. Utility bills
        2. Checks for home repair services
II. Painting
    A. Interior
        1. All Bedrooms
        2. Bathroom
        3. Kitchen-dining area

      B. Exterior
        1. Trim
        2. Car port
  III. Lawn work
      A. Mowing
      B. Re-sodding
      C. Garden
      D. Removing dead trees
  IV. Building plans
      A. Screened in porch on front
      B. Tool storage shed out back
      C. Add on to car port for boating gear

Here is a second example of a topic outline:

Thesis: The sheepdog is a good pet for persons who want a loving furry friend that is not expensive and bothersome.

   I. Characteristics
      A. Size
      B. Weight
      C. Color
      D. Life Span
   II. Training
      A. Sit
      B. Stay
      C. Speak
  III. Housebreaking
      A. Indoor
      B. Outdoor
  IV. Grooming
      A. Brushing
      B. Clipping
   V. Feeding
      A. Food types
      B. Schedules

Debbie Walters

This example shows you why the use of an outline almost guarantees the essay that is based upon it will have structure and organization of primary and secondary ideas. This example also demonstrates the parallel structuring of ideas: primary ideas are indicated by the use of Roman numerals, and secondary ideas are indicated by the use of capital letters.

■ The Outline: the sentence outline

The sentence outline is very similar to the topic outline, with two important distinctions. One, as its name implies, the sentence outline is written in complete sentences. Each idea presented in the outline, whether primary or secondary, is expressed in a complete sentence. Two, the sentence outline shows the amount of development to be included in the essay. Because it goes into depth, the sentence outline is a good indicator of the relationship between ideas and paragraphs and of the approximate length of an essay. Like the topic outline, the sentence outline follows the same parallel system of numbering and lettering.

Both types of outlines establish a system of using the lefthand margin and consistent identation patterns to structure and organize the ideas to be presented in essay form. Because of its length and depth, the sentence outline is the most-thorough.

Here is a sample sentence outline:

Thesis: There are four types of eaters in our house.

   I. The first type of eater is the picky eater.
- A. This type puts hardly any food on the plate.
- B. All foods are separated into little sections with nothing touching.
- C. Each item is eaten clockwise.
- D. After twenty minutes, the plate is still half-filled.
- E. Most of the food goes into the garbage disposal or to the dog.

  II. The second type of eater is the garbage pit eater.
- A. This type heaps food until the plate overflows.
- B. The foods are just heaped one on-top of the other in a pile.
- C. The food is inhaled in gulps, not eaten in any kind of structured way.
- D. After twenty bites, the plate has been emptied and is ready for another load.
- E. Most of the food in the kitchen goes into the garbage-pit eater; there isn't a crumb or a scrap for the dog.

III. The third type of eater is the gourmet eater.
- A. This type carefully chooses any foods that have a foreign name.
- B. The foods are selectively arranged by shape, color, consistency, nutritional value, and/or calorie count.
- C. The food is sniffed, whiffed, nibbled, and savored.
- D. After twenty minutes, the plate is systematically half empty: half of each food.
- E. Most of the meal, the dog camps out under this eater's chair; during all the sniffing and whiffing, frequent bites escape the fork and fall to the floor.

IV. The fourth type of eater is the snacker eater.
- A. This type hardly takes any food because he/she has been snacking before dinner.
- B. The foods are placed on the plate in any fashion since appetite is of no concern.
- C. The food is played with and rolled around or poked, but not eaten.
- D. After twenty minutes, the plate is placed on the floor for the dog.
- E. After dinner—an hour later—this eater and the dog are in the kitchen raiding the refrigerator and snacking.

Here is a second example of a sentence outline:

Thesis: There are a variety of reasons why students do not do well their first semester of college.

   I. Some students do not do well because they do not have the academic ability to do college-level work.
- A. Students do not always have the writing skills that they need.
  1. Grammar skills are not up to college standards.
  2. Vocabulary has not kept up with their learning in other courses, or it is too informal for college papers.
  3. Spelling is another problem for many students.
- B. Students do not always have the mathematics skills that they need.
  1. Basic skills in adding, subtracting, and dividing are not present.
  2. Students have not learned to do basic computations because they have relied upon the calculator and other electronic learning aids.
  3. Students have not learned the logic that is part of the mathematical frame of mind.

    C. Students do not always have the reading skills that they need.
      1. Students sometimes find it difficult to read for long periods of time and be able to maintain concentration.
      2. Comprehension is also difficult for many students.
      3. Reading in technical areas is also difficult because of a limited vocabulary.
      4. Skimming often results in misunderstood or incomplete understanding of material.

II. Some students do not do well because they find themselves in a new environment.
    A. Students who go to a live-in college frequently miss their family and friends.
    B. Students who go to community colleges often find themselves among strangers and find that they feel alienated from the rest of the student body.
    C. Students who attend a private college frequently find that they are thrust into an environment where they are one of only a few students, which means that they constantly feel compelled to excel.
    D. Students who live on a resident campus sometimes find themselves living with a roommate, a situation which frequently leads to personality conflicts.

III. Some students do not do well because they discover that they do not want to or cannot attend college.
    A. Some persons simply want to try college for a semester to see if they will like it or be able to succeed at it.
      1. This includes those students who did not do well in high school but still want to attempt college.
      2. Some students are forced to attend college for a semester because they come from a family in which everyone attended college.
      3. Some students attend for a semester to escape the world of full-time work.
      4. Some students earn financial aid to college and feel obligated to at least try for a semester even though they do not want to attend.
    B. Some students are forced into situations that require that they drop out.
      1. Many married students must withdraw because of personal problems such as divorce or separation.
      2. Long-term illness is another factor which forces many students into dropping out.
      3. Lack of financial support causes many students to withdraw because they no longer can afford the cost.
      4. Lack of support from family members can place many students, especially older students, in an uncomfortable psychological situation which in turn leads to withdrawal.
      5. Some students must choose between full-time employment and full-time education.

IV. Some students do not do well in college because they fall victim to a lack of discipline.
    A. It is easier to play cards or shoot the bull with roommates instead of studying.
    B. It is more fun to cut classes and shoot pool or throw a Frisbee than it is to do homework and dig through the stacks in the library.
    C. It is easier to go out drinking with friends than it is to sit inside and study with friends.
    D. It is more fun to read the latest issue of <u>Ms.</u> or <u>Playboy</u> than it is to write a term paper.
    E. It is more fun to go with friends for the weekend skiing trip than it is to do an extra chemistry lab on Saturday morning.

Patti Martin

PART THREE: THE TITLE

Another way to add unity and coherence to a work—and a way that is often overlooked and under-rated—is the title.

 ## GUIDELINES FOR WRITING OR CHOOSING TITLES FOR EITHER PARAGRAPHS OR ESSAYS

- **One,** do not underline your title or place it in quote marks. Capitalize the first word and all important words: The Best Bargain in Town.

- **Two,** keep your titles short, usually a half a dozen words or less.

- **Three,** make the title related to the essay or its thesis. The best source of titles, in fact, is to read your own introductory and concluding paragraphs and look for a catchy or significant phrase or word. Most of the titles of the essays which appear in the rhetoric section of this text include titles that came from the essay itself. This truly adds unity and coherence to the writing.

- **Four,** if possible (and, believe me, it is not easy to do), write your title in such a way that it is a "hook." That is, the title "grabs" or "hooks" the interest of your reader and makes that reader really want to find out exactly what that title means. Once, as I was glancing through a set of student papers, one title really caught my attention: *First Time Camping: I Was Chomped on, Stomped on, and Whomped on. . . .* I couldn't wait to read it. This was his first sentence: *The first time I went camping, having two fingers bitten off was the second worst thing that happened to me.* Well, that was it; I was definitely hooked!

- **Five,** if required by your instructor, place the title on a title page. Although guidelines differ, the title page usually has the title centered. Other information appears below the title: date, class, section, name of instructor, etc. The title, obviously, should be placed in a position of emphasis.

THESIS STATEMENT AND OUTLINE—YOUR TURN

1 Think of a topic or a subject.

2 Narrow the topic. Choose a limiting idea. If possible, construct three or four thesis statements. Then decide which limiting idea would be the easiest and most-satisfying to develop into an essay.

3 Write a rough outline of the main points to be presented in the paper.

4 Write some detail beneath the major headings of the outline.

5 Check the organization. Will the outline produce an organized essay? If so, you are ready to write. If not, try to do some revision.

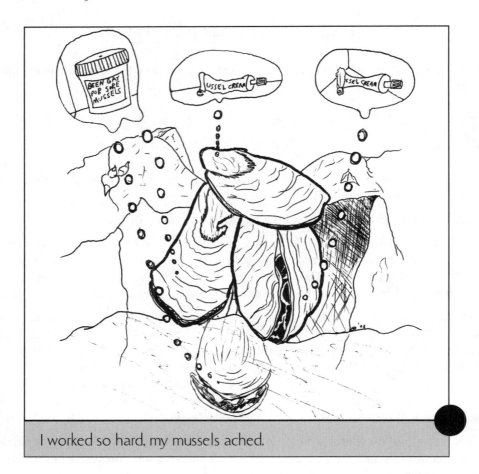

I worked so hard, my mussels ached.

My uncle always wore a cowboy hat with leathery tonsils on it.

THESIS STATEMENT AND OUTLINE PLAN SHEET

EXERCISE ONE

> **Part One:** Choose a topic for an essay and write it in the blank provided. Then try to construct four or five thesis statements dealing with the topic.

Topic: _____

1. _____
            topic   limiting idea

2. _____
            topic   limiting idea

3. _____
            topic   limiting idea

4. _____
            topic   limiting idea

5. _____
            topic   limiting idea

> **Part Two:** Choose one of the thesis statements you wrote in Part One and write it in the blank. Next try to break it down into a preliminary outline.

Thesis Statement: _____

_____

Outline: _____

_____

_____

_____

_____

_____

_____

Part Three: Using the outline you made in Part Two, write a more-complete outline, including some of the information which would appear in each paragraph.

Topic: _____

Limiting Idea: _____

Outline: _____

_____

_____

_____

_____

_____

_____

_____

_____

_____

_____

_____

_____

_____

_____

_____

_____

_____

_____

_____

_____

_____

_____

THESIS STATEMENT AND OUTLINE PLAN SHEET

EXERCISE TWO

Part One: Choose a topic for an essay and write it in the blank provided. Then try to construct four or five thesis statements dealing with the topic.

Topic: _____

1. _____
            topic   limiting idea

2. _____
            topic   limiting idea

3. _____
            topic   limiting idea

4. _____
            topic   limiting idea

5. _____
            topic   limiting idea

Part Two: Choose one of the thesis statements you wrote in Part One and write it in the blank. Next try to break it down into a preliminary outline.

Thesis Statement: _____

_____

Outline: _____

_____

_____

_____

_____

_____

Part Three: Using the outline you made in Part Two, write a more-complete outline, including some of the information which would appear in each paragraph.

Topic: _____

Limiting Idea: _____

Outline: _____

_____

_____

_____

_____

_____

_____

_____

_____

_____

_____

_____

_____

_____

_____

_____

_____

_____

_____

_____

_____

_____

_____

_____

Special Paragraphs

PART ONE: INTRODUCTORY PARAGRAPHS

THE INTRODUCTION

Most essays can be broken down into three distinct sections:

Introduction	(Beginning)
Body	(Middle)
Conclusion	(End)

Think for a second about the meaning of the word *introduction*. It is a formal greeting, an announcement or proclamation of something new. The dictionary defines an introduction as "anything that introduces or prepares the way."

In essay writing, the introduction is that section between the title and the body (or support sections) of the paper. The introduction has two important functions to perform: to **state** and to **narrow** the topic of the essay. A secondary function of the introduction is to **interest** (or "hook" the reader). As you learned in the last chapter, the thesis statement (and sometimes the title) states the topic of the essay, and, through its limiting idea, narrows or limits the topic. This is why the thesis statement is usually contained within the introductory section.

Obviously, the introduction is vital. It may consist of one or two sentences, one or two paragraphs, or even one or two pages. Regardless of its length, the introduction is kept separate from that portion of the essay which begins to support, explain, or illustrate the thesis. When a reader finishes your introduction, he or she knows what your topic is, what specifically about that topic you are dealing with, and perhaps the manner in which you will examine the topic.

You might be thinking that you don't always want your reader to know your topic or your main idea. You might wish to write inductively in order to create suspense or interest or curiosity. All of this is possible, and will, in fact, be explained and illustrated in later chapters.

For now, however, I recommend you follow the traditional approach to essay writing: introduction, body, conclusion. Most writers find it easier this way. If you sometimes struggle with "what goes where" or "where do I place all of these ideas," then it probably would be easier to begin with the main idea (an intro containing a thesis). When you have more practice and are feeling more confident, feel free to experiment.

DIRECT INTRODUCTIONS

There are two types of introductions: direct and indirect.

A **direct** introduction is simply what its name implies—it is an introduction which is direct. It is blunt; it is to the point. It is exceedingly informative and is usually quite brief. Frequently the direct introduction is nothing more than the thesis statement, such as:

> The purpose of my paper is to explain why college is expensive.

Some students and some teachers tend to look upon this type of introduction with disfavor; because it is so direct, it tends to be flat, dull, and perhaps boring. However, the direct introduction does announce and narrow a topic, as well as give both writer and reader a focus. Using this type of introduction is definitely better than writing a paper that begins without a clear focus or that runs together the introduction and the body.

Some direct introductions go beyond just the simple statement of thesis. Here are some samples:

A. In the following few paragraphs, I will explain the steps that a loan processor applies when doing a credit check on a married couple applying for a first-time mortgage.

Bill Addler

B. On your next vacation, why not relax for eight days and seven nights aboard an elegant ocean liner? Booking a cruise is easy. Here's how to do it.

Gary Jankovich

C. When I was seventeen, I dropped out of high school. There were four reasons for this decision, and I would like to explain each of them.

Jason Scheger

D. From my years of observations, I have discovered that there are basically five types of people you will encounter if you work as a bank teller.

Bill Jenkins

E. So! The class you just gotta have is closed, and the instructor says no to your request to get signed in. Don't be sad or mad. Just follow these directions, and you can get any instructor to sign that permission-to-register form.

Mary Bertinelli

F.　　You are in the batter's box and feeling pressure because you are the strike out king of the softball league. I can't promise round baggers, but the following steps will help you improve your batting average.

Carl Kelly

As you can see, the direct introduction is truly direct, but the writer does have a certain amount of flexibility. The direct introduction may not be interesting, depending upon the individual reader's taste, but the direct introduction most definitely gives the paper a focus, and that is the primary function of an introduction.

INDIRECT INTRODUCTIONS

An **indirect** introduction is just what its name implies—an introduction which is indirect. Like the direct introduction, the indirect introduction states the topic and narrows it—that is, it contains a thesis statement—but it goes one step further. The indirect introduction attempts to interest the reader, attempts to delay the blunt presentation of the thesis statement.

There are a variety of ways to write an indirect introduction, as some student examples will illustrate.

One of the most-common methods of indirect introduction uses **deduction,** a thought process that moves from very general to more-specific information:

A.　　Ever since Eve decided that one fig leaf was not enough and she experimented with other varieties, the female of the species Homo Sapiens has wanted to look just a little different from other females. One way to accomplish a "different look" is to sew your own clothes. Sewing is both a hobby and a financial necessity for me. My most recent project was to make a long gown for my daughter to wear during choir performances. I'd like to tell you how this gown was born.

Pat Reynders

B.　　As a young boy, I loved to eat, and after each meal, I prided myself on being a member of the "clean plate club." I especially loved sandwiches because no matter how a sandwich was prepared, bread had to be involved. Then one day, while sitting patiently at my grandmother's dinner table, starving as usual, I experienced for the first time her homemade bread. Fresh out of the oven and still steaming, the loaf was a mouth-watering work of art—but I was hardly content to just look at it. Biting into that first slice marked a turning point in my eating habits, as my naive taste buds were introduced to a whole new world. A discovery had been made, and needless to say, store-bought white bread was no longer on my favorite foods list.

　　As I grew older, my love for bread grew stronger along with a sincere concern for good nutrition, which led to another discovery. Not only were store-bought brands inferior in taste, but their ingredients were not exactly healthful either. In fact, most were not even pronounceable.

> Pondering these discoveries, I reasoned that if I were to bake my own bread with only the natural ingredients I saw fit to include, all of my standards of taste and nutrition could be met. So, I proceeded to experiment with a number of recipes, during which time I allowed myself to become creative. Due to this creativity factor, I have never baked the exact same bread recipe twice. However, I have developed a somewhat basic pattern that I always follow. If you would like a basic idea of how to bake your own bread, here is how baking bread is best accomplished for me.
>
> Louie Beuschlein

Both of these student examples illustrate the pattern of going from a general thought to a specific thought/statement. Notice, too, that the second example is three paragraphs in length. It is an excellent and interest-grabbing opening to a process essay that is well-written.

A second method of indirect introduction is **comparison-contrast:**

> Webster's New World Dictionary defines the word twin as "either of two persons or things much alike." Micki and Dave, being sister and brother, were both born on November twelfth. Micki, now seventeen, a senior at Reavis High School, was born on November 12, 1971; Dave, now fourteen, a freshman at Reavis High School was born on November 12, 1974. The fact that they were born exactly three years, eight hours, and forty seven minutes apart is still amazing to both of their parents. I suppose you could say that they are "three-year-apart-twins," or are they? Having been born on the same day, though three years apart, Micki and Dave are similar in some ways and very different in other ways, such as their appearance, their taste in music, and their ambition in life.
>
> Sharyn Sobanski

A third method of indirect introduction is to use a **quotation:**

> A.　　The dictionary defines the word clerk as "one employed in an office, shop, etc., to keep records or accounts and attends to correspondence, etc." As a clerk in a junior high school, I feel both of these definitions are too cold and impersonal for me to accept. A clerk is a person who performs various duties and takes a personal interest in every student, teacher, and parent.
>
> Paulette Obradovich

B.   In 1778 Samuel Johnson (<u>Boswell's Life</u>) wrote, "Take a hundred ladies of quality, you'll find them better wives, better mothers, more willing to sacrifice their own pleasures to their children, than a hundred other women."

I doubt that either Mom or Grandma Stella would have termed it "sacrifice." It was just their way of life. These two wonderful women, each so dedicated in her major commitment as wife and mother, were utterly different in most ways. Different as they could be in appearance, personality, and life-style but equal in dispensing love and encouragement to their husbands and children.

Kathryn Osterman

The use of a **rhetorical question** (one which goes unanswered by the writer, a question left directed toward the reader) is still another form of indirect introduction, as in the following examples:

A.   Have you ever wondered what causes the extraordinarily brilliant and beautiful coloration of many birds, butterflies, fishes, and insects? Or, more specifically, have you ever wondered how it is possible for these spectacular colors to change, for example, from a metallic-green to a deep violet, simply by changing the angle of view? If so, you will be interested in knowing about the two causes of iridescent colors.

George Tarpanoff

B.   Are you tired of sleeping in a wet blanket that pretends to be a sinking boat? Have you had it with gnats and mosquitos in your outdoor cooking? Does the phrase "back to nature" mean that you sit and rest in a patch of poison ivy? Have you ever considered that your next vacation should follow my plan of renting a camper?

Kevin Griggs

Another interesting way to write an indirect introduction is to use **conversation or dialogue:**

"Hey, mister. Which way is second base?" "Coach, can I go get another drink and go to the bathroom?" "Do I throw with this hand or with this hand?" "I'm supposed to play shortstop—where's that?" These are only a few of the comments you will hear if you ever decide to coach pee wee baseball. Although it is a job that requires a great deal of patience, there are a few special moments in each season that make the job very rewarding. Let me share a few of these special moments with you.

J. J. Garner

Repetition can be an effective device to use in an indirect introduction:

> Drip. Drip. Drip goes the leaky bathroom faucet. Gurgle. Gurgle. Gurgle goes the leaky powder room toilet. Bang. Bang. Bang goes the flapping rain gutter against the eve of the house. Squeak. Squeak. Squeak goes the loose hinge on the side storm door. This litany of noises is a foreshadowing to the homeowner, one which signals how the spring will be spent. Doing home repairs is a never-ending responsibility. With my method of organizing your chores, however, you might find yourself with spare time for the swimming pool or the golf course. Here's how I do it.
>
> Paul Metcalf

An **example** can be used in an indirect introduction:

> The bright green and orange envelope caught my attention the instant I opened the mailbox. In the corner was a gold star with a registration number of my guaranteed prize, perhaps maybe a million dollars or a yacht or a new vacation home on a lake. In a few moments, I had the envelope open and was—cynically—beginning to read the directions for the contest. I was also looking for the "come on" that I knew had to be buried within the several page letter. Now, most people I know hate junk mail, but I love it. I have found a variety of uses for all of it. Surprised? Read on (unless you think this is a junk essay, of course) and learn how to convert your mailbox trash to mailbox treasure.
>
> Paul Bradley

Another method of indirect introduction is **induction:** to go from specific to general:

> Cab drivers seem to have gotten very friendly lately. So have store clerks in the malls. And yesterday, as I was walking to work, a stranger yelled at me to tell me that I had dropped something from my purse as I ran up stairs to catch the elevated train. The more I think about it, the more I am convinced that people really are starting to care more about each other and be friendly toward one another. Let me provide a few more examples.
>
> Lana Lehman

PART TWO: CONCLUDING PARAGRAPHS

THE CONCLUSION

Too many writers, I feel, regard the conclusion as nothing more than the place to stop. This is unfortunate, because the conclusion is as vital to a paper as is the introduction. It is the final chance to reach the reader, a final chance to explain, reinforce, or summarize the ideas presented in the paper. A good conclusion will remain with a reader, just as a weak conclusion will detract from the effectiveness of an otherwise well-written essay. It is unfortunate when a student spends a great deal of time writing an essay and then ends it abruptly or ineffectively, or fails to give it a conclusion at all. Obviously, a well-written paper deserves to be well-written to the last punctuation mark. The conclusion should be a contributing part of the paper and not just a sentence or a paragraph tacked onto the end.

TYPES OF CONCLUSIONS

There are several kinds of conclusions, most of which use the same techniques used in introductions. Possibly the most-commonly used type of conclusion is **the summary.** Here are a few summary concluding paragraphs:

A.   As you can see from the preceding examples, you only need to be steady and confident when you approach that first customer. A neat appearance, a pleasant smile, and a non-pushy attitude certainly contribute, but self-confidence really is the biggest factor.

Jack Hudson

B.   Yes, Christmas is a very special time because of the very special people who have provided me with a multitude of extraordinary memories. The pastors, choir members, deacons, and even strangers have added hectic and frantic joy to my life. This year, as our choral preparation for this blessed holiday begins, I wonder what marvelous surprises Midnight Mass will provide. Will it be calm serenity, frantic chaos, or lofty comedy? I can't wait to find out!

Melodie French

C.   Waitressing is not a fulfilling job or even a fun job unless you like to be burned, spilled on, or blamed for mishaps you had nothing to do with. If that is the case, I say, "Go for it," but if you are turned off by what you have just read, I suggest a different line of work.

Tracy Moe

D.   Yes, gardening can be hard physical work, but it is also mentally satisfying and emotionally soothing. A quiet morning spent close to nature does wonders for your equilibrium. Although my garden is now a thing of the past, many memories remain to bring a smile or a tear, or just a quiet sigh of thanks to "Mother Nature."

Pat Reynders

Another effective way to end a paper is to use a **rhetorical question.**

A.   Unfortunately, that old adage is correct. You have two choices: you can change your car's oil yourself or you can pay someone else to do it. If you neglect this maintenance operation, you will be facing some very expensive overhaul operations in the future. Is it worth giving up an occasional Saturday afternoon or paying twenty-five dollars at the local gas station? Or would you rather spend hundreds of dollars for major repairs? The choice is yours.

Tom Cupic

B.   Well, as I stated and then tried to illustrate, I will never understand the human being's ability to "talk more than walk." Why is it that we find it easier to discuss recycling than to recycle? Why it is that we find it easier to discuss energy conservation than to conserve? Why is it that we find it easier to discuss community service than to serve? I'll never understand.

Robert Anders

C.   Well, after these experiences, as you might have anticipated, I am somewhat hesitant to accept arranged dates, especially if they are arranged by my family. Now, when someone says, "Hey, Jane. I have a date for you!" I immediately counter with my questions: "Is his name Bubba or Biff?", "Can he count to ten without using his fingers or toes?", "Can he drive and talk at the same time?", and, "Can he pass an entire evening without mentioning his last girlfriend, wife, sister, or mother?".

Jane Smith

Another type of conclusion makes use of **a quotation**.

A.   The dictionary defines the word teacher as "one who educates; gives lessons to" or as "one who disciplines." I entirely agree. I have written this essay to show the various ways a human being can experience these procedures. I believe we encounter learning experiences every day of our lives and that all of us are teachers of others.

Sandra Schmidt

B.   Well, you must admit, although the context of the quotation is entirely different from my perspective as a waitress at a pie counter, "Let them eat cake!" still has a lot of meaning no matter what the context!

Kim O'Connor

C.   After reading about the exploits of our dog, you must be convinced that members of our household definitely believe the old adage that "a dog is man's best friend." Indeed, our old mutt Max is as much a part of our family as those cousins we only see on holidays. And, as the examples have illustrated, Max has increased his ability to serve our family, whether making us laugh at his adventures or learning how to fetch the morning paper. Who says, "You can't teach an old Max new tricks?!"

Walter O'Flynn

Another type of conclusion is the **comparison-contrast**.

A.   Spring is a freshness and a new beginning with soft, vibrant colors, when nature says, "See what I can do after a long rest!" Fall is a burst of unequaled, spectacular color, when nature says, "Enjoy me now, for tomorrow I rest in preparation for spring!" Nature is surely at its best during these two seasons of the year.

Loretta Shicotte

B.   In conclusion, iridescent colors are produced either by the interference of two light waves when reflected from the two surfaces of a clear membrane, or by the reflection of light from multiple, microscopic, opaque reflectors. The end result of the two causes of iridescent colors is the same: to produce brilliant, pure colors which change color depending on the viewing angle.

George Tarpanoff

INTRODUCTIONS AND CONCLUSIONS: A SUMMARY

As you have probably observed from reading the various examples and types of introductions and conclusions, one of the more-effective means of opening and closing essays is to use the same technique—and frequently the same words and/or phrases. The following **sets** of openings and closings illustrate this concept:

A.

Rationalization 101:
Cleaning Your Closet, Clearing Your Conscience

You've been meaning to do it for a long time. You promised yourself that once school let out you would set your mind to it. You have to do it before you leave for college in August, anyway. Now it's a boring summer afternoon, and the little voice in your head leaves you no choice but to clean out your closet.

————

There! You're finished cleaning your closet. Step back and take a look at your accomplishments. You still have an overflowing closet, but more importantly, you have a clear conscience. The little voice inside you seems to have found someone else to nag. You even have lots of energy left. Maybe now you should tackle your dresser drawers. You've been meaning to do them for a while. . . .

Michelle Kairies

B.

Dark Moods Defined:
The Three-Syndrome Excuse

My dark moods can be classified and defined in three phrases: Pre-menstrual syndrome (PMS), Full-moon syndrome (FMS), and Ugly-mood syndrome (UMS).

————

My family became thankful over the months and years for my being able to define what was happening. The mood transitions became easier for everyone to handle when they could say, "Hey, Mom. What's Wrong?" and I could answer, "Oh, not much. Just a little PMS or FMS or just plain old UMS." These syndromes also created a myriad of wealth for "cranky Mom jokes." There's nothing like humor to get one through a period of FMS, PMS, or UMS. Just ask my family.

Chris McCabe

C.   The True, Special Meaning

We have all used a variety of delineative words to express a thought or feeling about a person, place, or thing. However few descriptive words in the English language are avoided as much as the word "old." An old person is referred to as a "senior citizen," an old place is "quaint," and an old object is an "antique." My grandmother Claire would therefore, be depicted as a senior citizen who lives in a quaint home filled with antiques. In reality, though, her life, reflecting that of so many others like it, exemplifies the true, special meaning of the world "old."

The dictionary defines "old" as "dating from the past—showing the effects of time or use," but taints this definition with synonyms like "archaic," "trite," and "obsolete." These words need to be replaced with words like "wisdom," "pride," "character," "value," and "loved," for the true, special meaning of the word "old."

Lynda Flanagan

D.   It's Only the Basement

Imagination can be a wonderful tool, but in the mind of a seven-year old, it can run rampant. As a small child, my imagination worked overtime whenever I dared to venture into the mother of all pits, the resting place of ghouls, the hideaway for demons, better known as "the basement." My grandparents (we lived with them) and my parents openly expressed their adult views.

"It's so *silly* to be afraid of the basement."

"There's nothing down there that could hurt you."

"For goodness sake, it's only the basement!"

Only the basement. If only they knew what I knew. If they could only see what I could see. Then they wouldn't refer to that deep, dark, damp, underground tomb as "only the basement." What did they know, anyway? Ghouls, ghosts, and demons appeared only when little kids were around.

Today, my sister and I are in our forties, but we often reminisce about "the basement" on Wilcox Street in Chicago. We now know how our childish imaginations played tricks on us. After all, it is just "the basement". . . isn't it?

Mari Jayne Tittle

PART THREE: TRANSITIONAL PARAGRAPHS

There is a third kind of special paragraph which you need to be aware of and know how to write—the transitional paragraph. At this point in your writing, you might not use transitional paragraphs very often, but you may occasionally.

A transitional paragraph has one primary function: it announces a shift, a change, a transition from one section of an essay to another section, from one idea to another idea. Many writing teachers use the analogy that transitional paragraphs are like bridges: the first section of an essay is one riverbank; the second section is the other riverbank; the transitional paragraph, like a bridge, links them. This analogy is close to being corny, but it graphically illustrates the function of a transitional paragraph.

Let's take a look at an example from one student's essay. Notice how the second paragraph functions in relation to the two which surround it.

1 . . . My first-semester, senior-year English class was the same way. I once again found myself with a teacher whose idea of "grading" my paper was to put lots of red marks and circles and strange abbreviations all over what I had written. She always assumed that I knew what she meant by all her comments. She never offered to explain to me what all those little marks and squiggles and scribbles meant. I was beginning to feel even more doomed because of my weak background.

2 The first hint I got that there might be hope for me came when my regular teacher got very sick and a substitute was called in to teach the second semester. From the first day on, I knew it was going to be different.

3 The first day of class with the new teacher, she asked us to do some writing. Instead of picking up the homework and grading it later, she came around the room to help us as we were working. If she saw we were making mistakes, she helped us find them and correct them. If we didn't understand what she was talking about, she would take the time to explain the rules or terms that she used. If necessary, she referred us to the correct section in a textbook or she would work with us after class. For the first time in my school years, I was learning from an English class.

4 After two or three months with this new teacher, I began to see some real progress in my. . . .

The second paragraph illustrates how a transitional paragraph functions. These paragraphs are taken from an essay describing a student's problems with English classes. Early in the paper, the student explained that she had moved frequently from one school to another and had missed most of the explanations of English that a student normally acquires in elementary school.

Next she addressed herself to the problems she had in high school because her teachers assumed she had these basic skills. As the first paragraph printed here explains, the problem continued to exist, if not grow worse. The transitional paragraph (#2), however, tells us that a change occurred, that something different happened. What that something was is the subject of the final page and a half of her essay. The transitional paragraph alerts the reader to this shift in the subject matter. It lets the reader know the writer is going to take the topic in a different direction.

Here is a portion of another student-written essay. The transitional paragraph is the second one.

1   . . . The final step in stripping the furniture and getting it ready to stain is to make sure that the wood is clean. Use a slightly damp piece of cheesecloth (or any old rag that will be free of lint or fuzz) and rub it on the furniture in the direction of the grain. Be sure to get in all the grooves and notches and make certain there are no little build-ups of dust left over from sanding. Don't forget to do underneath shelves, drawers, and tops; dust always collects there. Once you've gone over all surfaces with the damp cloth, repeat the process but use a soft, dry rag. Then let the furniture sit in a warm, dry, dust-free place for an hour.

2   So far, we have been doing what most people consider the "hard" part or the "dirty" part of furniture refinishing. From here on is where the "fun" comes in. The next step is staining.

3   To get the finish you want from the staining process, you'll need to work fast and consistently. You'll also need some more cheesecloth and a paint brush and a clean place to work. Follow all directions on the can of stain which you bought. When applying the stain, it's best to begin at the top and work your way down. Apply the stain with the brush. . . .

Deep in the woods, you can hear the animals talking, the trees scratching.

Although we are married now, at first our relationship was purely plutonic.

Skinning is one of my very favorite forms of exercise.

DIRECT AND INDIRECT INTRODUCTION
AND CONCLUSION PLAN SHEET

EXERCISE ONE

Part One: Think of a topic for an essay. Construct a thesis statement for the essay and write it in the blank provided. Next try to write a direct and an indirect introduction for that essay.

Thesis Statement: _____

_____

Direct Introduction: _____

_____

_____

_____

_____

_____

Indirect Introduction: _____

_____

_____

_____

_____

_____

_____

_____

_____

_____

_____

_____

_____

Part Two: Try to write two different conclusions for the same essay.

Concluding Paragraph: _____

_____

_____

_____

_____

_____

_____

_____

_____

_____

_____

Concluding Paragraph: _____

_____

_____

_____

_____

_____

_____

_____

_____

_____

_____

_____

_____

DIRECT AND INDIRECT INTRODUCTION
AND CONCLUSION PLAN SHEET

EXERCISE TWO

Part One: Think of a topic for an essay. Construct a thesis statement for the essay and write it in the blank provided. Next try to write a direct and an indirect introduction for that essay.

Thesis Statement: _____

_____

Direct Introduction: _____

_____

_____

_____

_____

Indirect Introduction: _____

_____

_____

_____

_____

_____

_____

_____

_____

_____

_____

_____

Concluding Paragraph: _____

_____

_____

_____

_____

_____

_____

_____

_____

_____

_____

Concluding Paragraph: _____

_____

_____

_____

_____

_____

_____

_____

_____

_____

_____

_____

_____

The Description Paper

DESCRIPTION OF AN OBJECT
DESCRIPTION OF A PLACE
DESCRIPTION OF A PERSON
DESCRIPTION OF AN EVENT

OVERVIEW

Description, one of the four basic types of writing, is writing that shows. Its purpose is to help the reader see what you see—be it a person, a place, an event, or an object. The subject you are describing may be something which the reader knows but does not "see" quite the way you do. On the other hand, you may be describing something totally unfamiliar to the reader.

At times you may want to express your feelings in descriptive writing. If you are describing your memories of your grandmother's kitchen on Christmas Day, you will probably want to communicate not only how the kitchen appeared, but also how you felt—your feelings—about those special times. At other times, however, it might be essential that you keep your feelings out of the description as much as possible. If you are a patrol officer asked to describe an accident, your job is to record the details of the accident. You are required to be objective and to keep your feelings out of the description you write on the accident report form. Most teachers refer to these two types of description as **subjective** (that which is personal, that which communicates feeling) and **objective** (that which is neutral, that which lacks feeling).

EFFECTIVE DESCRIPTION

A popular misconception about good descriptive writing is that it has to be filled with adjectives. This is simply not true. There is nothing wrong with the discriminate use of adjectives. Good description, in fact, relies upon well-chosen adjectives. Good description also relies upon the use of well-chosen concrete and specific details. Some sample passages of writing should illustrate these concepts.

The following is a description of a condominium. Notice how many adjectives it uses.

A.   My condominium's carpeted throughout with warm, dark, earthy colors of brown, beige, and cream colors. The old, hand-carved, hand-polished, oil-rubbed furniture my grandfather made also adds to the warm feeling the condo gives me. It is accented with big, leafy, healthy, ever-growing green plants. Some of the plants are in hand-woven, brown and tan baskets. Others sit in gleaming and shiny brass pots. On one wall of the living room rest sturdy, handcarved and hand-etched oak and maple bookcases. The bookcases hold dusty and somewhat aging and musty books of all colors: reds, oranges, yellows, blues, rusts. . . .

As the last paragraph illustrates, description that uses too many adjectives does not do a very good job of communicating, and it is boring to read. The next example is a description that "takes inventory." Instead of describing, the writer makes "lists."

B.   My condominium is approximately 1800 square feet; it consists of a living room, a dining room, a kitchen, two bedrooms, two bathrooms, a large walk-in closet, and a den. It also has a patio approximately six feet by twelve feet. Inside the living room is a couch, a love seat, three oak tables, four bookcases, and approximately a dozen plants. The plants are in six wicker baskets and five copper and brass kettles and buckets. . . .

Obviously, the presentation of lists is not very interesting and not very descriptive. At this point, you might be wondering how to write effective description. Actually, effective description combines some of the features of the two previous examples. Good description uses **some** adjectives and **some** detail. A final suggestion is to write by focusing your ideas—including the adjectives and the details—to communicate a specific impression of what you are describing. The next example combines all of these suggestions. I think you will find it better reading.

C.   What I like best about my condominium is that it is filled with possessions that are special to me. My bedroom furniture was hand-made by my grandfather. The dresser, like his personality, seems contradictory. Its size is massive and overpowering, yet it contains delicate work of hand-pieced veneer. This same contrast is evident in my plants. The delicate and lacey leaves contrast to the heavy and squatty copper pots in which they reside. As the light shines in the patio doors and bounces across the leaves of the corn plant, the crystal paperweight on the shelf behind the plant catches the sunlight and breaks it into little rainbows on the plants' leaves. . . .

In my opinion, the third version (C) is the most-effective and the most-interesting of the three. Its writer made some use of detail and included some adjectives. The writer of the third version used description to say something to the reader. The writer was not just writing to describe; he was describing to communicate. The writer's values (such as his admiration for his grandfather and his grandfather's furniture) and the writer's feelings (such as the contrasts in his own personality) are communicated to the reader.

THE DESCRIPTION OF AN OBJECT PAPER

Hardly a week of our lives passes that doesn't find us describing an object of some sort to someone. Just yesterday, I overheard myself describing to the guy behind the auto parts counter the type of widget I was looking for to repair the dome light in my truck. Later, in the lumber supply store, I heard a woman and a clerk engaged in conversation about the part she needed to repair her sliding patio doors. On my final stop, I wandered the aisles of the beauty supply store looking for the exact diffuser that my daughter had told me to pick up for her to attach to her blow drier to protect her perm. It would seem, then, that describing objects is not just something we do for writing classes or writing teachers, but is something we do for ourselves. This is only one of the reasons that I find my students have little problem in writing descriptions of objects. Such description is a good way to begin the process of learning to describe.

Read the following essay and study how the writer was able to communicate through description:

Simple by Design

1   It was a well-worn timepiece, simple by design.

2   As I gently, even reverently, removed it from its encasement in that rectangular box where it had been placed long ago, I noted how it weighed heavily in the palm of my hand. Fine craftsmanship was indicated by the almost seamless fusion of front to back. No unnecessary ornamentation, for it was meant to be functional, and I knew it had completed its task well over the years. There was a smooth, well-worn, polished feel to the back of this timepiece, as though it had been cradled, lovingly, in someone's palm many times, just as I found myself doing now.

3   The face of the pocket watch had tall, straight Roman numerals to mark the hours. Their size was not imposing, and because there was space between each number, the figures neither crowded nor overpowered the face of the watch. Balance and symmetry had been achieved in the simplicity of the design.

4   At the one and two o'clock positions on the top of the watch were two thick stems. Arising from each of these stems were two grooved knobs. They appeared like sentinels standing guard. One knob was used to set the time, the other to set the alarm. I wondered how many times these knobs had been twisted, backward and forward to set and reset the time, yet they remained unbroken. The grooves on the knobs were still clearly distinguishable, like well-worn time lines in an aged face proudly displaying character against the test of time.

5   My fingers slid down the black leather strap that connected the timepiece at one end and the fob on the other. The condition of the leather surprised me because it was still very soft and pliable despite its age. When I unbuckled and opened the strap, the hole where the fastener had been was stretched, just a bit, but was not loose enough to let it unbuckle at will. When I refastened it, it held tightly. Two deep, distinct creases, where the watch itself and the fob had been attached, showed the strains of the weight it had carried, but there were no signs of being worn through. That leather strap was the connection and the strength needed to hold all the pieces together and make it function as one unit.

6   The only ornamentation on this quietly functional unit was the fob that hung at one end of the leather strap. A circular piece of heavy metal portrayed several men of an obvious blue collar working class. They stood with tools in their hands, railroad-type caps on their heads, and across the top of this piece of metal, three words proclaimed: 30 Years Service. At the bottom, there was a name inscribed of the worker who had been

recognized for achieving this length of service. Two of these service awards—one for 30 years, and one for 25 years—had been attached. These ungilded adornments added a quiet dignity, and did not take away from the serviceability of the timepiece.

7   It was simple by design, yet was it? Complex tangible and intangible qualities made up that timepiece, just as they made up the man it belonged to: my dad.

Bea Paller

This example illustrates many of the principles of how to write a good description of an object. Let's analyze it, and in doing so, establish the guidelines you might follow in writing your own paper.

GUIDELINES FOR WRITING A DESCRIPTION OF AN OBJECT ESSAY

- ■ **One,** analyze the object you have chosen as subject matter and try to determine how you are going to structure and analyze the ideas into paragraphs. Had Bea outlined her essay, it would resemble this one:

simple by design

   1: introduction

   2: first impressions

   3: face

   4: knob/stems

   5: the leather strap

   6: ornamentation

   7: closing

   In this essay, the structure and the organization are based mainly upon spatial principles. With some objects, this works well. With other objects, the writer must find another method, such as function, parts, the senses, etc. Just be sure you have a method besides just writing what comes to mind. For example, if you were describing an item of food, the senses might seem a natural method of organizing/structuring. You might be able to write one paragraph on sight, one on smell, one on taste, etc. Or, if you are describing a more-mechanical object, perhaps you might organize by parts of the whole or by functions of the various parts. A third method might be to arrange your observations chronologically, that is, the order in which you observed them. These methods are only suggestions; feel free to "invent" your own, but be certain you have a method.

- ■ **Two,** follow the guidelines/suggestions concerning development which were presented earlier in this chapter: use "lists" and adjectives sparingly; instead, rely upon the use of concrete and specific details and examples which will appeal to the senses of your reader. Bea's essay on her father's watch is a good example. Paragraph six on the watch's ornamentation is quite specific and concrete; the information in that paragraph helps the reader envision the ornamentation on the watch. Much of the description in Bea's essay is objective; she presents a literal description of the watch. Yet, she is also subjective in her description. The introduction and the conclusion include her feelings; so, too, does paragraph six which describes the service awards received by her father. The essay is not just a straight-forward description of an object, of a watch; it is also a description of the writer's feelings for her father.

■ **Three,** try to use an occasional **analogy** to enhance the description. An analogy is a brief comparison between two concepts, one which the reader is most likely familiar with and the other which the writer is describing. In paragraph four, for example, Bea writes the two grooved knobs appear like sentinels standing guard.

DESCRIPTION OF AN OBJECT PAPER—A FEW STUDENT EXAMPLES

Miraculous Metamorphosis

1   Though revived anew each springtime, Mother Nature and her tiny creatures' extraordinary, everchanging beauty go unappreciated. Brilliantly staged, colorful performances, intended solely for the audience of man, too often pass into time unnoticed. One such apt entertainer is the Monarch butterfly.

2   The Monarch evolves through a miraculous metamorphosis. It changes from an insignificant, crawling caterpillar to a splendorous, airborne butterfly. Inheriting the wealth of nature's beauty, it moves from pauper to nabob. This legacy, however, is shadowed by brevity, for this new life will end in only a few months.

3   When the butterfly is motionless and perched on a bough, nature's finest artistry can be seen. Its black, slender body, with two knobbed antennas, vaunt wings that are painted vivid, fire-flame orange. These wings, spanning six inches across, appear divinely transparent and reflect the sun like fine stained glass. The pinions are ebony, and like soft French velvet cut into a chantilly lace pattern.

4   A hush surrounds the butterfly. When in flight, it is as if wings and air become one, leaving no audible trace. So featherlight, the Monarch can pause on a delicate rose with nary a petal bent, or sound heard.

5   A true Thespian, the Monarch is always entertaining. Darting about, fluttering, or catching a breeze in free flight, it performs a superb aerial act. As if mimicking a shy, curious child, the butterfly dares to approach closely, but cautious of its freedom, it swiftly retreats.

6   Perhaps this springtime, life might pause a moment to watch this creature's bittersweet finale and appreciate the beauty and serenity it offers. A bit of poetry by Nathaniel Hawthorne states: "Happiness is a butterfly which, when pursued, is always just beyond your grasp, but which, if you will sit down quietly, may alight upon you."

Lynda Flanagan

Mr. Coffee and Family

1   Hey, what's up? My name is Mr. Coffee. As you know, I live in a kitchen. I'm almost eight years old, about a foot tall, and I'm brown and beige. In the Tokarczyk family's kitchen, I sit on the brown and white speckled Formica counter between the toaster and the dishdrainer, and I'm just kitty corner from the cookie jar. Over the years, I've come to learn just how much I'm valued and depended on.

2   I'm usually of most importance to this family early in the morning. Candy is usually the first to wake each day, and I know she's coming straight for me. The first sound I hear upon her arising is the toilet flushing, and then I hear the soft thumping of her bare feet touching each wooden stair as she makes her way into the kitchen. She enters the softly

lit room, looking as though she's trying out for the lead role in *Night of the Zombie.* Her eyes are half-closed still, her pajamas wrinkled, and she has hair that's practically screaming for the attention of a brush. While pouring cool water into the back of my head and scooping coffee grounds into my plastic filter holder, Candy stretches and yawns repeatedly, muttering certain four-letter words under her breath. And boy, could she use a Tic-Tac! However, after drinking a hot, fresh cup of Maxwell House Coffee, which I produced, mixed with lots of sugar and cream, Candy smiles, just like in the commercials, and I pat myself on the back for a job well done.

3   I'm not used only in the morning though. Duty calls late at night sometimes when Candy stays up late reading a book, doing homework, or cramming for a test. Once again, I'm responsible for providing the best-tasting coffee. I help keep her energy level high, so she can get the job done without falling asleep at the table. There's not much for me to do late at night, except watch the crazy cat Tessie chase her tail, so it's at these times I enjoy Candy's company the most.

4   Holidays, barbecues, birthdays, and other special events are the busiest days, and it's on these days I really bust my filter! The entire family comes over, and it's as chaotic as a circus! There are children running this way and that, ignoring their parents' orders to calm down and behave. There are about seven different conversations going all at once, each person engaging in the game called "I can talk the loudest." These are the times when my services are requested throughout the entire day, from beginning to end. It gets a little hectic, sure, but I love every minute of it!

5   "What would I do without my coffee?" Candy asks all the time. I never tire of hearing those words. Knowing that I help out in this family's lives, I feel appreciated, and I look forward to greeting them in the morning. I wouldn't give up my job for anything in the world!

Candy Tokarczyk

My Life in a Drawer

1   The top drawer of my dresser holds chapters to my life. When I pull open my top dresser drawer, I see momentos that carry me back over the past twenty years of my life . . . and then some.

2   Sometimes, when I can't get the drawer open, I have to reach my fingers in and push papers down and rearrange objects that flow ever higher in my drawer of memories.

3   My current payroll stubs are first to attract my probing eye. Every time I see these payroll stubs, I think of some of the arrests I have made at work, some of the people I have worked with that no longer are there, all the hours I have worked, the promotion I received. Behind the payroll stubs is all the correspondence from the police departments that I have applied to dating back to 1984. When I look at this bundle of letters from so many different police departments, I can recall filling out applications that were as many as 25 pages long. I can remember every written test, every physical agility test, every oral interview, every psychological test. I remember waiting for each test result to come in the mail. With a strange loving care, I protect these letters. I put them in order by date and store them right in front so that I see them every time I go into my drawer.

4   Directly behind the police letters are my unemployment papers, bringing back memories of hard times, memories of being out of work, standing in line for hours at the un-

employment office, filling out those forms, seeing all the various unemployed people. I remember watching these people search for names of businesses in the phone book so that they would have something to put on the benefit application forms where it was marked "Places I have looked for employment." Without this information, their precious benefits could not be received.

5   Jammed in behind the unemployment papers are the rest of my payroll stubs dating all the way back to 1974. Visions of all my past jobs, the people I have worked with, the buildings I have worked in, the bosses, all the different wages I have earned, jobs I liked and didn't like all come floating back to me. I wonder what those people are doing now and how the people and places have changed.

6   Tossed in behind all those pay stubs and envelopes is the aluminum cast of an antique 1906 Cadillac I made in the foundry in my metals shop class when I was in high school. I remember the choice of what we could cast: an Indian head nickel, a couple of different antique cars and a Lincoln head penny.

7   In the center of my drawer, my high school diploma has somehow risen to the top of the heap causing me to reflect on graduation and all the pictures that were taken after the ceremony. I recall holding on to my mortarboard when everyone else threw theirs into the air because I wanted to save mine. Where is it now?

8   Below the diploma is a plastic bag jam packed with photo I.D.'s. There are a few firearm owner's cards, expired college I.D.'s, old driver's licenses, employee identification cards. Looking at these I see my different hair styles and my facial hair changes: beard, moustache, sideburns.

9   Beneath the plastic bag is a bumper sticker saying "Steve Martin is a Personal Friend of Mine." There is also a certificate saying that I belong to the Steve Martin fan club. These relics date back to 1978 when I really was a "wild and crazy guy."

10   Back to the front of the drawer. I see a jewelry box that was given to me as a gift for standing up to my sister-and brother-in-law's wedding. Inside this box are various pins from my rock-a-billy days. (I still love rock-a-billy music and wonder why I don't listen to it any more.) Thoughts of The StrayCats, Dave Edmunds and Gene Vincent bring back memories of seeing Robert Gordon in 1980. At the time, he was a new wave rock-a-billy artist, and I went to see him in concert at the Park West in downtown Chicago. I was close to the stage and asked him to sing a tune called "Rock-a-billy Boogie" and he said, "I already did, man." I was so drunk I didn't even know he sang the tune. Somewhere I still have some great pictures of him rockin' that night. . . .

11   To the left of the jewelry box is a cardboard box full of little odds and ends from cars that I have owned. There is a headlight switch from my 1948 Plymouth Business Coupe. That Coupe was my first car. Everybody loved the car and would want to cruise with me because they felt like Elliot Ness. (Not a good statement on Reavis High School's history curriculum.) Here are the keys to my 1966 Ford Fairlane. The gas pedal always stuck at full throttle on that car because of a broken motor mount, so until I could get the pedal released, I would have to hold the brake pedal down hard. If I let go to get better place-ment of my foot, the car would jump like a frog.

12   Here we are at the back of the drawer again. There are mass cards from the wakes of friends and family members. They cause me to remember the day that each person died and the funeral. I especially remember when my cousin died. He was killed in Viet Nam in 1969. When he was waked, it was a closed casket with his photograph next to it. When he was buried, they played "Taps" and had a 21 gun salute that tore my heart out. When my uncle died last year, my wife called me at work, and I went to his house and saw him laying on the floor. My kids saw him on the floor and thought he was sleep-

ing. When my youngest boy saw my uncle being wheeled into the funeral director's van, he called out, "Goodbye, Uncle Bill." Thinking about it now still makes me cry.

13　　Travelling still further back in the drawer, I see my dad's police patch and my grandfather's police notebook. I remember going to work with my dad and seeing the police dog "Baron" and having my picture taken in the processing room where they take mug shots and fingerprints. I never met my grandfather, but I have read about him in a couple of newspaper articles, and I have read his police notebook.

14　　This dresser drawer holds so many memories; most are happy, some sad. It is my life, and I think anyone could read all about me if they opened my dresser drawer and flipped through some of the pages of my life pressed and tucked away inside.

Timothy McPhillips

"The Most-Advanced Ever"

1　　Whenever I see an advertisement saying something is the most-advanced ever, I wonder what kind of electronic gadget someone has come up with. One day when I was looking through a catalog I saw the Casio Pathfinder watch. The advertisement stated that it was the most-advanced outdoor watch ever. I went to my local electronics store to examine one for myself. The watch impressed me with its features, so I purchased one.

2　　I could not believe that a watch could have so many features. The Pathfinder watch has a thermometer, multiple alarms, an altimeter, a digital compass, a barometer, a stopwatch, a calendar, and it tells time in standard or military time. The Pathfinder gets all of its information from two sensors, on either side of the watch. The sensors make it look bulky, but the bulky appearance is to be expected from a watch with so many features. The instruction manual has over fifty pages of instructions! I am going to highlight just a few of the best features.

3　　My favorite feature is the barometer. The watch automatically measures barometric pressure every two hours. Then twelve readings for the past twenty-four hours are also shown on a graph. The graph is very helpful in predicting a trend of rising or dropping atmospheric pressure. Another atmospheric measurement the watch can make is temperature readings in Celsius or Fahrenheit.

4　　The digital compass or bearing sensor can detect up to sixteen directions. The directions can be very specific, such as west-northwest. A reading can be observed in less than one second after pressing the bearing sensor button, showing the direction the watch is pointed. Up to five sets of directions can be stored in memory. These readings help to make the user well-informed on or off the trail.

5　　The altimeter can measure altitude from zero to four thousand meters or zero to thirteen thousand one hundred twenty feet. Changes in altitude are also displayed on a graph. There is an altitude alarm that can be set to go off when a certain altitude is reached. Of course you can save altitude readings on the watch's memory. The altimeter is not accurate enough for industry, sky diving, or hang gliding, but it is perfect for the outdoorsman.

6　　I have been very satisfied with my Pathfinder. I enjoy knowing the altitude of hills I've conquered. The barometer has helped me to try to predict weather on camping trips. The watch has been my travel alarm on vacations. It is a gadget I think any outdoorsman would enjoy and should for its price.

Nick Brosnan

THE DESCRIPTION OF AN OBJECT PAPER—YOUR TURN

1 Look around and find an object. Remember that this is an exercise in detail, so choose something that gives you enough to write about.

2 Very carefully study the object.

3 Jot down the ideas and observations that step two produced. Jot down details—all details, large and small. Jot down the analogies that come to mind. Be certain that your list is as thorough as possible, for this list will eventually generate your paragraphs and the entire essay.

4 Organize and structure the detail.

5 Write the draft of your paper.

After Christmas, all winter clothing goes on clarence.

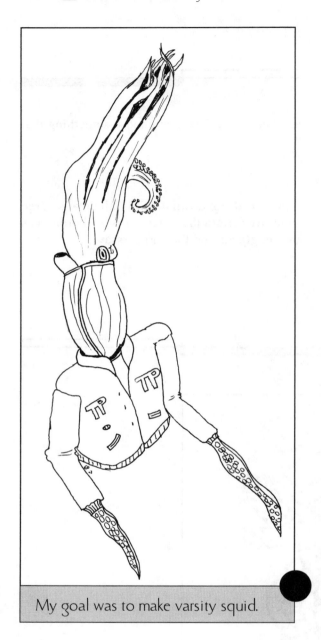

My goal was to make varsity squid.

On Friday nights, my friends and I love to chow down on big burros.

DESCRIPTION OF AN OBJECT PAPER PLAN SHEET

Part One: Choose an object (topic) for your essay and write down some of the detail and some of the analogies which might appear in the essay.

Topic: _____

Jottings: (Use these blanks to jot down details you observed while examining the object.)

_____   _____   _____

_____   _____   _____

_____   _____   _____

_____   _____   _____

_____   _____   _____

_____   _____   _____

_____   _____   _____

Analogies: (Use these blanks to jot down some of the analogies you might use in the paper.)

_____

_____

_____

_____

_____

_____

_____

_____

_____

Name _____ Section _____ Date _____

SELF-EVALUATION SHEET: PART ONE

Assignment: _____

Strong points of this assignment:

_____

_____

_____

_____

_____

_____

_____

Weak points of this assignment:

_____

_____

_____

_____

_____

_____

_____

General comments:

_____

_____

_____

_____

_____

_____

_____

(over)

SELF-EVALUATION SHEET: PART TWO

What were the strong points of your last writing assignment?

_____

_____

_____

_____

_____

_____

What were the weak points of your last writing assignment?

_____

_____

_____

_____

_____

_____

What have you done to correct those weaknesses in this assignment?

_____

_____

_____

_____

_____

_____

PEER-EVALUATION SHEET: PEER-EVALUATOR #1

Writer's Name _____ Essay's Title _____

> **Directions:** (1) Remember not to write on another student's paper. Instead, use this form. (2) Offer concrete, specific comments using the terminology of writing (e.g., "The development in paragraph four might be improved by adding a brief example." or, "Check structure on page 3.")

What do you see as the strong points of this writing assignment: _____

_____

_____

_____

_____

What areas do you feel might need additional work: _____

_____

_____

_____

_____

Do you see any areas of grammar/mechanics (e.g. usage, spelling, fragments) that might need attention: _____

_____

_____

_____

_____

General comments: _____

_____

_____

_____

PEER-EVALUATION SHEET: PEER-EVALUATOR #2

Writer's Name _____ Essay's Title _____

> **Directions:** (1) Remember not to write on another student's paper. Instead, use this form. (2) Offer concrete, specific comments using the terminology of writing (e.g., "The development in paragraph four might be improved by adding a brief example." or, "Check structure on page 3.")

What do you see as the strong points of this writing assignment: _____

_____

_____

_____

_____

What areas do you feel might need additional work: _____

_____

_____

_____

_____

Do you see any areas of grammar/mechanics (e.g. usage, spelling, fragments) that might need attention: _____

_____

_____

_____

_____

General comments: _____

_____

_____

_____

_____

THE DESCRIPTION OF A PLACE PAPER

Have you ever tried to describe to a friend the small town where you grew up? Before beginning, you try to decide where to start and what to say. Should you describe the location of the town in the state, or should you describe the population and the ethnic make-up? Next you think of all the other bits of information: the industry, the restored city hall building and courthouse, the city flower gardens, the new park complexes, the industrial park and the new business district, the scenic view of the hills and the river valley, the clean air, the antique shops, the marina, the new airport. . . . Suddenly you feel overwhelmed. It is difficult to decide where to begin, where to focus, what to include, and what to exclude. Yet it is not unusual for us to be asked to do this in some way almost everyday: a neighbor asks us about the new Chinese restaurant that opened nearby, our mother-in-law wants to know about the new boutique in the mall, or our son asks about the new school that he will be going to at summer's end.

To avoid the feeling of being overwhelmed by the task—and to answer the where-to-begin question— you simply need to keep in mind one concept: focus your description. That is, when you describe a place, you want your reader to see that place in a certain way; you want one idea or impression of that place to stand out, to dominate. That one, overall impression which you wish to communicate to your reader through your description is called the **dominant impression.**

THE DOMINANT IMPRESSION

The term *dominant impression* means what the two words imply—it is the one impression of a place which stands out (is dominant) from all other impressions. The dominant impression of a place is a generalization or a conclusion based upon observed details and facts.

For example, imagine that you and I went to a restaurant for lunch before class. Afterwards, as we walk into class, one of the other students asks us what we thought of the restaurant. At the same time, we both give a response. You say, "It was a real dump!" while I say, "It was a charming place." What happened? We both ate at the same place—the same table, in fact. So why are our impressions so different?

Well, while we were dining, you observed various details that led you to the conclusion that the restaurant was in fact a "dump." Perhaps the chair you chose had crumbs on it. Add to this the fact that your water glass was chipped, your fork had egg on it, etc., and you will soon convince anyone that the restaurant was indeed a "dump."

On the other hand, I noticed that the help was polite, that the tablecloth was clean and crisp, and that each table had fresh-cut flowers and scented candles. The more positive details of this type that I can relate, the better I could convince someone that the restaurant was charming.

If both of us can support and illustrate our impressions by providing detail, then we both have succeeded in describing the same restaurant. It is quite possible that the student who asked us about the restaurant might go there and come back with a third impression, and as long as he could support his opinion, who could say which of the three of us would be right or wrong?

Needless to say, each person will choose the details that best support his overall impression. Even if I had noticed a rumpled napkin under the table, I would not mention it if I were trying to convince someone that the restaurant was charming. Nor would you mention the exquisite quality of the food in trying to convince someone that the restaurant was less-than-high-class. Each of us would use only the detail that supported, illustrated, and clarified our dominant impression. This is the principle you need to apply in selecting detail.

When describing a place, then, you really begin with a generalization. That generalization is called the dominant impression. The dominant impression serves the same function as the thesis statement. It is the one point or the limiting idea of a particular topic, in this case a place, that you want to communicate to a reader.

 GUIDELINES FOR WRITING A DESCRIPTION
OF A PLACE ESSAY

■ **One,** apply those principles of descriptive writing which have been covered in the previous pages of this chapter: write with concrete and specific detail and example; only sparingly use "lists" and adjectives. Also, try to incorporate some effective analogies.

■ **Two,** as explained in the last section, focus your description around a clear dominant impression.

■ **Three,** learn how to select information to be included. This works according to two principles. One, make certain the details you include support the dominant impression and thereby maintain the overall unity of the essay. For example, if you are describing your cottage as a beautiful, rustic place, don't mention the rusty cans bobbing around under the dock or the old beater decaying in the back yard. True, they are great details/examples, but unless you have a personality disorder, they don't have a lot to do with the beauty of nature. Those details have to hit the cutting room floor. Two, select detail which seems to be most-critical or most-significant. Obviously, not every last piece of information about a place can be included or the reader will be overwhelmed with detail (and probably a boredom-induced coma as well). Include that information which best supports the dominant impression; exclude that information which does not.

■ **Four,** provide structure and organization for the detail which you have selected for inclusion. This is not always easy because, in most cases, places don't automatically divide themselves into paragraphs. It becomes the writer's responsibility to place information into paragraphs which are unified and coherent. The first three examples which follow will illustrate three common methods writers use to organize and structure: senses, time, and space.

■ **Five,** as with any type of writing, try to write to communicate with your reader. As you read the following essay, notice how the writer uses description not just to give an impression of a place; the writer had something to say and used description to say it.

You Are Almost There

1   I think that most people, during their lives, have a special place, a home away from home. This is a place where I feel inner peace, a place which holds so many memories I could picture heaven being just like it. This is the way I feel about the Boy Scout Camp in Whitehall, Michigan. This reservation consists of three section camps for Boy Scouts— along with a family camp. The family camp is named Reneker. It is a little more modern than where the Boy Scouts must stay. Boy Scouts sleep in tents and cook outside. They walk outside, down a path, to the KYBO (outside bathrooms). At Camp Reneker, we have cabins with small kitchens. However, I still have to hope there is not much wildlife outside in the middle of the night while I make my way to the community bathroom.

2   Driving to Whitehall takes anywhere from three and a half to four and a half hours, depending upon my speed and the traffic. The feeling starts after my arrival in Muskegon, which is a little south of Whitehall. The road travels through a terrible looking swamp area, but then I know camp is near. There is that feeling! Only a few more miles, and I will have arrived. What exciting things will take place on this visit? This could be just the quiet and peacefulness I have been looking for. There it is! There is that slow chill that goes down my spine and puts goosebumps on my arms. "Welcome to Owasippe" the sign reads. Welcome home!

3   I always hope that on the day I arrive the sky will be blue and clear. When it is, I can see forever, or so it seems. The trees and grass are greener, the sky bluer, the flowers brighter, and even the weeds look like they were hand painted just for me. I look around to see what has changed since my last visit. A tree has fallen across the path. Some new cacti are growing in a new section. (Yes, Michigan does have prickly pear cactus.) A tree which had fallen last year is now overgrown with vines and wildflowers. The area appears beautiful as always.

4   As I look around, a scent of something not smelled for a long time greets my nose: fresh, non-polluted air. Taking a deep breath, I start noticing all of the other fragrances wafting around me. The flowering vines, the shaggy weeds, the sweet-smelling flowers, the smell of water from the lake close by, and even the smell of horse manure from the nearby corral bring back memories of past years.

5   In the woods are many sounds. Everyone pretends they know what kind of animal or insect may be making a specific sound. Is it a raccoon or another furry animal? Was that a deer we heard on the path or just some children running? The wind through the tops of the trees has a different sound than that same wind along the path. The storms are even different. The rain falls harder and louder than at home, the lightning is brighter, the thunder is louder, and the wind is scarier. The sounds of nature never stop; they just change their tune depending upon the time of day.

6   Even the taste, yes the taste, of Owasippe is different. At home, it is great to barbecue outside. When you bring out the charcoal at camp, there is a whole new meaning given to the words "cooking outside." The grill might be the same, the briquettes may be the same, the favorite food on the grill may be the same, but it's not. There is a special taste at Owasippe: a fresher, cleaner, more-wholesome taste, a "you'll never taste anything like this again" taste. Everyone's appetite soars. It is good that there are so many trails to hike. We can exercise off all that we have eaten.

7   Owasippe is my special place, a place to think of when I'm down, when everything is going wrong. Everyone wonders why I am smiling. Everyone should have their own special place to keep inside of them, a place that helps them through the more-mundane parts of life. Owasippe is my home away from home. I would be happy to give you directions to get there. Maybe you could find a little place to keep in your heart so you could have your own home away from home.

Sharon Tiberi

When reading Sharon's paper, we are invited to share her impressions of and her love of Owasippe and what it means—and has meant—to her in her day-to-day life. It is a good essay for several reasons. First, she used description to say something to her readers; this place is important to her. She has a clear dominant impression: this place is special, and I hold it in my heart. All of the information in her paper is focused in support of this concept. She does not overload us with detail, but provides the necessary development to communicate and support her point.

Sharon's essay is also structured and organized very efficiently. This is not always easy with description. One method that works for some writers—as it did for Sharon—is to use the **senses.** If you study Sharon's essay, you'll notice that most of the body paragraphs are focused on a specific sense. The following scratch outline illustrates:

1. intro & statement of dominant impression
2. the drive there
3. sights

4. smells

5. sounds

6. tastes

7. closing parag.

A second method of organization is **chronological** organization, organization by the passage of time. In the following example, the writer used the passage of time (or different times during the day) as the limiting idea in each paragraph. Although the essay is very structured, it almost appears to be free-form. The observant reader, however, will perceive the use of time as a structural device.

A Day on the U.S.S. Detroit

1   The United States Navy provides very busy days for its crews onboard ships at sea. The U.S.S. Detroit is a Naval ship that has a very full day for its personnel. The people onboard the U.S.S. Detroit, in particular—the deck unit, are always doing something, from early in the morning, until late in the night.

2   The U.S.S. Detroit is a United States Naval supply ship. It is responsible for supplying other ships with food, fuel, ammunition, and clothing. This vessel is one of the biggest in its fleet. It is as long as three football fields combined and as wide as a quarter of a football field. It is not only big, but it has one of the biggest crews as well. This support ship can hold a crew as big as an average high school population. This ship has many obligations, so the crew is always doing something.

3   Knowing what the U.S.S. Detroit is, let us begin with a typical morning for one of its crew members. At the crack of dawn, there is a loud ear-popping bugle played over the ship's intercom. A startling reaction to this noise is a usual response, which results in a jumping out of his or her rack (bed). After a few seconds of being awake go by, there is usually a rush to the head (bathroom) to get cleaned up for the beginning of the day. It is most likely that more time is spent *in* a line to get to the head, than time actually spent *inside* the head. After quickly washing and shaving the face, and brushing the teeth, the sailor typically dashes back to the rack to get dressed and leave for quarters.

4   "Quarters" is a roll-call process to see if all crew members in a unit (group of personnel that have the same responsibility to the ship) are awake, present, and ready to work. The leading petty officer (person in charge of his/her unit) is the one who calls roll and makes sure everyone is there. This part of the day usually takes about forty minutes because not only does it take time to listen to the ship's announcements, but there is always someone in the unit that oversleeps. The unit then has to wait until that person gets to quarters and is also ready to work. Once everyone is present and accounted for, the leading petty officer puts the unit to work. For example, if it is a deck unit, they are responsible for the upkeep of the ship. This unit is then put to work for an eight-hour period sweeping, mopping, painting, and chipping rust.

5   In the middle of the crew member's eight hour work day, there is a thirty-minute allowance for a lunch break. When the clock strikes twelve, the workers are released and there is a sprint for the chow line. This is not only to get to the front of the line, but also to satisfy the hunger that began with skipping breakfast to get to quarters on time. The first half of the allotted time for lunch is usually spent crunched up between fellow crew members. Once the food is served, there is a hurry to a table to inhale the meal. Then it is back to work!

6   The next half of the work day for the deck unit personnel is spent doing the same thing as done earlier—cleaning the ship. The sailor is usually supervised the entire time while working, so a break is more than likely out of the question. Once the drudgery of the eight hour work day is finally done, the worker of the ship is usually exhausted. However, the day is not quite finished yet.

7   Dinner is served when the work day is finished. Once the seamen gulp down their dinner, they are assigned by their leading petty officer to stand a five hour watch. There are three watches after the work day that must be served—the 5:00 P.M. to 10:00 P.M., 10:00 P.M. to 3:00 A.M., and the 3:00 A.M. to 8:00 A.M. watch. The sailor prays he/she gets the 5:00 P.M. to 10:00 P.M. watch so a full night's rest can be accomplished. Of course, the mariner will more than likely get one of the other watches, which means a good night's rest is out of the question. Watches are mandatory for all crew members of the vessel. The deck crew members' watches are held on eight outer posts of the ship. The seamen are responsible for reporting any unauthorized objects that may seem too close to the ship. They must be reported to the person in charge of all watches so it is properly dealt with.

8   Clearly a sailor's day on a Navy vessel at sea can be pretty busy. Sleep is something that a Navy person gets little of because of all the responsibilities that must be fulfilled, remembering that the U.S.S. Detroit's fleet is needing of supplies. The replenishing process must be squeezed into that filled day. Keep in mind the sailor needs time to keep in touch with home and his/her personal needs. It is definitely hard to find time for that. Once the day is finally over and the crew member goes to sleep, it is just a matter of hours until that startling bugle will be played and the same daily routine will be repeated.

James P. Godfrey

Had James outlined the main ideas in his essay, his outline might have resembled this one:

    I. introduction
       dominant impression: a place of activity
       a place of never-ending work

   II. limiting idea: general info about the ship

  III. limiting idea: dawn

  IV. limiting idea: "Quarters" & beginning of work day

   V. limiting idea: lunch

  VI. limiting idea; second half of work day

 VII. limiting idea: dinner time & watch assignments

VIII. closing paragraph

A third method you might find useful is **spatial** organization, organization by space, physical layout, or arrangement. When reading the following example, notice how the writer presents information; just as a photographer might pan from one section of a room to another, the writer uses this same kind of movement to structure the limiting ideas for the various paragraphs.

A Shockingly Horrible Place

1   When you are somewhere pleasant you can go anywhere in the world. While you sit on a sunlit beach you can be the President of the United States, on a stage, giving your inaugural speech to all of America. But when you are somewhere shockingly horrible, it seems as if your mind is paralyzed. It forces you to go through and to experience where you are. This is how I felt when I was visiting Dachau, West Germany. Dachau—concentration camp from 1933 to 1945—was one place my mind wished it could have escaped.

2   I remember I was standing at the main gate of Dachau. The gate is made of thick, black, intimidating iron, about 14 feet high in places. Almost as intimidating is the coarse wire strung across the top of the gate, wire so coarse it dares anyone to try to climb it that does not want to be ripped to shreds by little razors.

3   I walked with a group of people, all like me, who had come to see Dachau. We came to see if we could find a shred of evidence that would tell us all of the terrible tales we had heard about Dachau were not true. I think we didn't want to believe the stories of the execution-style murders we had heard. It's easier to think that human beings are not capable of this barbaric behavior. Our guide led us to a large brick building. The building was full of long, slim, wooden troughs. They were 2½ feet wide by 6 feet long. They are set one right next to the other, by width, with only one board to separate ten or twelve troughs. These rows were stacked three high with only a few feet between the stacks. It resembled a crude bunk bed. My guide informed me that this was where the half-conscious bodies slept, the few hours they were allowed to sleep. I felt my stomach tighten thinking of these poor people scrambling to get to their slim, crude bed with a gun pointed at their heads. It is unfair for human beings to have to live in these frightening, hard conditions.

4   Our guide led us to another building, but my thoughts drifted back to the crude bunk beds, trying to get them out of my head. The building we were in had showers in it. "How undignified to shower with a lot of people," I thought. My guide informed me this was not a shower, but a gas chamber. At that moment I became aware of the vise that had hold of my stomach. The echoing of my guide's voice is all I could hear as we quickly filed one-by-one out of the cement building.

5   I found myself in another room, although I don't remember walking there; I could not get the gas chamber out of my thoughts. I had a vivid image of people trying to breathe while a poisonous gas poured out of the shower spout. I forced myself to focus on the building I was in now. It had rows and rows of ovens. My first thought was, "What were these ovens used for? Maybe they made prisoners cook or labor. This could be some sort of a factory or bakery." The voice of my guide overpowered my thoughts. As I tuned him in he was saying that this was a crematorium. He no sooner completed his sentence and I became aware of a sour, ashy odor; it was making me nauseous. "My God! this smell was actually charred human flesh. I couldn't believe after all these years I could still smell this terrible odor." My guide was speaking again, if I could only hear what he was saying. My head felt like an empty tunnel, and my ears were full of a pulsing pressure that was making it very difficult to hear anything. As I fought to tune him in, he was saying you can still smell an odor much like sour cauliflower. I don't know what I expected; definitely not this. It was worse than I could have ever imagined. How could people think of these terrible murders, not to mention actually carrying out these murders!

6   As I fought to pull myself together—I could not stop the vise in my stomach—I felt something wet hit the hand I had clutching my abdomen. I realized I was crying. I looked around to see if anyone else was crying. Most of us were.

7   Before I walked through the gates of Dachau, these murders were inconceivable. Tens of thousands of people actually were executed there, in larger proportions than most people realize. My mind was definitely frozen in time when I visited this startling horrible place I wished I could have escaped. As I passed back through those gates of Dachau that day, I glanced back at the gate for one last look at the gates I was lucky enough to leave under my own control; I know it could have very easily been me. The gates looked so proud and strong. Ironically, I thought, "Why shouldn't they? They defeated tens of thousands of people, all for being born a certain race."

Kathleen M. Blume

Had Kathleen written a scratch outline of the main ideas in her essay, that outline might have resembled this one:

Dominant Impression:	Dachau Concentration Camp is a shockingly horrible place.
limiting idea:	the main gate at the front of the camp
limiting idea:	the first building in the camp: living quarters
limiting idea:	the second building in the camp: gas chamber
limiting idea:	the third building in the camp: ovens
limiting idea:	the catharsis of tears
Concluding Paragraph	

These are only three of the various methods of organization available to you. There are others, and you should feel free to create your own. Just be certain there is a reason for each paragraph's beginning and ending and for each detail's placement. In other words, remember what you have learned about paragraphing and apply that knowledge here.

Suggested Topics

Most of my students select topics (places) that are real and readily accessible: a favorite room in their house, a classroom, a grocery store, a boutique, a cave, a shopping plaza, a restaurant, a lounge, a bar, an ethnic neighborhood, a park, a favorite spot or hideaway, a pond, a backyard, a school playground, a carnival, a circus, a spot in nature, a theatre, a place of business.

Some students have selected off-the-wall topics where they have placed themselves in strange or unfamiliar surroundings. These students have described such places as a phone booth, a confessional, a bathroom, an outhouse, a pup tent, the inside of a refrigerator, an airplane cockpit, a coffin, a tree house, a diving bell, and a riverboat.

Others have used very creative topics, such as the mind, heaven, hell, an emotional high, an emotional low, a dreamed or imagined place, or a utopia.

STUDENT EXAMPLES

Recuerdos de Cajamarca

1   When my husband and I traveled to the Northern Andean city of Cajamarca, Peru, to adopt our daughter, we were not prepared to fly from Peru's capital of Lima to our destination in an antiquated, 40 passenger aircraft. The departure of the flight was delayed, as we would later come to find out, was the case with most everything in Peru. "Mañana" would have been a fitting word to describe Peruvian lifestyle.

2   The plane was filled to capacity. We were the only "gringos" on board. For the first time ever I knew what it felt like to be a minority, different from everyone around me. I was very uncomfortable, and I think it showed. The two-hour flight was very turbulent. Being packed in like sardines with people who all looked, spoke and smelled different from what I was accustomed to added to my anxiety and discomfort. The pilot's cabin was visible to the passengers. As he prepared our flight for landing, I could see the Andes Mountains through the plane's front windshield. The view was magnificent, but now I was really scared, sick, and didn't care to look. My ears began to buzz; my head was pounding as if a locomotive were traveling through me. With my head in my hands, I began to sob and pray. I think I may have had a blackout, because the next thing I knew, we were on the ground deplaning onto the landing strip. We had to walk the equivalent of about a block to get into the airport, which was nothing more than an oversized airplane hangar. Our interpreter was waiting there for us. He could see that I wasn't well and explained that the "soroche," or altitude sickness, would go away once I got used to the altitude, 9,800 feet above sea level.

3   It wasn't long after our arrival before we got settled into our hotel, and at long last, had our new baby with us. We had prepared for and anticipated this moment for so long that having her with us felt natural from the start. We were a family. We had her, and she had us. We just had to wait for the court to process our adoption—mañana. We spent the next six weeks getting to know Cajamarca, a thriving metropolis by early 20th century standards.

4   We passed much of our time in the historical Plaza de Armas (town square). There, we could behold the beauty of tropical flowers that seemed to grow wild. The shrubs were sculpted into busts of Inca warrior heads by pinching off new shoots by hand. At any given time of the day or night there would be people congregating in and around the Plaza. The Plaza was the hub of the city. Most people didn't own cars, nor did they need them. All roads led to and from the Plaza, and most everything was within walking distance.

5   The people of Cajamarca were friendly yet guarded of strangers. Their ethnicity was Native American, descendants of the Inca and Quechua Indians, or mestizo, a mix of Spanish and Indian. Most people spoke Spanish, Quechua, or both. The Indian women wore full woolen skirts to just below the knee, brightly colored shawls slung across their backs and high, wide brimmed hats made of straw, to protect them from the hot Andean midday sun. As they strolled through the streets, Indian women often spun llama or alpaca wool into yarn, by twisting it through their fingers onto what looked like an elongated top. It was common to see a baby's head poking out from within the shawl on a woman's back. Sometimes little Indian girls would share the load of carrying infants on their backs the same way. The men wore the same style hat, a sack type white shirt and dark col-

ored drawstring pants. Indian men, women, and children alike wore sandals or no shoes at all. The non-Indian people dressed more or less like we do in the U.S. There were many non-violent demonstrations held by students from the nearby university in the Plaza. Every Sunday there was a parade procession of school children whose families could afford to send them. All school children wore a uniform of a white shirt or blouse, dark blue pants for boys, and gray wool jumpers for girls. The jumpers looked so hot and itchy. There was a man who earned his living taking pictures in the Plaza. His camera was old and decrepit. He had to cover his head with a dark cloth and hold a big flash bulb off to the side to shoot the photograph. His camera only took pictures in black and white. The Indian people were very camera shy. They believed that if photographed, they would lose a part of their soul. Little boys offered shoeshines for a few cents, even if your shoes were Hush Puppies like my husband's were. Poor Indian women and children, referred to as campesinos, begged for money. Moneychangers stood at every corner surrounding the Plaza shouting "cambio" (change). The rate of monetary exchange was different from day to day.

6   Across from the Plaza, against the backdrop of the Andes Mountains, stood the Cathedral San Francisco. Built in the 17th century, the facade of the Cathedral was trimmed with ornamental moldings and vaulted peaks. The architecture reflected the colonial days of the Spanish conquistadors. The main altar in the Cathedral was completely covered in gold leaf. There were life-size religious icons and paintings. A noticeable dichotomy existed in the portrayal of wealth by the ornate decorations in the Cathedral compared to the abject poverty of the peasant worshipers.

7   On another side of the Plaza was the Salas restaurant. The front was open to the street and to the cats or chickens that would occasionally wander in. That was where we tried the traditional Andean dish of "cuy." It was roasted guinea pig in rich yellow gravy. The flavor and texture was like . . . chicken! Some of the locals raised cuys in their homes. Another restaurant that we frequented was the Cajamarqués. It was more upscale than the Salas, with a small courtyard full of beautiful flowers, plants, peacocks, and other tropical birds that made it their home. On all of the tables were dishes of salty fried corn kernels that were as big as thumb nails. It would always sneak some into my bag for later. If we were in the mood for fast food we would buy it from the street vendors. The anticuchos de corazón, marinated and skewered beef hearts, were my favorite. The candied peanuts, cooked up over burning wood fires in big aluminum pots, were a close runner up.

8   A short way up the street from the Plaza was the market, a place that was like walking through the pages of a National Geographic magazine. It was where many of the campesinos, who traveled down from their mountain villages, came to sell their fruits, vegetables, and live fowl. Cattle, sheep and goats were butchered and sold right there. When all the parts were sold, the animals' heads were left on display. Yuk! Curanderos, or medicine men, sold herbs, oils, and bottled llama fetuses. Our interpreter never accompanied us to the market. There, more than anywhere else in Cajamarca, I was truly reliant on the few Spanish phrases I had learned. I didn't understand how much was needed to pay for things. I must have looked so odd holding out whatever money I had in my pockets to allow merchants to take what was needed from me. I still don't know if I was ever ripped off.

9   During the course of our stay, we visited three of Cajamarca's many historical sights. We took an eight-mile taxi ride outside of the city to Ventanillas de Otuzco. It was a harrowing ride up a mountainside in an old jalopy that had a hole in the back floorboard, allowing exhaust to rise up under us. Ventanillas means little windows. They were little crypts carved into rocky cliffs where the pre-Incas buried their dead. I enjoyed the view from high upon the mountain where we stood more than the attraction we had come to see. The bus ride to Baños del Inca was slightly better. Like the taxi, it was old, but there were no holes in the floor. It was crowded with as many people as could sit, stand, or hang on to the open doors from outside. The Baños were the Baths of the Incas where thermal waters come up from out of the ground. It is said that during Inca times, solely Inca rulers could enjoy the properties of the curative waters. They have since been converted into individual little bathhouses for all to enjoy, for a small price of course. Within walking distance from the Plaza was El Cuarto del Rescate, or Gold Room, the principal monument in Cajamarca. It was the only remains of Inca architecture left there. Inside the granite block walls was where Francisco Pizarro held Inca leader, Atahualpa, captive to be ransomed only when the room was filled with gold and silver. When his demands were met, Pizarro killed the Inca anyway. A larger than life mural depicts the events of that fateful day.

10   Having been able to visit these sights has allowed me to appreciate the city of Cajamarca's historical significance.

11   Eight years have passed since our six-week stay in Cajamarca. The memories of my experiences in that intriguing city, so full of history and wonder, will always have a special place in my heart. Someday we plan to return with our daughter so she can become acquainted with the land of her birth: Mañana.

Heidi A. Foster

The Fisherman's Ultimate Dream

1   When people come to our home for the first time, and I give them the tour, it is always our bedroom that gets the same reaction.

2   When you stand in the doorway, the first thing you see is our queen size bed. The bedspread is a country plaid in taupe, teal, white, burgundy, and navy blue, with taupe and teal being the dominant colors. A stuffed Amish couple, dressed in burgundy and black, sit comfortably resting their back on our bed pillows. To the right of the couple, back by the headboard, are two small decorative pillows, with sayings I feel describe my husband pretty well—#1 dad and I'd rather be fishing.

3   On the wall above the bed is an eucalyptus spray. The shape of this arrangement is like an upside down letter u, only more circular. This piece is made up in layers, beginning with long, thin, tree branches. Green eucalyptus lay upon the tree branches, followed by pale yellow and burgundy roses. Finally, a cream bow, and baby's-breath, as filler, finishes it off.

4   Your eyes continue upward until they rest upon the border. Now the border is what I call an outdoor theme. When I began my search for a border for this room, I used the bedspread as a guide for the colors, so it ties in very well. The pattern on the border repeats itself around the room beginning with a male mallard. Laying next to the mallard are matches, not a pack, but the little box type that you don't see much anymore. The lantern and binoculars, positioned next to each other, look like they are just waiting for their next outing. My favorite item in this border is the wicker fishing basket. It reminds me of the one they carried in the Andy Griffith show. Attached to the top left of the basket, sort of hanging off of the side, is a fishing license. A few fishing lures are scattered here and there amongst these items.

5   I have figured out that it is this border that people follow around the room, bringing them to the wall opposite our bed. This is where they kind of look at the wall and cock their heads slightly and then look at me and say, "Fish?". For above Dan's chest of drawers, hang not one, but two, largemouth bass.

6   Both bass were caught in Canada on two different fishing trips. Together the two weigh approximately 18 pounds, each expanding 29 inches in length. After the first catch he brought home and mounted, I prayed during the second trip, that he wouldn't catch the "big" one. Well, that week, my prayers were not answered.

7   When we first hung the fish we had a pretty good laugh. We had hung them facing each other at the same level. They looked like fish that belonged on a fountain. I told my husband all that was missing was the water shooting out of their mouths. We then re-hung them still facing each other, but at different levels. Now they look as if they are going to swim right across the wall past each other!

8   Now the look of puzzlement and the "fish?" reaction is from our female visitors. They don't understand how I could have hung fish in the same room where our romance takes place. But the way I figure, the majority of the time my eyes are closed (except for the really steamy parts), and I tell them it was either here, or on my living room wall. "Oooooooh!" is what I hear next, as if they totally understand.

9   The reaction I get from men is quite different. They are surprised that I would allow this, but for a different reason. They always tell Dan that their wives would never let them hang fish on their bedroom walls. Secretly, they are jealous of Dan, because he has his best catches in one room at the same time. One in bed and the other two on the wall. The fisherman's ultimate dream!

Cheryl Kaner

Memories of Our Migros Market

1   After three long weeks in a hotel, we were ready to settle in and begin our new life abroad. Our home for the next two years was in a town called *Adliswil*. It was a small working class community, about thirty minutes outside of *Zurich, Switzerland*.

2   It's one thing traveling around the beautiful countryside as a tourist. It's another story living in a foreign country and trying to adapt to their way of life. I discovered the meaning of culture shock the day my family and I entered the Swiss grocery store.

3   Tiny cheese and sausage shops lined the main road leading into town. The outdoor market was filled with fresh flowers and wooden carts piled high with fruits and vegetables. As we stopped at the only red light in town, bold, red letters caught my eye. A *Migros Market* sign was displayed on the side of a gray, two-story cement building, not like the Alpine cottages with flower boxes and green shutters on the windows.

4   We turned the corner and followed the narrow road, which led us to the entrance of the underground *Park House*. We slowly drove into this poorly lit lot. It was difficult maneuvering the car around the narrow aisles. The ceiling was very low, which made this area seem smaller. We eventually did find a spot to park, and we only had to drive around a dozen times. A little like holiday shopping at the mall. Once we wedged our car into a space, I noticed a parking meter in front of us. We had to pay for this spot! This didn't really surprise us. We did have to pay extra for the rolls we ate at dinner last night. I fed the meter one Swiss franc and headed for the elevator.

5   There are many *Migros* stores throughout the Zurich area. This particular one sold household goods and had a restaurant on the second floor.

6   The elevator doors opened; we entered the first floor of the *Migros*. Directly in front of us were many large, green buckets full of red and yellow tulips. I couldn't resist picking out a bouquet of pink roses to brighten up our new home. A tall woman stood behind the counter of the floral shop. "Gruezi Mitenand," she greeted us with a smile. "Gruezi," I replied. I paid for the flowers, smiled and hoped I didn't sound too silly.

7   Next we needed a shopping cart. There was a row of shopping carts neatly lined up near the registers. Our son was pulling on the carts, but they seemed to be locked up. Our groceries wouldn't be the only thing we'd be paying for on our trip today. A two-franc coin had to be inserted in the coin slot in order to unlock the cart. The good news is it's only a deposit; we'll get our coin back when we lock it back up.

8   I pushed the cart through the turnstile, and we headed down the first aisle. Bottles of *Orangina* and *Citro* filled the shelves. Not one of the name brands looked familiar to us, but we had to drink something besides water or coffee. We picked one and continued on our way. The kids ran ahead. As we turned the corner into the next aisle, our daughter came running towards us yelling "cookies!" She did hit the jackpot! The top shelf was full of hand painted tins, each one depicting the beautiful Swiss countryside. Inside were carefully wrapped chocolate covered butter cookies. It's not like the *Oreos* back home. Next to the cookies were Swiss chocolate bars the size of license plates. There were many types to choose from: white, dark, and milk chocolate, some with hazelnuts, or almonds too. I placed a *few* bars in the cart. I confess. I was familiar with this particular Swiss product.

9   The smell of freshly baked bread led us clear across the store. Rows of bread were carefully arranged in a glass-enclosed case. Stacks of bread were beautifully braided and baked to a golden brown. Loaves with hard crusts resembled mountain ranges, which ran along the length of the counter. Large wicker baskets were filled with rolls of all kinds: hard, thick crusts dusted lightly with flour, poppy seed rolls, and soft, flaky *Gipfelis*, which is a Swiss croissant. We bought a dozen rolls and wiped the drool from our chins.

10   Heading to the back of the store toward the meat department, my family and I were taken by surprise. Cartons of milk and eggs were displayed on the top shelf, but none of those items were refrigerated. I picked up an egg carton to look inside; tiny, white chicken feathers flew out from the sides of the carton. Now those were fresh eggs! We still don't know how the milk stayed so fresh!

11   We slowly walked past the deli counter. My husband and I looked at each other. "How many pounds equal a kilo?" The meat selection was much like we had back home, with the exception of a few frozen rabbits encased in plastic. "Yum." We watched the Swiss butchers behind the counter. A burly man wearing a bloody, white apron stood chopping a side of beef; while the smaller man neatly wrapped all the meat in heavy, brown paper. We successfully ordered a kilo of meat and continued on our way.

12   Our two children ran by us holding their noses. Not to cause us further embarrassment, we knew stopping at the cheese counter wouldn't be wise at this time. A Swiss friend later told us, that the cheese with the strongest odor was the best tasting. We'll take his word for it.

13   We didn't give any thought about getting our cart to the second floor, until we came upon four escalators. The customers had two escalators, one going up and one down. In the middle of these two escalators were two more just for the grocery carts. We watched the customers push their carts on to the center escalators, then ride the other (customers escalator) along side the grocery cart to the next floor. When it was our turn, we also took the ride up (with our grocery cart) to the second floor.

14   The second floor was made up of many departments: a houseware and toy department, and a clothing department for men, women, and children. It's amazing the variety of items that we found on one floor. Everything from ironing boards to recycled toilet paper (that's another story) can be found at the *Migros*. We picked up a few necessities and decided that it was time to head home.

15   Our children turned the escalator ride down into a game of, *who can reach the bottom floor first*? Children get bored shopping even in Europe.

16   We wheeled our cart toward the cashier; there were only four checkout lanes. At each lane a woman sat comfortably on a high back cushioned chair. While standing in line I noticed that everyone was carrying his or her own shopping bag. Some of them held canvas bags; others had paper shopping bags. I guess we would have to buy a few (souvenir) shopping bags, if we wanted to get our groceries to the car. While bagging our own groceries I realized how much I missed the little conveniences of home.

17   Walking toward the elevator, I thought of this once-in-a-lifetime opportunity to experience Switzerland and its customs. It was not *Orland Park*, but what wonderful memories my family and I would have for a lifetime.

Sheila Keating

Condemned

1   "OK, I'll amuse myself. If you don't want to go fishing with me, I'll find something to do," I tossed my angry words at my companions. As I headed out of the cabin door, I lifted my hiking pack off of its nail. Walking down the access road, I mumbled to myself, "Let them sit around the table and play cards. I keep my own company very well, thank you." It was a beautiful day, and I was looking for adventure.

2   An interesting walking trail caught my attention. My hesitation was brief; investigation was the order of the day. Entering the forest, I was surrounded by the perfume of sweet sumac and wildflowers. I truly enjoy walking in the woods, and I have a tendency to lose track of time and distance traveled. I had no clue how far I had traveled, but I now seemed to be peering into someone's backyard. Curiosity overtook me; I had to see who lived here.

3   The yard was overgrown with vegetation, making my approach to the house difficult. The closer I came to the structure, the more it was apparent that much work was needed in the form of repairs. Heedless of any danger, I climbed the stairs and strode across the porch. There was no response to my rapping on the door. Foolishly, I tried the doorknob. It turned and the door opened; I entered into a dark, dank hall. Trouble was waiting around the corner.

4   Enough light made its way through the filthy windows that I was able to see my way without my flashlight. I scanned what had once been a kitchen. Small, furbearing creatures scampered out of my way as I crossed the floor. I confronted a heavy oak door. It was ajar; I tugged to open it further. I needed to see what was on the other side, for curiosity sake. Suddenly I heard a creak. Was someone in this house with me? Several more creaks followed the first. I quickly spun around to see who was behind me. Suddenly, the bottom literally dropped out of my world. I found myself plummetting into darkness. As I hit bottom, my feet slid out from under me, and I landed on my behind in slimy muck.

5   In the still darkness, I became aware of the fact that I had found the cellar the hard way: through the floor boards. I was searching my pack for my flashlight, when something flew past my face. "Oh no!" I whispered to myself, "That can't be a bird. Birds don't come into dark places like this." I switched on the light and gently scanned the ceiling. My fears were confirmed as several bats hung upside down from the beams. Looking down, I discovered that I was standing in about three inches of muck. I refused to even think of what its ingredients were.

6   Carefully, I inched my way, scanning for the stairs leading out of this dungeon. To my dismay, I happened upon the stairs. Long before this day, the lumber had rotted and the stairs had detached. Ironically, the door above me was the same door I had tried to open. There was my exit from this hole; sadly, I could not reach it.

7   Panic set in as it occurred to me exactly what my plight was. No one knew where I was. I was trapped in a slimehole with bats and other unsavory creatures for companions. I knew I should have let someone know where I was going: I wander off constantly without a word. This was a lesson hard learned; was it too late?

8   The thought of eating multilegged bugs to keep from starving prompted me to seek an alternate exit. At the front of the house, there appeared to be a small window. Closer investigation confirmed that I would fit through this space. There was one problem: dirt and weeds had piled up to cover part of the opening. If I stood on my toes, I could reach high enough to grab handfuls of dirt. Slowly the opening cleared, as I reached, pulled and was bombarded by dirt, stones and plantlife. Pulling myself up, I wiggled through the window, but not without difficulties; my bruises and cuts attested to this.

9   Picking up my pack, I picked my way through the growth. I must have looked like a survivor of a war. "Never will I wander off by myself," I promised myself.

10   As I walked away, it came to me that I had not seen the front of this house. Though it may seem silly, I had to know what my tomb looked like. Slowly I turned, scanning the top floor first. It had been a pretty white house. The intricate woodwork was still visible. Continuing to look down, I noticed carved pillars supporting the porch roof. Suddenly, I glimpsed the color red. "What is that?" I queried. Skirting a bush that blocked my view, I came face to face with the answer to my query: a large red sign with black letters that read CONDEMNED!

Cindy Schneider

THE DESCRIPTION OF A PLACE PAPER—YOUR TURN

1 Select a place to describe. As with any topic, choose carefully. The place should be rich enough in detail to produce a paper but not so large as to overwhelm you. It might also be beneficial to choose a place that is accessible. It is sometimes hard to rely upon memory, although it can be done. Similarly, some students like to create or fantasize places.

2 Sit and observe. Sharpen all your senses and notice all details, large and small.

3 Jot down the details you observed in step two. Do not fail to note analogies that would help you describe the place.

4 Formulate a dominant impression. What is the one quality or impression of this place that you would most want the reader of your paper to have? If the place you are describing is one very familiar to you—or if it immediately popped into your mind—try to determine why. Is there one quality about the place that seems to stand out? Be certain that the dominant impression grows out of the details you gathered in the last step.

5 Select the details which will support the dominant impression. Any detail that does not support, illustrate, explain, or clarify the dominant impression should not be included in the paper. Do not forget about unity.

6 Organize the details into clusters that will eventually become the paragraphs.

7 Write the rough draft.

While she was on her trip, my sister got a taboo.

My rabbit was a pig when it came to carats.

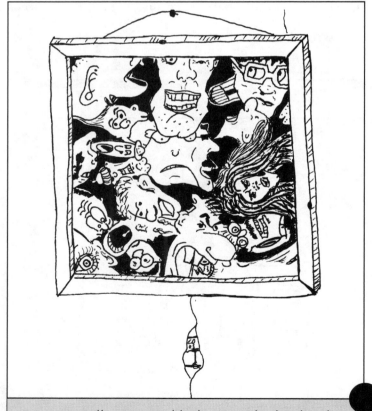

Being in collage is not like being in high school.

DESCRIPTION OF A PLACE PAPER PLAN SHEET

> **Part One:** Choose a place (topic) for your essay and decide upon a dominant impression; then write down some of the detail and some of the analogies which might appear in the essay.

Dominant Impression: _____

_____

Jottings: (Use these blanks to jot down the details you observed.)

_____   _____   _____

_____   _____   _____

_____   _____   _____

_____   _____   _____

_____   _____   _____

_____   _____   _____

_____   _____   _____

_____   _____   _____

_____   _____   _____

Analogies: (Use these blanks to jot down some of the analogies you might use in the paper.)

_____

_____

_____

_____

_____

_____

_____

Part Two: Write the outline for your essay.

SELF-EVALUATION SHEET: PART ONE

Assignment: _____

Strong points of this assignment:

_____
_____
_____
_____
_____
_____
_____

Weak points of this assignment:

_____
_____
_____
_____
_____
_____
_____

General comments:

_____
_____
_____
_____
_____
_____
_____

(over)

SELF-EVALUATION SHEET: PART TWO

What were the strong points of your last writing assignment?

_____

_____

_____

_____

_____

_____

What were the weak points of your last writing assignment?

_____

_____

_____

_____

_____

_____

What have you done to correct those weaknesses in this assignment?

_____

_____

_____

_____

_____

_____

PEER-EVALUATION SHEET: PEER-EVALUATOR #1

Writer's Name _____ Essay's Title _____

> **Directions:** (1) Remember not to write on another student's paper. Instead, use this form. (2) Offer concrete, specific comments using the terminology of writing (e.g., "The development in paragraph four might be improved by adding a brief example." or, "Check structure on page 3.")

What do you see as the strong points of this writing assignment: _____

_____

_____

_____

_____

What areas do you feel might need additional work: _____

_____

_____

_____

_____

Do you see any areas of grammar/mechanics (e.g. usage, spelling, fragments) that might need attention: _____

_____

_____

_____

_____

General comments: _____

_____

_____

_____

_____

PEER-EVALUATION SHEET: PEER-EVALUATOR #2

Writer's Name _____ Essay's Title _____

> **Directions:** (1) Remember not to write on another student's paper. Instead, use this form. (2) Offer concrete, specific comments using the terminology of writing (e.g., "The development in paragraph four might be improved by adding a brief example." or, "Check structure on page 3.")

What do you see as the strong points of this writing assignment: _____

_____

_____

_____

_____

What areas do you feel might need additional work: _____

_____

_____

_____

_____

Do you see any areas of grammar/mechanics (e.g. usage, spelling, fragments) that might need attention: _____

_____

_____

_____

_____

General comments: _____

_____

_____

_____

_____

THE DESCRIPTION OF A PERSON PAPER

Within the course of a day, most of us probably find ourselves describing a person to someone: to our friends we describe the blind date that we have arranged for them; to our parents we describe the blind date who will soon ring the doorbell; to our spouses we describe the strange person we encountered at work or on the commuter train; to our neighbors we describe the person who just bought the house across the street; to our bosses we describe the new employee who was hired while the big boss was out of the office for a day; and to our classmates who couldn't make the reunion we describe the homecoming queen who has gained thirty pounds and the most likely-to-succeed guy who is now out on parole. Although describing a person is something we obviously do frequently, it is not easy, especially when it is done in writing.

One of the reasons this task is challenging is the nature of the subject matter; people, more so than either objects or places, are complex. They have appearances and personalities and characters and moods; they also act. The very complexity of people, however, is also what makes them interesting and what can make the actual description of a person easier for the writer. Keep in mind what it was that attracted you to a person as subject matter. Was it a trait that is visible in both personality and physical appearance? If so, use that as a focal point.

GUIDELINES FOR WRITING A DESCRIPTION OF A PERSON ESSAY

- **One,** apply those theories of description that you have learned in the previous sections of this chapter. Avoid over reliance upon adjectives. Instead, rely upon concrete and specific details, including details which will appeal to your reader's senses. Don't just *tell* your reader about the person you are describing; try to *show* your reader the person as well. Also rely upon an occasional, effective analogy to communicate a lot of information in a few well-chosen words. Sometimes, one well-thought-out, concrete image can communicate a lot more feelings and ideas than are communicated in an entire paragraph of general statements. For example, don't write, "My mother was really mean to me." It doesn't tell us a lot about how mean your mother was. But if you write, "My mother was so mean that she bit the head off my hamster!" you have made a striking impression!

- **Two,** when describing a person, apply the same principle of the dominant impression that you used to describe a place. Try to find a trait which is dominant in the person's appearance, personality, and actions. By writing about all three areas, you will describe and communicate the person's complexity. Also use the selection process to gather supporting detail. Use that information which best communicates the dominant impression of the person. Eliminate that information of lesser importance.

- **Three,** the essay should be organized and structured. As you learned in the previous description assignments, structure and organization are the responsibility of the writer. Just as places and objects don't automatically lend themselves to easy or natural paragraphing, neither do people. The writer must find a method to use to provide the description of a person with both structure and organization. There is not a certain, prescribed method that is always used; the writer, however, should be certain that he is using a method, that he is in control of beginning and ending paragraphs.

- **Four,** in order to show the person in action, learn to write the anecdote. An **anecdote** is a brief story or action narration; it is usually focused on an incident in the person's life. This brief incident, however, reveals the whole person, reinforces the dominant impression. When writing the anecdote, make certain that it blends with the rest of the essay's style and purpose. The function of the anecdote is to provide a brief glimpse of the person in action; the anecdote isn't just an opportunity to showcase the writer's skills at storytelling. A very focused anecdote related in just one or several paragraphs really communicates quite effectively.

The following essay illustrates how one student was able to apply these guidelines in describing a person.

My Father

1　　Recollections of my childhood days bring back memories of my father. He was, in my mind, one of the finest individuals I have known. My father was always ready to lend an ear for problems or a hand to those in need. My father, was in fact, my stepfather, although I never really thought of him in that way. My real father died when I was seven, and I really don't remember him. My stepfather married my mother when I was eight, and he has been the only father I have really known.

2　　I think back to the year I was eight when I first met my father. He was a tall man, about 6'1" with dark curly hair, dark brown eyes, and a rugged complexion. When he smiled, his mouth would turn up slightly at the corners. His walk was slow and steady, and he never seemed to change his stride. I remember that his hands were large, and I was afraid that if I didn't behave, he would hit me, although he never did.

3　　My father was a steamfitter for the railroad, and I remember that in the winter he would always wear a plaid flannel shirt with dark gray corduroy work pants and a heavy quilted cap, similar in style to a baseball hat. In the summer, he would wear a light blue or gray chambray work shirt with lightweight blue or gray pants and a lightweight cap. As I recall, he took a clean pair of overalls to work everyday to work in, and he always changed back to clean clothes before he came home from work. There was always a treat for me in his black metal lunchbox.

4　　As the years passed, I became very close to my father. We were inseparable. He would take me golfing, bowling, and ice skating. He even took the time to show me how to do minor repairs on cars. He was also handy around the house and was always "touching up" as he called it, with a paint brush in hand. There was never any peeling paint or rusty metal. He never let it get that way.

5　　His workshop, which was a long, narrow, shed-type structure attached to the garage, was neat, clean, and organized. His tools were either hung on a pegboard or neatly packed in boxes in drawers under his workbench. Shelves lined the walls at the upper third of the workshop on which he had neatly stacked boxes of screws, bolts, nuts, and other hardware sorted by style, each box plainly marked. Nails were in baby food jars or larger jars, depending on the size of the nails, with the lid of the jars bolted to a board which was attached to the underside of one of the shelves; he could simply screw the jar and the lid remained attached to the shelf. Lawn equipment was either hanging on the wall with special brackets or in its own special place on the floor. Extension cords were wrapped so precisely that they never twisted or turned. There was never anything out of place.

6　　He could also dance and sing beautifully. Whenever we were at a party, he would be asked to sing ballads from the 40's, 50's, and 60's. When it came to dancing, he was right there. If he would see that some of the women weren't dancing, because their husbands didn't dance, my father would whisk them away for one or two dances. It didn't matter if it was a waltz, jitterbug, tango, or any other type of dance; my father could dance all of them. When he and my mother would dance the tango, everyone in the room would watch them. They danced beautifully together.

7   My father also had a good sense of humor; he was always laughing and telling jokes. The younger people he worked with used to come to our house on the weekends just to visit; they used to call him dad. He would be outside either washing his car, which was always immaculate, or working in the yard and before long, the fellows from work would be helping him with whatever he was doing. He was likable, lovable, and a pleasant person to be around. He had many, many friends, and I attribute that to his personality.

8   If anyone needed a hand with anything, my father was right there. I recall that one of his neighbors was bedridden with cancer. John, my father's neighbor, was a big man, and his wife had a hard time changing the sheets. My father would go over there every day after work and lift John out of bed so his wife could change the sheets. He would also cut their grass and help with the outside work, as needed. John and his wife were struggling financially and apologized to my dad for not being able to pay him for his time. My father, I'm told, said in response, "I don't want your money; I'm your friend."

9   If anyone had plumbing problems my father was right there to lend a hand. He would get his toolbox and off he would go to the neighbors, friends, or relatives who asked for his help. I remember one particular incident that happened in 1953 on Christmas Day. One of the neighbors had some plumbing problems, and they were going to have company for dinner. They had called several plumbers; however, due to the holiday, they couldn't get a plumber to come out to do the repairs. They called my father to see if he would come over to help them, and he said he would be right over. My father took his toolbox and extra plumbing fittings that he had in his shed and off he went at 6:00 A.M. He spent over six hours doing the repairs. The neighbors offered him money but he refused. He would never take money from anyone; his favorite comment was, "Some other time," but, of course, some other time never came.

10   Whenever I had problems, I could sit down and talk to him, and he was never too tired to listen or give advice. He told me when I was very young, "No matter what happens, don't ever be afraid to talk to me. Whatever it is, come to me, and we will work it out together." As I grew older, we had many, many conversations. He always encouraged me to participate in school activities and told me that if I continued to be a good student and to study hard, he and my mother would buy me a car for graduation. In May of 1955, just before graduation, he and my mother took me outside to the garage, and there to my surprise was a 1949 Ford. It was dark green with a beige interior. I was thrilled. I had already had my driver's license, but I was told I could only drive the car with his permission.

11   I remember one Sunday shortly thereafter in particular; my friends wanted me to go to a ball game. My father had gone golfing with his friends, and I knew he would not let me have the car. I waited until after he left and then begged and pleaded with my mother to let me take the car. She finally relented after an hour of my pleading and told me to be back before my father got home. I pulled the car out of the garage, picked up my friends, and we left for the ball game. On the way, one of my friends called my attention to something while I was driving. Not thinking, I turned to look and the next thing I remember, I hit a parked car. I was petrified. No one was hurt, but there was damage to the parked car, as well as my car. After the police left, I drove the car home and put it in the garage. I told my mother what had happened, and she was extremely upset. One thought raced through my mind: how was I ever going to tell my father? My mother was upset because she gave me permission to take the car, and I was scared to tell my father because I had not gotten his permission to drive the car.

12   When my father came home from golfing, he put his car in the garage and came into the house. He looked from me to my mother and then back to me. He said, "Does somebody want to tell me what happened today?" I told him how I had begged my mother to let me have the car and about the incident that led up to the accident. My father did not get mad; however, he said, "You disobeyed my instructions." He told me I would not be allowed to drive my car until I could pay for the repairs from the money I would earn after graduation when I began working. It was six months before I was able to earn enough money to get my car fixed, but I did learn a valuable lesson. I respected him for his guidance and his patience to raise me as if I were his own daughter.

13   Throughout my teenage and adult years, even after I was married, he always had time for me and my problems. After I was divorced, he was like a father to my children, taking an interest in them and teaching them how to do projects around the house. He would sit and talk with them when they had problems, and he would show the same patience he had extended to me during my growing years. His patience was limitless. He never complained about anything. There are times when I think back to those years and wonder how he managed to be so supportive throughout the years with the seemingly unending problems that arose. I wish I had his patience.

14   My father has been dead nine years now, but he is not forgotten. His work cap still hangs in the shed where he used to keep it. His memory is vivid in my mind. I miss him.

Loretta Shicotte

The preceding essay illustrates the steps discussed earlier in this chapter. The essay on Loretta's father is clearly written in support of a dominant impression: "my father was one of the finest individuals that I have ever known." Every idea expressed in the essay communicates the love, respect, and admiration she has for her father. The essay is well-structured and well-organized in support of the writer's main idea. Each individual paragraph in the essay is coherent, unified, and well-developed. Finally, the essay demonstrates the principles of descriptive writing advocated in this chapter: the selective and effective use of well-chosen, concrete and specific details and adjectives, the use of analogy, and the use of anecdote. What I most like about her essay is its warmth. In reading it, I gain a clear picture of the man who was her father; I gain an understanding of the loss she feels now that he is physically gone from her life. Although I never met her father (I would have liked to), I feel as though I know him.

Had the writer outlined this essay before writing it, the outline would have appeared similar to the one below:

1   introduction
       dominant impression: my father was one of the finest individuals that I have ever known.

2   limiting idea: when I was eight and first met him

3   limiting idea: his work

4   limiting idea: we grew close

5   limiting idea: his workshop

6   limiting idea: his dancing and singing skills

7   limiting idea: his sense of humor

8   limiting idea: his helpful attitude

9   limiting idea: his plumbing skills/helpfulness

10   limiting idea: his willingness to listen to me/the gift of the car

11–12   limiting idea: the anecdote of the car accident

13   limiting idea: his continuing support in my adult years

14   closing paragraph

Obviously there is no single way to organize or structure an essay that describes a person; there are as many ways as there are people to describe and people who write. Just be certain that you use some method of organizing and structuring the description you write.

SUGGESTED TOPICS

This is one assignment for which you probably will have little difficulty in choosing subject matter! You probably already have someone in mind. If not, think about the people you know best. (This could be your chance to "get back at" someone!) Some of my students have simply created persons from their imaginations. Other students have described movie stars, professional athletes, and musicians they know about but do not know personally. You might also find inspiration by looking through the family photograph album. If all else fails, go look in the mirror!

STUDENT EXAMPLES

Last Lesson

1   The lessons of my childhood are divided into gender-based categories.

2   The lessons of my mother differed from the lessons of my father in their practicality. My mom's instructions, always lovingly given, were mainly centered on food and the preparation of it, hygiene and my friends' lack of it, and the constructive use of time. My mother's special gift was her ability to incorporate Jesus into every lesson she ever taught. Her messages were the language of base survival tinted with the promise of heaven.

3   My father's lessons removed me from the ordinary and mundane and taught me about life in the world. He was a literal authority on how to buy things, how to drive things, how to travel, and how to read social situations.

4   I trusted his advice in almost all areas. His weak spot was animal advice, and unfortunately, this was one of his favorite arenas. I knew his actual experience with animals was very limited. (Marlon Perkins was his source for most facts, and that would have been fine, except we didn't have any lions or bears on Washtenaw Avenue.) We couldn't have a dog or cat because my mother was allergic to every single type of domesticated animal, and this frustration led my father to "care" for the neighbors' pets.

5   He overfed the Burns' dog and aggravated Mrs. Lynch's cat. He attempted to teach things to Mrs. Bellezini's bird, and the man across the alley point blank ordered my father out of his yard while tending a "sick" squirrel.

6   My father, simply, did not have a "way" with animals, and I had a tendency to turn a deaf ear to his animal lessons. This knowledge would haunt me later, while he lay in a coma. Desperate to fill the hours and days near the end of his life with sounds recognizable and comforting to him, I spoke to him of his beloved—if not misguided—animal sagas.

7   I reminded him that he was wrong about birds. They do not smell human hands. I reminded him that he was incorrect about dogs. They do not look you straight in the eyes. Wolves—not dogs—do that. I filled his last days with corrections. My siblings took their turns, but mine was primarily animal chatter. I disputed all of his animal misguidance.

8   Two days before he died, he came out of his coma and cast a narrowed eye on me. "You're wrong," he whispered, "and I'm takin' my fish."

9   The fish he referred to represented the only animal to actually thrive in the light of my father's care. For four years it happily swam, in a fish tank, set up in my parents' bedroom. It was found dead and floating on the morning of my father's funeral—snatched away from skeptics.

10   He may have had a better way with animals than I thought.

Mary Signorelli Kreisl

The Unknown and the Insignificant

1   It was just like one of those days. There was a traffic jam as usual. The broad daylight was a torment, like a burning fire on my skin. The crowd was still massive as ever. Those were the hurdles I had to undergo before I could reach the university I attend. The mix of manifold perfume scents, perspiration and all kinds of human body odors lingered in the air, creating a tightness in my stomach. Everything seemed to be perfect and on due course. The University Belt, that's what they have called the place. Five big universities, private educational centers and exclusive colleges for boys and girls can be found in the vicinity. The University Belt was known not because it was the center of intellectual learning. Rather, it was known for the immense number of abandoned kids who lurked in the street of Recto, day and night. It was a place outsiders dared not sojourn, particularly at night, for in the shadows, the unknown hid like animals waiting for their prey.

2   It was just one of those days. I was walking down the street of Recto deep in thoughts. I was fully aware of those little, dirty, bare feet sprawling on the sidewalk, shouting and cursing. There were about six of them, aged from five to fourteen, dressed in tattered, soiled shirts and shorts. They were the unknown, the insignificant, the nuisance to the pedestrians, the eyesore, the abandoned and the homeless. They were all part of the scene, a normal sight to behold and nothing extraordinary. People never bothered to look at them, talk to them or even talk about them. Sadly, I was one of those people.

3   On that particular day, however, the feelings between me and one of those kids wasn't mutual. Unexpectedly, an arm with a palm open wide came out of nowhere, nearly hitting me on the face. A voice said, "Alms!" Startled, I halted and felt my body grow rigid. My heartbeat seemed to pop out of my chest. My reaction seemed to be obvious that it infuriated her. She withdrew her arm and slapped me on the back of my left shoulder, pushing me a step forward. It seemed like an eternity when I stood there after she left. As I regained my composure, I looked back and saw her walking away calmly, as if nothing happened. I realized that she was just a kid of eight to ten years old. She had a dark complexion, or perhaps it was layers and layers of dirt and soot that had accumulated in her skin for months that she had not taken a bath. Her hair, coiling on her back down to her waist was as black as the color of the night. She was wearing a skirt that she had outgrown and a shirt that appears to have been handed down to her from three generations. The color was unrecognizable for it was filthy and overused. She had some wounds on her legs and blisters on the soles of her feet. Some of the sores were still fresh, discharging a reddish and yellowish fluid. On her feet she had a tsinelas (rubber thongs) that were very worn out. The stench that she left lingered and overpowered the smell of the sweat. She was more pitiful than disgusting.

4	For consecutive days, I saw her standing beside a street post that she claimed as her territory. With a small plastic bag in her hand, she raised it to her nose and started inhaling and exhaling the air inside the bag. I realized that she was sniffing an inhalant that gave a euphoric effect, subduing her hunger and stomach pain.

5	For some specific reason, I had a sudden opportunity to talk to her. I found her outside the university gate sitting on the bench, staring into nothing. As I sat beside her, I took out from my bag a burger and offered it to her. Without any hesitation, she took it and feasted on it as fast as she could, as if it would be taken back from her. In just a minute or so, the burger was gone. She smiled and was satisfied. That Burger Day started our never ending conversation.

6	Grace was born poor not knowing who her father was. At the age of six her mother died, leaving her with nothing. She became homeless, until she found herself in a place where everything was free. The house she called home was built out of free materials: pieces of cartons and plastic grocery bags for the walls and scraps of old and rusty metals for the roof. The only sturdy material she owned was an old piece of wood one foot shorter than her, that she called bed.

7	Every morning, be it a sunny day or a rainy day, Grace was greeted by a familiar scent that adhered to her skin like a fragrant perfume. It was not a perfume, but a stinky, disgusting stench of rotting garbage that the infamous Smokey Mountain emits unceasingly. Smokey Mountain—an enormous and mountain-like garbage dump that continually emitted smoke from decomposing waste—was a haven for people like Grace.

8	It was there in the Smokey Mountain, in one of her garbage digging escapades, that she met 8 year old Joann. Grace found her sitting on the earth hugging her legs close to her chest and crying, "Stop it, Papa, stop!" Innocently she asked me why there were bruises on her arms and the blood stains on her ragged clothes. For a moment I was silent, not knowing what to say or how to say that Joann must have been raped by her father. Nevertheless, she went on hastily with her narration about her other friends.

9	Olan, one of the very few friends of Grace, was just a little older. He was bigger and taller than the other boys of his age in Recto. Super Olan, as he was widely known since he arrived in Recto, was one of the swiftest purse snatchers in the University Belt. Of all the people Grace knew, she liked Olan the most because of his generous heart. He had a liking of giving her tokens such as different kinds of wallets: big or small, new or torn, stylish or ugly, empty or not. Casually, she reached for her pocket and pulled out a Hello Kitty wallet, with pictures of college students she had never seen in person. She looked at them admiringly.

10	Inspite of her destitution, Grace considered herself as fully blessed, particularly when Johnny was around. He seemed to have more money collected from begging than Grace, enough to afford a burger meal from McDonald's for the two of them. He also had new clothes to boast every Saturday. Grace said that a blue eyed man gave clothes to Johnny every time he spent the night in the man's house. Grace thought that Johnny was so blessed to meet such a generous person, to be supplied with new clean clothes and be given an opportunity to sleep in a soft, cozy bed in the comforting arms of this blue eyed man.

11	For days, I carried the burden that Grace never realized to have ever existed. The burden she never carried was haunting me for days and nights, often left me wondering if she had some more stories left to tell. Just thinking what was in store for me for the next days, I wasn't enthusiastic anymore. I never felt so hopeless in my life as I was feeling then.

12   On that very cloudy and gloomy day, when I was waiting for her on that same bench, with burgers on my lap, she never showed up. For days I searched the streets of Recto for that familiar face to no avail. Days turned into weeks, weeks into months, but there was no Grace. On the street post where once stood a drug-sustained girl, now stood a boy of eighteen years old, the new claimant.

13   I realized that any day would just be like any day in the University Belt. As students come and leave their alma matter, as recognized, significant new intellectuals of their generation, so do the unlearned, who remained to be insignificant, a nuisance and an eyesore of society. It would still be just one of those days, when the traffic would still be jammed, the streets would still be crowded and life would still go on, in the University Belt.

MA. Christine Joy Blase

Simply Courageous

1   "May Joseph's soul rest in peace."

2   Soon enough, these grim words will be a reality for me, as my grandpa, my best friend, fights a horrible disease just to survive to see another day. Grandpa suffers from Periarteritis Nodosa, a rare liver disease that causes the arteries in his liver to "bead" and eventually will cause his bowel to die. Complicating his condition further, he is a level 4 heart failure, who has undergone 25 heart procedures. But to him, the hardest part of dying is knowing that soon enough he will have to say his last goodbyes to his family and loved ones.

3   As you can see, Grandpa is my hero. His strength and courage leave me in total amazement, and his faith always remains strong. Gramps has endured a lot of pain the past few years, but he has lived an amazing life.

4   Gramps was born on Valentine's Day, 1931, in the middle of the Great Depression, to a family with an abusive father. At the young age of 6, my pal caught a case of the chicken pox so badly it left him blind. Doctors said that he would never see again, but two years later, on Easter Sunday, he regained his sight. Looking back, I believe this was a foreshadowing of the odds he would beat to live. During high school, Grandpa played many sports and yet remained at the top of class academically. In his senior year, my hero amazed many by breaking George Mikan's basketball scoring record. (Mikan went on to be one of the NBA's 50 greatest players.) With such an accomplishment came many college scholarship opportunities, but he did not accept any because he was afraid to leave his mom alone with his father. A few years later, my grandpa was offered the land his grandfather owned in Lithuania, but again he said no; he chose to stay home. Instead, he joined the Chicago Police Department and quickly moved up the ranks by solving murders, saving lives, and working beyond his call of duty. (He even arrested Hugh Hefner for showing too much Marilyn Monroe.) Eventually, he was named the Asst. Deputy Superintendent and became friends with Presidents Carter, Reagan, and Kennedy. In addition, Grandpa went on to be a professional wrestler and eventually to manage his own business, so it is easy to see how successful he has been.

5   So why is he my hero? Well, because he is much more than his accomplishments show. He is a man made of love, generosity, and care. He volunteers for his church and cooks Thanksgiving dinners for those who cannot afford to buy their own. He tutors kids, teaches appraisal classes and reads in church. The whole family looks up to him. He offers me advice dealing with relationships and friendships, offers new ideas for me to propose to the American Cancer Society, and always shows me ways to better the world around me. He understands who I am and is someone I can call if I do not understand life's obstacles or if I just need a "boost." Even though he is terminally ill, and knows that his life is nearing its final stage, his determination and will to live are at an all time high.

6   Gramps is a man made of courage and strength. I can see it everyday when I look into his eyes, but there is one story that exemplifies his character. Back in 1981, he needed quadruple bypass surgery to fix a few blood clots around his heart. By this time in his life, he had a rather extensive medical history, so we could not find a doctor that was willing to perform such a dangerous surgery. Then one day Gramps heard that the world's best heart surgeon happened to be flying in from Spain to study in America, and he was bringing about 30 of his patients from Europe (many were European royalty) with him. So Gramps asked his nurse if he could have that doctor do the procedure, but the nurse said that he only worked on the rich and famous. Feeling let down, Grandpa decided to take this into his own hands. He called that doctor's secretary and said, "This is Dr. Smith from Cambridge University. May I speak to Dr. Piffer?" Soon enough the doctor was on the phone. "Yes, doc. Well, whatever I told your secretary was a lie. I am not a doctor, but rather a heart patient here at Loyola. I hear you are the best surgeon around, so I want you to do my surgery. They say I have a severe heart problem so I beg you to help." He was put on hold, and a few minutes later the doctor showed up at his door. Needless to say, the doctor performed that surgery and even a few more during Grandpa's life.

7   Doctors from around the world have come to Gramps' aid (sometimes to help and other times to study such a rare case of illness.) While being sick and hospitalized, he has helped society because he has been the first to test many new medications and drugs. For example, Grandpa was the first man to have a drain to be installed into his stomach to drain excess fluid because of a malfunctioning liver. As a result of his willingness to experiment, many new technologies have been proven a success and since then have been placed on the market, and in addition, those medications have allowed Gramps to enjoy life's luxuries.

8   Grandpa introduced me to the game of golf about three years ago. Since then, our friendship has blossomed and my life changed. He taught me how to play and soon enough I made the high school team, qualified for state, and then went off to play for college. While I was at college, he drove up to visit me one weekend, and we were both excited to spend time together. The next morning, our plans changed. An emergency struck, and instead of going to the golf course, we ended up at the hospital. He had started to pass blood. At the hospital, they medivaced him to a larger unit because of his deteriorating condition. Doctors told me he had passed 19 liters of blood and was dying. Furthermore, my family was three hours away, so I was watching him die, alone. That night we transferred him to Loyola by ambulance, but of course, I had to stay at school to get my schoolwork done. Within the next few days, I realized how fragile life is, and that he needed me to be by his side. So, I withdrew from college and spent the next month with him. Again, he beat all odds and told me, "If I had to do it all over again to see you, I would." Immediately, tears filled my eyes, and my love for my friend overwhelmed me. So, that weekend, he taught me not only what love meant, but how to show it.

9   Well, according to doctors, I will lose my buddy within the next few months. His disease has left him without any white blood cells, so infection has taken over his body. He still projects a positive attitude to us all, continues fighting to hang on, and continues to be there for us. I have had to deal with seeing my pal in agonizing pain and suffering, but no matter what happens, he will always be a part of me. I know that someday soon I will have to continue living my life without the guidance of my best friend, but yet I have realized that he will always be watching over me. He will never be forgotten and will always hold a special place in my heart.

Rich Bajner

First, I'll Cry

1   Every time someone (anyone) gives sympathy to my daughter Sam, I have the urge to strangle that person. If you knew the situation that Sam is in, you would understand why this happens. Sam is disabled, and people are of the misconception that Sam deserves sympathy. If you are a member of the tenderhearted club, please be aware that Sam needs empathy, not sympathy; understand Sam, don't pity her.

2   June 17, 1979, Father's Day, I presented my husband Joe with a great present: an eight pound, six ounce girl. My labor was hard, and the delivery was worse (comparable to squeezing a watermelon through a keyhole), but after nearly nine childless years, we were parents. Samantha Ann had finally arrived.

3   Nature can be cruel, bordering on vicious. Sam was perfect in our eyes, with long, black hair and eyes like coal. Our desperate yearning for a child was now fulfilled. We had no way of knowing what a devastating disorder was escalating within Sam's tiny body, nor the difficulties (some are insurmountable) that awaited her.

4   Sam's first eighteen months of life were fairly uneventful. Her physical and mental development was accelerated; however, not having any reference point to compare Sam to, we assumed that her progress was normal. Shortly after her eighteenth month, Sam began to exhibit abnormalities involving her connective tissue. It took another eighteen months to obtain an accurate diagnosis. Sam had passed her third birthday, and I was informed that it was doubtful that she would see her fifth birthday. Worse yet, she would become both a mental and physical vegetable before death took her from me. I have never felt such hurt; it was as if a piece of ice was driven deep into my soul. I cried; then I got angry. I believe it is my anger, my refusal to give up, that has molded Sam, in body and spirit, into who she is today.

5   Sam was spared the devastation of mental retardation. She progressed rapidly and was very advanced for her age. By her first birthday, Sam was speaking compound, complex sentences. At her birthday party, she opened her presents by herself. Sam acknowledged every person there and thanked everyone for her presents; she was able to match the person with the present given to her. I thought this was normal. Much later, the daughter of friends, had a birthday party. Seeing the child sit and play with the ribbons and paper, instead of opening the presents and thanking everyone, gave way to a rise in concern. I voiced my concern that I thought the baby was retarded to my husband. Joe in turn chuckled and informed me that our friends' daughter was not retarded; she was normal. Sam was advanced. Today, Sam is mainstreamed in a public high school and excels in many subjects.

6   A statement that I have repeatedly quoted to Sam has become her motto which she lives by: "You can do anything that you want to do, if you want to do it bad enough!" By the time Sam was four years old, she had developed severe contractures of her knees and hips; walking became nearly impossible. Sam's legs would buckle after a few steps and she would crumple to the floor. Her shoulders, elbows and wrists were contracted; she was no longer able to raise her hands above her head. It would have been easier to help Sam to her feet or retrieve objects above her head. I refused, knowing that if she was going to have any quality in her life, she had to learn to overcome her handicaps. As Sam would crawl to a piece of furniture to use for leverage and painfully struggle to stand, I would turn away from her so she could not see the tears that I shed. Criticism free-flowed from many people, who did not understand, because I prodded Sam; I taunted her; I did whatever I had to do to instill determination within my child. Besides physical therapy, I enrolled Sam into ballet and tap dance classes. I forced her to do stretching exercises, which were so painful that often she would scream. Sam's determination became so great, that by her fifth birthday, she had acquired several trophies and ribbons for first and second place in dance competition. She was only beginning her struggle for life.

7   Sam is amazing. One would expect her to be introverted, selfish, disrespectful, depressed and, generally speaking, a very nasty person. Sam is not any of these things. She is very outgoing, always joining groups, usually in a leadership position. Sam belongs to a group of girls called Rainbow. It seems that they attempted to have a carwash to raise money, without much success. Sam suggested that they try again, only at a different location. No one wanted to organize another carwash, for fear of another failure. Sam accepted the challenge and within a few days had orchestrated the new fund-raiser. The girls turned a large profit; Sam beamed at her success.

8   Sam has learned to accept people as they are, and she likes to try new things. It is the combination of these two traits that led Sam to join the International Club. When a new foreign student joined the club, Sam befriended her immediately. It seems that the new girl felt out of place and avoided making friends. From ignorance, grows fear; from fear, grows hate. Many students criticized Sam for associating with the new girl. Sam's persistence, along with her wonderfully dry sense of humor, helped the student get through her adjustment period. Sam did not realize what a wonderful act she had committed, only that she had another friend. Sam is very loving, very giving, very selfless.

9   If you had to face going through at least one, sometimes two or three, surgeries per year, how would you feel? You would probably be depressed. Add a handful of resentment and fear to the depression and you have a boiling cauldron of hostility. I'm not going to claim that Sam did not experience these feelings; I am going to claim that she rose above them. She questioned her physicians, hospital staff and anyone who would let her harass them, gathering information starting with how the procedure would be performed to what to expect post-surgically. From this knowledge, she drew strength.

10   Physical strength and dexterity are not attributes of Sam (through no fault of her own). Her contractures have worsened, and new contractures have appeared. Consequently, Sam cannot walk for any distance without frequently resting. Running is out of the question, unless she wishes to turn blue and faint. Walking up stairs is a definite problem. Sam does not look at these situations in a negative way; rather she finds advantages in whatever it is that she cannot do. Instead of saying, "I can't take gym with the other kids," she says, "I don't have the hassle of undressing and dressing." She does not complain about not walking far; instead she points out that with her parking permit, we very rarely have a problem finding a parking space. The kid never quits!

11   I can only surmise how Sam feels about what is happening to her. I know how fearful I would be knowing that my life could end tomorrow. That's quite a burden for anyone to carry around with him or her and largely accounts for her stubbornness and her insatiable appetite for life. Surprisingly, Sam is a happy person, which is reflected in her quick smile and hearty laugh. Does Sam sound too good to be true? Guess again; Sam is still with us after sixteen years and is still going strong.

12   Many of my friends state that it is a miracle that Sam was born. Sam's birth is not the miracle; Sam is the miracle. There are times that I wish that I could enfold Sam into my arms and protect her from what lays ahead. No matter how hard I wish, I know that this is not possible. How long does Sam have to live? I don't know. Do not forget, she was not expected to live past five years of age; she is now sixteen. How does Sam feel about her situation? I don't know that either; I can only surmise; I am not Sam. What I do know is that Sam struggles to do simple, every day tasks that we take for granted. I would be lying if I said that Sam has only good feelings about herself. Once in awhile Sam verbalizes, "Why me?" To this I respond, "Why not you?" Sam then gives me a quizzical look, shrugs her shoulders and walks off.

13   At least once a day, the hurt that resides within my core, twists deeper into my soul as it reminds me of its presence. It asks me, "What will you do when Sam's gone?" First, I'll cry.

Cindy Schneider

To the memory of my student
Sam Schneider
1979–1999

THE DESCRIPTION OF A PERSON PAPER—YOUR TURN

1 Select a person to describe.

2 Sit and think about the person. If it is someone you know and you can observe, sit and study the person. If possible, watch the person without the person's knowing you are watching him or her.

3 Jot down some detail and some information about the person.

4 Formulate a dominant impression of the person. What is the one quality or impression of this person that you would most want to communicate to your reader?

5 Be certain that the dominant impression applies not only to the physical description but to the character and personality description as well. If necessary, be willing to alter the dominant impression.

6 Organize the body of the essay; begin to work the information into clusters of ideas that could become paragraphs.

7 Outline the essay.

8 Write the rough draft.

DESCRIPTION OF A PERSON PAPER PLAN SHEET

Part One: Choose a person (topic) for your essay and decide upon a dominant impression. Then write down some of the detail and some of the analogies you could use in the essay.

Dominant Impression: _____

_____

Observations about physical appearance:

_____   _____   _____

_____   _____   _____

_____   _____   _____

_____   _____   _____

Observations about personality:

_____   _____   _____

_____   _____   _____

_____   _____   _____

_____   _____   _____

Observations about actions:

_____   _____   _____

_____   _____   _____

_____   _____   _____

_____   _____   _____

Analogies:

_____   _____   _____

_____   _____   _____

_____   _____   _____

_____   _____   _____

Name _____ Section _____ Date _____

SELF-EVALUATION SHEET: PART ONE

Assignment: _____

Strong points of this assignment:

_____

_____

_____

_____

_____

_____

_____

Weak points of this assignment:

_____

_____

_____

_____

_____

_____

_____

General comments:

_____

_____

_____

_____

_____

_____

_____

(over)

Name _____ Section _____ Date _____

SELF-EVALUATION SHEET: PART TWO

What were the strong points of your last writing assignment?

_____

_____

_____

_____

_____

_____

What were the weak points of your last writing assignment?

_____

_____

_____

_____

_____

_____

What have you done to correct those weaknesses in this assignment?

_____

_____

_____

_____

_____

_____

PEER-EVALUATION SHEET: PEER-EVALUATOR #1

Writer's Name _____ Essay's Title _____

> **Directions:** (1) Remember not to write on another student's paper. Instead, use this form.
> (2) Offer concrete, specific comments using the terminology of writing (e.g., "The develop-
> ment in paragraph four might be improved by adding a brief example." or, "Check structure
> on page 3.")

What do you see as the strong points of this writing assignment: _____

_____

_____

_____

_____

What areas do you feel might need additional work: _____

_____

_____

_____

_____

Do you see any areas of grammar/mechanics (e.g. usage, spelling, fragments) that might
need attention: _____

_____

_____

_____

_____

General comments: _____

_____

_____

_____

_____

Evaluator's Name _____ Section _____ Date _____

PEER-EVALUATION SHEET: PEER-EVALUATOR #2

Writer's Name _____ Essay's Title _____

> **Directions:** (1) Remember not to write on another student's paper. Instead, use this form. (2) Offer concrete, specific comments using the terminology of writing (e.g., "The development in paragraph four might be improved by adding a brief example." or, "Check structure on page 3.")

What do you see as the strong points of this writing assignment: _____

_____

_____

_____

_____

What areas do you feel might need additional work: _____

_____

_____

_____

_____

Do you see any areas of grammar/mechanics (e.g. usage, spelling, fragments) that might need attention: _____

_____

_____

_____

_____

General comments: _____

_____

_____

_____

_____

THE DESCRIPTION OF AN EVENT PAPER

Almost every day of my life, I find myself walking several miles on the biking/walking/rollerblading paths that dissect metropolitan Chicago. When a person spends this much time alone, there is a lot of opportunity for reflection. It's probably a sign of aging, but I spend much of this time reflecting upon my life (only occasionally do I ponder why it's been 1985 since the Bears were the Monsters of the Midway). More and more, I see my life and myself defined by certain events—and my reactions to those events—which really helped to mold me into who I am: experiencing my first kiss in kindergarten, witnessing the birth of my children, reconciling the death of friends in an auto accident, walking into a book store for the first time and buying a magazine containing an article I'd written, delivering the eulogy for a loved one, losing it when my youngest announced that he had just flushed his deodorant down the toilet—at the most exciting moment in the Bears-Packers Monday Night Football game, looking into the faces in the crowded lecture hall and discovering that the mysterious woman whose beautiful face was frequently in my childhood dreams was sitting in the fifth row, receiving the phone call announcing I was soon to become a grandfather. . . .

These events, to me, are the individual threads in the tapestry that is my life. And I have a feeling that you and I are alike in this way. These events and our memories of them represent the stages of life we all experience as we change, develop, and grow (although—in my particular case—some of my family members might argue that growth part!). We recognize certain events in our lives as significant, and we usually try our best to cling to their memory in detail; why else would we have so many photos, home movies, and souvenirs tucked into books, drawers, and curio cabinets?

Because most of us reminisce about events in our lives, and because we recognize their significance and therefore remember them in great detail, these events become very good subject matter for writing, especially description. Over the past thirty years, many of my students have shared with me their memories of life-shaping events: a first kiss, a first arrest, a first date, a first job interview, a first sexual experience, a first birth, a first day in a new country as an exchange student, a first wake, a first experience with violent crime, a first marriage, a first day as a returning college student. . . . Or: a last dance, a last chance, a last goodbye, a last divorce, a last vacation fling, a last cigarette or drink, a last New Year's Eve party and resolution, a last Christmas with the family, a last day before retirement, a last bruise at the hands of an abuser, a last day before "coming out" to the world, a last "free" day before entering basic training. . . . In between all of these "firsts" and "lasts" have been many other meaningful events which my students have described.

Like my students, you will probably enjoy writing this paper, assuming that the event made a positive difference in your life. But even if the event was negative or difficult, maybe there is growth and learning in writing about that as well—if you are ready. As one of my students once shared with me in her self-evaluation,". . . writing about [being an abuse victim] has helped me to face some of my fears and my anger. I can't say I enjoyed writing this paper, but I sure as hell got my tuition's worth of learning!" Trust me, it was a very powerful piece of writing, a very powerful event in her life.

 ## GUIDELINES FOR WRITING A DESCRIPTION OF AN EVENT ESSAY

- **One,** apply those principles of descriptive writing which have been covered in the previous pages of this chapter: write with concrete and specific detail and example; only sparingly use "lists" and adjectives. Also, try to incorporate some effective analogies. As with any kind of descriptive writing, your purpose is to show, to help your reader experience this event from your perspective.

- **Two,** as explained in a previous section, focus your description around a clear dominant impression. Don't just focus on an event, but on the significance of the event.

■ **Three,** also focus on the time element of the event. Unless you intend to write a very long paper, it will be necessary to restrict the amount of elapsed time of the event you describe. A mother's depiction of the birth of her first child, for example, could cover the entire nine-month "wait." By focusing on the moment when the contractions begin, however, she is probably more able to hook the reader and will have less information to sort through and present.

■ **Four,** provide structure and organization for the detail which you have selected for inclusion. Frequently, chronology is a natural method for this assignment, as you'll discover when you read the student examples.

■ **Five,** as with the other types of description presented in this chapter, try to communicate with your reader. Use your description skills and your description of an event to say something to your reader.

The following essay illustrates how one student was able to apply these guidelines in describing an event.

Too Young

1   It was a beautiful summer day. The sky was clear as the sun shone through my kitchen window. I looked long and hard out the window as I do every morning. As I gathered my thoughts for the day, I realized that today was the day I had hoped would never come. This day I had to attend a wake. Having attended many wakes I knew what to expect, or so I thought. This time it would be different. We had lost Mellissa.

2   As I prepared for my day, I also tried to prepare myself mentally. Looking in the closet, I decided to wear an outfit with some color. Black seemed to be such a violent color. Yellow was my choice. Mellissa had liked yellow. I would wear it in her honor.

3   Before I left the house, I made sure my two young daughters had breakfast. When my mom arrived to baby-sit, I kissed each of my girls and said good-bye.

4   The drive to the funeral home was pleasant. I turned the volume up after putting in a favorite tape. The thought of where I was going escaped my mind for the time being. When I saw the funeral home about a block ahead, reality kicked in. Suddenly I felt sick to my stomach. My whole body grew tense, and I started to tremble. Before I reached the parking lot, tears were rolling down my face and my hands were shaking.

5   While parking my car around the back, I tried to get control of myself. I sat and cried for a few minutes, thinking that if I could get it out now I would be able to control myself and comfort Mellissa's family when I went inside. After about ten minutes and some pep talk, I stepped out of my car. My knees were weak, and now I was more nervous than ever. Telling myself over and over to relax, I started walking toward the front of the building.

6   Turning the corner, I saw the front door and the hearse. As I looked away, I noticed a crowd of people near the front door. Some were crying and others just making small talk. Taking a deep breath, I reached for the handle and pulled the door open.

7   When I stepped inside the reception area, I could not help but notice the flowers and candles. The flowers were pink and yellow lilies, sprinkled with baby's breath. The many candles scattered around the room once again appeared in pink and yellow. I could not help but think of Mellissa.

8   As I entered the chapel, Mellissa's grandpa caught my eye. This is a man who is hard working, always happy and full of life. He was very different today. When I approached him, I saw a man filled with grief. His eyes were red and his stance was some-

what off balance. We greeted each other with a hug. My condolences were given. His reply came weakly with a whisper of his normally deep voice. I wondered if he would ever recover from such a great loss.

9   The next person I spotted was Sue. She was the reason I was at the wake. We have been best friends for fifteen years. Never in all those years had I seen her so devastated. Sue and I held each other and cried for a short time. Mellissa was Sue's niece. I was very worried about Sue. Sue had been diagnosed with cancer a short time ago. Now she had lost her niece to the same disease she had to fight. Being a very petite girl, she appeared more fragile than ever before. Puffy black circles under her eyes led me to believe she had not slept for days. Her hands were shaking and her voice was hoarse from crying.

10   As I approached the casket, I was overcome with what I was looking at. The casket was lavished with hundreds of flowers, mostly yellow ones. It was as if I had walked into a floral shop. The sight of it all was breathtaking. One arrangement in particular caught my eye. It sat directly on top of the casket. It was huge white spider mums in the shape of a teddy bear. A straw hat with yellow ribbons hanging from the brim sat on the bear's head. Across the front of the bear was a banner with the words "Darling Daughter." This sight brought a real sadness to my heart.

11   Walking closer, I realized how much bigger I was than the casket. As I knelt at the casket to say a prayer, I looked at Mellissa. She was wearing her favorite pink and yellow party dress. It had been her favorite because when she twirled in it, the rows of lace blew up in the air like a princess dress should. When I looked closer, I could see that under the dress she was wearing her treasured Barney nightgown. The casket was adorned with some of her best friends. Sally her doll, Barney, and Fred, her favorite yellow teddy bear, would all stay with Mellissa to keep her company and make her happy. Carefully tucked under her arm was her blanket. This blanket was torn and very faded, but Mellissa would never go out without it, not even today. When I looked at this little girl, I thought to myself she was too young to die. Mellissa was only three years old. After saying a prayer I took one last look at Mellissa, not to look at a little girl who no longer had a full head of brown curls, but to say good-bye.

12   Having said my good-bye's to Mellissa and her family, I stepped to the back of the room. Knowing all the painful treatments and hospital stays this little girl had endured, I tried to convince myself this was for the best. Having two girls of my own, it seemed so unfair and cruel for a child to have such a short and painful life. Mellissa would never again be able to dress up like a princess, play at the park, eat ice cream on a warm summer day or lay awake at night waiting for Santa to arrive the next morning. I closed my eyes as the tears fell on my face and thanked God for blessing me with healthy children.

Laurie S. Hrebenak

Laurie's essay exemplifies the previously listed steps for writing about an event, most strikingly illustrating that description—when used to communicate thoughts and feelings—can have a very dramatic effect. When we read Laurie's description of the wake, the details which she included demand our attention and deliver a message because they are so vivid, concrete, and specific. The description of the teddy bear floral arrangement in paragraph ten, for example, focuses our attention on one specific object in the room that becomes a symbol for Laurie's anger and grief at the very nature of the event she is describing. In the next paragraph, Laurie's description of the party dress, of the Barney nightgown, and of the favorite childhood companions (Sally, Barney, and Fred) brings all of our attention onto the casket and what it represents. Finally, Laurie focuses on Mellissa's blanket and uses it to communicate one of her main ideas: Mellissa would never go out without it, not even today. . . .

By focusing on a few significant observations, Laurie is able to reach inside our chests and squeeze our hearts. In paragraph twelve, Laurie "pulls back" as she literally steps back—to the back of the room. Her other ideas about this event are then offered to the reader as she closes her essay. They are statements that we sometimes say almost sound like cliches because they are all we have to cling to during events such as a wake, especially the wake of a young child: it is really for the best that she is no longer suffering, we should all appreciate our lives and the lives of those around us and the nature of life itself, and we are all left to wrestle with what we sometimes perceive as the unfairness of life.

Laurie's essay is also well-written in terms of how it is focused, organized and structured. Although she spends a little time at the beginning "setting up" what the paper is really about, most of the essay is about the actual time spent at the wake. Although we have no exact way of knowing, I would guess that the essay portrays a time period of two or three hours. Time, in fact, is mainly how Laurie structured and organized her description. Had she outlined her paper, it might have been similar to the following outline:

1 introduction
2 getting ready & getting dressed
3 taking care of my girls
4 the drive to the funeral home
5 trying to gain self-control
6 making it to the front door
7 entering the reception area
8 entering the chapel
9 meeting Sue
10 approaching the casket
11 saying good-bye to Mellissa
12 stepping to the back/closing comments

Obviously, Laurie was very much in control of her writing, and that is what we want for you as well. As you work on paragraphing your own description of an event, you should find your old friends of time and space (chronological and spatial organization) should help you.

SUGGESTED TOPICS

I don't believe you will have difficulty choosing subject matter for this assignment. But if writer's block should strike, grab yourself something to drink, curl up on the couch in front of the T.V., and imagine that you are about to watch a mini-story of your life on the tube. Which event would it be? Where would it begin? How would it end? What is the significance of this event? Why—out of all the events in your life—are you remembering this particular one at this particular moment? What would your reader learn about you from reading this? What might the reader learn about himself or herself from reading about this event? What—if anything—are you saying about life?

If the tube gives you nothing but static, try making a lifeline. That is, sit down at the keyboard (or with pen and paper) and draw a line from left to right. Pretend the line is your life, birth being the left-hand margin. Along the line, jot down events from your life. When you've finished, analyze what you have chosen to include. Why have you chosen certain events? What is their significance? What—if anything—did they teach you about life and yourself? What events did you omit? Maybe those events are the most meaningful ones.

STUDENT EXAMPLES

The Repo Man

1   For as long as I can remember, I was taught and believed wholeheartedly that Father's Day was, next to Christmas and birthdays, the one day a year that belonged only to fathers, husbands, and brothers in recognition of the hard work and devotion they had given throughout the year to their families. Only they received cards and gifts, their favorite meals are prepared, and absolutely no manual labor is asked of or provided by them. But, on Father's Day in the summer of 1997, my children and I came to the realization that we were totally wrong about our conception of Father's Day. Regardless of what the calendar read or the Hallmark cards at the corner grocery store had printed on them, it really was Independence Day.

2   Now, don't get me wrong. I'm not talking about the Independence Day that our country celebrates on the Fourth of July, when friends and family share burned hotdogs and warm beer in neighbors' backyards on freshly cut grass and sit on newly bought yard furniture or underneath the trees in city parks waiting for the ritualistic fireworks display provided by various townships and municipalities. This Independence Day was made solely for my children and me, brought forth in the third week of June.

3   I'll never forget that day for the rest of my life, and to be honest, I hope I never do. The sound of my five-year-old son's voice mingled with the monotone rumblings of my husband Rich's conversation woke me from much-needed sleep. In my sleepy state, I remember how I felt the warmth of the sun coming in through the open windows, intermingled with the scent of summer air. You know that smell, the scent the air has only through the months of May through early September. It's the scent of clean-cut grass mixed with the smell of earthworms drawn up from the dew on the lawns during the night before. If you keep your windows open while driving down the roads through the forest preserves after a light rain or if you forget to close the windows in the house after leaving them open in a failed attempt to catch the light breeze, you might be lucky enough to catch that warm, earthy smell. The memories of those scents of summer are the ones that get you through those long, subzero, winter days and nights that seem never-ending.

4   I remember that as I awoke, the voices started to separate themselves and the undercurrent of sounds came through. The low, steady hum that I at first thought was a garbage truck, even though I knew in the back of my mind that the garbage man didn't come on Sunday's, brought itself out over the argument that was occurring in my small kitchen and made me realize that something had happened. I heard, "But Daddy, that's Mommy's van!," and the unmistakably callous remark of, "Just don't worry about it, Mike," as I walked deliberately through the bottom half of the house waking more and more.

5   As I got into the kitchen, through the open back door I saw "my" minivan being towed out of my driveway, to the corner, and down the street, never to be seen again. In its wake I noticed that whatever of my children's or my belongings that had been in the van were haphazardly strewn into the yard, because Barbie dolls, Power Rangers and Anne Rice novels are of no use to the repo man.

6   I remember looking at Rich and soaking in the smug, uncaring and above-all-else, victorious look that he had on his face. At first, all I wanted to do was grab the front of his over-washed black-turned-grey tee-shirt and yell, "How could you do this? How could you let this happen? Don't you know that van was mine?" But instead, all I could do was laugh. I sat at the table in the tiny, cramped, rented kitchen and laughed and laughed. I laughed because I realized that even though I had used my old van as a trade-in for this van, only Rich's name was on the title, and even though I tried as hard as I could to pay the small loan payment on it so we wouldn't lose it by spending half of my public assistance check on the loan, Rich still hadn't made the first six payments, and even though it was bought "for me," I was hardly, if ever allowed to drive it—even to take the kids to the doctor or to the grocery store.

7   But, most of all, I laughed because I was relieved. I was relieved to finally know that I tried as hard as I possibly could to do right by my family. That no matter what I did, it still didn't change the fact that we would never have anything, do anything, BE anything if we lived in a house with a man who could casually offer a cup of coffee to a repo man who would always know where we lived.

8   Instead, I looked at my "husband" who was now surrounded by our now-very-awake, crying children and said, "Happy Father's Day. Thanks for my present. This was better than a card."

9   Now that I look back on it all, I realize that I thanked the wrong person. I should have thanked the repo man.

Beth Stokes

The Painful Interview

1   This was the morning of the second interview, the interview with the owner of the company. I was nervous, but I was also ready. After nine months of interviewing with many different companies, this was the company where I was going to work. All I had to do was convince the boss that I was what he needed.

2   I was to be in his office at 8:00 a.m., so not to interrupt his many daily appointments. That would work out fine with me. My current boss, who was not a morning person, sprinted into the office around nine or nine-thirty every day. I would probably be back before she got in. If not, all the other gals I worked with knew what I was doing, and they would cover for me.

3   I wore the greatest navy suit my money could buy, with a crisp white blouse and polished navy pumps. I carried my purse and a leather portfolio that held extra copies of my resume and noted questions that I had for my new boss. I left my desk and headed downstairs to catch a cab. There was a foggy mist in the air, but not enough for an umbrella. Due to this misty mess, it was hard to get a cab. When one finally stopped in front of me, a nicely dressed gentleman, who was also trying to flag a cab, asked if he could share the ride. Having a cab mate was fine with me. He was headed further north on Michigan Avenue, so I was the first stop.

4   I was at my stop in a matter of minutes. Cabbies want fares to get out curbside, but my cab mate seemed in a hurry and was not moving to let me out curbside. I paid my portion of the fare and got out street side. I stepped out of the cab onto a freshly grated street waiting for its new surface.

5   I took one step away from the cab, closed the door and fell. The heel of my right shoe became caught in this roughly grated street. I twisted my right ankle falling out of my shoe. Next thing I know, I have this rutty street digging deep into my left knee and both palms of my hands. At that point, I heard my own voice. "No," repeated over and over, slowly and determined. The cab pulled away.

6   I got myself to the curb and threw the purse and portfolio on the sidewalk. I heard the portfolio slap against the pavement. I could not believe this was happening. I had this black sticky gravel on everything, my purse and portfolio, my hands, and dug deep into my pulsating knee. Both ankle and knee throbbed.

7   I had to think fast. Did I mess up my suit? No. There were no tears in the bottom of the skirt. It did not come between the rutty street and my knee. The sleeves of the jacket did not rip out either. I can't explain it, but at that moment I thanked God that the suit was still in great shape. With this black sticky gravel everywhere, I had to find the ladies room and get cleaned up. I was running out of time. I had to make this interview.

8   I got myself inside the lobby of the building, my knee and ankle constantly on my mind. As I held out my hands to show the doorman and ask where the ladies room was, I saw small spots of blood in my palms. Am I going to make it through this? My head swam with panic, and it must have shown in my face. The doorman immediately pointed around the corner and down the stairs. I moved as quickly as I could with the agony that I was in.

9   Hurry! Go! Get moving! My mind was racing. I ran cold water into my hands. I just had small scrapes in my palms, no continued bleeding. This was good. I wasn't going to leave blood in his hand as I shook it. I washed off my purse, portfolio and shoes. Then I tried to do something with my knee. The panty hose were gone. The whole knee was out. I wet some paper towel with cold water and held it on my knee, in hopes of relieving some pain. This did not work. The knee just throbbed under my hand. There were small pieces of black gravel and strands of nylon imbedded in my skin. It was hard to look at. God, did it hurt! There was no running-down-my-leg bleeding, just oozing, clotting blood. One thing was good, if I could call any of this good: the panty hose did not run down my leg. The length of my skirt would hide everything except the pain. I just had to keep that from showing.

10   I headed back up the stairs trying to block out the pain and to get focused on this interview. An elevator took me up to the 26th floor, as I inhaled deeply and asked for help from above. I walked into the office just as another man was coming out. He turned and yelled back into the office that someone was here. Yes, I was here. I made it. The boss greeted me and shook my hand. I could feel the soreness in the palm, but I smiled as if nothing was wrong. We went into a small conference room with a large round table. As we sat down, I made sure my skirt was draped nicely over my legs. He sat on my left, with his chair turned so his legs were not under the table, which allowed him to face more in my direction. I pulled my chair as close to the table as I could and kept my knees under the table in hopes of him not seeing my injury.

11   I don't know what happened, but they say the mind rules. I was so focused and in tune. I listened with an intrigued ear, gave the correct answers and asked the appropriate questions. I was prepared for this, and I did well. This was where I soon would be working.

12   The interview lasted about forty minutes. Then I had to stand up. The pain flooded my entire being, except for my face. I smiled and said good-bye. The boss went back to his office. Sheri, the enthusiastic lady I interviewed with the first time, walked me out. As she chatted and asked how I thought it went, she walked slowly. My painful ankle and

knee thanked her. We said our good-byes, and the elevator doors closed. Tears streamed down my cheeks. Was I glad it was over or was the pain that bad? Probably a combination. I got in a cab and looked down at my ankle. It was twice its size. I wondered how I was going to make it back to my desk, or for that matter, through the rest of the day.

13   I survived that day and healed well. About three weeks later I was working at that new job. I never told the story to anyone there until the boss took me to lunch on my first anniversary. After I told him the story, he looked at me and told me to never change.

Cathy Phillips

That First Kiss

1   Everyone tells you what the labor and delivery will be like. Mothers on playgrounds share their horror stories and their pain. Some newly delivered mothers at the obstetricians office tell you, while holding their six week old babies, to get the epidural; others tell you the drugs are bad for the baby. Everywhere a pregnant woman goes, experienced mothers seem to be on a mission to give her the nitty gritty on the physical aspects of having a baby. They tell her how long their labors were; they tally the stitches they received. The experienced mothers discuss ill fitting nursing bras, stretch marks and burping babies. As important as all of these things are, most mothers do not share the most important aspect of having your first baby. No one truly prepares you for the emotional impact of holding your firstborn child for the first time.

2   From the moment I first held my son, I knew I loved him. I was in love with him. I was that amazed he was in my arms and no longer wiggling around inside my belly. I counted his fingers and toes, I caressed his tiny ears and nose. I inspected his little face, waiting for his sleepy eyes to open. I was so happy; I was flying on a post-birth high. I felt invincible. I was now a mother. Now what? As I kissed the top of his little misshapen head, bruised from the difficult delivery, it occurred to me that I am "it." I am the one responsible for this other tiny life. What on earth was I thinking nine months ago?

3   My mother always said that having children is not something you just do. She said being a mother is someone you become. As I held that little bundle for the very first time, it occurred to me that I was going to become part of a special group of women. Because of this six pound, thirteen ounce, squirming bundle, I was on my way to becoming a mother. Although I had all the right "gear" for the baby at home, I wasn't convinced that having diapers, a crib, newborn clothes and a few noisy rattles were going to help me become a mother. Sure, I knew I could feed this child. I knew I could change his diapers and bathe him. But how would I do the really important things?

4   As I cradled my son against my breast, I had no idea how I would teach this little guy how to live! This tremendous job of raising this child consumed me. How could I protect him from the scrapes and bruises of life? What if he chokes on a grape? What about the inevitable bullies at school? How would I protect him from the frightening claps of thunder during a summer storm? So many thoughts and nightmares swirled in my head. What would I do if he has the same eye problems his dad has? What if his foot doesn't turn back the right way? Would he be able to walk properly? What if he is allergic to my old faithful dog? Am I crazy? How did my mom cope with this? How on earth did she do this six times?

5   This is the precise moment I realized my own mom was most likely afraid during a raging storm. It is also the moment I realized that as a child, I did not see that she was probably afraid when the lightning flashed and the thunder shook our house. I always saw her as a strong, brave woman. I knew I could always trust her to keep me safe. Somehow, she was always there to make everything all right. Would my own son look at me the same way? Would he blindly trust me to protect him always? How could I let him trust me when I was so afraid and unsure?

6   As I continued holding my son, something inside told me it was going to be all right. I had made it through the labor and the delivery (with lots of help from an epidural). I survived all the physical pain. Although no one had told me what to expect when I held and kissed my firstborn child for the very first time, I realized no one really could. This was one part of life I would have to experience and discover on my own. As I kissed my son for the second time, I just knew somehow I would become a good mother. After all, I had my own mother show me how to do it in just the right way. I just wish someone would have warned me that the first kiss is harder to handle than the delivery.

Karen Z. Hoogland

My Buddy

1   "It's beyond me how anyone can rest in this place," I tossed at my companion, Barb. I stared out of the window; I saw nothing. My thoughts flitted between the past and the present. I turned around in time to witness Barb wiping away a lone tear. Next to her, in a hospital bed, was her husband Mark. It was an insult to see him so still. In my mind, I heard Mark's infamous greeting, "Hi, kid! How's my buddy?" I sighed as a tear escaped me. The rhythmic beep of the cardiac monitor had a hypnotic effect; my consciousness drifted back eight years in time. . . .

2   . . . Within the medical community, it is an unwritten law: Never become personally involved with a patient. To adhere to this law is sound practice; however, you can count on at least one person to make you breach your vows. Mark was the person who undermined me.

3   It was very fitting that I managed the office of a diabetician; I am an insulin dependent diabetic. I empathized with patients; I never sympathized with patients. When Mark first entered the office, I related to what he felt. Despite the fear and the devastation that he felt, Mark displayed an easy manner and a warm smile. I could not help liking him.

4   I guided Mark to an examination room and settled him into a chair opposite me. As I began to write his case history, I informed Mark that I shared the same plight as he did. Mark's questions gushed forth: "When am I going to go blind? Will I have a heart attack or stroke? How many years have I got before I lose my legs?"

5   "Slow down, Mark. What kind of horror stories did they tell you in the hospital?" I queried. I continued, "There are no guarantees that you won't go blind, lose a leg, or have a heart attack. With good control of your blood sugars, you can delay, or perhaps avert, complications from developing." Mark calmed down; we were able to have a long, intelligent conversation. The doctor entered to give Mark a thorough examination and to refine Mark's treatment plan. As I exited, I knew that Mark was going to be fine.

6   One hour later, Mark emerged from the room, calmer, less fearful, but apprehensive about what was expected of him. I then broke the cardinal rule. "Mark, here is my home phone number. Feel free to call me any time." Mark took the paper with my number written on it and tucked it into his wallet. I believe that knowing he had someone to talk to helped Mark. He seemed to have a new spring in his step as he strode away from me. . . .

7   . . . "Cindy, have you heard anything I've said?"

8   Barb's voice drew me back to the present. "I'm sorry, Barb," I replied, "I was just thinking about Mark. Talking to him always cheered me up, regardless of how rotten my day was. I am going to miss those conversations; Mark had a way of making me feel better." Barb nodded acknowledgment; sorrow prevented her from speaking. At that moment, I realized that we had entered into a death vigilance.

9   "There it goes again; there is something wrong with the monitor," Barb's voice rose in volume with each word.

10   She was right; Mark's monitor had developed a hiccup. The monitor rapidly beeped twice, then there was a long pause. "I wonder if they're seeing this at the desk," I inquired, panic quickly rising within me. "I'm going to get a nurse." Before I reached the door, the monitor changed, emitting a constant tone; we were deafened by the screech of alarms.

11   Personnel rushed into the room from all directions. Barb and I retreated to a far corner; we were completely unnoticed. There must have been a team of a dozen people working to bring Mark back to us; they did their jobs very well. Only minutes had passed, though it seemed like hours. Everyone backed away from Mark as the monitor resumed its rhythmic beep. I slipped closer, observing the stillness of Mark with tubes running into every orifice. There was an I.V. in each arm and one in his neck. This is not how I wished to remember Mark. Emotion threatened to take me over as I mumbled, "Barb, I can't take this; I have to get out of here."

12   I left Mark's room without looking back. Dashing down the hall, I was aware of the tears streaming down my face. Slamming open the door to the stairwell, I rushed forward, taking two stairs at a time. I didn't want anyone near me; I needed to be alone with my sorrow. Running blindly, I descended six flights of stairs; I crossed the lobby and ran out of the front door. I continued running down the sidewalk, passing one street after another. My aching legs screamed in pain; my burning lungs begged me to stop. Finally, I collapsed on someone's lawn. Leaning against a huge oak tree, I realized that exhausting the body does not numb the mind; I could still think. I kept visualizing Mark in his futile struggle to live. I couldn't run away from this scene, any more than I could run away from the pain that I was feeling. Oh, how I hurt! The pain gnawed at my heart, sending cold chills through my very essence.

13   Wallowing in self-pity, I had not noticed the approach of a gentle soul. He touched my shoulder as he inquired, "Missy, are you OK?"

14   With a wane smile, I nodded assent. Watching him depart, I once again heard Mark's voice: "Hi, kid. How's my buddy?" "Not so good, Mark. Not so good!" I whispered. As I attempted to sort out a multitude of emotions, I walked back to the hospital. Memories of Mark's antics consumed me. . . .

15   As Mark came skulking into the office, I heard, "Hi, kid. How's my buddy?"

16   I looked up at him as I asked in concern, "Mark, what are you doing here? You don't have an appointment. Is something wrong?"

17   "Nope. Nothing is wrong," he replied, "I was just passing by and thought that you might need some cheering up." After having made that statement, Mark plopped a large box of Fanny May candy on my desk.

18   Needless to say, this action triggered my scolding him. "You know that I can't have candy, and neither can you. What's the matter with you?"

19   A devilish grin spread across Mark's face as he unwrapped the box. Revealed beneath the paper was a beautiful box of sugar free Fanny May chocolates. My act of sternness was less than effective, as a smile crept across my face. Laughter emanated from me as I scolded, "Mark, you're a brat! You suckered me again. Thanks. The candy is much appreciated and so are you." Mark smiled and bounced off, undoubtedly looking to perpetuate more mischief.

20   As I left the office that night, a cold, semi-solid projectile came into contact with my person; I was knocked onto my behind into a snow drift. Profanities flowed through my mind; however, being a professional, and a lady, I restrained myself. I looked up to see Mark standing over me; mischief glittered in his eyes.

21   Laughing, Mark inquired, "Are you OK?"

22   "Terrific, Mark! I'm terrific," I retorted. "Give me a hand up, will you?" Mark bent down to take my extended hand. I saw the opportunity for retaliation and swept my leg across the back of Mark's leg. He fell headlong into a snow drift. Before he could extricate himself, I started piling snow on Mark from head to foot. The fight was on. Like two children, we pushed and rolled each other into the snow.

23   When we finally finished playing, we appeared as two snow people. I crept to my car, cold and wet, when I heard Mark call to me, "It's OK to be a kid once in a while. How else can you remind yourself how much fun life can be?"

24   . . . Mark was the sunnyside of life. I could have used some sunshine as I re-entered the hospital. I took the elevator to Mark's floor; reluctantly, I entered his room. Barb looked at me with eyes swollen from the many tears she had shed.

25   She sighed, "There's no change; he's resting comfortably."

26   I returned to my vigil at the window. I heard a phone ring in the distance. . . .

27   . . . In my daydream, I answered the insistent phone. I heard a familiar voice.

28   "Hi, kid. How's my buddy?"

29   "I'm fine, Mark. What's up?" I sensed in Mark's voice that something was wrong.

30   "Well, kid, I followed your advice and got checked out by a cardiologist," Mark continued. "You were right. My chest pains weren't from low blood sugars. I'm going for angioplasty tomorrow. I'm scared, kid!"

31   Fear crept into me too. I fought to keep concern out of my voice as I told Mark, "You're going to be fine. Angioplasty is performed every day without problems. You're going to have to stay in the hospital for a few days. Call me when you can."

32   Mark should have called me by Wednesday. When Friday came and I still had no word from him, I became worried. I was pacing when the phone rang. I didn't want to answer for fear of impending bad news. When I heard Barb's voice, I knew it was bad news. "Cindy, you had better come to the hospital. Mark had a triple bypass yesterday, and he's not doing very well, Barb choked, then hung up. Dumbfounded, I stood listening to the hum coming from the receiver. My mind reeled, "What went wrong? This should have been a routine procedure." Numbly, I hung up the phone. . . .

33   . . . My name being called brought me out of my daze. Barb's voice beckoned to me, "Cindy, come here. Mark is awake; he wants to talk to you."

34   I glided over to Mark; he looked up at me. I noticed his bright eyes that once sparkled with mischief were now glazed over with pain. Struggling for every breath, he whispered, "Hi, kid. How's my buddy?"

35   "Terrible, Mark," I whimpered, "I'm worried about you. You have to rally, Mark."

36   "Not going to happen," Mark whispered, "remember there's no guarantees."

37   I fought to control my emotions and quietly listened. Painfully, Mark took a breath. He wistfully smiled as he instructed me, "As long as you remember me, I'll be alive. Who knows, maybe I'll come back and haunt you." Mark then closed his eyes, and with a sigh, all of his pain slipped away.

38   The pain of my sorrow tore my heart apart. Time does not heal; it merely dulls the pain so I can tolerate it. The ache always surfaces when I encounter a reminder of Mark; he haunts me nearly every day. There is a chance that someday I'll get over waiting for his voice on the other end of the phone line, but it's not likely.

Cindy Schneider

Although my parents promised me a magic sow for my tenth birthday party, I never got it.

Name _____ Section _____ Date _____

DESCRIPTION OF AN EVENT PAPER PLAN SHEET

Part One: Choose an event (topic) for your essay and decide upon a dominant impression. Then write down some of the detail and some of the analogies you could use in the essay.

Dominant Impression: _____

_____

Jottings: (Use these blanks to jot down the details you observed.)

_____	_____	_____
_____	_____	_____
_____	_____	_____
_____	_____	_____
_____	_____	_____
_____	_____	_____
_____	_____	_____
_____	_____	_____
_____	_____	_____

Analogies: (Use these blanks to jot down some of the analogies you might use in the paper.)

_____

_____

_____

_____

_____

_____

Part Two: Write the outline for the essay.

Name _____ Section _____ Date _____

SELF-EVALUATION SHEET: PART ONE

Assignment: _____

Strong points of this assignment:

_____

_____

_____

_____

_____

_____

_____

Weak points of this assignment:

_____

_____

_____

_____

_____

_____

General comments:

_____

_____

_____

_____

_____

_____

(over)

SELF-EVALUATION SHEET: PART TWO

What were the strong points of your last writing assignment?

_____

_____

_____

_____

_____

_____

What were the weak points of your last writing assignment?

_____

_____

_____

_____

_____

_____

What have you done to correct those weaknesses in this assignment?

_____

_____

_____

_____

_____

_____

PEER-EVALUATION SHEET: PEER-EVALUATOR #1

Writer's Name _____ Essay's Title _____

> **Directions:** (1) Remember not to write on another student's paper. Instead, use this form. (2) Offer concrete, specific comments using the terminology of writing (e.g., "The development in paragraph four might be improved by adding a brief example." or, "Check structure on page 3.")

What do you see as the strong points of this writing assignment: _____

_____

_____

_____

_____

What areas do you feel might need additional work: _____

_____

_____

_____

_____

Do you see any areas of grammar/mechanics (e.g. usage, spelling, fragments) that might need attention: _____

_____

_____

_____

_____

General comments: _____

_____

_____

_____

_____

Evaluator's Name _____ Section _____ Date _____

PEER-EVALUATION SHEET: PEER-EVALUATOR #2

Writer's Name _____ Essay's Title _____

Directions: (1) Remember not to write on another student's paper. Instead, use this form. (2) Offer concrete, specific comments using the terminology of writing (e.g., "The development in paragraph four might be improved by adding a brief example." or, "Check structure on page 3.")

What do you see as the strong points of this writing assignment: _____

_____

_____

_____

_____

What areas do you feel might need additional work: _____

_____

_____

_____

_____

Do you see any areas of grammar/mechanics (e.g. usage, spelling, fragments) that might need attention: _____

_____

_____

_____

_____

General comments: _____

_____

_____

_____

_____

The Narrative Paper

OVERVIEW

Narration is one of the four basic types of writing; its purpose is to tell, usually in story form. Narration is story telling. Its purpose is also to illustrate/communicate an idea, a feeling, or both. Because most of us are natural story tellers (think back to the last time someone asked you why you were not where you were supposed to be the night before—or the last time your writing teacher asked you why you missed your eight o'clock class again), and because most of us love to hear a really good story from a really good story teller, narration seems to come easy to most writers.

GUIDELINES FOR WRITING A NARRATIVE ESSAY

■ **One,** keep in mind that you are telling a story. The subject matter is usually something that has happened to you or to someone you know. A single incident from your life (or someone else's life) generally makes the best subject matter. You should also keep in mind that you are writing a narrative essay and not a biography or autobiography. Be certain to focus on a specific time or event or action. The incident should have a beginning, a middle, and an end; that is, the essay tells a complete story. Most narrative essays emphasize the middle portion of the story. Although the beginning (the set up) and the ending (the wind up) are important, the middle usually focuses the reader's interest on a conflict.

■ **Two,** the conflict becomes the pivotal part of the narration. A conflict is some type of struggle between two forces. The conflict might be an **internal conflict**: Should I tell my math professor that the person next to me is cheating? Should I accept this date or should I decline? Should I tell my boss to shove it and look for a new job or should I just be glad I have a job? Should I take early retirement next year or should I go until I am ninety? Such conflicts are referred to as internal because they take place within a person. An **external conflict** is one between a person and some force outside (external to) the person: Can I outrun the person in the lane next to me and bring home first place? Am I capable of landing this marlin? Can I survive this war and go home to tell about it? Will I be able to drive through this ice storm and make it home safely? The conflict and its **resolution**—the moment the conflict is solved or faced or eliminated—

provide the focal point of the narrative paper. Once the conflict is resolved, the narration usually ends very quickly.

■ **Three,** narration is usually told from a first person point of view, the person which uses the first person pronoun **I**. (The second person pronoun is **you**; the third person pronoun is either **she** or **he**. There is also the objective voice **one**.) Narration is usually most-effective when it is written in the first person, using the pronoun **I**. The use of the first person pronoun creates the most intimacy between the writer and the reader.

■ **Four,** narration, like description and other types of writing, relies upon the use of concrete and specific detail. The use of detail will help the reader to see what you saw, hear what you heard, taste what you tasted, etc. If you have ever sat around a late-night campfire telling ghost stories, then you are aware that the storyteller who tells the best story and sends goose bumps scurrying along your flesh is the one who can present the most graphic descriptions of settings, events, characters, and feelings.

■ **Five,** narration—as does all writing—has structure and organization. The usual—and most-natural—method is chronological. The chronology, as you will see in some of the examples to follow, can be straight forward, reverse action, or employ the use of flashback.

■ **Six,** narration communicates a message, but does not have to do so blatantly. The message can come through without being bluntly stated in either the introduction or the conclusion. If you follow the first five steps, your message should come through clearly.

THE NARRATIVE PAPER: A STUDENT EXAMPLE

As you read the following student essay, try to analyze how she combined her natural storytelling abilities with her knowledge of the preceding principles of narrative writing.

Good Bye, Johnny

1   Past the hub of the city and the sprawl of the suburbs lie vast expanses of land called the boondocks. The boonies, as they are affectionately named by their inhabitants, are some of the farthestmost regions of civilization. Far removed from the density of urbanization, the boonies are as close to country living as can be; they are not as remote as farm country, but the ambiance is similar. Two lane roads come to mind, winding along endlessly through wide open spaces. Unspoiled wilderness parallels the road at random intervals, with intermittent warnings posted of wildlife crossing. The county seat of each village is marked by small clusters of buildings along the way. Homes, prairies, and fields of corn dotting the landscape add to the rural atmosphere. Lighting along the roads is sparse, and at night one travels with trepidation. That fear and doubt is not entirely unfounded, for at night the roads can be deceiving. Clipping along in the dark, one never knows where the next bend in the road might be. At night, the woods are vaguely outlined pitch-black against the darkness of the sky above. The headlights reflect a glimmer of light in the shadow. Was that a dew-covered leaf or the eyes of a deer? Driving past the open fields, one can see the faint glow of lights from the street lamps and houses far off in the distance. A lone car traveling on the road is guided by the glare of its own headlights on the pavement. On foggy nights, one's view is misted and obscure in spots. It was on a road much the same as this that my cousin and I were driving along on our way home one night.

2   Marie and I had been to a party in Lemont, and afterwards I was going to spend the night at her house. It was well past midnight when we left the party for the long journey home. Once we left the sub-division and were on the main road, I was genuinely surprised by the darkness enveloping us as we drove along in her tiny pick-up truck. The only other time I had experienced a similar tableau was when I drove through the farm counties of Wisconsin and Indiana.

3   Now, it was four o'clock in the morning, and I was totally unfamiliar with my surroundings. I had not expected such a blackness-of-night, and to be quite honest, it gave me the creeps. My cousin was a bit unnerved too, and to allay our fears, she tuned the radio in to our favorite oldies station and cranked up the volume. Occasionally we passed another vehicle or a lighted intersection, but for the most part, we drove along alone and in darkness, singing at the top of our lungs.

4   As we passed one intersection, I saw the street sign bearing the name of the road we were traveling on, Archer Road. I stopped singing and asked Marie what direction we were heading. A feeling of uneasiness came over me when she told me we were heading north. My heart began to pound as we passed 135th Street, and I thought to myself, "God. I know where I am." Looking out into the darkness, scores of thoughts filled my mind, racing about and tumbling over one another. Even though I had never been here before, I knew where we were, or rather, I knew about the place where we were.

5   I had heard many stories and had read much about the area in the newspapers. Now that I was here, something did not seem right. I thought to myself, "This could not be the same place; it was too dark, too remote. What would anybody have been doing in such a God-forsaken place, and where would an overpass be in the middle of all of these prairies and woods?" This was all happening too fast, and I was very confused. We were driving along at a pretty good pace, and the radio was still blaring. I felt as though I personally was racing too, to what I didn't know—my own destiny perhaps? My apprehension grew, and I reached over and turned down the radio.

6   I wanted Marie to slow down so I could get my bearings and figure all of this out. What I had thought to be true did not fit in with what I was seeing. As I turned the knob on the radio, I looked up and saw that we were fast approaching a bend in the road. I could see a faint light coming from around the curve, and before I could move or speak, Marie had maneuvered the truck around the bend. In an instant the truck was barreling through the intersection. I was immediately aware of the brightness, although I did not actually see the lights. A streak of silver on the left caught my eye, and I kept my gaze on it, turning my whole body as we shot past it. I screamed, "Stop! Marie! Stop the truck!" I was frantic. She must have sensed the urgency in my voice. She slammed down hard on the brakes, and we came to a screeching stop.

7   I was trembling all over, and my heart was pounding so hard I could hardly breathe. I was practically turned around in my seat, staring into the blackness behind me. Now she too was frantic. "What's wrong?" she yelled as she shifted the gear shift into park. I could feel the tears burning in my eyes as I took a deep breath. I turned to face my cousin, and in a voice barely above a whisper I said, "Do you know where we are?" As the realization sank in, she slumped back against the seat; of course she knew. "Peggy, I'm sorry," she said quietly. "I never even gave it a thought." We sat there in total silence for a while, then she asked me what I wanted to do. I was a lot more calm by now, and I said, "I've never been here before. I want to go back."

8   We must have overshot the intersection by about seventy-five feet. When she put the truck in gear and turned it around, the bend in the road looked the same as when we had approached it from the other side; just a faint glow of light radiated into the darkness from beyond the curve. She slowly drove around the curve and came to a stop at the street where 112th Street intersects with Archer. I saw the overpass then, and I was amazed at how small it was. It could not have been more than twenty-five feet long, tiny by city standards. She crossed over 112th Street and came to a stop next to the guardrail that had so caught my eye in those few frenzied seconds, only minutes before. I took in my surroundings as I opened the door and slowly stepped into the street. The night was very quiet and still; neither my cousin nor I spoke a word. A feeling of absolute awe washed over me as I crossed the street and stood for the very first time on the spot where my brother had died almost thirty years before.

9   I approached the guardrail quietly, staring out over the void before me. Suddenly my breath caught as I felt the chill from a cool, dank breeze emanating from the ravine below. I looked down into the chasm then, and I was almost mesmerized by the shadowy darkness. "That was where he died," I thought to myself. My thoughts drifted back in time to May 28, 1962. . . .

10   . . . My cousin Marie was spending the night with me. The next day was a legal holiday, Memorial Day. The day would have been filled with backyard cookouts, neighbors visiting, and children playing. Marie and I had planned to hang around with our friends later in the day. I was fourteen years old at the time; Marie was a year younger. My brother John had gone out with his friends that holiday eve. I remember them picking him up at the house that night in a car that they had borrowed from another friend. His best friend was behind the wheel, and my mother told him to drive carefully. John poked his smiling face out of the back window and waved. Marie, mom, and I stood on the porch and watched them leave. We never saw John alive again. He was seventeen years old.

11   Early the next morning, two men in black suits came to the house and brought the sad news that Johnny had died in an automobile accident sometime during the night. My mother was devastated; his friends could not be consoled. I was saddened by the loss of my brother, and I was frightened when I saw him lying in his casket at the funeral home. My most vivid memory of his wake was walking into an entrance hall and seeing many shadows on one wall. The shadows were of people with their arms flailing about wildly through the air. The shadows were cast through a huge window in a brightly lit waiting room. I was startled when I entered the room and saw all of his friends, both boys and girls, screaming and beating the walls with their fists. Frightened, I ran from the room.

12   The day we laid Johnny to rest was the saddest I have ever known. The final good bye. . . . So many people, sobbing and holding one another, and flowers everywhere. His friends threw rose petals and pictures of themselves on his casket as it was lowered into the ground. That day was the last time my mother was ever in Holy Sepulchre Cemetery. She has never gone back there; she has never seen his headstone. She never spoke of John again.

13   When my brothers and sisters asked questions about him, she was reluctant to answer; over time, they stopped asking. My siblings do not really remember Johnny; they were very young when he died. My brother and three sisters ranged in age from seven years to five months old at the time of John's death. As adults, they were curious about the brother they never knew; most of what they do know about him, I have told them.

14   I showed them mementos of John that I had put away; among them were letters he had written to his girlfriend and her responses, and his death notice and the newspaper article about the accident. The article stated that a car traveling at a high rate of speed and carrying three teenage boys crashed through a guardrail, sheared off the tops of three trees, and plunged into a ravine fifty feet below. One boy died and two were hospitalized in serious condition. His friends said that they had been out joy riding and that they had gone to that remote area for the thrill of racing down the long, winding roads. When they reached 112th Street, however, the curve in the road was sharp. They were doing over 100 mph when they came around that curve; the coroner said Johnny went through the windshield on impact and died instantly. "God. I certainly hope so. I would not want to think that he suffered," I muttered softly to myself. . . .

15   . . . The sting of my own tears burning in my eyes brought me back to reality. I was no longer standing though; I was on my knees, holding onto the top of the guardrail, with my face pressed against one of the metal slats. I cried freely then as I imagined the last moments of my brother's life. I was overcome with grief as I pictured him lying in the bottom of the ravine, dead or near death, alone and so far from home in this desolate place. My cousin was crying too as she tried to comfort me; I stood up and composed myself then.

16   Looking around, I thought that this place had not changed since John's accident. We were surrounded by forest preserves, and the street lights above us in that tiny intersection cast the only light. The ravine on either side of the road was overgrown with shrubs and foliage of all sorts. The three trees that had been sheared off were now fully grown back and jutting out of the ravine. Marie and I walked back to her truck and got in. "No," I thought, looking around, "the passage of time has not altered this place at all." My heart was heavy as we drove away; I did not look back. As we headed home, I silently vowed that I would not carry this burden alone; it was time my siblings met their brother.

17   On May 28, 1990, my brother, my sisters, and I, and all of our children, gathered at Johnny's grave in Holy Sepulchre Cemetery. We placed flowers and balloons with streamers on them on his headstone. My siblings and I set white roses down the center of his grave and sat alongside of it, while my son took pictures. It was a strange family reunion, but it was long overdue; when we left, we had one more stop to make.

18   The reunion on top of the overpass was more somber. We must have been a strange-looking sight to anyone driving by that day. We were twenty people standing in front of a ravine in the middle of nowhere, holding a wreath of flowers and gaily colored balloons with streamers billowing off them. The wreath was made of white mums, with five red roses forming an arc at the bottom and with a single white rose on the top. As my brother Frank threw the wreath into the ravine, we all released our balloons. There was no need for words. A card enclosed in the wreath read:

> "In loving memory of our brother
> John J. Burns
> who died here on May 28, 1962
> at age seventeen
> Your spirit has been here alone for so long,
> It is not alone any more. . . . We are all here with you"
> Good Bye, Johnny

Margaret Peggy Burns

The preceding example illustrates the qualities of a well-written narrative essay. Let's examine some of these qualities.

First of all, the subject matter is extremely well-chosen. Peg's personal essay on the death of her brother and on how the family dealt with Johnny's death touches all of us. It touches us first of all because of the power of how well-written it is. It also touches us because we can all—most likely—relate to the subject matter: the death of someone we were close to, the sense of loss and grief that we all experience because we are human. Peg's vivid descriptions really pull us into her narrative and really put us on the overpass that dark night, put us graveside with the family, and put us at the scene of the accident as they truly celebrate their grief, their loss, and their love for their relative and for each other.

Peg's story clearly has a beginning and an ending. The middle of her story—the events of the accident—dominate the paper and are effectively communicated through flashback. The use of the first person (I) point of view is also effective. We feel the closeness, the intimacy which first person narration establishes. The use of the first pronoun I creates the most intimacy between the writer (narrator) and the reader.

The use of the flashback and the use of the first person point of view are only two of the choices Peg made in planning her essay. Her planning is also evident in the excellent structure and organization. Had she outlined her essay before drafting it, her outline might have resembled the one printed below:

1 introductory comments about roads, night driving, and perceptions
2 Marie & I leave party
3 4 AM jitters and singing
4 approach Archer & 135th
5 growing apprehension & awareness of location
6 screech to a stop at moment of recognition
7 I tell Marie where we are
8 We do a U turn & stop at 112th & Archer: the spot where my brother died 30 years before
9 I approach the guardrail . . . begin flashback to night Johnny died
10 Johnny & friends leave the house & wave goodbye
11 news of Johnny's death/the wake
12 the burial
13 questions—but no answers—about his death/time passes
14 mementos of Johnny/report of the accident
15 end flashback. . . .
16 Marie & I leave for home, making a vow to return
17 family visits Johnny's grave
18 family visits overpass/scene of accident/caption on card to close essay

Student Examples

His Deep Love

1   "No, you can't go to America! You are already in a college now. Having an Associate Degree is enough education for a girl." These were my father's answers when I told him my plan to study in the U.S.A.

2 My father and I rarely talk about private things, and when we talk about them, we usually don't agree with each other because he is always the one who has the right to decide everything.

3 My father, who is fifty, is a typical Japanese "old-fashioned father." Strictly following Japanese customs, he never says directly "I love you," to his children. Japanese fathers also don't kiss or hug their children after they grow up. In our society, these are not the ways to express our affections, but we sense them. Because of these Japanese customs, my father and other Japanese fathers can't communicate very well with their children, especially with their daughters.

4 My father is not only an old-fashioned father, but also a "Kyusyu-men." Kyusyu is the most southern main island of Japan. The "Kyusyu-men" is an expression for men who live on this island in that they have strong characteristics. The word "Kyusyu-men" refers to a man who has dignity, is strong, and is a man among men. Kyusyu is a male-dominated society region. For the "Kyusyu-men," it is also difficult to accept new ideas or other opinions. Especially, when they become husbands and/or fathers, they assume that they should always have the dignity and respect of husbands and/or fathers. My father is one of these types of men. Because of this male-dominated mentality, he always uses the word "women" when he explains the reason why I should or shouldn't do something. For example, I am obligated to do the housework, but he never tells my brothers to do it. I couldn't go to a college out of my prefecture, but my oldest brother could. I am not allowed to drink alcohol, but he enjoys drinking with my brothers because they are men, and I am a woman.

5 In addition, my father is a person who doesn't like to work under supervision, but he likes to supervise. Because of his strong personality, he started to run his own construction company at the age of 21 when he got married to my mother. He has a really loud voice because he is also a site-foreman of his company. This strong voice makes him appear to be scarier to me. His company is not big, but he loves his job. He works very hard and also takes care of his employees. For instance, my family had been eating dinner every day with each of the single employees until they got married. My mother also cooked their box lunches the same as my father's. My father had a hard time when he was young, so he wants to help his young employees. I'm proud of my father and what he does in his life. Although his parents didn't have enough money to give him any education after he graduated from junior high school, he gives us everything that he didn't have in his childhood. The things he does makes me proud of him, but he never speaks proudly. He is known as the "black-tongue" president of his company. His jokes are spicy, and no one knows whether he is joking or telling the truth. However, it is funny that everybody around him likes him a lot, even though he has a foul mouth. Almost every day, my father has guests in our house to drink with him. Moreover, his company is always busy because everybody wants to ask a service from him.

6 On August 15, 1996, I was in Kansai International Airport with my parents. My flight schedules were from Oita to Kansai International Airport, from Kansai to Los Angeles Airport, and my final destination was O'Hare Airport. My father was still unwilling to let me travel to the U.S.A. My mother was the one who financially supported me and managed to persuade him to change his mind. My brothers and my friends had given me a good send-off at Oita Airport. When we were waiting for our flight at Oita Airport, I was surrounded by my friends telling me good-bye. On the other hand, my parents were sitting on chairs without any words, so I suggested that we drink coffee together. The three of

us walked into a coffee shop at the airport. My parents looked nervous, and my father rarely opened his mouth. He asked me, "Will someone pick you up over there?" I said, "Yes, but I have to transfer my airplane at LA." He didn't say anything. My mother asked me, "Can you do that by yourself?" I said, "Of course." After we arrived at Kansai International Airport, my father's sister and her daughter were waiting for our arrival.

7   After we had lunch together, I found a long line of people who were waiting for check-in. That day was the biggest summer holiday in Japan. My mother, my aunt, my cousin, and I were standing at the very end of the long line. Suddenly, I wondered where my father was. I looked for him, and he was sitting on a bench a little far from me. When I looked at his face, he moved his eyes to a different position. His big swollen stomach seemed to be telling him that he was no longer young, and his short gray hair made him look older than his real age. Even his short but powerful body, due to his job, looked weak at that time. When I progressed very close to a check-in counter, I looked for him again. He had already followed me and was sitting on another bench. A serious expression appeared on his dark face. He might have wanted to tell me something, but he didn't. My mother called him to come to me when I was about to pass the gate. My father slowly stood up and came close to us. I looked at his wrinkled face, and I lost my words. His big eyes, maybe twice as big as mine, turned to red, and unexpectedly tears were dropping from them. My father was crying in front of me.

8   If I had not come to the United States, I wouldn't have seen this different side of my father. He couldn't even make any jokes, and his voice was very soft. He just told me to take care of myself. I thought that he must have never expected to send his daughter to a foreign country. He might be telling himself that he didn't have any more control over his daughter and holding indescribable feelings in his mind. Without any words, I strongly felt his deep love for me which was more than any words people use to express their love.

Miwa Oda

Memorial

1   Anyone who has been driving for any length of time has probably driven past one of those "roadside memorials." Sometimes, the memorial is a simple wreath of flowers propped up with wires on the grass alongside of the road. Sometimes, accompanying the wreath is a picture of a person whom you've never met and never will. At an intersection not too far from where I live and work, there's a light pole on the corner. It would be like any other light pole, except that attached to this one, is a wooden box with a Plexiglas window. Inside of the box is a picture of a man. At the base of the pole, there are flowers.

2   Do you ever stop and think about the people for whom these memorials are left? Do you wonder what happened to them? Who they were? What they left behind? Do you know someone for whom one of these memorials has been left? Until October 31st, 1997, I don't think that I ever gave it much thought. But on that night, I became part of the story behind one of those memorials.

3   I was working the afternoon shift with the police dept., and I was due to get off at 10:45 p.m. It was a quarter past 10:00 p.m., and I remember thinking that we had made it through the shift without anyone dying. Perhaps that might seem like a morbid thought, but I had been present for two deaths in the three days prior to that particular night.

4   One of the deaths involved a 16-year-old boy who, after having an argument on the phone with his girlfriend, hung himself in the basement of his home. (Little did anyone suspect that almost one year later, this boy's mother, despondent over the loss, would hang herself from the same beam in that basement.)

5   The other death was that of a man in his late 40's, who had three young children. He had been complaining to his wife throughout the day that he was having chest pains. She finally managed to convince him that he should go to the hospital. As he was getting his coat on, he suddenly collapsed. While the paramedics worked on this man, I took the three children into one of the bedrooms and talked to them about school, computer games, and police work. All the while, they were laughing and excitedly telling me about their favorite games. All the while, I could also hear the paramedics just outside of the bedroom door futily attempting to bring the father of these wonderful children back to life. Every minute or so, I would hear, "Clear!," coming from one of the paramedics, as they used the defibrillating paddles on him. Once the paramedics removed him, I was free to go.

6   By Halloween night, I'd had my fill of death. With only half an hour left on my tour of duty, I had fooled myself into thinking that I had made it. At 10:16 p.m., I could no longer fool myself. A call went out that there was a "car vs. pedestrian" accident on Roosevelt Rd. I was literally seconds away.

7   As I pulled up to the scene of the accident, I saw a teenage girl lying in the roadway with her head resting in a pool of blood, almost exactly on the center dividing lines. She was resting on her left side, facing the south side of the road. I was the first officer to the scene, so I ran from my car to check on her condition. Not knowing the extent of her injuries, I was afraid to move her unless I absolutely had to. As it turned out, she had no pulse and was not breathing. I had to move her.

8   Right about this time, several other squad cars were arriving on the scene. My friend Erv was getting out of his car, so I yelled to him, "Grab an ambu bag to vent her." As Erv was coming over to where I was kneeling over the girl, I was carefully rolling her onto her back so that I could do chest compressions on her.

9   Her eyes were open and there was blood trickling not only from the corners of her eyes, but also from her ears. She was wearing bib overalls with a T-shirt underneath. I noticed that the left shoulder strap had come unsnapped, and her T-shirt had gotten pulled up, exposing her left breast. She had apparently been wearing a jacket at the time of the accident, but it was now in the road approximately 60 feet west of where she was lying. Along with the jacket were the gym shoes that she had been knocked out of. There was a large crowd gathered on the roadside, so I adjusted her clothing to cover her exposed breast. With all that was going on, I was surprised that I was so concerned with this girl's dignity, but somehow it seemed important to me.

10   Erv had run back to me with the ambu bag, and apparently reading my exact thoughts, he looked at the girl and said, "I don't think we're doing her a favor if we bring her back." I agreed and knelt over the girl's body, straddling her, to begin the chest compressions, to try and start her heart. I counted out loud with each compression, "One, two, three, four, five," and then directed Erv, who had by now placed the ambu bag over her nose and mouth, "Vent!"

11   I remember thinking, "Where the fuck is the ambulance? God, please don't put this girl's life in my hands. She needs professionals." All the while, I kept on working. "One, two three, four, five. Vent!" I was scared and kept thinking, " I know that I've been trained to do this, but I've never had to, until now. What if I'm doing it wrong?" "One, two, three, four, five. Vent!"

12   I don't remember from where this woman appeared, but I looked over and she was taking the girl's pulse. Without looking up, perhaps sensing that I was staring down at her, she said, "I'm a nurse. You're doing fine." After a couple of seconds, she said, "She has a pulse." I was in such disbelief, that I kept up the chest compressions for another count of five, until the words sank in.

13   She still was not breathing, so Erv continued to vent her periodically. I didn't move from my position of kneeling over this young girl as I looked up at the large crowd standing on the sidewalk on the south side of Roosevelt Rd. and yelled, "Does anyone know this girl?" A few people answered, "No," but most of them were too much in shock at what they were seeing to react. I couldn't imagine a young girl like this, who should have had her whole life ahead of her, having to die in the middle of the street with two police officers trying desperately to keep that from happening.

14   After what seemed like an eternity, but I'm sure was much less, the ambulance arrived. As the paramedics got out of the ambulance, I noticed that one of them was carrying a clipboard to gather information about the victim. I rather unceremoniously yelled, "Forget about that! She needs to go NOW!" They quickly rolled the gurney from the back of the ambulance, and as easily as they could, they slid the girl onto a "backboard" and placed her on the gurney.

15   In moments, she was on her way to the hospital. It was only after the ambulance had left that I noticed the gray 1985 Chevy Cavalier stopped in the left-hand lane, about 30 feet down the road from where the girl had been laying. The windshield had been "spiderwebbed" from a large indentation directly in front of the steering wheel. The driver, a 24-year-old man, was standing on the side of the road being questioned by another officer.

16   My specialty within the police department is accident reconstruction. In the event of fatal or near-fatal accidents, it's my job to photograph and measure everything at the scene. From the measurement of skidmarks, it's possible to determine the speed that a car was traveling at the time of an accident. I began to walk through the accident scene to determine what needed to be done first.

17   Starting from the spot where I found the girl laying, I walked back in the direction where her shoes and jacket were still sitting on the roadway. Approximately 48 feet from the spot where the girl had been, I noticed something unusual. Something that I could not as yet identify was stuck in the pavement. I walked over, set my flashlight down next to it, and saw that it was a tuft of the girl's reddish-brown hair embedded in the asphalt.

18   I began measuring the distance between where the Cavalier was now sitting, to the point of impact. The point of impact in "car vs. pedestrian" accidents is usually made apparent by scuff marks on the street, left by the victim's shoes. The distance in this particular case was 90 feet. I measured the distance from the point of impact to where each of her shoes had landed, as well as her jacket. Finally, I measured the distance from the point of impact to the patch of hair which was embedded in the asphalt. That turned out to be forty-two feet and six inches from the point of impact.

19   From the caved-in windshield of the Cavalier, as well as a deep gouge in the hood of the car, which was caused by a metal button on the girl's bib overalls, the obvious conclusion that I arrived at was that the girl was first hit by the car, which never achieved full braking. (This was obvious, because of lack of skidmarks on the road.) As she slid across the hood of the car, her head impacted with the windshield. After she hit the windshield, she was thrown over the driver's side of the car, where she landed on her head, leaving a patch of hair. She continued tumbling down the street for an additional forty-seven feet and six inches, where she finally came to rest.

20   Once the measurements were taken, I had an opportunity to speak with the driver of the car, who was understandably shaken. According to him, he never even saw the girl. He stated that he had just left the traffic signal at Main St. on Roosevelt Rd. He had only gone about 2 blocks, when he heard a short scream which was immediately cut off. He said that right after the scream was cut off, his windshield exploded inward. At that point, he applied the brakes, but was afraid to jam them, because he could no longer see where he was going. It was only after he came to a complete stop that he realized what had happened.

21   Several other witnesses, who had been driving in the opposite direction, came forward to tell me that they had observed three teenagers running across Roosevelt Rd. from the north side to the south. One witness stated that he, himself, had been westbound and had to skid to avoid hitting them. He stated that his car had come to a complete stop in the middle of the road and that a moment later, he heard the sound of a car hitting something. As he looked over his left shoulder, he saw something that "looked like a rag doll" flying through the air.

22   Another woman told me that she was a little further back in traffic and that she had also seen the teenagers running across the street. She stated, "The cars were swerving out of the way, trying to avoid hitting the kids. They should've been hit right there. Somehow they managed to get to the middle. Then, that girl walked right out in front of that car. It was like they were playing "chicken." They looked like they saw the cars and were taking the chance. You know how sometimes you see a chance to get across the street? It wasn't like that. There was no way they were gonna make it."

23   So now we were faced with some questions. Who were the other two teenagers? Where did they go? Who was the girl who had gotten hit by the car? The answers came rather quickly. We received a call from the hospital saying that there was a young girl in the waiting room who was asking questions about the injured girl. One of our officers immediately went to the hospital.

24   At the hospital, the 18-year-old girl admitted that she and her boyfriend had been with the victim, who was only 16 years old, when the accident occurred. According to her, a group of friends had been driving around, looking for fun on Halloween night, when someone in the car came up with the idea of getting someone to buy beer for them. Apparently, someone in the car had a friend who was at The Red Onion, a banquet hall and bar. It's located on the north side of Roosevelt Rd., directly in front of where the accident occurred.

25   The "friend" was of legal age to buy alcohol. So they went to The Red Onion and got their friend. From what this girl told me later on when I interviewed her myself, this friend came out into the parking lot of the bar, saw a carload of teenagers and said, "I'm not pulling up in front of a liquor store with a car full of kids. Some of you need to get out and wait here."

26   So, this 18-year-old girl, her boyfriend, and the 16-year-old girl got out of the car to wait for their friends to return with the beer. After waiting for a little while, the three of them were getting cold, so the 16-year-old girl said that she knew a guy who had just gotten a job at the Burger King, just across Roosevelt Rd. So, the three of them decided to run over to see him.

27   According to this 18-year-old girl, "We were all trotting across the street, and me and my boyfriend stopped at the median, but she kept running." I asked her, "Did she stop at all? Even for a moment?" She told me, "No. She just kept going." When I asked why her friend didn't stop, she said, "I don't know. Maybe she just got scared because another car had just missed us." She also told me that she and her boyfriend were standing alongside of the road while Erv and I were doing CPR on her "friend." She was willing to let her friend die alone in the middle of the street, even after I had shouted to the crowd, looking for someone who could tell us who this girl was, and how we could notify her family.

28   Before I went home in the early hours of November 1st, I asked our dispatcher to call the hospital to check on the 16-year-old's condition. The hospital told us that she was in critical condition. By now, we had identified the girl with the help of her so-called friend, and the girl's parents had gone to the hospital to sit throughout the night. Because there is a legal case pending, I won't print the girl's name, or that of anyone else who was involved that night. But then, names really aren't important. What happened that night could happen to anyone.

29   At 6:45 in the morning, I returned to work, having slept very little. The first thing that I did was to ask the day shift dispatcher to call the hospital to see how she was doing. We were told that she was on life support with no brain activity. She also had a broken neck. At exactly 3:30 p.m. that afternoon, November 1st, 1997, with her family by her side, she was taken off of life support and slipped away. Her family donated the girl's organs so that others might have the chance that their little girl never would. I completed my calculations from the evidence that I had collected the night before. I determined that the car that had struck her was traveling at approximately 37 mph. The speed limit on that part of Roosevelt Rd. is 35 mph. I don't fault the driver of the car for what happened, but I know that he probably goes over the events of that evening and wonders what he could have done differently. Just as I'm certain that the dead girl's friends ask themselves over and over again, "Why?"

30   I don't know anything about that girl. I don't know what her voice sounded like. I don't know what she wanted to do with her life. But she's now a part of my life that I cannot escape. She's now a part of the outlook that I have about my job. Every time that I pull over a speeder on a street where the speed limit is 35 mph, and I get the lame excuse, "I was only going 48 mph.," I think about what 37 mph did to that girl and all of those who knew her, and some, like myself, who never knew her.

31   Her picture is attached to a light pole on the south side of Roosevelt Rd., just east of Main St. There are always flowers lying at the base of that pole. I don't know who leaves them there, but I suspect that they're from her family, friends, and perhaps even from the man who hit her. I don't know. It isn't really important. What is important, is that they represent a life that was carelessly thrown away. So, when you see those memorials, think not of who they are for. Think of yourself and those you love. Let it serve as a reminder to live every moment to the fullest, because you never know if you'll ever have the chance to tell those you care about how much they mean to you.

Scott Sodaro

Under the Lights

1   Who says dreams can't come true? Whoever said it doesn't know what he or she is saying because a dream of mine came true my senior year in high school. My dream was to play football under the lights in front of a large crowd. I always wanted to play on a football field in front of lots of people who were there just to watch a good football game. I wanted to look up and be astounded by the number of people that took interest in a game that I was a part of. I never expected this to happen, but it did, and when it happened, it was even better than my dream. I wasn't just playing under the lights in front of a large crowd, but I was the captain of a team that was about to play against its most bitter rival. I was one of two captains for the 1998 Brother Rice Crusaders, and we were about to play the Marist Redhawks on a brisk Friday night in early September at Marist High School.

2   Being a captain, I led our team out of the locker room onto the field. I remember looking back and seeing everyone packed in tight. We were one big unit that night, striving for a common goal. That night we chose to wear our all-white uniforms, a combination that we normally don't wear. We had on our brand new shining white pants and jerseys. Looking back I also saw that our entire team had their game faces on; no one had a smile or a grin on his face. We were ready for our upcoming battle.

3   As we approached the gate to the football field, I stopped the team, looked back and said, "This is what we have been waiting for our whole lives. We have worked hard for this. All these people that you are about to see have come to see us. Now let's give them something to be proud of!" With that having been said and seeing the lighted field, we walked through the gates onto the illuminated battleground. We began to get antsy, and we wanted to play. The adrenaline was pumping fast through our veins.

4   We were now in the south end zone getting a pep talk from our coach. As I looked around I first saw our opponents running on the field. They were wearing their red jerseys and white pants. I noticed the Marist captains and knew that they would have their team prepared, just like I had ours. They ran by and gave us a stare down. They were attempting to get our minds off the game. As many Chicago high school football fans know, this is a very bitter and long-lasting rivalry between Brother Rice and Marist. Since the schools are only two miles apart, this game is essentially a battle for the neighborhood bragging rights. We had gained the bragging rights the previous year, and we all knew it was going to be a battle to retain those rights.

5   As my eyes followed the Marist players to their sidelines, I glanced up into their home stands. They were overflowing with people. There were at least 3,000 people on that side alone. There were family, students, friends, teachers, sports lovers, and newspaper reporters packing those stands. I was in awe. I could not believe how many people were in the home stands alone.

6   Our coach had finished his speech. Our team now surrounded my co-captain and myself. Seeing as I had already said something, my co-captain said a few words of his own. As soon as he finished, our entire team shouted, "Go Crusaders!" We then began to walk right down the center of the football field. We walked hand-in-hand, my co-captain and I leading the way. We heard a resounding roar from our crowd. As I looked over I was dumbfounded. Seeing the 3,000 plus Brother Rice fans and knowing that I was the leader of the team that they were proud of my knees got a little weak, and I got the strangest feeling inside of me. I saw many of my classmates all dressed up in their Rice apparel and with their bodies painted for this game. I saw teachers and family members,

and then I saw people who did not even go to our school but were there on our side just for entertainment. This was a dream come true for me, and I said to myself, "You will not let all these people down; you will do the best you can to win this game for them, for your team, and for yourself."

7   As we got to the fifty-yard line, we turned and sprinted to our sideline. Our fans went crazy, and so did we. Now the long-awaited battle could begin. The captains from each team were led out to the middle of the field for the coin toss. As I was walking out there, I thought to myself how honorable it was to be selected by my own coaches and team-mates to be one of two guys leading this team. We got to mid-field and completed the coin toss. Brother Rice was going to have the ball first. The referees told us to shake hands and to keep our players in order. So we shook hands, turned, and sprinted back towards our sideline. I shouted, "Offense, you guys have to set the tone! It's your turn to show what you have!" While running back, I looked up into the crowd once again and knew that they had a great respect for me and my ability to be a team captain.

8   That was the last time I noticed the crowd or any other distraction that night. After the kickoff, my mind was focused on winning that game. Although I played my hardest and did my best, I could not help our team achieve victory that night. That night was not a complete loss though. Our team grew closer and for most of us, one of our dreams was lived out. I know it was more than a dream come true for me. I don't know if I will ever again be able to lead a team in such a brutal rivalry, under the lights and in front of 6,000 or 7,000 people. If I don't, oh well. I was fortunate enough to have had that night. That night will live on in my memory for the rest of my life. To this date that has been my most-treasured achievement in my life.

Scott Staros

The Right to Fail

1   The right to fail sounds like a pretty negative phrase, coming from a person who believes the glass is always half full. But it has worked, in a very positive way for me. I am a woman in a man's world. My job as an offset printer operator is held mostly by men wherever I have worked, on the east coast, down south, and now here in Chicago. I do not consider myself a feminist; I have no intention of burning my bra. I would be willing to stand and fight for anyone's right to fail, choose, try, or succeed, whatever they want to call it. You may choose to call me a feminist, which is your right. But I want to tell you about my first success, using the statement the right to fail, and maybe you can explain to me why it works so well.

2   When I was in high school, in the early 70's, I wanted to take auto mechanics as one of my classes. I was told girls are not mechanics. I should sign up for home economics, learn how to cook and make dresses. Since I did not like to wear dresses and I already knew how to cook, it seemed to me to be a waste of my time. I wanted to be able to change the oil in my car and know if a mechanic was BS'ing me or not. Growing up on a farm, I already knew a lot about machinery. You cannot leave a broken down tractor in the middle of a field. When I insisted on the auto mechanics class, I was told I could not have the class because of my long hair; it was a safety risk. In the 70's my male class-mates had hair as long as mine or longer, and they got to take the class.

3   That night at the dinner table my parents asked me if I had gotten all the classes I wanted. I told them what had happened and now I have a two-hour block to fill, and did not know what to take. My dad told me, "I think the hair thing is a poor excuse too. With all the long hair you kids wear today, who can tell the boys from the girls?" The next night at dinner, my parents asked again about what I was going to do. I told them that the school counselor had made an appointment with me for tomorrow. My mom then told me that there was a school board meeting in two weeks, and we could go and present the issue to them. This would not mean that I would get what I wanted, and chances were that I would fail, but I would never know if I did not try. This told me she had already called the school and could not get them to change their minds either. Mom told me to think about it for a few days, because they would support my efforts, but I would have to plead my own case to the board.

4   I went to school the next day and talked to a few of my friends about going to the board and trying to change the unfair practice. I went to the appointment with my counselor and told him that I was thinking about going to the board meeting and stating my case. He told me that he would like to help me with my presentation to the board. A cold chill ran down my back, and the little hairs stood up on the back of my neck. I was not planning to make a big deal out of this; I thought I would just need to tell them that it was unfair to prejudge people by their sex. All of a sudden I was not so sure I wanted to do this. My counselor told me I was the first student ever to challenge the rule and that he would do everything in his power to help me. I told him I had better think on this some more.

5   That night at dinner, I told my parents what had happened. They did not shove me, but they did do a little pushing, telling me to speak my convictions to the board; I had a right to try and that is all I could do. If I really felt that it was unfair, the board would not know unless I told them. Besides if I did fail the first time I could try again the next year. In the morning I asked my mom if I stayed after school with the counselor to work on my presentation, if she would pick me up on her way home from work. She said she would, and if she could do anything else just ask. I am not sure that was the answer I wanted from her.

6   I was just your everyday average student. I was a good student who did not rock the boat. The news that I was taking on the man (or the system) spread through school like a *wild fire*. I was so busy working on my presentation that I did not realize what was happening. It was the shortest two weeks of my life. I had practiced my presentation in front of my family and the counselor. They all told me to speak a little louder and to look up. The Big Day arrived. I was going to do it if it killed me; too many people had done their very best to help me. My parents and I went to the meeting. The room was packed, standing room only. A lot of fellow students were there, including seniors that would not be attending school in the fall. My counselor had saved seats for me and my parents near the aisle. I sat next to him and said, "You told me that there would only be about ten to fifteen people here." He told me, "All the kids are here to support you." I must have had a complete look of horror on my face, because he said, "You may not win this time or even the next, but eventually you will. They are here to let you know, and the board, that they believe you are right."

7   As I waited for the board to ask about new business, my hands started to sweat, my heart was beating so hard and fast that it was making my whole body shake. When they asked for new business, I went up to the front. One of the mothers (I presumed) got there first and was complaining about how short the cheerleaders' skirts were; they should be knee length and no shorter. It took what seemed like forever. I did not notice the group gathering behind me, the other students.

8   When my turn came, a gentleman at the big table asked, "Who is the spokesman for the group?" I looked behind me and saw all the other students, telling me to, "Go get them; you can make a difference." All of a sudden I felt empowered. I did have the right to ask for a chance, and even if it was the right to fail. It meant the right to succeed to me, and the right for others to succeed. I introduced myself to the board and told them about the double standards that were being practiced in the school. If they wanted to give an entrance exam to everyone I would be willing to take it. It was my education, and I should be able to try new things. That was what an education was for, to learn something new. I believe that you learn just as much from failure (your mistakes) as you do from success. When I said thanks for listening and I hoped they would change the double standards, a cheer went up in the room. Then different students stepped up and said they were representing different groups in the school and stood behind every word I said. The last student, a senior, told the board, "If they did not change the rules they better start holding their meeting in a bigger room, because we would be back until there was a change." The board members said that they would have to take it under consideration. There were other issues involved. There were a few other new business items, and then the meeting was adjourned.

9   On the way out of the building that night, my counselor told me that I might not be in auto mechanics in the fall, but some other girl would have to thank me because she got to take auto mechanics, in the future. He also told me that my presentation was honest and simple; they did not even ask why I wanted to take the class. It was almost a month later before my counselor made another appointment with me. I figured I was going to have to fill my two-hour block with whatever classes were still open. But to my surprise he told me I was taking auto mechanics in the fall. He also told me that now was the hardest part; I was going to have to back my words with action. The first few weeks of class were rough, but when teacher and students saw that I could do it and learn, it got a lot easier. I got an **A** in the class.

10   I do not know why the statement the right to fail works in a positive way for me. Is it the system or the men who run it? Is the thought that I will fail a favored idea? I do not believe that most men want to see me fail, but do they want me to be successful? I have played the game long enough to know that I better be more than I say I am. And that there are days I need to have tough skin and a warm heart, to have the life I have chosen to live.

Kandice Perry

THE NARRATIVE PAPER: POSSIBLE TOPICS

Generally, the best subject matter for a narrative paper is a personal experience. Those experiences which seem to produce the best narratives from my students seem to revolve around some of the following situations. Maybe they will give you some inspiration as you decide on subject matter:

- an embarrassing incident
- a threatening incident
- a frightening incident
- a time-suspended incident
- an hysterical incident

- your first _____
- your last _____
- learning how to _____
- teaching someone to _____
- getting caught _____

- an out-of-control incident
- a dramatic incident
- a tragic incident
- a comic incident
- a sad incident
- a joyful incident
- a sorrowful incident
- a growing incident
- a tender incident
- a sharing incident

- catching someone _____
- crying about _____
- laughing over _____
- remembering to _____
- forgetting to _____
- succeeding at _____
- failing at _____
- avoiding entirely _____
- wishing for _____
- trying to avoid _____

THE NARRATIVE PAPER—YOUR TURN

1 Select an incident to use as the subject matter for your narrative paper.

2 Sit and think about this incident. Why did you select it? Out of all the events and incidents that have occurred in your life, why have you chosen this one moment, event, or situation? What is its significance? What does it mean to you even today? How did it contribute to making you who you are?

3 Jot down some of the detail and example that could help to recreate the scene for the reader.

4 Think of the conflict in the situation. What was the conflict? Was it internal? Was it external? How was it resolved?

5 Think of the incident in terms of a story line. What is its beginning? What is its middle? What is its ending? Where would be the best place to "pick up" the story line? Where would be the best place to end it? How involved is the middle part of the story? Is there information that could be included but that might have to be cut in order to shorten the paper/incident?

6 Determine which person (point of view) to use to narrate the essay.

7 Shape the beginning, middle, and ending into an outline.

8 Write the rough draft of the narrative paper.

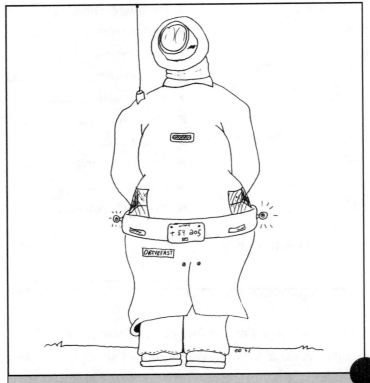

My new rear end is great. My lights all blink and my bumper has no rust.

My old boyfriend always put me on a pedalstool.

NARRATIVE PAPER PLAN SHEET

Part One: Fill in each of the following blanks with basic information.

Incident to be described: _____

What you learned from this incident or want your reader to learn: _____

_____

Person to use in narrating the incident: _____

The conflict: _____

_____

The beginning of the story: _____

_____

The ending of the story: _____

_____

_____

Some of the ideas to include in the middle: _____

_____

_____

_____

_____

_____

_____

_____

_____

_____

_____

Part Two: Write the outline for the essay.

Name _____ Section _____ Date _____

SELF-EVALUATION SHEET: PART ONE

Assignment: _____

Strong points of this assignment:

_____

_____

_____

_____

_____

_____

_____

Weak points of this assignment:

_____

_____

_____

_____

_____

_____

_____

General comments:

_____

_____

_____

_____

_____

_____

_____

(over)

SELF-EVALUATION SHEET: PART TWO

What were the strong points of your last writing assignment?

_____

_____

_____

_____

_____

_____

What were the weak points of your last writing assignment?

_____

_____

_____

_____

_____

_____

_____

What have you done to correct those weaknesses in this assignment?

_____

_____

_____

_____

_____

_____

PEER-EVALUATION SHEET: PEER-EVALUATOR #1

Writer's Name _____ Essay's Title _____

> **Directions:** (1) Remember not to write on another student's paper. Instead, use this form. (2) Offer concrete, specific comments using the terminology of writing (e.g., "The development in paragraph four might be improved by adding a brief example." or, "Check structure on page 3.")

What do you see as the strong points of this writing assignment: _____

_____

_____

_____

_____

What areas do you feel might need additional work: _____

_____

_____

_____

_____

Do you see any areas of grammar/mechanics (e.g. usage, spelling, fragments) that might need attention: _____

_____

_____

_____

_____

General comments: _____

_____

_____

_____

_____

Evaluator's Name _____ Section _____ Date _____

PEER-EVALUATION SHEET: PEER-EVALUATOR #2

Writer's Name _____ Essay's Title _____

> **Directions:** (1) Remember not to write on another student's paper. Instead, use this form. (2) Offer concrete, specific comments using the terminology of writing (e.g., "The development in paragraph four might be improved by adding a brief example." or, "Check structure on page 3.")

What do you see as the strong points of this writing assignment: _____

_____

_____

_____

_____

What areas do you feel might need additional work: _____

_____

_____

_____

_____

Do you see any areas of grammar/mechanics (e.g. usage, spelling, fragments) that might need attention: _____

_____

_____

_____

_____

General comments: _____

_____

_____

_____

_____

The Process Paper

OVERVIEW

Process/instruction is a method of development which a writer uses to explain how to do something. A process description is a general explanation of the process by which some task is completed. Process is intended for a general audience. An instruction description, however, is a detailed, step-by-step explanation of how to perform the process. Instruction is for a specific audience, an audience with special skills. Anyone, for example, can read and understand a process description of how a riverboat pilot navigates a series of locks and dams. It takes a person with very special skills, however, to read and perform such a maneuver with a towboat and fifty barges of coal. This distinction between process and instruction is important and is usually emphasized in technical writing classes. Since this text's purpose is more introductory in nature, it will simply use the label process/instruction for that broad category of development which explains how to do something.

THE PROCESS PAPER

Process/instruction is a method of development we obviously use a great deal. Hardly a day goes by that someone does not ask us to explain how we made that delicious-tasting banana bread. Or, we are asked how we got such a nice finish on the antique table we just purchased. Or perhaps someone asks us how to study for a final in calculus. All of us have certain skills, and we are usually not shy when it comes time to share our knowledge, whether it is how to water-ski, bake chocolate chip cookies, tune the car, keep score at tennis, lay carpet, throw a good surprise party, sneak in the house after curfew, or change the circuit breaker in the house's master panel.

 ## GUIDELINES FOR WRITING A PROCESS/INSTRUCTION ESSAY

■ **One,** since process/instruction entails explaining how to do something, choose a topic that lets you write about a process with which you are familiar.

■ **Two,** provide the essay with structure and organization. Generally, each step in the process functions as a topic sentence. When you change steps, change paragraphs. Be careful, however, to apply knowledge of paragraphing; don't let paragraphs become too choppy or too lengthy. Be certain each paragraph is unified and coherent.

■ **Three,** develop each step in the process with detail and example. As the writer or explainer of the process, you are providing information to a reader who is not as accomplished at this process. Try to give the reader complete information and try to give suggestions or hints for completion of the process; the latter are not a direct part of the process, but are ways of making the process go more smoothly. Such suggestions also indicate that the writer is aware of audience.

■ **Four,** pay attention (as always when you write) to audience analysis. As mentioned in an earlier chapter, audience analysis is always an important part of the pre-writing process; this is especially so in a process essay. The process paper presents an opportunity to strengthen your concept of audience. For example, perhaps it is wise to tell what supplies (if any) are needed so that the reader knows ahead of time and can procure them. For instance, don't tell your reader to drain the oil from his car and then later tell him to add several quarts. It could be a long walk to the service station! Or if you are explaining a certain way to create lasagna, don't surprise or puzzle a reader by telling her to add a teaspoon of Beau Monde. Your reader might not know what Beau Monde is or where to buy it.

The process paper is also the perfect opportunity to try a directed-audience essay. That is, focus on a very specific audience and write to that audience, perhaps even in letter form (as suggested in an earlier chapter). For example, explain to Aunt Lucy the process of how to buy you a Christmas gift that you really want. Or explain to your maid the way you would prefer to have your windows done and your diamond collection dusted. Or describe the process of how the curve breaker in your Calculus class cheats and never gets caught—and send this process explanation—anonymously—to your Calc. professor. At the risk of sounding like a doddering, middle-aged fool, I'll repeat: good writing engages the reader and the writer with its energy; most good writing does not "happen" just for the sake of earning a good grade. Have something to say; the good grade is more apt to follow.

Let's take a look at an example. We'll examine it and analyze it to learn what goes into a good process paper.

For the Love of Bread

1   As a young boy, I loved to eat, and after each meal, I prided myself on being a member of the "clean plate club." I especially loved sandwiches because no matter how a sandwich was prepared, bread had to be involved. Then one day, while sitting patiently at my grandmother's dinner table, starving as usual, I experienced for the first time her homemade bread. Fresh out of the oven and still steaming, the loaf was a mouth-watering work of art—but I was hardly content to just look at it. Biting into the first slice marked a turning point in my eating habits, as my naive taste buds were introduced to a whole new world. A discovery had been made, and needless to say, store-bought white bread was no longer on my favorite-foods list.

2   As I grew older, my love for bread grew stronger along with a sincere concern for good nutrition, which led to another discovery. Not only were store-bought brands inferior in taste, but their ingredients were not exactly healthful, either. In fact, most were not even pronounceable.

3 Pondering these discoveries, I reasoned that if I were to bake my own bread with only the natural ingredients I saw fit to include, all of my standards of taste and nutrition could be met. So, I proceeded to experiment with a number of recipes, during which time I allowed myself to become creative. Due to this creativity factor, I have never baked the exact same bread recipe twice. However, I developed a somewhat basic pattern that I always follow. If you would like a basic idea of how to bake your own bread, here is how baking bread is best accomplished for me.

4 To start, combine in a large mixing bowl all the dry ingredients, which consist of: six cups of whole wheat flour (preferably organically grown), 1/8 cup of soy flour, 1/8 cup of rye flour, 1/8 cup of cornmeal, 1/8 cup of quinoa flour (pronounced keen-wa; it is an ancient South American grain available in some natural food stores), 1/8 cup of sesame seeds, three tablespoons of wheat germ, two tablespoons of wheat or oat bran, and two teaspoons of salt. Except for the whole wheat flour and salt, any of these may be omitted if they are unavailable. Also, you may add any other dry (hopefully natural) ingredient you wish, since creativity makes baking an adventure instead of a chore. I often add a teaspoon of brewers yeast along with a pinch of torula yeast, which increase nutritional value without affecting taste or the way the dough rises.

5 Next are the liquid ingredients. Dissolve two packets of active, dry yeast in a half cup of 110 degrees water (warm to the touch). In a separate container, dissolve two tablespoons of honey in three cups of lukewarm water. Now add the liquids to the dry ingredients and mix well by hand.

6 In order to become dough, the mixture will require still one more important ingredient: grease. Before you start asking what in the name of health food is grease doing in this recipe, relax. I'm not talking about lard or bacon fat, but a special type of grease, known as elbow grease. If you truly desire good bread, there's no getting around it: you *need* to *knead.* And working the dough properly often means working up a sweat.

7 Don't let this discourage you, though, because it's actually a lot of fun (and my favorite step). Just dump your mixture onto a clean surface and squeeze, twist, pound, punch, pull, push, stretch, and fold for at least twenty minutes. Once again, be creative! It's really a great stress reducer!

8 Having been kneaded, the dough is ready to rise (though you might be ready to collapse). Simply sprinkle a little flour on your working surface and on top of the dough to prevent sticking, and cover with a clean towel. About two hours later you will find that your innocent, little ball of dough, now fully risen, has taken on the appearance of a huge, menacing blob, hungry and anxious to engulf your entire kitchen.

9 Before calling an exorcist or *The National Enquirer,* keep in mind that by casually pressing out the gas within, which just so happens to be the next step, the blob collapses back to its original size. A pair of floured hands will do the job nicely, since flour will prevent the dough from sticking and, in this case, from swallowing you alive.

10 Hopefully, surviving your initial encounter with the blob will boost your confidence level and provide you with the courage needed to face him a second time. Because now the dough must be reshaped into a ball, given another flour treatment, and covered. Once again, the stage is set for his inevitable return, but this time the blob will attain monstrous proportion in only an hour.

11 In the meantime, get your bread pans ready. You'll need two of them, approximately eight inches by four inches. Pour a small amount of oil into each, enough to coat all surfaces of the pans. Any type of vegetable oil will do; just use your imagination. Failure to add any oil, though, will result in loaves of bread that are very stubborn, and sometimes downright ornery, when attempting to persuade them from their cozy shells.

12   By now the dough should be as big and scary as it was previously. Take a deep breath and deflate it just as before. The conquered blob is now ready for division into two equal portions, each of which is to be shaped into a loaf and placed into the oiled pans. At this time, the dough is allowed a half hour to rise for a third and final time. Don't worry. Two small blobs are not nearly as ferocious as one large one.

13   Nevertheless, the yeast will undoubtedly cause yet another transformation, and while this is taking place, preheat your oven to 425 degrees. The arching of the dough over the sides of the pans, as if trying to escape its confines, will signify that the transformation is complete. This will occur nearly simultaneously with your oven reaching the desired temperature.

14   After about ten minutes at 425 degrees, lower the oven to 325 degrees and continue to bake the precious, little loaves for forty-five minutes. These figures are merely very loose guidelines, which can be altered as determined by your creative nature. I've found that longer cooking times and higher temperatures generally produce a thicker, crispier crust.

15   Even if you lose track of time altogether, you'll know when your long-awaited end product has finished baking, for your entire home will be filled with a heavenly aroma. Upon removing the pans from the oven, and then the loaves from the pans, the magnificent smell of freshly baked bread will intensify until it simply becomes overpowering, making the bread itself irresistible. So what are you waiting for? Let the feast begin!

16   Believe me, there's nothing like homemade bread, especially when it's still warm from the oven. The fact that the bread was made by your own hands and creativity and that it contains only natural, healthful ingredients makes it all-the-more satisfying. If you're concerned with good nutrition and love bread as I do, I'm sure you'll agree that this bread is far superior to anything you can buy in the store. I hope I have now inspired you to partake in the ancient art of bread making, just as I was inspired by my grandmother's bread many years ago.

Louie Beuschlein

There are many reasons why Louie's process paper is an excellent example to study. First, the paper has an attention-grabbing, multi-paragraph introduction which leads to a very focused thesis statement: If you would like a basic idea of how to bake your own bread, here is how baking bread is best accomplished for me.

After the introduction, Louie begins his step-by-step explanation of how to prepare and bake bread. His explanation of the process is written in well-organized, well-structured, and well-developed paragraphs. Each paragraph is unified and coherent; the entire essay is also unified and coherent. Louie's outline reflects his control over his writing skills:

    Introduction:
   Thesis Statement: If you would like a basic idea of how to bake your own bread, here is how baking bread is best accomplished for me.

   Body
      mix dry ingredients
      mix liquid ingredients
      knead
      let rise
      deflate
      let rise

prepare pans
deflate
let rise
preheat
bake

Conclusion

Notice that the major steps in the process become, in effect, the topic sentences for the paragraphs. Although not all process papers can be structured and organized in this manner, many of them can be. Simply listing the steps you want to explain is a good starting place for generating the scratch outline or the rough draft.

Louie has developed his essay well. He has written for his audience a clear process which can be followed and then savored. Trust me. Although my wife prefers to use her bread machine, I still toil as does Louie. I have, in fact, tried and enjoyed Louie's recipe; I invite you to do likewise. The process can be completed while you are shackled to your computer writing a process paper for your teacher; besides, when you turn in your paper for grading, you can also give your teacher a loaf of Louie's bread and gain a few brownie (whole wheat?!) points.

Louie's paper also has some personality in it; the essay just doesn't explain the bread-making process, but does so with a voice. In paragraphs six and seven, for example, Louie's sense of humor is quite evident. His use of narration and anecdote in the introduction also adds to the personal voice which is strong in this essay. When the process is complete, when the bread is ready for savoring, Louie provides a nice closing with a personal comment about his grandmother; by mentioning his grandmother, Louie ties the closing to the opening. All in all, Louie's process paper is as unique as his recipe.

THE PROCESS PAPER—A FEW MORE EXAMPLES

Trail and Error

1   **"Warning: Do not attempt to hike from the rim to the Colorado River and back in one day. Many people who attempt this have suffered serious illness or death,"** Kevin read from the sign. I looked out across the canyon. I could not even see the Colorado River. Kevin's voice broke my train of thought, "Well, we'd better get going if we want to hike this puppy before dark!" I shrugged my shoulders, gave Kevin a big grin and said, "Let's do it!"

2   We were barely prepared for the entire trip, let alone a fifteen mile hike into a huge hole in the ground. Kevin and I decided to make the trip to Arizona one month before our spring break began. We could stay with my godfather in Phoenix. While using the Automap on my computer, we realized that we could make a quick stop at the Grand Canyon. We decided that hiking the Grand Canyon would be fun, so we made reservations for two nights at the Grand Canyon Squire Inn.

3   We did not do much planning. We went to a surplus store, found a trail on a map and decided to hike it the following day. It wasn't until six grueling hours later that we realized how we had misjudged the power of this natural wonder. It was during the last couple of miles on our ascent when I realized that our lack of careful planning could have gotten us killed. We were sore and fatigued, but we made it to the top. Many people have not been so lucky. After reading this paper, you, the amateur hiker, will have learned from our mistakes and should be able to successfully hike the Grand Canyon without any major problems.

4 The first step in this process is planning the trip. You need to decide when you want to go to the Grand Canyon. There are many factors to consider when trying to arrange your trip. The south rim of the canyon is open year-round, but the north rim is only open April through the middle of November. During the warmer months, the canyon is packed with tourists, and reservations for many lodges and tours are booked several months in advance. To get information about facilities, services and programs, you can go to the library or to a travel agency. We went to the library and found information about lodging within the Grand Canyon National Park. Since we decided to go in early March, which is not a busy time of the year for the canyon, we were able to make reservations for a four star hotel only a month in advance. Once you have made your plans to visit the Grand Canyon, you need to prepare your body for the hike.

5 In order to hike the Grand Canyon, you must be in good to excellent physical condition. Before we took our trip, I was well into my fourth month of an exercise program that required one and one-half hours of exercise four times a week. My workout included cardiovascular and weight training exercises. I was also playing volleyball two times a week and had done some mild hiking. I thought that I was in excellent physical condition. After hiking the canyon, however, I was completely exhausted. I was sore for two weeks after our hike. This example illustrates why you need to be in good physical condition to hike the Grand Canyon

6 The next step can either take place at home or once you arrive at the Grand Canyon. This step is researching. You need to decide which trail or trails you want to hike. We found it easier to do our research once we arrived at the Grand Canyon. Souvenir and surplus stores, park checkpoints and even hotel gift shops have many free pamphlets and newsletters which give information about the canyon, trails, climate, programs and safety procedures. Most of the surplus stores supply tourists with free maps showing the most-popular and least-difficult trails. The employees are very knowledgeable and can answer almost any question you have about the canyon. We collected all the information we could and decided which trail we wanted to take.

7 There are many things to take into consideration when deciding which trail you want to hike. The amount of time and experience you have are two major concerns. A newsletter, "The Guide," lists all of the major trails that are open for that particular season (in our case March 5–May 25). This guide gives trail names, locations, difficulty levels, distances, and lists of facilities available. Once you have picked the trail that you want to hike, make sure you know the exact distance, location, difficulty level, and location of water and toilets (if there are any). You should also check the current condition of the trail. This last point is especially important in the spring months because there may be icy paths and mudslides due to melting snow. Once you have decided on a trail and have made sure that it is safe to hike, you need to gather the proper equipment for your hike.

8 There are many steps for preparing for your hike. It is best to have your equipment prepared the night before your hike since you most likely will be leaving early the next day. The first thing you should do is find out how the weather will be on the day of your hike. You can get this information from the front desk where you are staying, from a surplus store, from the television or from a newspaper. Once you know the temperature, you should figure that the inner canyon temperatures will be about twenty degrees warmer than the rim temperature. If thunderstorms are in the forecast, a long hike should not be planned. How you plan on dressing depends on the weather. When we went, the rim

temperature was about fifty and the inner canyon temperature was about seventy. Since the temperature at the rim was relatively cool, we dressed in layers. You should wear two pairs of socks to cushion your feet and to prevent blisters. You should pack extra socks in case yours get wet or real sweaty. Good hiking boots are a must. I made the mistake of wearing boots that were too big and ended up with blisters the size of quarters. Depending on the season and which trail you take, sun protection for your skin and a hat for your head are important.

9   The right kinds and amounts of food are another thing to consider when preparing for your hike. You need to pack nutritious, high-energy, low-sugar foods. Bananas and sandwiches are good choices. Avoid high-fat foods because these will make you sluggish. Water is another necessity. It is recommended that the hiker bring at least one gallon of water with him. There have been numerous deaths because people dehydrated.

10   Another necessity for your hike is a small first aid kit. You can purchase one from the surplus store, or you can make your own. The kit should include Band-Aids, gauze, anti-bacterial ointment, Ace bandages and foam pads to put on blisters.

11   You also need a watch to pace your hiking, a flashlight in case the sun sets before you are finished hiking, and you need a camera to capture all of the breath-taking views.

12   The final step in preparing for your hike is to make one final check on the condition of the trail you plan to hike.

13   Now that you have carefully planned and organized your equipment for the hike, it is time to start your adventure. You should probably get started as early as possible. You should figure that the ascent will take approximately twice as long as the descent. Leaving early allows you to hike the trail without the fear of being caught in the dark.

14   As you begin your hike down the canyon, read all of the caution signs which are posted on the trail. There are several signs which warn hikers about the dangers of hiking from the rim to the Colorado River and back in one day. I did not take this information seriously and by the time I had reached the top of the canyon, I was ready to die. Other signs warn about the dangers of feeding the wild animals. Not only can the animals bite, kick or chase you, but giving them human food is bad for their digestive system. When hiking the Grand Canyon, you need to stay on the trails at all times. Every year several people fall to their deaths because they go onto rock outcrops, outside guardrails and attempt dangerous short-cuts. Pace yourself and stop for rest if you become too tired. Another thing that is helpful is to talk to hikers making the ascent. Ask about the condition of the trail and how far they have come. Pay attention to their breathing and body language. If they are struggling, you may want to re-think how far you had planned to travel. The uphill climb is the most difficult part of your hike. Before you begin your ascent, make sure you rest, eat and drink. If there is a place to get water, make sure you refill your supplies. If you are traveling with a slower hiker, make sure you stay with that person and encourage him. The trip uphill is difficult, so you may need to help someone with a backpack. If you or your companions are getting tired and cranky, think positive and provide physical and psychological support to him. I was miserable the last three and a half miles because I had huge blisters on my feet. Kevin got me up that canyon by having a positive mental attitude. He made me believe that I could make it to the top. He helped me with my backpack and constantly mumbled the words, "hot tub," and "foot massage," to get me going. You may have to do this for your companions. Whatever happens, do not get discouraged. You will make it to the top!

15   "If I slip on this ice, I am not going to try to stop myself from falling down this canyon!" I moaned. Kevin trudged behind me mumbling something about hot tubs and mas-
sages. We finally reached the top. My legs were throbbing; my spirit was broken. I slumped
over the sign that had warned us not to attempt this trip in one day and laughed like a
mad woman. "I did it, you bastard! I defeated you! You are nothing!" I yelled as I shook
my fist at the hole I had just climbed out of. I knew that if I could defeat the Grand
Canyon, I could conquer just about anything.

16   Even though my hike was a memorable one, I was miserable. We should have
never attempted to do the whole fifteen mile trip in one day. I hope that by reading my
paper and the mistakes that we made, you will be better prepared for your hike. This way
you can enjoy the breath-taking beauty and mystique of the Grand Canyon without the
nagging pain in your legs.

                                                                                    Jen Caponi

Harder Than It Looks

1   Over the years, I have worked on many cars. From rebuilding an entire car to something as simple as changing the oil, I've done it all. The last job I did was on a 1995 Ford
Mustang, 3.8 liter with a V-6 engine. When I actually sat down and thought of the process
to changing oil, I realized how involved such a simple job is. It takes a lot of time, energy,
and preparation to do this.

2   First of all, you need to determine what types of supplies and equipment are necessary to complete the job. The grade of oil and part number of the oil filter are found in the
owner's manual under the appendix section. If the car did not come with an owner's
manual, this information can then be found by either buying a Chilton's or Haynes Service Manual from an auto parts store or by looking up your car in the parts book near the
oil filters at the auto parts store. Either way, you have several options when it comes to
types of oil and filters. Basically, you need to determine what your driving style is and the
mileage and condition of your engine. Usually, you would want to get supplies that are at
least one step up from the stock replacement. If your driving style is mainly city driving or
a racing style, then a higher performance filter would be necessary. If the engine has
more than 50,000 miles, then an advanced oil such as a synthetic blend would be a good
recommendation. Once you have established what type of supplies you need, purchase
an oil filter and six quarts of oil. The engine and filter hold a total of five quarts combined,
but the extra quart is there just to have if needed.

3   The next step is to determine if you have the recommended tools for the job. Your
checklist would consist of the following: a 15 mm wrench or a preferred 15 mm socket for
ease of use, a pan or bucket capable of holding six quarts of fluid, plenty of clean rags,
an oil filter wrench, WD-40 in case the bolt is stuck, a jack and jack stands, gloves, safety
glasses and a funnel. If some of these items are not on hand, they may be substituted.
An old belt or a long screwdriver may be used to remove the oil filter instead of the oil
filter wrench. Although difficult, it may be possible to remove the filter by hand instead.
The funnel is basically used to keep from spilling oil along the block, but is not necessary.
Since metric wrenches are not as common as standard sizes, an adjustable wrench or
vise grips may be used. Be careful you do not strip the bolt.

4   You must also make sure that the area you choose to work is safe and clean. The ground must be flat and level and as free from debris as possible. A level surface prevents the car from rolling or falling on you as you work. Keeping the area clean prevents contaminants from entering the engine at any time and causing severe damage.

5   Once everything has been established, you are ready to start. Since your oil will drain better when warm, it is a good idea to drive to the parts store to get the necessary supplies. If you already purchased them, you can warm up the engine by first making sure the gear selector is in park, setting the parking brake, and starting the engine and letting it run for about ten minutes at idle. Once the engine is warm, get your supplies and tools together and set them aside.

6   Park your car on a flat and level surface, set the parking brake, and pull the hood release lever. Next, get the jack and jack stands. Position the jack on any part of the front of the frame or on the control arms. Jack it up high enough to get the bucket underneath with a couple of inches to spare for clearance. Position the jack stand near the frame and lower the jack. Now that the car is supported, get in front and open the hood, then support it with the prop rod. Remove the oil filler cap and the dipstick. They are both marked "engine oil," so they are easy to spot. Put them aside on a clean table. Grab your wrench, bucket, and some rags. Lie down next to the passenger side and look directly behind the tire to find the oil drain plug. Start loosening the bolt with the wrench enough so you can do it by hand. Place some rags on the ground and the bucket on them. Remove the bolt completely, being advised that the oil is hot and will spurt out quickly. Allow all the oil to drip drain and then replace the drain plug. Remove the bucket from under the car and set it aside. Grab the oil filter wrench, slip it on the filter and begin loosening slowly. The filter is tough to remove at first, but get it loose and twist it the rest of the way off by hand. Since it is full of oil and very hot, it is advised that you use a rag to help you remove it. Slowly pull it back and up out of the engine compartment and set it next to the bucket.

7   Taking the new filter, place some clean oil on the gasket with your finger and replace it. Be sure to tighten it per the manufacturer's recommendations. Pour four quarts of oil into the engine. Replace the dipstick and filler cap. Check the oil level by removing the dipstick again. It should read low, so add about half a quart. Start the car and check the oil pressure gauge to make sure it rises and settles in the "Normal" range indicated. Let it run for about one minute and shut the car off. Wait one minute for the oil to drain back into the pan and check the level once again. The level should be slightly low, so add the remaining half-quart. Wipe off any oil that spilled onto the valve covers and headers. Close the hood. Jack the car up to remove the jack stand, putting them aside. Lower the car. Put your tools away after cleaning them with a rag. The used oil and filter can later be transported and dropped off at an oil-recycling center.

8   As I have shown, a simple act like changing the oil in a car takes a lot of time and preparation. Having the knowledge is also a necessity. The detail involved can be so tedious, yet if you miss a step, it can cause severe problems for your engine.

Robert Harland

Distressed Waitress

Dear Restaurant Patrons,

1   As a distressed waitress sick of your abuse, I thought I would write you this letter to inform you that I am not a superhuman and can't take anymore of it. My job is very demanding, and putting up with your crap for an hour doesn't help it any. I think you purposely devise a plan to make me crazy and then leave an awful tip, or no tip at all. Haven't you ever heard of leaving at least 10%, maybe even 15%? If you have a bill of $100, please leave something. Contrary to what you think, I am not only there to serve you, but to make some money too. I am now going to describe what we have to go through to make you happy. Hopefully, you will understand why I am so frazzled and cranky by the time you leave, and you may leave just a little more.

2   Although it looks easy enough to get your order, it isn't. Sure, you see me go to a computer, punch a couple buttons on the screen and leave, but that isn't the end of it. I still have to hit the salad bar, the bartenders and then the cooks. After dealing with all of these things, I don't want to have to listen to your complaints about everything. Keep in mind that I am only the server, not the cooks or bartenders. If you don't like something, take it up with them.

3   Before your meal, you usually get a salad. Please have in mind what kind of dressing you want before you come and don't make me stand there and repeat what we have five times. I don't have the time, or the patience, for it. The best kind to get is either coleslaw or applesauce because it takes about three seconds to throw it in a bowl and leave, but if you do have to get an actual salad, don't get really picky because then I will deliberately put everything on it just to piss you off. And do any of you know what a Caesar salad is? If you don't, please ask because it has its own dressing, Caesar dressing, and I hate when you ask for a Caesar salad with French dressing, because then it's a tossed salad. Anyway, getting a salad is no easy task. There are about 20 servers at the salad bar at one time, and it's only made for two or three at the most. There is just way too much pushing and shoving for a salad. After I do get your salads, and a couple broken bones and a bloody nose, I put on a huge (fake) grin and come back to you.

4   OK, so now you have your salads. One step of the process is over, and I have to go to the bar now and get your drinks. Please keep in mind that even though some of these bartenders know what they are doing, some of them don't, and none of them have a bartending license. They are there for the same reason I am, to make some money. Remember how I told you about the computer we punch a couple of buttons on and then leave? Well, that's how everyone gets the orders, and depending on who's working the bar is how fast your drinks come out. Sometimes they are made in about thirty seconds, and other times it takes twenty minutes to get a beer. If your drink comes out in a melted blob with something that resembles whipped cream on top, the bartender made your drink before I even put in the order. I'll try to get them to remake it, but they usually won't. If you don't like it, go to the bar yourself and tell them about it. I don't want to hear it because now I have to go battle with the cooks about your food.

5   Let me tell you a little something about our cooks. They have no idea about what they are doing. Don't ask how they got the job, because I have no clue. We have three expos, or head cooks, and they all have their faults. One of them is just stupid. If there are more than three tickets in the window for him, he starts flipping out and calls a manager back there to help him. The other one is good but he's slow. It takes him about five

minutes to put out a cup of soup, and when he finally does, he whines that it's in the window. There is one that's really good. I don't really have any complaints about him. Depending on who's in the kitchen is how long it will take for your food to come out. Since you have ordered about six plates of food, I have to try and find someone to help me walk all of it, and you don't even eat it all. If you can't eat all of that food, then don't order it because two things happen. I have to hunt down large to go boxes, and I get my hopes up for a larger tip, just assuming that someone will leave me 10% . . . yeah right. And if you want extra ketchup, dressing or any of the condiments that come with your meal, please use what I bring to you, because I really don't appreciate running back to the kitchen and getting it to find that you don't use it. Same goes for drinks; if you don't think you'll drink a refill of what you have, then don't ask for it. It's a huge waste of time.

6   OK, so you have your food and your to go boxes for the wasted food you didn't eat, and it's time for your check. It says right on there that you pay me, so please don't ask if you pay the cashier. Did you see a register on your way in? I usually have enough change to give you, but sometimes I don't, so if you don't get back twelve cents, don't ask. I'm sorry if you are that cheap you can't afford to swallow an extra twelve cents. And try not to give me any big bills, like $100's or $50's, because I probably won't have change for them, and then I have to go hunt some down, which takes awhile, and then you get angry. If you do give me a $100, then leave a decent tip because I know you have it since I just gave you $40 in change. Don't try and pretend you are broke.

7   All right, so now you know what I have to go through to get your food and keep you happy. It may seem like a simple process, but it's really not. I know that I mentioned you leaving a big tip a few times, and I would like to add that sometimes I don't deserve it, but if you think that, just look and see for yourself what I have to do to keep every table I have happy. And this letter isn't meant for every person who goes to a restaurant, but it is meant for about 75% of you. So just keep in mind what your next server has to do and be nice to her because you never know what she/he may be doing to your food in the back. Thank you.

Gwen Clancy

An Incredible Journey to Familyhood

1   Having successfully completed two international adoptions, I feel that I have some useful firsthand information to offer anyone who is thinking of pursuing this avenue as a means of creating, or adding to, a family. The road to the successful completion of an international adoption is long and winding. However, anyone who is well prepared and committed to engage in this kind of an adoption process should not be intimidated by the following procedures.

2   Before getting started, I think it is important to mention that: you will not doubt that you can love an adopted child, a child who does not look like you; that you have considered how this child will be accepted by your extended family; and, if there are not future plans of moving, how well the child will be integrated into your neighborhood and schools.

3   Where to begin? Some people choose an agency and then a country based on their agency's programs or vice versa. With both of my adoptions I chose the countries and later sought out agencies that had programs working in those countries. Make contact with support or international family groups in your area. The Internet is a good starting point for gathering this kind of information. Attend their meetings or social gatherings. Talk to people about their experiences and what worked for them. This is an excellent way to meet people and their kids. Find out who the intercountry adoption co-coordinator in your state is. A call (or several calls) to that person will inform you of what different countries' requirements and/or restrictions are. Your age, if you already have children, religion, prior divorce, if you're single or if you want to specify sex of the child will help you narrow things. With many countries it's most likely that you'll need to spend some time abroad to complete the adoption. Ask about anticipated length of stay for different countries. If time and expense can be managed, traveling to your child's birth country can provide a special immediate bond as well as an understanding of the culture he/she comes from. If travel is not an option for you, look at countries that allow children to be escorted to the United States.

4   As with deciding on a country, choosing an agency can begin by talking to people or networking. Keep in mind that you are not limited to agencies in your own state. Let your fingers do the walking through the Yellow Pages to locate agencies in your area. Go to the library where they will undoubtedly have different publications for adoptive families in their periodicals section. These will contain listings of agencies and what international programs they have. Attend seminars and workshops that are available to you. Gather whatever information you can from these forums by taking and sorting through all pamphlets and brochures. This is how I found the agency for our first adoption. When making inquiries to agencies, you will be asked if you are open to a child with disabilities. Ask how the different countries they work with define disabilities. They can range from mild to severe. Russia, for example, considers a crossed eye to be a disability; this is something that is easily correctable in the U.S.

5   Once you've found an agency that's a good "fit," the next step is to begin the process of complying with state and federal requirements for international adoptions. Contact your nearest INS office (Immigration and Naturalization Service) and request an intercountry adoption packet. This packet will contain the necessary information and forms that must be completed before the U.S. consulate abroad will issue the child a visa and legal alien registration card (green card) to immigrate into the United States. Your agency will be able to guide you through this part of the process.

6   The next step, and perhaps the most daunting, is the paperwork for your dossier. Not only is this to satisfy state and federal requirements, but also the requirements of a foreign government. You will have to have a homestudy done by an adoption caseworker. This involves a series of meetings at your caseworker's office and in your home to explore your motives for adoption, your ability to parent a child, and your family history. Essentially, the homestudy probes into every aspect of your life. Try to keep in mind that when conducting the homestudy your caseworker is trying to help you reach your ultimate goal of becoming a parent, not judge you. You may be asked to write an autobiography. You'll have to have letters that verify your employment and income along with bank statements of your accounts. You will need letters of personal reference from your family, friends, church, employer, and anyone else who can attest to your good character and moral fiber. A doctor's letter to verify good physical and mental health will also have to be included. Some countries will require adopters to have a psychological evaluation. Some may require documentation of infertility if it applies.

7   The final course, which might even take place after that long awaited phone call ("We have a child for you.") is legalization of all your documents. Each one must be notarized, and then certified by your county clerk's office. There they will attach a paper to each document certifying that the notary public is in full force and effect. Then each document must be authenticated by the foreign country's consulate here in the U.S. This is to say that the notarization and certification are authentic and legal. It is imperative that every document has all three.

8   The road to international adoption is indeed long and winding. You will meet many people who will have a profound influence on you, and their contributions in the process will never be forgotten. The road has no end, for once you become a parent, Mom or Dad, you have that privilege for a lifetime. Enjoy the ride!

Heidi Foster

How to Plant a Perennial Garden

1   As I sit on my deck, drinking my morning tea, there is nothing more relaxing than looking out over my blooming perennial garden. Although a lot of hard work and patience are required to prepare a garden of yearly bloomers, the end result is well worth it. If you plan ahead, low maintenance and a chance of spring thru fall blooms are your rewards. Spring is the best time to plant, but fall planting can also be done. Summer planting is not recommended due to high temperatures and dry ground. Here goes; I'll walk you through the basics of preparing a perennial garden.

2   Naturally you need a place to plant or you need to create one. You may choose to remove some grass, or you might already have some space available. If possible, I believe your garden should be visible from your home, so you may view its beauty. If that's not an option, try to choose a location that will allow your garden to be seen from the deck or patio. Being able to see what you've grown and nurtured is the most rewarding part of gardening. Don't worry if the chosen area is only full sun or full shade. There are a tremendous amount of plants to choose from that adapt well in either location.

3   Although digging in the dirt may sound like fun, you may need to shop for the proper garden tools. You'll need to head to your favorite garden center. K-Mart or Wal-Mart offer the best deal, but Franks or Home Depot may have a larger selection. A shovel and rake are a must, and a pad to kneel on is also important. A set of small hand tools for planting is easy to work with, so keep that in mind when making your selection. Important items are a hand shovel, a hand held set of clippers, small edgers and a trowel. If you decide to plant bulbs, a bulb planter is another handy tool.

4   A good solid pair of gardening gloves are a necessity. We must protect our nail polish! You may want to pick up a gardening hat if you're sensitive to the sun or just to stay cooler while working outside. I find it easy to put all my tools and essential items in an old wagon and pull it behind me. It saves a lot of trips to the shed and back. If you don't have any fertilizer at home, put this on your list too. I use the same in my garden as on my lawn, and it works just fine.

5   Preparing your soil is our next task. It's a hard and dirty job, but someone has to do it. You may wish to pay someone to rototill for you if you don't own a machine of your own. Renting a tiller is not very expensive or time consuming. You'll be done in less than an hour depending on the size of your garden. If you choose, the dirt can be turned over with a regular shovel and raked smooth. All the lumps and bumps must be evened out of the garden so you can plant. After the area is smooth, I sprinkle a light layer of fertilizer on the soil and work it in with the tiller or rake.

6   Now is the best part of all, buying the plants! Read through all those great gardening books and catalogs and find out what works well for your area. Different states are in numbered zones which is explained in most books on gardening. Some plants will not tolerate the cold winters, so choose well. Friends and other gardeners are a great source of useful information. Color is another area to think about. You may only want or like certain ones. A really nice garden also has different heights to it, with the taller plants in back, medium in the middle and shortest in the front for best visibility. Any plant you buy from a garden center has a tag to inform you of the plant height, blooming time, and how long it will be in bloom. A planned garden can have color from early spring until late fall. This is the time to plan, plan and plan some more. So choose and buy your plants and get ready to play in the dirt again. It's time to plant.

7   Pick a cool day to start planting and wear old clothes so you don't ruin any good ones. The tags with your plants will indicate how far apart to space them. Please follow these directions. I know they look small and innocent now, but in a few years you'll be cursing as you pull out an overgrown plant. Believe me, I know. Bulbs can be planted now for blooming next spring or you can wait and do that in the fall. Anything you plant underground and cover up should be marked. You don't want to plant over it or worse yet, pull it up next year thinking it's a weed. I use popsicle sticks. They're cheap, and they don't rot away over the winter. If the sticks don't appeal to you, ready-made markers are available.

8   Decide if you want a border around your garden and what you would like to use to make it. You may choose from some options, such as: a low fence, bricks, stones, wood or plastic edging. Just remember, where grass meets border means you will have some edging to do. Your next step is to mulch around your plants to keep the weeds to a minimum and the moisture in the soil. I prefer cypress mulch because of its rich red color and durability. Use approximately a 2–3 inch layer over the entire garden, except over the plants of course. By next spring you'll have to replenish and revive it a little because the mulch will disintegrate over the winter.

9   Don't forget to water your new garden (unless Mother Nature does it for you). Water every day for about 45 minutes for 3 or 4 days straight and then twice a week after that depending on rain fall amount. Make sure you periodically pull any weeds so they don't overrun your garden. Now, brew up that cup of tea or coffee and sit back and enjoy the beauty of your new addition.

Sharon Chorzempa

PROCESS—POSSIBLE APPROACHES

- how to _____
- how to rebuild a _____
- how to forget a _____
- how to break a_____
- how to plant a _____
- how to can a _____
- how to earn a_____
- how to lose a _____
- how to tell a_____
- how to return a _____
- how to cheat on a _____
- how to win a _____
- how to mend a_____
- how to bake a _____
- how to eat a_____
- how to save a_____
- how to report a _____
- how to clean a _____
- how to take a _____
- how to deliver a_____
- how to "steal" a_____
- how to wash a _____
- how to eliminate a_____
- how to seduce a_____
- how to roll a _____

- how to hunt for a _____
- how to see a _____
- how to close a _____
- how to open a_____
- how to discover a _____
- how to hide a _____
- how to overcome a fear of_____
- how to ride a _____
- how to handle a _____
- how to view a_____
- how to build a _____
- how to apply for a _____
- how to paint a _____
- how to start a _____
- how to quit a _____
- how to make a _____
- how to plan a _____
- how to buy a _____
- how to fix a _____
- how to change a _____
- how to please a _____
- how to catch a _____
- how to enjoy a _____
- how to avoid a _____
- how to select a _____

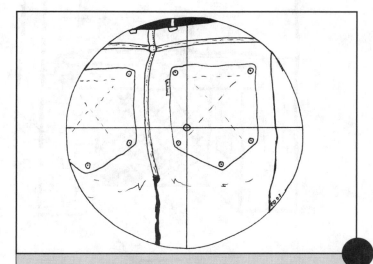

In Steinbeck's <u>Of Mice and Men</u>, George shoots Lenny in the end.

THE PROCESS PAPER—YOUR TURN

1 Choose a process you want to explain or describe. Select something with which you are familiar—such as a hobby, an interest, or a process you perform on the job.

2 Analyze your reading audience. Think of what terms or steps might require extra definition or clarification.

3 Think through the process and try to logically break it down into steps.

4 Jot down the major steps of the process. This should be your outline. Examine the steps you have listed. Are they in proper order? Will they produce paragraphs? (Try to avoid numerous short, choppy paragraphs or a lot of short, numbered steps.)

5 Write the rough draft of your paper.

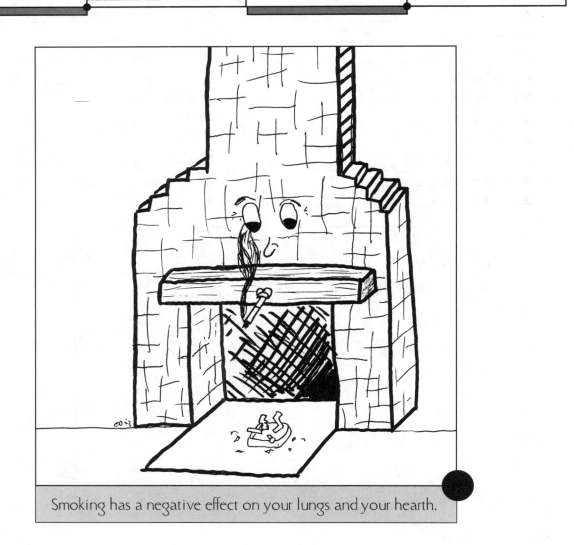

Smoking has a negative effect on your lungs and your hearth.

PROCESS PAPER PLAN SHEET

Part One: List several processes you are interested in or that you perform at home, school, and/or work and that could be the topic for your paper.

_____

_____

_____

_____

_____

Part Two: Choose one of these processes, construct a thesis statement, and list the major steps in the process.

Thesis Statement: _____

_____

Major Steps in the Process: _____

_____

_____

_____

_____

_____

_____

_____

_____

_____

Part Three: Write a more-complete outline for your process paper. Use the extended lines for the major steps, the shorter lines for supporting information.

SELF-EVALUATION SHEET: PART ONE

Assignment: _____

Strong points of this assignment:

_____

_____

_____

_____

_____

_____

_____

Weak points of this assignment:

_____

_____

_____

_____

_____

_____

_____

General comments:

_____

_____

_____

_____

_____

_____

_____

_____

(over)

SELF-EVALUATION SHEET: PART TWO

What were the strong points of your last writing assignment?

_____

_____

_____

_____

_____

_____

What were the weak points of your last writing assignment?

_____

_____

_____

_____

_____

_____

What have you done to correct those weaknesses in this assignment?

_____

_____

_____

_____

_____

_____

Evaluator's Name _____ Section _____ Date _____

PEER-EVALUATION SHEET: PEER-EVALUATOR #1

Writer's Name _____ Essay's Title _____

> **Directions:** (1) Remember not to write on another student's paper. Instead, use this form. (2) Offer concrete, specific comments using the terminology of writing (e.g., "The development in paragraph four might be improved by adding a brief example." or, "Check structure on page 3.")

What do you see as the strong points of this writing assignment: _____

_____

_____

_____

_____

What areas do you feel might need additional work: _____

_____

_____

_____

_____

Do you see any areas of grammar/mechanics (e.g. usage, spelling, fragments) that might need attention: _____

_____

_____

_____

_____

General comments: _____

_____

_____

_____

_____

Evaluator's Name _____ Section _____ Date _____

PEER-EVALUATION SHEET: PEER EVALUATOR #2

Writer's Name _____ Essay's Title _____

> **Directions:** (1) Remember not to write on another student's paper. Instead, use this form. (2) Offer concrete, specific comments using the terminology of writing (e.g., "The development in paragraph four might be improved by adding a brief example." or, "Check structure on page 3.")

What do you see as the strong points of this writing assignment: _____

_____

_____

_____

_____

What areas do you feel might need additional work: _____

_____

_____

_____

_____

Do you see any areas of grammar/mechanics (e.g. usage, spelling, fragments) that might
need attention: _____

_____

_____

_____

_____

General comments: _____

_____

_____

_____

_____

The Example Paper

OVERVIEW

When I sit at my old roll-top desk reading and evaluating my students' papers, sooner or later—usually sooner—I find myself writing either the abbreviation **ex.** or the word **example** in the margin of many of the essays. Although I have accepted this act as part of my destiny, I still try to change the course of human events and prevent these marginal scribbles. In other words, I nag my students in class to try always to impregnate examples (That phrase always wakes them up!) into their writing. Besides simply enjoying the role of nag, I urge my students to use examples for several reasons. Examples aid communication by clarifying and illustrating main points. Examples make writing vivid and memorable. Examples also add interest. They grab the reader and say, "I bet I can make you remember this point."

So allow me to nag you. Always remind yourself to use examples to clarify, to illustrate, and to support main ideas and/or general statements. Not only will your writing and your communication improve, but as I always tell my students, "If you nag yourself, then I don't have to. And mono-nagging beats stereo-nagging any day."

THE EXAMPLE PAPER

Using examples is one of the most-effective ways of illustrating and explaining ideas. An idea that is general and perhaps abstract can be made very concrete and very clear through the use of an example or several related examples. This is a principle that you are aware of and make use of in everyday communication.

The next time you find yourself in a conversation or an argument with someone, listen to what you say. You will likely use examples to explain ideas. Perhaps you have just bought a new house and moved in. You are talking to the builder and telling him you do not like some of the finishing work inside the house. He might ask for specifics. You reply that the trim does not all have the same finish and that some of the doors have problems. If this is not enough information to communicate your dissatisfaction, use detail to develop the examples. Tell the builder that the door to your daughter's bedroom will not stay open because it is hung incorrectly and slowly creeps shut. Tell him that the baseboard around the upstairs hall is lighter than the baseboard in the rest of the house. At this point in the conversation, the builder should have a clear understanding of your original statement: *some of the finishing work inside the new home is not done satisfactorily.*

This is the basic premise behind the use of examples to explain ideas. The writer has a general idea in mind that he or she wants to communicate to the reader; this general idea is called the thesis statement. To develop the thesis statement, the writer uses a series of related examples. To develop the examples, the writer uses detail. Mastering this process is the first step in learning to write exposition. Examples are obviously very effective for explaining, clarifying, supporting, and/or illustrating a thesis statement.

 GUIDELINES FOR WRITING AN EXAMPLE ESSAY

- **One,** be certain that each example is related directly to the thesis statement. Choose at least two and no more than four. Theoretically, the number of examples to choose from is infinite. Select the three or so that would be most-effective in developing the main idea. Trying to explain an idea using only one example is possible, but it means that the example must be exceptional.

- **Two,** develop the examples with specific, concrete detail. Without the development, the examples are not effective. In our example situation of the house that needed work, one example is the doors. Merely mentioning "the doors" does not communicate what the speaker really wanted to say. The details had to be added to the examples. Call upon the detailing skills you developed in the description unit; good examples mean your reader understands fully the points you are making; understanding is aided by detail.

- **Three,** structure and organize the essay. You have at least two choices: deduction and induction. **Deduction** is the thought process that begins general and becomes specific. **Induction** is the thought process that begins specific and becomes general. In an example essay, the general section is the thesis statement, and the specific section is the examples. The following outlines illustrate how deduction and induction are used to organize and structure an example essay:

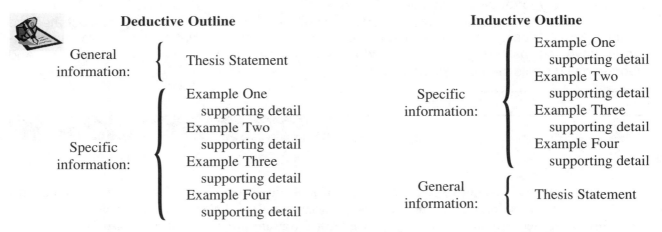

Deductive Outline

General information: { Thesis Statement

Specific information: {
Example One
  supporting detail
Example Two
  supporting detail
Example Three
  supporting detail
Example Four
  supporting detail

Inductive Outline

Specific information: {
Example One
  supporting detail
Example Two
  supporting detail
Example Three
  supporting detail
Example Four
  supporting detail

General information: { Thesis Statement

As you learned in the chapter on paragraphing, deduction and induction can be applied to any type of writing. The example essay, however, is simply a good opportunity to reinforce these skills and to acquire some practice with these basic techniques of organization. As with many of the other concepts you'll learn about in this text, deduction and induction will be useful to you in various writing assignments.

DEDUCTION

You may be familiar with the deductive process because of exposure to it in the study of philosophy, science, math, or logic. *Deduction* implies thought or understanding that moves from the general to the specific. The generalization is stated first, followed by the specifics which led to that generalization.

When an essay is organized deductively, the generalization serves as a thesis statement. The examples serve as the specific support for the generalization. The overall movement of thought in the paper is from general to specific. To illustrate deduction, let's look at an example.

Christmas Eve: Calm Caroling or Lofty Comedy

1   *Joy To The World, O Come All Ye Faithful* and *Silent Night* are traditional carols which are especially meaningful when sung as part of the Christmas Eve Midnight Mass celebration. For this ceremony, the organist and choir members have put in many hours of practice trying to reach a performance level close to perfect. When the time to begin arrives, the church is dimly lit by candlelight, and every seat in every pew is filled in hushed anticipation of the coming of the Holy Child. But, did you ever wonder what is going on behind the scenes in the choirloft? Do you think it is as calm and serene as the music? To be honest, it can be calm serenity, but it can also be controlled chaos or comic relief. Perhaps you think I jest, but as organist and choir director, I have memories of Christmas Eves past that are delightful and humorous.

2   Our choir begins caroling at 11:30 P.M. and continues until Mass begins with a formal procession at midnight, after which the pastor places the baby Jesus in the manger. One year the choir had concluded caroling, and it seemed everyone was ready to begin. The deacon, however, did not approach the microphone to greet the congregation and announce the processional hymn. We waited a few moments and to avoid an awkward silence, began singing another carol, then another, then another. Latin, English, Polish . . . we sang anything to fill the void. Finally, the deacon came bustling up the stairs and whispered in my ear, "Keep singing. The pastor isn't here yet. We sent the altar boys to the rectory to get him. He must have fallen asleep." Our pastor eventually showed up, and the service proceeded as usual, although it was earmarked by an unusually short and sweet sermon.

3   The snoozing pastor was a time to remember, but the year the lead soprano arrived at 11:29 is unforgettable and comical in retrospect. At the time, I seriously considered strangulation as a possible remedy to the situation. You see, she not only arrived at the last minute, but she had begun her celebrating a little early. Her distinctive voice is usually loud, and the liquor she had consumed made her sing even louder. That same "joy juice" also helped her reach the decision that the organist should pick up the tempo. Of course, no amount of pleading looks, gentle shushing, or pointed glares produced any results. She was off in her own little world of fast and furious Christmas music. Finally, the ladies on each side of her gave a polite (or not-so-polite) nudge to the ribs each time she got carried away. When the final alleluia was sung, and *We Wish You a Merry Christmas* was concluded, this darling diva had sobered up enough to get down the stairs and out the door very quickly. She must have realized that she was fingered as the victim of a serious crime.

4   If the memory of that tipsy soprano makes me chuckle, recalling the young man who tried to join in the choir's Christmas Eve performance makes me pensive because of his sincerity. Because Midnight Mass is well attended, the overflow crowd fills the vestibule, the aisles, and the choirloft. Once, a young fellow was standing in the side aisle, gently swaying as he loudly prayed with the congregation and with the celebrant. His hair was long and unkempt, his clothes were dirty, and he looked like drugs were a part of his lifestyle. The ushers asked him to leave, but instead he found his way to the loft, and proceeded to "sing along with Melodie." Consequently, I had to go over and carefully

explain to him that to sing with the choir he would have to attend the practices. His glassy eyes looked at me, and in a slurred voice, he asked for copies of the music because that would be helpful to him. I repeated that he couldn't sing with us because he had not attended the rehearsals and that I would not give him the music. He looked me in the eye, slowly nodded his head, and quietly went down the stairs. He didn't leave the building, however, but went up the center aisle to the front altar and proceeded to pray and sing with the priests. This really woke up the congregation. One of the assistants eventually took him by the hand and escorted him to the door. I sometimes wonder if that young man remembers his actions that memorable Christmas night.

5   Obviously, the choir does most of the singing on Christmas Eve, but some parts of the service are designated to be sung by the deacon. We once were blessed with "good ol' George" who conducted himself in a pompous manner every time he donned his deacon robes. George's speaking voice was pleasant and his enunciation was clear, but despite these facts, his mission every time he sang was to seek out and find strange new notes. As a result, no matter how the choir tried (and try they did), they always sounded awful because the women responded in high notes and the men responded in low notes. Of course, "good ol' George" thought he was Mario Lanza and always volunteered to do the chanting. He is gone now, moved to another state, and we miss the unique flavor he brought to our pastoral celebrations. We are genuinely pleased, however, that he took his strange notes with him.

6   Yes, Christmas is a very special time because of the very special people who have provided me with a multitude of extraordinary memories. The pastors, choir members, deacons, and even strangers have added hectic and frantic joy to my life. This year, as our choral preparation for this blessed holiday begins, I wonder what marvelous surprises Midnight Mass will provide. Will it be calm serenity, frantic chaos, or lofty comedy? I can't wait to find out.

Melodie French

Melodie's essay is an excellent example of an example paper. There are several features about Melodie's essay that I would like to analyze for you. These are the features that all example papers, whether deductive or inductive, should possess.

First of all, the paper is fun to read; it has energy, energy that leads me to believe that Melodie enjoyed writing her essay. I don't think she wrote it just for me as her teacher; rather, I think that she had some thoughts and feelings that she wished to share with her readers. Her desire to communicate her "memories of Christmas Eves past" gives her a purpose and a focus for writing.

Secondly, the paper is well-organized and well-structured. Melodie's essay begins with an introduction that clearly focuses on a thesis/purpose. The body of the essay consists of four unified and coherent paragraphs, each one developed in support of an example that supports and illustrates her main thesis. The paper also has an excellent closing paragraph.

The development of the paper is also quite good. Each body paragraph is well-developed. Notice—and this is very important—the amount of specific and concrete detail in each paragraph. In paragraph four, for example, Melodie describes the young man very specifically for us. He "sways gently and prays loudly." "His hair was long and unkept, his clothes were dirty, and he looked like drugs were a part of his lifestyle." He has "glassy eyes" and he speaks in "a slurred voice." As Melodie continues to describe the young man and his actions, I can picture him—vividly—in my mind's eye as he celebrates Midnight Mass in his own way. Melodie's description makes me glad to be a writing teacher and not a choir director.

Finally, Melodie's essay is a good example of the use of deduction, the thought process which moves from general to specific. Melodie's essay begins with a very general idea: "I have numerous memories of Christmas Eves past that are delightful and humorous." This is indeed a very general statement about all of the Midnight Masses at which Melodie has participated and celebrated as organist and choir director.

To support her generalization, Melodie gets very specific. She writes about the snoozing pastor, the tipsy soprano, the strange young man, and the pompous deacon. These single, specific examples support the general idea (thesis) which Melodie has reached about being an organist and choir director at Midnight Mass.

INDUCTION

Induction is the reverse of deduction. *Induction* refers to the thought process that moves from specific to general. The specifics or the particulars are presented first, and they lead up to the generalization or the thesis.

Some writers believe induction is harder to write, since the paper actually begins with its support, or body, and thus lacks a formal introduction or statement of purpose. Many writers feel that induction is a more-creative approach, however, one that may intrigue or interest a reader more than the deductive approach.

Although induction is actually not any harder to write than deduction, there are a couple problems with it that you might be able to avoid. Some writers find it difficult to maintain unity. Outlining should help you solve this problem. A second problem is that the paragraphs that end or begin examples are frequently hard to write, since you might not want the reader to know the point you are trying to communicate. (Perhaps you want the reader to be in suspense until you state your generalization.) The best advice I can give you is to write the rough draft and follow the outline. Then go back and smooth out the rough spots between paragraphs and between examples.

One of the biggest problems my students face is with the last section of the induction paper—the combined statement of purpose and the conclusion. The most-often asked question is, "How much do I have to write?". This is hard to answer, because it depends upon your topic and your approach. The best answer I can give is that if the examples are well-detailed and well-developed, *they will* do most of the communicating, and the essay's last section will be easier to write.

To understand induction a little better, study the following example.

Building Character

1   I was twelve, and it was the first week in May; my catechism class was given the opportunity to vote for one boy and one girl who would have the privilege of placing a wreath of flowers on our statue of the Blessed Virgin Mary. I wanted to be chosen very much. Each of us was given a piece of paper to write down the name of the pupil we felt worthy to partake of this honor. The boys were told to vote for a boy and the girls to vote for a girl. I proceeded to whisper to two of my classmates, "You vote for me and I'll vote for you." I then voted for myself. My dream came true! I won! After crowning the Blessed Virgin Mary, the boy who won and I kneeled on the floor in the front of the classroom and said prayers with the entire class. Sadly, I didn't feel honored. I felt I had achieved my goal by being dishonest, and I felt unworthy and unhappy.

2　　　One Saturday afternoon a few weeks later, my girlfriend and I decided to visit the neighborhood dimestore. We dared each other to steal something. I took a scarf and a roll of Tums. I felt very daring and smug as I walked out of that store! Later that day, I realized I had broken the seventh commandment: "Thou shall not steal." I knew I would have to go to confession to tell a priest what I had done. In addition, I had one week to worry and feel guilty before I could confess. I approached each oncoming day with more dread than the day before. Finally, with a heavy heart, I made my confession. Father told me to give back what I had stolen. It was too late for me to return the Tums, but I replaced the scarf as quickly as I had taken it. With a sigh of relief, I had cleaned my slate and cleared my conscience.

3　　　Last but not least, the piece de resistance! My school was competing in a "Clean Up Week" slogan contest with other elementary schools. Each classroom was to send in three entries that the students thought were best. My slogan wasn't picked, and I felt very disappointed and unfairly treated. I strongly felt my slogan was better than the three my classmates selected. A few days later, two girls and I were asked to sort out the slogans. My room sent in four slogans because I slipped mine in with the winners! One month later our school had an Awards assembly. I sat in the back of our large auditorium with my class. There were two winners in the slogan contest from our school. I was one of them. I had been accurate when I had sensed my slogan was good, but now that seemed unimportant because I was sitting in the middle of classmates who had not picked my slogan! I felt paralyzed with fear from the top of my head to the tip of my toes. Amidst clapping, I walked the long way down to the stage to receive my "Honorable Mention" certificate from the principal of our school. When I returned to my seat, a classmate turned around and said aloud, "We didn't pick her slogan." The girl next to her told her to be quiet. Later on, I wondered why the girl told her friend to be quiet instead of agreeing with her. Years later, looking back, I realized that the girl who told her friend to be quiet had also been one of the girls who had sorted the slogans. I theorized that she may have seen me slip my slogan in with the winners, and perhaps she related this to our teacher. Our teacher may have told her not to say anything knowing that if my slogan won that would be reprimand enough. Nothing else was ever said.

4　　　I was very unhappy, frightened and sorry when I encountered these predicaments. I look back now and smile, because I experienced moral growth through these episodes that helped me to become the kind of person I'd always wanted to be: honest!!

Sandra Schmidt

An outline of the preceding example shows its inductive organization:

Specific
information:
{

Example One: Voting for herself instead of her friends
　supporting detail
Example Two: Stealing with her friend
　supporting detail
Example Three: Submitting her slogan after her
　classmates voted against it
　supporting detail

General
information:
{

Thesis: These episodes helped me to become the
　kind of person I'd always wanted to be:
　honest!!

Note that when an essay is organized inductively it does not have an introductory paragraph; the essay begins with the support section. The essay ends with the thesis. Sometimes the thesis is stated in one paragraph and the essay concludes with a separate paragraph; this is a matter determined by the amount of information which needs to be communicated and the personal preference of the writer. Transitions are important in all writing, but especially so in induction. The writer did a good job of using transitions between paragraphs to lend coherence to the essay.

STUDENT EXAMPLES

Here are a few more examples of example. You'll find induction and deduction and a variety of topics and styles.

A Cat Tale

1   Cats are highly intelligent and able to communicate very clearly and effectively their responses to people. They are known to be very independent, free spirits and are often inaccurately accused of being aloof and distant. From our first cat Clochard (which means "tramp" or "hobo" in French), we learned a great deal about effective communication.

2   Clochard was the first in a series of "gift cats" and thus our first experience in living with a cat. He was small and black, with beautiful green eyes and an especially thick, bushy tail. He was a tramp—alone, hungry, frightened, and obviously very much in need of a home. Quietly but persistently, he arrived in our midst late one night, just after our marriage, as we were in the process of packing and preparing to move to Chicago. He was affectionate, purred loudly to convince us of this, and quickly charmed us into taking him along.

3   Clochard, we were to discover, was an unaltered male cat with very definite ideas and a distinct personality. He apparently decided early in our acquaintance that he didn't approve of my husband, Frank, didn't want to encourage his presence in the house, and was prepared to be very direct in making his feelings abundantly clear. At the same time, he was openly affectionate with me, and I gradually realized what he wanted was a "ménáge á deux."

4   Like all cats, Clochard was most alert in the middle of the night. One of his favorite activities consisted of racing wildly through the house at strange times in the early morning hours. We never knew what prompted these frantic outbursts of activity, but they seemed to occur frequently. What made them quite distinctive, however, was the way Clochard would include our bed as part of his itinerary. He would arrive very suddenly, leaping very deliberately on Frank's sleeping form and at the same time uttering a bloodcurdling "attack meow," then streak off triumphantly. This was something Clochard obviously enjoyed because he did it repeatedly. It was an effective way to get a response from Frank, too.

5   Clochard obviously felt the need to express his feelings in a more-direct way, however, and he soon came up with an innovative approach, which I was fortunate enough to observe. It was early evening, and Frank had arrived home from work after a long and very tiring day. He sat down quietly to read the newspaper, legs crossed, looking relaxed and peaceful, totally absorbed in the news of the day. Clochard walked over to him very purposefully, turned around, lifted his thick, bushy tail high in the air, and proceeded with great accuracy to "mark" Frank's leg. There was a startling sound of water as a small stream sprayed through the air and trickled down the pant-leg, dripping on the carpet below. This prompted a rather-dramatic response from Frank, and Clochard was wise enough to disappear quickly and totally until calm was restored.

6   Having discovered how entertaining and gratifying his behavior could be, Clochard decided to refine his skills. He waited, of course, until an appropriate amount of time had passed, hoping our collective memories would fade. This time, he chose a Saturday afternoon when Frank was taking a nap on the sofa. Frank had removed his shoes and left them next to the coffee table. The telephone rang, and Frank, suddenly awake, groped for his shoes before answering the phone. I was in another room but heard the piercing scream as Frank discovered that while he slept, his shoe had been carefully and quietly "filled" by Clochard. It was quite a remarkable feat of accuracy, in fact, because there was not a drop outside of the shoe itself. Once again, the cat, triumphant, went into hiding until the air had cleared.

7   But Clochard saved his best effort for one last spectacular display. In our bedroom we have a wonderful canopy bed. Clochard had discovered he could leap up into the canopy and from there have a very comprehensive view of his surroundings. If he felt we were sleeping too late and might perhaps forget about his breakfast, he could pounce down on us and thereby get our attention very quickly. On this particular occasion, however, Clochard felt inspired to try a new approach to the morning wake-up call. In a remarkable display of agility, even for a cat, he positioned himself directly over Frank's head and proceeded to urinate down on him from his perch on the canopy above. I woke from a deep sleep with the strange sensation of being near a tropical rain forest but quickly realized my error. As I recall it, Frank's response was immediate, quite verbal, and in addition to a number of colorful expletives, included several loud death threats directed at Clochard. I must confess that I had actually grown very fond of the cat and felt considerable relief in the knowledge that cats have nine lives. I sensed somehow that he would need them all.

8   Although Clochard remained with us for the rest of his natural life, he subsequently spent his nights in a separate room. When he eventually came to the end of his ninth life, it was from complications of cystitis—which Frank called "poetic justice!" From Clochard we learned that cats can communicate clearly and directly (one might even say "pointedly"), without any need for words.

Nina Thorp

Anything a Boy Can Do . . .

1   When I was about 10 years old, my mother was always telling me I was a tom-boy, and I was always rolling my eyes at her. Was I really a tom-boy? I can remember the crying fits whenever I had to put on a dress for a special occasion. I can also remember my red-hooded sweatshirt that was so torn up and old, that every time I wasn't looking, my mother threw it in the garbage. And I remember digging in the garbage to retrieve it every time she did. Thinking back on some of the situations I got myself into, I guess I really was a tom-boy. Let me share.

2   The railroad tracks were always a popular hangout for me and my friends. At the bottom of one of the tracks was a big area with high grass and small paths through it called Farmers Field. Both the railroad tracks and the field were private property with big "No Trespassing" signs posted all over. But this didn't stop us from walking along the tracks looking for adventure, or putting pennies down on them to be flattened. One day while we were on the tracks, we heard the railroad police yelling at us (was there ever such a thing?), and we all knew that they carried pepper guns to shoot trespassing kids.

So, we ran down into Farmers Field and, on our hands and knees, crawled out as fast as we could. When we were sure of our escape, we all stood up. My friends were staring at me. I screamed "What!" at them. They informed me my long hair was full of burs (those sticky-round things that are common in woody areas). We pulled and pulled, but could not get them out. My hair looked like a rat's nest! Oh, why didn't I put my hood up! My mother would take one look at me and know where I had been. And since I was not allowed on the railroad tracks, we went to my girlfriend's house to figure out a way to get the burs out. Our bright idea was to coat my hair with an entire economy size jar of Vaseline and slide the burs out. It worked, but if you did not know this, Vaseline does not wash out of your hair. So, after about 20 hair washings, I had to take my greasy head home to my mother and confess everything. After being yelled at for what seemed like forever, and after dumping three bottles of baby powder on my head to absorb the Vaseline, I was cured. I became known as bur-head for a long time after that.

3   The next incident that comes to mind is when my friends and I thought it would be fun to hop across garage roofs on our way home from school. Now, don't let me forget to mention it was winter time. Smart, huh. Well, after climbing up onto the top of a garage roof, we were to jump across to the next roof, all the way down the alley. I was last. After all my friends successfully made their jump, I walked to the edge of the roof to make sure how far across the jump really was. As I turned to head back up the garage roof, I slipped on a sheet of ice. I fell off the roof onto a big chain-link fence, hung there a minute, and then fell onto the asphalt of the alley. Was I ever in pain. I had blood running down my face, out of my hand and from my knees. Luckily, it was nothing too serious. As I walked home, I thought about how my mom was going to kill me this time. When I got home I started crying really hard, and with the quick thinking of a 10-year-old, told her how I had been run over by a herd of eighth graders rushing out of the alley. I don't know if she believed my story, but she felt sorry enough for my battered appearance that she accepted it.

4   Lastly, what comes to mind is the flag-pole swinging incident. I went to a city grammar school with a huge front school yard. Around the school yard was a four-foot high iron fence that had spiked poles spaced about ten inches apart, all the way around. In the corner of the school yard was a giant flag pole. After school, my friends and I would go back and hang-out at the school yard. Well, the flag pole had all this rope hanging down from it on this particular day. We thought up the brilliant idea of taking this rope, backing up as far as we could, running towards the fence, and with a flying leap sailing over the fence, clearing it, and then letting go to end up on the other side. After many successful attempts at this, I decided to do it one last time. I ran, jumped, sailed and let go. Only, this time, my pant leg got caught on the iron spike and ripped my jeans all the way up the back and landed me flat on my face. Amazingly, I hurt nothing but my pride. As I tied my red-hooded sweatshirt around my waist, I headed home to mom again. I couldn't think of anything to tell her, so I told the truth. I was grounded for a month, and a phone call to the school got that rope taken care of for good.

5   I am sure I did much more than this (I vaguely recall a garbage-picking stage), but these incidents stick out the most in my mind. I cringe now to think of how dangerous these things were and how lucky I am to have survived with only a few bumps and bruises. Thank goodness I discovered boys were more fun to be with than to act like. When my mother reminds me now of how much of a tom-boy I was, I look at my precious 6-year-old little girl. And I swear, I will never buy her a red-hooded sweatshirt, and I will dress her in frilly dresses as often as I can. I don't think I can survive a tom-boy. By the way, Mom, whatever did happen to my sweatshirt?

Chris Bowman

Dishonesty Hurts

1   Lies can get you into so much trouble. Being dishonest seems like the easy way out at times, but usually it is the worst way out. Pretty soon you are telling lie after lie just to cover up the other ones. Eventually, you'll mess your story up somewhere, and when you do, it all blows up in your face. And boy, does it hurt! You not only hurt yourself, but you hurt the others that were involved. I now see why being honest from the beginning is the best way to deal with situations that come your way.

2   One of the worst lies that I have ever told was one that should have gotten me into a lot of trouble, and now that I think about it, I have no idea how I got away with it! I was in fourth grade, and I was mad at my mom one morning. I ended up walking home from school that day, and on the way home I decided to plan something that would upset her. Don't ask me how or why I came up with the idea, but using sick creativity and imagination, I did. I told her that while walking home, someone had tried to kidnap me. I gave her a brief story of the "events" that took place and then sat and watched her reaction. She flipped out. I didn't want the lie to go that far, but when she started crying, I decided that I was too scared to tell her I had lied. Before I knew it, the police were sitting in my front room asking me all kinds of questions. Somehow, I made up a full description of the "kidnapper" and gave them my story. I cried the whole time because I knew what I had done was wrong. In the end, I even had to go down to the police station to make a record of what happened. I felt horrible, and that night I decided this was a secret that no one must ever find out. Now, after all these years, I still find it unbelievable that I made up that lie. How could I hurt my family like that? I decided that the best thing to do would be to come clean, and so a few years ago I told my mom what really happened. Not surprisingly, she told me that I should have been honest from the beginning, but what could we do now?

3   Another incident that comes to mind when I think about being dishonest is the hit-and-run accident. Yes, I did say hit-and-run. I had just gotten my driver's license a month before and was still pretty nerve-wracked about driving. On this particular day, it had been raining so badly it had started to flood. I decided to head for the mall to go shopping. I parked, shopped, and then decided it was time to leave. As I was backing out, I accidentally hit the car next to me (gently, I might add). I didn't know what to do. I kinda just froze with my hands on the wheel and my foot pressed hard on the brake. I looked quickly around the lot to see if anyone had seen what I had done. Nobody appeared to be around, so I finished backing out and left (going down the wrong way)! A week went by, and I thought I was in the clear. I had told my best friend about it because I felt terribly guilty. Yet, I thought I had gotten away with it. Boy was I surprised when my mom asked me if I had gotten into any accidents with the car. "No" was the only word that seemed to escape my mouth. She showed me a letter she received in the mail from the police department. It said someone had witnessed what I had done. We had to go down and file an accident report. We went a few days later, and I was really scared. I gave him my version of the story, and he told me I would need to go to court. Court was a horrible experience. The judge found me guilty and had me pay for the damage done to the woman's car. In addition, I had to attend traffic school and write a five hundred word essay on what I learned from the experience. Boy, did I have a lot to write!

4   Being dishonest has gotten me nowhere, but the hit-and-run incident taught me a lot. It showed me that I need to be responsible for my actions. I need to be willing to face the consequences when I screw things up. I don't want to live my life dishonestly, and I certainly don't want to be looked at as a liar. In the end, I can honestly say that I was punished for my actions. I didn't deserve to get away with my dishonesty, especially when I am being the most dishonest with myself.

Lauren Allie

True Friends

Dear Brian,

1   For the past few hours, I have been sitting here in my room attempting to get caught up on some homework I have successfully avoided all weekend. But my mind keeps returning to an analysis of our friendship. Particularly, I keep thinking of how I am beginning to get the impression that our friendship works only if I am there to serve your needs and only if I don't ask you to do the same. You might not want to hear what I need to say, but I do need to say these things.

2   Approximately two months ago, you had your car in the shop for repairs. For nearly a week you were without transportation. Well, more accurately, for nearly a week my car and I were there to take you many of the places you had to be. I took you to work and picked you up; I got you to school and back; I made sure that I checked with you before I made plans to go anywhere because I didn't want to leave you stranded. On one occasion, I gave up going to a movie because I knew you had an interview for a summer internship and my getting you there was important to you. It's true that you always thanked me and contributed some funds toward gas. But this past weekend when I really needed a lift to work because my car wouldn't start, you said that you were sorry but that you were "tied up" and couldn't get away for a couple of hours. I had to take a cab because I couldn't reach anyone else. I spent almost as much getting to work as I earned at work. Then, I found out that your being "tied up" was so you could watch a playoff game on television. I felt angry and used.

3   Another incident comes to mind. Do you remember when you cut your hand at work and had to stay home from school for several days? Do you remember who your lab partner was that took extra notes, grabbed extra handouts, made certain to tell the instructor and assistant why you weren't there? That same lab partner also went out of his way to see your Soc. Prof. and explain why you couldn't take the mid-term. Neither of these required a lot of effort or energy on my part, but they are gestures of my concern about you. They say something about my interest in you. Yet, last week, when I had to drive my mom to the clinic and couldn't go to my class, I asked you to put my paper in my Psychology teacher's mailbox so it wouldn't be counted late. And you forgot to deliver it! It sat on the frontseat of your car until you remembered it the next day. I know it was my responsibility to deliver the paper and to contact the instructor. However, I counted on you to do a simple favor for me. And you let me down. It wouldn't have taken a great deal of effort on your part to remember the favor I had asked you to do.

4   I used to think that we had a friendship; now it feels like a user-ship, and I am the one being used. If we are going to "hang together," it's going to have to be together. You have a lot of really positive traits that I appreciate, but I would really like for you to consider what I have said. I'd really like to stay friends with you, or maybe more precisely, really become friends with you.

Sincerely,
Paul (Adams)

Never Say Never

1   Although I tried for several nights to write my example paper, all I had to show for my efforts were the crumbled sheets of paper scattered across the floor. I was about to give up the whole assignment, but the words of my parents, teachers, and coaches, kept plaguing my mind. I could hear them saying wise proverbs like, "Never give up" or, "If at first you fail, try, try again." Since I was extremely frustrated, I tried to block their words from my mind. I couldn't, however, block the memory of what I had accomplished in the past because I had believed in those very words.

2   When I was learning how to print my name in kindergarten, I encountered a bit of a problem. I couldn't print the letter "S." First of all, I had trouble with all the curves in the letter. Secondly, I was constantly drawing it backwards; consequently, it looked more like the number "2" than the letter "S." My difficulty with that letter continued for several weeks. Not only was I becoming extremely discouraged, I was getting increasingly nervous. I was afraid I would never learn to print the letter "S"; therefore, I would have to change my name. I envisioned the name "Teresa" being replaced with "Terea" on all of my school records. Luckily, my teacher didn't give up on me, and I didn't give up on myself. For days, my teacher helped me trace the letter "S" over and over again. Eventually, I learned to print it perfectly.

3   As a freshman in high school, I decided to try out for color guard. The color guard is a group of performers who dance and twirl flags alongside the marching band. I attended both workshops before the initial try-out session. At the workshops, I realized that color guard involved much more than just waving colorful flags. I had to learn how to spin and toss a flag while keeping in time with the dance moves and the marching steps. Needless to say, color guard required coordination, patience, and concentration. I tried hard to master the routines, but I was very shaky on those flag tosses; I almost wiped out the band director during try-outs. I didn't make color guard that year. Heartbroken and devastated, I vowed I would never try out again. The following year, however, I was back twirling and tossing flags. I was determined to make the color guard this time. I practiced the flag routines until I could do them in my sleep. That year my performance at the try-outs was flawless; I made the color guard and remained a member throughout my high school years.

4   Driver's Education was another stressful endeavor for me. I had no trouble with the part of the course that involved classroom instruction. However, when the actual driving instruction began, I ran into a few obstacles; unfortunately, I mean that literally. I ran over almost every orange cone on the driving range. When I glanced over at my driving instructor, he was shaking his head sympathetically. The situation worsened in the driving simulation sessions. In one session alone, I ran two stop signs, sideswiped a car, and drove on the curb for almost two blocks. When my instructor told me I was not ready to drive on the road, I felt like quitting. When I realized that quitting would mean taking a bus for the rest of my life, I came to my senses. I repeated the driving range and simulation sessions. Gradually, I became comfortable driving a car on the highway.

5   Amazingly, I have completed my Com. 101 assignment. It's incredible what I can accomplish when I put my mind to it.

Teresa Balestri

EXAMPLE—POSSIBLE TOPICS

If you pay attention to yourself—truly listen to yourself—for a day or two, I'll bet you overhear yourself making statements which others might not fully comprehend or understand. These statements might be good subject matter for an example paper. If you think about it, an example paper is built by providing a series of related examples which—when connected—illustrate a general statement. Here are some general statements I overheard recently on campus. (OK, I admit it; I was eavesdropping!) I think that any of these statements would make for interesting reading when supported in an example essay:

- The best teachers are those who demand a lot.
- Creative people are strange.
- A hug always makes me feel better.
- My bad habits are about to catch up with me.
- TV ads are really stupid.
- Every sport I play leads me to the emergency room.
- Home-made is the best.
- You don't have to drink to enjoy a party.
- My horoscope is almost always right.
- There are a few movies I can see over and over.
- When no one else cares, your dog will always love you.
- Adverse conditions tell you who your true friends are.
- Getting lost can lead to adventures.
- It never pays to spread gossip.
- Whenever I buy something, it always goes on sale the next day.
- You can see some interesting sights at a red traffic light.
- Grandparents can be your best friends.
- I always do better when I trust my heart instead of my brain.
- Working nights means meeting society's weird ones.

THE EXAMPLE PAPER—YOUR TURN

1 Select a topic. As always, choose a topic you find interesting.

2 Think of examples you can use to support your topic.

3 Choose the examples you will actually use in the paper. Select those you can develop most-fully and perhaps those that are most-closely related to one another.

4 Decide whether you are going to organize deductively or inductively.

5 Write your outline. Try to list some of the details you might use to develop the examples.

6 Write the rough draft.

Above my dresser hangs a plaque I got in high school.

EXAMPLE PAPER PLAN SHEET

Part One: Choose a topic for an example paper. Write a thesis statement and then fill in the deductive outline for the paper.

Topic: _____

Thesis Statement: _____

_____

Outline: Body

Example One _____

_____

_____

_____

Example Two _____

_____

_____

Example Three _____

_____

_____

_____

Example Four _____

_____

_____

_____

Conclusion _____

_____

_____

_____

Body

Example One _____

_____

_____

_____

Example Two _____

_____

_____

_____

Example Three _____

_____

_____

_____

Example Four _____

_____

_____

_____

Thesis/Conclusion _____

_____

_____

_____

_____

_____

_____

_____

_____

Name _____ Section _____ Date _____

SELF-EVALUATION SHEET: PART ONE

Assignment: _____

Strong points of this assignment:

_____

_____

_____

_____

_____

_____

_____

Weak points of this assignment:

_____

_____

_____

_____

_____

_____

_____

General comments:

_____

_____

_____

_____

_____

_____

_____

(over)

SELF-EVALUATION SHEET: PART TWO

What were the strong points of your last writing assignment?

_____

_____

_____

_____

_____

_____

What were the weak points of your last writing assignment?

_____

_____

_____

_____

_____

_____

What have you done to correct those weaknesses in this assignment?

_____

_____

_____

_____

_____

_____

Evaluator's Name _____ Section _____ Date _____

PEER-EVALUATION SHEET: PEER-EVALUATOR #1

Writer's Name _____ Essay's Title _____

> **Directions:** (1) Remember not to write on another student's paper. Instead, use this form. (2) Offer concrete, specific comments using the terminology of writing (e.g., "The development in paragraph four might be improved by adding a brief example." or, "Check structure on page 3.")

What do you see as the strong points of this writing assignment: _____

_____

_____

_____

What areas do you feel might need additional work: _____

_____

_____

_____

Do you see any areas of grammar/mechanics (e.g. usage, spelling, fragments) that might need attention: _____

_____

_____

_____

_____

General comments: _____

_____

_____

_____

_____

PEER-EVALUATION SHEET: PEER-EVALUATOR #2

Writer's Name _____ Essay's Title _____

> **Directions:** (1) Remember not to write on another student's paper. Instead, use this form. (2) Offer concrete, specific comments using the terminology of writing (e.g., "The development in paragraph four might be improved by adding a brief example." or, "Check structure on page 3.")

What do you see as the strong points of this writing assignment: _____

_____

_____

_____

_____

What areas do you feel might need additional work: _____

_____

_____

_____

_____

Do you see any areas of grammar/mechanics (e.g. usage, spelling, fragments) that might need attention: _____

_____

_____

_____

_____

General comments: _____

_____

_____

_____

_____

The Comparison-Contrast Paper

OVERVIEW

Several hours a week, I work as a volunteer faculty tutor in our writing center on campus. That is, I meet with students who are writing papers for any of the hundreds of courses on our campus. Having done this for over a quarter of a century, I have reached some conclusions, two of which are important to the purpose of this chapter. One, lots of teachers other than writing teachers ask lots of students to write lots of papers. Two, of all the types of papers that I see students working with, comparison-contrast is one of the most-common.

Comparison-contrast papers are common because it is a rhetorical pattern (a way of thinking and organizing our thinking) which we use quite often. As students in a humanities course, we are asked to contrast two types of columns; as students in a science course, we are asked to contrast two approaches to problem solving an environmental issue. As students in an accounting class, we are asked to contrast two approaches to solving an investment procedure involving capital gains. Our literature teacher asks us to compare two poems by Anne Sexton; our history teacher asks us to compare two presidents on foreign policy approaches; our physics teacher asks us to compare and contrast two views of holograms. As a writing center teacher, I have seen drafts of all of these essays in the past semester.

As human beings outside the world of academics, we use comparison-contrast just as often. We make decisions based upon comparison-contrast: Should I grow a beard or shave? Do I want glasses or contacts? Should I major in business or biology? Am I going to transfer to the U. of I. or Eastern? Or should I not transfer and get married instead? Do I stick with Wild Turkey or switch to Jim Beam (Never!)? Most likely, none of us goes through a day when we don't compare-contrast songs, cars, teachers, managers, disc jockeys, TV shows, books, restaurants, friends, movies, classes, etc.

Because we do use comparison-contrast so often, most students don't find it all that difficult to write using comparison-contrast. If you follow a few simple directions and guidelines, you should find comparison-contrast an easy way to organize your thinking, a helpful process in decision making, and an efficient way to communicate with other people.

THE COMPARISON-CONTRAST PAPER

When a writer decides that it is necessary or beneficial to work with two topics or with two aspects of a single topic, he or she is developing ideas through the use of comparison-contrast. Generally, the phrase comparison-contrast is used loosely to describe any type of writing dealing with two topics. There is, however, a very precise definition of these terms. **Comparison** means that the writer is explaining the similarities, the likenesses of two topics. **Contrast** means that the writer is explaining the dissimilarities, the differences between two topics. **Comparison-and-contrast** means that the writer is explaining both similarities and differences. When you are given or when you choose an assignment that involves comparison-contrast, be certain that you have in mind a clear purpose for working with the two topics.

Let me give you an example. Suppose you are going to write a paper on AM radio and FM radio. Your purpose is to show how similar they are. If this is your thesis, you need only concern yourself with pointing out, in detail, the similarities between the two. In short, you would be using comparison and would not be using contrast. It would be possible for someone else to choose the same topic, AM and FM radio. Let's say this person's thesis is different. The writer wants to illustrate that they are different in a great many ways. He would point out, in detail, the differences or dissimilarities between the two. In short, he would be using contrast and would not be using comparison. It is possible that a third writer could also use the subject of AM and FM radio and explain that although they are alike in many ways, there are more differences than similarities. This third writer would be using both comparison and contrast and would be pointing out both similarities and differences.

How do you know whether to use comparison or contrast or both? What are you trying to communicate? Comparison-contrast is only a method of development; it is a rhetorical form. As a writer considering the use of comparison-contrast, you have several options, but basically there are two ways to organize a comparison-contrast paper. This text, similar to many others, advocates that there are two basic ways to write a comparison-contrast essay: subject-at-a-time and point-by-point.

COMPARISON-CONTRAST ORGANIZATION: A SUMMARY

For your convenience and for your perusal, here are two sample outlines in very reduced form. If you have lingering doubts about the ways to structure comparison-contrast, this side-by-side presentation of outlines should help.

Subject-at-a-Time	*Point-by-Point*
I. Puppies	I. Bringing one home
A. Bringing one home	A. Baby
B. Getting it to sleep at night	B. Puppy
C. Housebreaking	II. Getting it to sleep at night
D. Showing it off	A. Baby
E. Learning to love it	B. Puppy
F. Spoiling it	III. Housebreaking/Potty training
	A. Baby
	B. Puppy

Subject-at-a-Time	*Point-by-Point*
II. Babies	IV. Showing it off
A. Bringing one home	A. Baby
B. Getting it to sleep at night	B. Puppy
C. Potty training	V. Learning to love it
D. Showing it off	A. Baby
E. Learning to love it	B. Puppy
F. Spoiling it	VI. Spoiling it
	A. Baby
	B. Puppy

Obviously, the labels for the two methods are descriptive. Rather than belabor the obvious, I would like to point out the control and balance that exist in each method. The writer is in control of where information is placed and the order in which it is presented. This translates to an increased chance of communication taking place. Note, too, that either outline could be used for comparison, contrast, or comparison and contrast. The outline controls how information is presented; the thesis (or purpose) of the essay controls the development (the information which fills in the outline).

COMPARISON-CONTRAST: SUBJECT-AT-A-TIME

Subject-at-a-time is one of the basic ways to organize a comparison-contrast paper. The guiding principle in an essay organized subject-at-a-time is simply what the term implies. You deal thoroughly with one subject, saying all that you have to say about it. When you have finished presenting that subject, you move on to the other one. You do one subject at a time.

One of the big advantages of organizing a paper subject-at-a-time is that you do not have to constantly switch back and forth between the two subjects. This method saves you from writing sentences such as, "While the smoothness of artificial turf makes the baseball move faster, the roughness of natural grass adds to the unpredictability of when and where the baseball will hop.", or, "The Cadillac comfortably seats six, whereas the Volkswagen seats only four." Students frequently find this sentence-by-sentence, paragraph-by-paragraph comparison-contrast very awkward to write. If this has been your problem, subject-at-a-time organization might be the solution to your problems.

If you deal with each subject in an organized fashion and are certain that your main points are presented clearly and fully, then your reader should understand the ideas you are trying to communicate. In this type of paper, detail and development are very important. So, too, is a strong conclusion.

 ## GUIDELINES FOR WRITING A SUBJECT-AT-A-TIME COMPARISON-CONTRAST ESSAY

- **One,** as always, have a topic which interests you.

- **Two,** be certain that you are focused on whether you are comparing, contrasting, or doing both. Make certain you have clearly focused on audience and purpose.

- **Three,** since you have decided to use subject-at-a-time, you have already determined much of the structure and organization of your essay. Now, it is a matter of determining which subject you want to discuss first (or second) and what points you want to use to examine both subjects.

- **Four,** if you outline your writing before writing/typing the first draft, now would be a logical time to compose an outline.

- **Five,** begin to think about the detail and example which you will use to develop the main points of your outline when you write the first draft.

■ **Six,** try to maintain balanced treatment of all points, of both subjects. This does not mean that you cannot favor one subject over another; it means you should try to write approximately the same amount for each subject and each point. Avoid a drastic imbalance in the treatment of each.

Here is a student-authored example which nicely illustrates the preceding guidelines:

Wedding Days

1   The celebration of marriage often takes varied and wonderfully joyous forms. During the past year, I attended two extraordinary weddings, both of them absolutely beautiful but in totally different ways. Each was a unique experience and left me with vivid memories that cause those days to remain suspended in time and to live on as though painted on a canvas.

2   The first was the wedding of a very delightful, entertaining and talented friend, Katina, to Dmitri, and fittingly, it took place in the city of Chicago on a blustery afternoon in late March. The setting was a Greek Orthodox church, rich in Byzantine iconography and filled with flowers and incense. Ornately decorated, with candles flickering in the muted light, the church had an aura of profound mystery. Family and friends of the bride and groom, bejeweled and elegantly dressed, quietly filled the church. There was an attitude of joyous anticipation as everyone awaited the ceremony.

3   Suddenly, the wedding procession arrived in view, with attendants solemnly beautiful and flower girls enthusiastically scattering rose petals the length of the aisle. And then came the bride, resplendent in an exquisite white gown with a long train. Dmitri, formally dressed in tuxedo, awaited her at the altar. Both were radiant with barely suppressed excitement. The wedding service was very traditional, with two priests officiating, and was conducted both in Greek and in English. It was a long and very beautiful ceremony, incorporating rituals and a tradition that went back centuries in time. There was, in fact, a transcendent quality about the service; it somehow connected a distant past with the present day in an atmosphere of palpable celebration.

4   Following the ceremony, the bride and groom and their families left the church in an elegant procession of long, black limousines. Traffic was heavy as we all inched along, and it was a strange shock to find ourselves in the heart of downtown Chicago after the mystical, other-worldly experience of the church. The reception, which had been carefully orchestrated, was held at the Drake Hotel. The festivities there began with a long reception line, followed by cocktails, an elaborate buffet, and a formal dinner in the Gold Coast Room. Entering that room was like walking into an impressionist dream. The very elegant, gilded and spacious room was filled with extraordinary, towering flower arrangements in white and soft pastel colors. Each flower was a study in perfection, captured at its peak for this brief moment in time. The celebration was large and very joyous, with an abundance of Greek music, laughter, lively conversation, and dancing. The atmosphere was one of unrestrained joy as the wines flowed and the dancing achieved new levels of intensity. The pulsating, haunting Greek music, with its bouzouki providing captivating and mesmerizing rhythms, created a sense of timelessness as the evening unfolded. There were wonderful moments reminiscent of Zorba the Greek, with solo dancers— focused inward, totally absorbed in the music, arms outstretched, cigarette in one hand— proudly celebrating the very joy of life itself. As the evening wore on, the crowd gradually, almost imperceptibly, thinned, and we realized reluctantly, that even this day was destined to come to an end. On wings of song (Greek, of course), we returned to reality,

comforted in the knowledge that the memory of this day would remain with us, and the music and dancing would live in our hearts.

5   Soon after Katina's wedding, I received an invitation to the marriage of another treasured friend (and surrogate son), Lars, and Jen, to be held in upstate New York at the beginning of July. I had sensed that this was a wedding not to be missed, and the invitation confirmed my suspicion. Formally engraved, it announced the site of the wedding as "the upper hay field" on a farm near Gilbersville, New York.

6   From our vast, midwestern plains, I was transported to a landscape surrounded and protected by low, rolling mountains—a pastoral scene of quiet beauty. Driving to the wedding, I passed occasional farms and heavily forested, gentle mountains, sparkling multi-hued green in the bright, clear light of a perfect summer day. The farm where the wedding was to take place belongs to the bride's parents and had been lovingly restored by them as a vacation retreat over many years. The mood was one of relaxed informality as we gradually assembled for the celebration. A group of mountaineer friends, mostly bearded and dressed in t-shirts and cutoffs, headed for their campsite to a nearby spring for a quick bath before the wedding. The rest of us soon began the long ascent to the upper hay field across the road. It was a fairly steep climb, but for those who didn't feel up to it, a horse-drawn wagon was available, and in fact, made many trips up and down the hill. At the top of the hill, we found ourselves in a freshly mowed hay field, with rows of folding chairs arranged for the service and a spectacular view over the surrounding countryside. It was indeed a clear day, and we could see forever.

7   Lars arrived on the scene, striding up the hill with a big smile and a bouquet of flowers. He was wearing a white shirt with a bow tie and suspenders, baggy tan pants, and hiking boots. Jen, dressed in a lovely white gown, flowers in her hair, arrived with her family in the horse-drawn wagon. Gradually, the crowd assembled, and it was a diverse and festive group, dressed according to the dictates of a hayfield ceremony. Perhaps the style could be described as individualized casual elegance. There were friends and family members of all ages and from many different places, and all of us drifted, together, toward the area where the wedding was to take place. A solo flutist played as we were seated, the delicate sound wafting out over the countryside. The ceremony itself was designed by and composed by Lars and Jen and performed in the presence of a Justice of the Peace. Each of them made a very personal statement about marriage, a friend read poetry, and other friends sang a Cat Stevens song with guitar accompaniment. It was a very touching and unique ceremony, reminiscent of the sixties in its idealism and simplicity.

8   After the wedding ceremony, everybody slowly descended to the farm, savoring each moment of this magical time and place. There, a large tent had been placed next to a beautiful, sloping pasture. Classical music, violin and piano duets, performed by two gifted musicians, drifted forth from the tent, as appetizers and several varieties of punch were served. It was a nonalcoholic celebration, which in no way diminished the festive atmosphere. Outside the tent, people played badminton, volleyball, and pitched horseshoes. A delicious dinner was served, and the family Labrador retrievers made their rounds of the guests, hoping for hand-outs. Then came the multi-tiered wedding cake, which Lars and Jen had created. The music changed, as a bluegrass band came in, and the square-dancing began. At dusk, the cows, curious, wandered by, adding to the bucolic charm of the day. This day, too, had been one to treasure, and it was difficult to watch it fade into night, as of course it eventually did. It had been a day totally detached from the rest of life, and the memory of it remains a powerful source of peace and serenity.

> 9   The two weddings, one very traditional, the other equally nontraditional, vastly different in terms of setting, ceremony, and reception, nevertheless had in common an element of magic. Each in its own way captured a day, infused it with a celebration of life and joy, painted it in vivid colors and then set it apart, transformed into a living memory.
>
> Nina Thorp

Nina's essay is quite good, obviously written to convey her thoughts and feelings about these special friends and their wedding days and wedding celebrations. Her essay is a fine example of comparison-contrast used to communicate with a reader. That is, comparison-contrast was the means and not the end. Although this essay was written to fulfill requirements for a class, the essay was written for the student, not for the teacher. This is one of the factors that makes Nina's essay so effective.

Other factors contribute to the essay's effectiveness. Nina's use of subject-at-a-time organization reveals her knowledge of how solid structure and organization make writing clear and communicative. Had Nina outlined her paper before writing it, the outline might have looked like this:

Introduction
    Thesis Statement: Each [wedding] was a unique experience and left me with vivid memories that cause those days to remain suspended in time and to live on as though painted on a canvas.
Body
    Subject One: The traditional wedding
        The Setting
        The Ceremony
        The Reception
    Transitional Paragraph
    Subject Two: The non-traditional wedding
        The Setting
        The Ceremony
        The Reception
Conclusion

This is a perfect sample outline of subject-at-a-time organization and structure. And the essay based on it exhibits the good qualities of comparison-contrast we have discussed. It is not choppy, but presents each subject clearly and fully, in a balanced manner, allowing the reader to focus on the ideas and feelings Nina wishes to communicate.

Note, too, the vital function which development plays in the body paragraphs. Each body paragraph is quite specific and concrete. Nina has used her skills in narrative writing, descriptive writing, and expository writing. Her detailed observations add life and meaning to her writing. As I read her essay, I can hear the Greek bouzouki, I can see the black limos threading their way through heavy Michigan Avenue traffic in the Loop, I can smell the fresh-mown hay, and I smile at the thought of the family's Labs begging at the wedding reception. As I was always told by so many of my writing teachers, a writer is a person who observes the world and reminds the rest of us what we heard, saw, smelled, tasted, and touched. Nina's essay is a testimony to that statement's accuracy. When you write your comparison-contrast essay, work to achieve concrete development.

COMPARISON-CONTRAST: POINT-BY-POINT

Point-by-point is the other basic way of organizing a comparison-contrast paper. The guiding principle in point-by-point organization is simply what the term implies. You deal with each major point of comparison-contrast, examining both subjects in relation to each point as you work your way through the essay. You state one point, and then move on to the next point. In other words, you do one point, then another, and then another. The thesis or statement of purpose is explained or developed point-by-point.

GUIDELINES FOR WRITING A POINT-BY-POINT COMPARISON-CONTRAST ESSAY

- **One**, as always, have a topic which interests you.

- **Two**, be certain that you are focused on whether you are comparing, contrasting, or doing both. Make certain you have clearly focused on audience and purpose.

- **Three**, since you have decided to use point-by-point, you have already determined much of the structure and organization of your essay. Now, it is a matter of determining the order of the points and determining which subject will come first, which will come second. (Once you have established this order, stick with it throughout the essay.)

- **Four**, if you outline your writing before writing/typing the first draft, now would be a logical time to compose an outline.

- **Five**, begin to think about the detail and example which you will use to develop the main points of your outline when you write the first draft.

- **Six**, try to maintain balanced treatment of all points, of both subjects. This does not mean that you cannot favor one subject over another; it means you should try to write approximately the same amount for each subject and each point. Avoid a drastic imbalance in the treatment of each.

Here is a student-authored example which nicely illustrates the preceding guidelines:

On My Own

Dear Mom and Dad,

1   Well, it has been almost a year now since you gave me permission to move into my own apartment, work part-time, and go to school part-time. I don't know how you guys feel about it, but I am very happy. I think that matters have turned out quite well. How well, in fact, can be proven by looking at just a couple areas of my life that are important to me.

2   When I was living at home and just going to college, I really didn't have that many responsibilities. At twenty, I didn't really mind the fact that I didn't have to pay rent and other house bills, but, in a way, I also felt like a sponge at times. I did have my own car payments and car insurance and repairs to cover, but that was about the extent of it. I was working part-time, but it was the type of blow-off job that was okay to call at the last minute and say I wasn't coming in. If things were slow at the store, the owner didn't care if I took off or not. Now that I am living on my own (or at least with a couple of roomies), I don't have the luxury of calling in. Rather, I call in even on days I am not scheduled to see if I can pick up some overtime at time and a half. Now I like to work on the weekends

and on late nights if an order needs to be broken down and inventoried while the store is closed. The extra money comes in handy for the phone bill, the electric bill, the rent, the gas bill, etc. Remember how you use to nag me about my always leaving change around on the floor and in the washer? Well, I've discovered that even that loose coin comes in handy on trips to the laundry. I haven't missed a due date yet on a bill. I'm proud of that fact. I feel that I have become more responsible living on my own.

3   Do you remember how we argued over my grades? You guys were afraid that my grades would fall if I picked up more work to cover my bills and expenses. When I was living at home, I found it easier to put off my homework until the last minute. I was always running to the testing center at the last minute to take a test that had been waiting for me for several days. Every once in a while I would turn a paper in late and lose a grade or two simply because I was too lazy to meet deadlines. My grades were always B's and C's, but they also were never what my potential grades could have been. When there was lots of time and no pressure, I failed to pressure myself. Now that I am on my own, however, I get things done on time, or—sit down, folks—ahead of time. Yes, Me. I have turned work in early this semester. I was always on time with my homework so I could accept opportunities to take extra work (or even socialize) if the chance came about. Only once did I have to turn down extra income because I had put off a trip to the library. From that time on, I "got on top of things" so I would be flexible with scheduling work or pleasure. And, if my grades hold, I should come through with A's (yes, me!) and B's this semester. If that's true, it would seem that I have learned something about studying this semester while I was on my own.

4   Do you remember how tired you guys used to get having to settle petty fights between me and Linda? We were probably just typical brother and sister, but I know that our disagreements had to bother you guys at times. We seemed to always be fighting over stupid stuff like whose turn it was to drag the garbage to the curb on trash day, whose turn it was to mow the lawn or shovel the steps and walks, or whose turn it was to run Granny to the store on Saturday mornings. Even though we never had any major problems compared to some families I know of, I'm sure that our squabbles had to cause you stress. Now, Linda and I are actually friends, real friends. When we see each other a couple of times a week, we really talk and we really seem to enjoy each other's company. Last week for example, we went shopping for a gift for Father's Day (no hints, Dad, sorry) and took time out to have lunch and really talk about what was going on in both of our lives, like dating and school. So, although this wasn't something I had given thought to when I was trying to convince you to let me move out, it has happened. My sister and I have a pretty good relationship and seem to have become closer than when we lived together with you.

5   There is one more point I want to make. I feel better about myself. When I lived at home, I feel I was probably an okay kid. I did most of what you asked me to when (or almost when) you asked me to do it. (How's that for honesty?) And I always felt that you loved and respected me for loving and respecting you. But now that I am on my own, I feel that you love and respect me in a different way. You know I have lived up to my promises to you and to myself. And I appreciate your trust. I feel good about me, now, and I feel good about us. Thanks for giving me a chance. And do keep all this in mind when Linda wants to talk to you next week!!

Love,
Kevin (Meade)

Kevin's essay is an excellent sample of a comparison-contrast paper organized and structured point-by-point. First of all, Kevin had something to say to someone: he wanted to tell his parents that he has "made it" on his own, that he is thankful for their trust and belief in him. (He also seems to be laying a little ground work—in the closing—for his sister to have the same opportunity.) I think, in a very subtle fashion, he is also saying—without bragging—"See. I told you I could do it. And I did!" As I have suggested earlier in this chapter (and throughout this textbook), he has used comparison-contrast to really write about something important to him; the use of directed-audience helped him avoid a *burger-weenie exercise* in comparison-contrast.

Secondly, Kevin's skills in the area of development are quite apparent. In paragraph four, for example, he writes in detail about some of the squabbles that are normal between brother and sister. Although I was blessed with good children, I can recall heated discussions between them over whose turn it was on garbage day; Kevin's use of this example jogs my memory of having to sometime referee my own children's "discussions" over this very same issue. All in all, Kevin has done a good job in the paragraph of communicating to his parents his point about his relationship with his sister. The other paragraphs are equally well-developed.

Finally, Kevin's essay is very well-organized and well-structured. Kevin was clearly in control of his writing skills when he wrote the letter to his folks. Had he outlined his essay before composing the first draft, he might have had an outline similar to the one printed below:

Introduction

    Thesis Statement: Your permission for me to move into my own apartment, work part-time, and go to school part-time has turned out quite well . . . . This can be proven by looking at just a couple areas of my life . . . .

Body

    Point One: my responsibilities
        living at home
        living on my own
    Point Two: my grades
        living at home
        living on my own
    Point Three: my relationship with my sister
        living at home
        living on my own

Closing paragraph
        I feel better about myself
        pave the way for Linda

Kevin's paper and outline provide you with a good example of point-by-point comparison-contrast to analyze and study. The organization, structure, and development are excellent; the paper is balanced, it is written with a purpose, and it communicates. What more could a reader or a writer (or a teacher) ask for?

COMPARISON-CONTRAST: STUDENT EXAMPLES

No I *Won't* Come Back

Dear Lanie:

1   For the past few weeks, I've been thinking a lot about your offer to come back to McDonald's over the summer and work full time. As you know, I would have to quit my second job at Your Video Station to do so. After weighing my options, and comparing both of my present jobs, I've decided to decline your offer. At McDonald's, I don't get a lot of respect, feel extremely stressed out, have problems with scheduling, and don't receive worthwhile pay. At Your Video Station, I am respected, feel much less stressed, have set hours without scheduling problems, and feel I'm paid enough for the work I do. Therefore, I've decided not to work full time at McDonald's this summer and to stay at Your Video Station.

2   First off, the amount of respect I receive at work is very important to me. I feel I get much more respect when I work at Your Video Station than when I work at McDonald's. When I work at McDonald's, I'm treated like a new employee by the managers, even though I've been working there for over two years. I'm considered a "lowly crew person" and thrown in the same category as employees that have only been working there for a few weeks. The store owner doesn't even know my name! My fellow employees also treat me with little or no respect. If I need help and they aren't busy, most of them won't even help me. Plus, I never receive a thank you when I help them. The customers also give me hardly any respect. To them, I'm a stupid little girl with no skills that couldn't find a better job. McDonald's *can* be hard, and without the respect from the customers, working gets very annoying. When I work at Your Video Station, I am respected by the managers. They realize my potential and that I know what I'm doing. When the store owner comes in, he makes a point to say, "Hello, Kim, how is everything?", which really makes me feel respected. I'm not just a worker there. My fellow employees give me respect as well. We all help each other and are very friendly to each other. The customers at Your Video Station treat me like a human being, not like a stupid little girl with no skills. After taking care of a customer, I'll almost always receive a thank you, and it makes me feel good.

3   Next, I have much more stress when I work at McDonald's compared to when I work at Your Video Station. Even on a good day at McDonald's, I receive more stress than working a bad day at the video store. At McDonald's, I'm the person the customers scream at if their orders are incorrect or if it takes a while for them to receive their food. I've been in tears many times because of the rude things that they say to me, and usually it isn't even my fault! Almost every time I work at McDonald's we are short-handed, and I have to do two or three people's jobs. I have to constantly run around and try to keep the drive-thru going at a reasonable time. It takes a lot out of me! Managers at McDonald's don't understand just how stressful situations like this are. They yell at me to hurry up and ask me why it's taking more than ninety seconds for each order to go out. They hardly ever offer any help, which is obviously what I need! Plus, when I work an eight hour day, I only get one half hour break about two hours into my shift. By the fifth hour of work, I need another cigarette and feel very anxious to leave. At Your Video Station, I almost never get stressed out. The customers are usually very nice and understand if they have to wait a moment while I finish taking care of a different customer. However, they usually don't have to wait. I have never worked a day when we were short staffed at the video store. I

always receive help when I need it. If there ever *is* a problem with a customer, I never have to deal with it. If customers are upset with their late fees, the managers always come and take over for me. Plus, I can take a paid break any time I need one. I can go and have a cigarette, get food, or use the phone at my leisure, as long as it isn't busy. I feel hardly any stress when I work!

4   Then, I have many problems at McDonald's regarding scheduling and hardly any difficulties at Your Video Station. When I used to work five days a week at McDonald's, I had a lot of trouble trying to get the days I wanted off. My days were constantly changing each week, ranging from 5:00 in the morning to 12:30 at night. Also, it was very hard for me to get a full weekend off, since I was expected to work eight hour shifts on Friday, Saturday, and Sunday. Even when I tried to put in a request slip for a weekend off, I hardly ever got all three days. Right now I don't have this problem because I only work Tuesday mornings, but if I come back this summer, I'll have the same problems with scheduling that I had for the last two summers. At Your Video Station, I have a set schedule. I make my plans around the times I work. If I need a day off, I almost always get it. The only weekend day I normally work is Saturday morning from 10:00 to 4:00, so I have most of the weekend at my leisure. Plus, if I need some extra hours I can ask a fellow employee if I can take a day, and normally I'll get it.

5   Also, I don't receive worthwhile pay at McDonald's, but I feel that I do at Your Video Station. I have been working at McDonald's for two years and four months. I started at $4.75, and now make $5.90. In two years and four months, my pay has only increased $1.15. That is not good, especially with the low amount of respect and high amount of stress that I've had to put up with. Plus, there are no bonuses at McDonald's. The closest thing to a bonus is a book of five dollars in gift certificates for McDonald's food which is given to all of the employees for Christmas. That wouldn't be that bad, if we didn't get our food for free! A major reason why I feel that I don't make enough money is because I was told about a year ago that I was going to become a crew trainer. This promotion comes with a higher shirt and a quarter raise. I never saw a new shirt, or a raise on my paycheck, but I did start training new employees. I know that I do too much and have been there too long to still be receiving the pay I do. I have only been at Your Video Station for five months, and I'm already making $5.40. I feel that the payment I receive is worthwhile, because I receive a lot of respect and am not stressed at work. Plus, we receive a nice Christmas bonus each year. I received forty dollars from Tom, our store owner, after only working at Your Video Station for a little over a month. I also received a quarter raise after being there for six months. The largest raise I ever got at McDonald's is twenty cents after six months.

6   As you can see, Lanie, there are a lot of reasons why I would be best off declining your offer to come back over the summer and work full time at McDonald's. The low amount of respect I receive, the high amount of stress I get, the problems with scheduling, and the problems with pay and raises aren't even all the reasons that my decision is against McDonald's. However, I feel that they alone justify my decision. At Your Video Station, I am much happier because I receive a lot of respect, have a low amount of stress, have no problems with scheduling, and feel that my pay and raises reflect the amount of work I have to do accurately. I'll still work at McDonald's on Tuesdays if you need me to, but I will not come back as a full time employee.

Sincerely,
Kimberly Puchalski

Hell on Wheels

Dear Parents:

1   The past few weeks, I have noticed a startling trend in our transportation situation. As you may know, I currently share my car with my sister, Audrey. This arrangement has been tolerable; however, I believe it is necessary to change it. The problems all stem from my sister. She is managing to slowly destroy the car, mile by mile. I have found several reasons that suggest we must find another way to provide her transportation.

2   The first problem with Audrey is that she is very sloppy. This can also be said of her passengers. Every day, I must dig out piles of papers and wrappers. This colorful bouquet of scraps coats the interior. There is a blanket of waste, which I must brush away to sit down. Candy from the wrappers braids itself into the carpet fibers. The gooey caramel grabs hold of the mat and refuses to budge, no matter how much I scrub at it. I look under the seats, only to find mounds of old pay-stubs. Knowing Audrey's wages is an interesting fact, but quite useless. The car's cup holder always has a half empty beverage; most of the time it is a leaking cup. The ashtray below is filled with loose change coated with soda. Cassette tapes are crammed into the sides of the bucket seats. The car is simply in disarray after a few miles.

3   Once the car has been thoroughly cleaned and sterilized by myself, my tendencies can be observed. When the car is in my control, it is immaculate. The carpets are neatly vacuumed; a brilliant light blue shines below my feet. I leave a small plastic bag behind the driver seat for all the little messes that try to creep in. All loose change is placed in the coin holder in the center console. Not a single president struggles to maintain his dignity in the ashtray. The cup holder is tucked away. It is never used to hold soda bottles that look like a biology experiment involving new kinds of mold.

4   The other issue that highlights the importance of separating Audrey from my car is maintenance. Audrey ignores the desperate shrieks of the car. The car needs gentle care to keep it well off. She does not recognize how important this is. She would rather turn up the radio than go to a repair shop. Gears can grind, the steering wheel can rattle . . . all are easily ignored. The thought of losing access to the car overpowers her concerns for its condition.

5   The car, being my first, is my ward. I look for any flaw in it and desperately try to make sure all is well. The first sign of trouble raises flags. When there is the slightest rattling I dare not use the car excessively. I keep an eye on mileage, waiting for that next 3,000 mile oil change. The car needs to have a good exterior, so I find myself washing the car often. I am the one that wipes away the grit from the roads under repair on the way to the mall. I am the car's dedicated janitor. It is all for the sake of a decent automobile.

It is these differences in our treatment of the car that leads me to believe that something drastic needs to be done. I find myself taking the brunt of the work associated with running the car. It runs the gamut from oil changes, car washes, to filling the gas tank. The troubles this causes myself motivates me in the effort to get Audrey out of my car. A second car seems to be a feasible solution for this troublesome topic.

Your son,
Drew Rackow: concerned car owner

"The Three Wise Men . . . Three Visions"

Dear Mom,

1   Am I ever going to be as good as you? It was that voice. It was that voice and the smell of Cover Girl and Noxzema that I remember. Looking back, I realize you were the inspiration for my art. You were the one whose approval I sought time and time again. I choreographed so many dance pieces loosely based on you. I also choreographed some quite blatantly. But the voice, when you sang . . . the emotion you gave, and the lilting sadness. I will never be that.

2   You knew I was different and a bit of an actress. What I never knew until recently was that I was living a part of you. You got such a kick out of the shows that I put on in the back yard. I did it because you really watched me, and you really laughed at all of my six-year-old jokes. You taught me to appreciate the audience.

3   Do you remember the summer afternoon that I rang our bell and you answered the door and saw me standing there? You reacted to me as if it were very natural for your daughter to pretend she was someone else asking for *herself*! Then you invited me in for lunch until "I" returned. Did you realize that you were shaping my improvisational skills?

4   Do you remember us practicing our best cry for when we would accept the Oscar and how we practiced crying in front of the mirror for so long that dinner was late and Dad got mad? You were hilarious when we came out of the bathroom and told Dad that somebody famous had died and we were upset. He did not believe a word of it, but it was a brilliant performance worthy of the Oscar!

5   You always used to say that you were a shy kid and you hoped that I would not be afraid of my creativity. I know now that you were afraid you might stifle that creativity. You did the opposite for me. I felt encouraged, no matter how bizarre my ideas, or how against the grain I became, you let me figure it out. You nudged me into dance when my English teacher told you about scholarship possibilities. You always said, "Be true to yourself and always be able to support your art." I trusted you and got that scholarship, went to college, and fulfilled my dream of dancing and choreographing. You knew it, didn't you? Thanks, mom.

Dear Avalon,

6   Am I ever going to be as pure as you are? It was that face. It was that face and the smell of newborn baby that I will always remember. Looking back and knowing you were not "planned" and I was not ready, all seems a moot point now. You have filled my heart in places I never knew needed filling. The focus of my art has shifted onto a healthier plane. I can breathe again. That face, that face of sheer joy and happiness just "blows my mind." You are so pure and innocent; I now can see a part of me in you that my mother took hold of and nurtured. I know you look up to me, it is scary, but I will do my best to help you take shape. I pray I don't stifle that innate curiosity.

7   I remember the day I named you, it was the day you were born. An angel whispered in my ear, "Avalon." (Based on the book of *King Arthur* and *The Mists of Avalon*.) You are an old soul, Ava. I knew it the second after you were born when the nurses crowded around you. They were amazed at how articulate your hands and fingers were fanning about your face. "Babies usually clench their fists and cry; it is a natural response," one of the nurses exclaimed. That was interesting. You let out a loud cry, and as soon as you saw my face, you relaxed. We stared into each other's eyes for what seemed an eternity. That was when I heard the angel.

8   I remember fighting with Grandma. You, at the age of three-and-a-half, followed Grandma downstairs after the argument. I heard Grandma laughing uncontrollably, and when I rushed downstairs to see what was happening, Grandma was wiping tears from her eyes. There you were, rubbing Grandma's hand and reassuring her that everything would be just fine. You said that your mommy was wrong for "shouting," and not to worry because "sometimes my mommy gets crabby."

9   I remember you waking me every morning so excited about the new day and planning what we were going to do. You found excitement in every mundane little thing we did. Remember when my car was in the shop for four weeks during the summer and you and I would walk to the dance studio where I taught? Each morning you found a thousand things to talk about. Remember the brown hare we encountered on the same block every morning? How about the "roly-poly" bugs you loved to hold, or yelling at me not to step on any of the baby ants? All the bird calls that we both learned to recognize, (the *whippoorwill* was your favorite) and how we were saving the trees by not driving that "stinky car?" You taught me to see what was in front of me all along.

10   You have brought me down a few pegs and taught me that the finer things in life are free. I sleep better at night with you curled up next to me. I don't even mind your snoring or occasional arm flail that smacks me square in the face. You have taught me to laugh slower and shake off the residue of the day. You have given a stronger connection to my art and to stick to my convictions instead of adopting others' opinions. Thanks, Ava.

Dear Lord,

11   *Thank You for hearing my prayers. You have sent the best mentor, my mother, and the greatest teacher, my daughter, to me. I have been taught so much through them. The vision I had of myself as a child was the same vision my mother had as a child, and what my daughter already is today. I do believe in miracles. The photographs I have in my mind of my life experiences spill out into my art. I have always had a wealth of information to draw from. Most of it inspired through these two beautiful people. I aspire to be everything in my mother and instill all that I have learned from my daughter. There is definitely a female connection, which leads me to believe that You are more female than most would like to admit. Not to forget, I know You have an incredible sense of humor, too. My strength lies in how strongly I believe in You. Mom says we are not "of this world, but merely living in it." Thank You, Lord, for putting me with these two; I am greatly humbled.*

Michelle Marie Greaney

Grandmothers

1   Cousin Jennifer commented that she was terribly exhausted after a day of babysitting for her three grandchildren. "I was glad to see them, but extremely thrilled when they went home," she said. Considering the significance of her statement, I realized that in the future, I might become a grandmother, too. I also reflected upon the differences in grandmothers: some are traditional and old fashioned; others are modern and liberated. Both love their grandchildren dearly, and each is capable of opening different worlds to them.

2 The sixty-plus, traditional grandmother is a comfortable presence, indeed. With her ample figure clad in her floral housedress, she greatly resembles the legendary Mrs. Doubtfire, since this grandmother obviously disapproves of artifice in any form. Her hair, worn in a practical bun, has never been subjected to the rigorous treatment of the modern beauty salon. Therefore, it is gray and unpretentious. According to this grandmother, makeup is dishonest. Only brazen hussies wear it. She highly disapproves of its use, saying that she earned her wrinkles and gray hair; they are part of her individuality. She would never think of camouflaging them in any way.

3 The grandma whose appearance is round, warm, and comforting is also a willing baby-sitter, a resourceful homemaker, and a supreme cook. Frequently, this grandma takes in her little darlings while their mother works. At their grandma's house, which is filled with the delectable scents of devil's food cake, fudge brownies, and apple dumplings smothered in cinnamon sauce, they feast extremely well. Since her kitchen is the center of her universe, this grandma's culinary skills rival those of the corner bakery. When grandma is not cooking, she quietly knits in her favorite chair. Like a spider busily weaving a web, she knits for hours, creating Christmas presents and birthday gifts for all in the family. The old-fashioned grandma was taught that "whatever is worth doing is worth doing well," and she puts that old saying into practice every day.

4 Growing up in a culture that did not encourage women to be independent, this traditional grandmother is beyond doubt a very sociable lady. Usually, she has a great time at church Bingo games and luncheons with her friends from the Altar and Rosary Society. Occasionally, this grandma may need to ask for a ride because she does not drive; in her day, husbands had control of the family car as well as the family finances. However, lack of driving skills does not keep her home, since she has many friends who do drive. When going to ladies' luncheons, she is often the first to volunteer to contribute her masterpieces to the bake sales. What this grandma lacks in sophistication, she makes up for in generosity.

5 If an old-fashioned grandmother reminds us of "Mrs. Doubtfire," the modern grandmother seems like "Auntie Mame." This liberated grandma believes that "Life is a banquet."

6 She is the grandma that does not look like one. Working out in a gym, this grandma has no cellulite or "love handles." Looking sleek and stylish, she can still turn heads when she enters a room. Her diet usually includes plenty of fresh fruits and vegetables. Therefore, because of her lifestyle, she is in excellent physical condition, which rivals that of a much younger person. Modern grandma dyes her hair a becoming golden brown or chestnut color; she will also take full advantage of the many flattering cosmetics on the market. Her feelings are that a person does not have to look old just because she is a grandmother.

7 The modern grandma, who believes that maintaining a young outlook is an asset, is also very active in her career life. Though she does not have time to baby-sit, she has a great advantage over the more traditional grandma. She is frequently able to get tickets for sporting events. The children know that she will take them to see the Bulls or the Bears play. Sometimes, they will even get to see her play, because she joined an adult softball team. Though she is not domestically inclined, she'll always remember birthdays and Christmas with special gifts. Trips to the mall are frequent events when grandma and grandchildren can talk freely and share confidences.

8 This grandmother loves her family dearly, but believes everyone should be self-sufficient. Visiting her married children and her grandchildren often, she still has many interests of her own. Her social life is always colorful and adventurous since she likes to travel. Dinner and theater with friends are often on the agenda, and if this grandmother is

unfortunate to have been widowed, she is very likely to date occasionally. Romance, flowers, and candlelight have not been ruled out, and often such a grandma may even re-marry. Perhaps if she does, she will then act her age. However, modem grandma does not have to be married in order to lead a fulfilled life because she feels that marriage, while desirable, is not the only goal she has.

9   In conclusion, both grandmothers have much to offer. The traditional grandmother comforts and indulges. The modern grandmother teaches independence and survival skills. It would be truly wonderful if all children could have two grandmothers. Wouldn't it be even better if one of them could be old fashioned, and the other, modern?

Mary Ann Endre

Image in the Mirror

1   At the age of fifty-eight, I look in the mirror and stare at my reflection, and someone is playing tricks on me. The image is much older than I am. I know I have passed the age of getting just a few gray hairs, but I'm still able to keep a fast and steady pace. I think of myself as being in my late forties . . . or maybe early fifties. The mirror says otherwise.

2   A closer look leaves me wondering what has happened to my neck; the skin seems to be wrinkly and sagging. I reach back and pull the skin tight on the back of my neck. Ah! The front of my neck looks much better. My jowls seem to hang. I put my fingertips on my cheekbones, and I smooth the skin back to my hairline. The wrinkles around my mouth disappear. My fingertips move to my temples, and as I pull the skin back, my eyes lose that tired, droopy, look. Time has passed, and my face tells the story. I stop to reflect, and I realize my children are about to reach the age I still imagine myself to be.

3   The thought of a facelift passes through my mind. Several of my friends have gone through this procedure, and they look okay. I would want a really good plastic surgeon; we have all seen famous people's faces plastered in the headlines, "Face Lift Gone Wrong!" I wonder what would a facelift cost, and how much recovery time would I need? My busy schedule doesn't allow me much down time.

4   Then I look long, and hard, in the mirror. My father's face jumps out at me. His blue eyes are looking back at me. We are all so proud of our blue eyes. They have been handed down from my grandfather to my father, passed on to me, and I passed them on to my children. When my grandson, Morgan, was born, I was so thrilled to see our eyes had made it to another generation. My mouth is shaped like Dad's, and that smile is definitely his smile I see on my face as I look at my reflection in the mirror. My mind wanders, and I hear his laugh. I ask him, "Dad, what do you think of this drooping face?" I hear him say, "Carol Ann, you are perfect, don't change a thing." Okay, Dad, you can have the last word, for now.

5   Time has definitely passed, the face and body show the effects, but maybe I'm not ready to change that reflection in the mirror just yet. There is a certain amount of comfort in the image. And after all, I still have plenty of time to consider a facelift.

6   They say age is in the mind of the beholder. In that case, I think I will just continue to enjoy the rest of my forties, and maybe not look in the mirror quite so often!

Carol Pearson

Surviving

Dearest Brother Dan,

1   As Nov. 17 approaches, the anniversary of your sobriety, I am reminded of how different our lives are since you choose to live your life sober.

2   Before Nov. 17, 1993, I remember how strained our holidays were. I would show up at mom's house, with gifts in my arms and a smile on my face. It seemed like every other normal household. The kids would run into the house and look for Nanny and Papa, but as soon as I would hear, "Where is Uncle Dan?" reality would hit. I would either see the bedroom door closed, or one look at you, and I would know how that holiday would go. I would join everyone at the table and eat that wonderful meal mom made, but there would be such an underlined sadness. By the end of the evening, the tension would be enormous and sometimes tempers would fly. On the way home from every get-together, I had tears in my eyes, because seeing you destroy your life was too much for me to handle. I would be exhausted, because I felt as if I was acting in a play, with a smile on my face and an ache in my heart.

3   Before Nov. 17, 1993, I would not trust you with my children, no matter how much that would break your heart. Lauren and Mark loved you, because small children love unconditionally. You felt that love, and they seemed to be the only ones you felt comfortable with. Unfortunately, when you were drinking, you did not know your own strength, your balance would be off and your common sense was not there. I would not allow you to take them for a walk to the candy store, for I was afraid, because you had to go across the street with them. I would not let you hold them, because I was afraid you would drop them. When you wrestled with them I would have to stop you, because sometimes you did not know your own strength. This hurt me, as much as it hurt you.

4   Long before Nov. 17, 1993, I watched you go through your teen-years and your twenties and saw you emotionally stop somewhere around sixteen. You could not handle any kind of responsibility. You could not keep a job, you lost your driver's license, and you could not pay any of your bills. You even smashed a few bikes, by pedaling under the influence. I was so concerned that you would get hurt or killed through these years. Naturally, the co-dependent that I was, I would financially, emotionally, and physically help you. I thought that was love, but now I know that was guilt, because I could not help you stop drinking.

5   Before Nov. 17, 1993, when I would look at you I would not see a young man, but an old man who lived a hard life. You never cared about your appearance, but I guess you never cared about yourself. Your hair was unkempt, your clothes were out-of-date, or unwashed, and your outward appearance showed how much your life was in turmoil. That didn't frighten me as much as your physical well-being did. Your health appeared to deteriorate, as the years went on. Your skin color was so pale, there were dark circles under your eyes, and you were so very thin. I could tell your health was suffering, because of what you were putting into your body.

6   Before Nov. 17, 1993, our family was still close, but I felt the tension whenever I would see or speak with someone. I think everybody thought one of us should be doing something. You would always be in our minds, in our conversations, and in our hearts. I know we all felt the same—guilty—because we could not help you—angry—because we did not like what was happening to our family—sadness—because at the rate you were going we thought you were going to die. Our family was going through the same emotions that a family goes through, watching someone they love die of cancer, heart disease or diabetes. This disease that was affecting our family was called Alcoholism.

7   After Nov. 17, 1993, our holidays are so different. When I walk into mom and dad's house, and the kids run off to find Nanny and Papa, they also now find you, with a smile on your face and your arms open wide. I sit at the dinner table and truly say a prayer of thanksgiving, for the changes in our lives. I don't feel the tension that was there before, and the laughter that goes on all evening is real. I go home with the feeling of contentment and happiness, knowing that God is hearing my prayers.

8   After Nov. 17, 1993, there is such an enormous change in you. Not only do I see it, but my children see it also. They love to be with you, and I feel comfortable with that. Not only will I let them go to the candy store with you, but allowed you to take them to the Sox game, with your AA group. That is a big step for me. I not only trust you with Lauren and Mark now, but I feel they are lucky to know their Uncle Dan and how hard he is fighting to survive this disease. I now feel confident that anytime they are with you, they are being taken care of. I cannot tell you how happy that makes me feel.

9   After Nov. 17, 1993, you have taken on such a large number of responsibilities. Your AA group comes first, and you take that very seriously. Slowly, I see you grow into a very responsible adult. You have found a job and started a career, which I know is difficult, because your work record is so bad. You are going to court to prove yourself responsible, so you can get your driving privileges back. You consolidated your bills and started to pay them off. It is a long road, for you have fifteen years to catch up on. I now watch, as you put your life back together and feel such pride. You have been going on an uphill climb, but because of your determination, support of your AA group, and support of your family and friends, you are doing it.

10   After Nov. 17, 1993, all I have to do is look at you, and I know things are going to be OK. You have a sparkle back in your eye and the zest of life back in your step. You now look like the handsome thirty-three year old man that you should. You care about your outward appearance and your health, but most of all you care about your emotional well-being. This shows, not only by the growing love and respect you are getting from your family and friends, but by the first true healthy and happy relationship you have with Sandy.

11   After Nov. 17, 1993, our family is truly happy. Sure there are times when we have some problems, but they are normal family problems. Now instead of you only being in our thoughts, our prayers, our conversations, you are at our dinner table, our parties, and part of our lives. We all feel proud that we made it through some difficult years and still stayed close. Mostly, we feel respect, happiness, and love for you, because you are surviving a disease that could have taken your life.

12   Nov. 17 will be a date that will always be in my mind, because of Alcohol Anonymous, Alonon, the Higher Power, and your will-power, you and our family are surviving this horrible disease. Before this date, I felt as if I was a victim, and it consumed our entire family, but now I feel peace and happiness. I am proud of you and respect you, because I know being sober took dedication and hard work. I love you.

Your Sister,
Chris (Gniadek)

COMPARISON-CONTRAST: FOOD FOR THOUGHT

Well, here we are at that part of the chapter where I am supposed to help you find something to write about. So, I'll try.

As you might remember from earlier sections of this book, I strongly advocate writing about something which is important to you (thereby avoiding the burger-weenie syndrome). I also advocate—if the situation, topic (and teacher) allow—writing directed-audience essays. If you examine the student-authored examples in this chapter, you'll discover all of them have a purpose (whew! no burgers/weenies lurking here) and many of them are written directed-audience.

As I wrote in the opening section of this chapter, we all use comparison-contrast for decision-making. What decisions have you made lately that involved the use of comparison-contrast? What decisions are you trying to make? Any potential topics lurking within all of that decision-making?

Whatever you decide upon as subject matter, remember that you are writing to communicate ideas, thoughts, and/or feelings; you are not writing just to show your teacher that you know how to write a comparison-contrast paper. Say something to someone.

THE COMPARISON-CONTRAST PAPER—YOUR TURN

1 Think of a topic for your comparison-contrast paper. At this time you probably should also decide whether you will be comparing, contrasting, or both.

2 Decide which method you will use: subject-at-a-time or point-by-point.

3 Jot down your outline and try to think through the paper. This will insure that you have chosen the right form to structure the paper.

4 Write the rough draft of your essay.

5 Proofread your draft, paying particular attention to development and structure. At this time review the other suggestions made about comparison-contrast.

6 Write the final draft of your paper.

My father is an avid haunter.

A good freethrow shooter must be able to consummate.

COMPARISON-CONTRAST PAPER PLAN SHEET

Part One: Choose a topic for a comparison-contrast paper. Write a thesis statement. Then fill in the subject-at-a-time outline for the paper.

Topic: _____

Thesis Statement: _____

_____

Body Outline

    Subject One _____

        Point One _____

        Point Two _____

        Point Three _____

        Point Four _____

        Point Five _____

        Point Six _____

    Subject Two _____

        Point One _____

        Point Two _____

        Point Three _____

        Point Four _____

        Point Five _____

        Point Six _____

Conclusion _____

_____

_____

_____

Body Outline

Point One _____

Subject One _____

Subject Two _____

Point Two _____

Subject One _____

Subject Two _____

Point Three _____

Subject One _____

Subject Two _____

Point Four _____

Subject One _____

Subject Two _____

Point Five _____

Subject One _____

Subject Two _____

Point Six _____

Subject One _____

Subject Two _____

Conclusion _____

_____

_____

_____

_____

_____

_____

Name _____ Section _____ Date _____

SELF-EVALUATION SHEET: PART ONE

Assignment: _____

Strong points of this assignment:

_____

_____

_____

_____

_____

_____

_____

Weak points of this assignment:

_____

_____

_____

_____

_____

_____

_____

General comments:

_____

_____

_____

_____

_____

_____

_____

(over)

SELF-EVALUATION SHEET: PART TWO

What were the strong points of your last writing assignment?

_____

_____

_____

_____

_____

_____

What were the weak points of your last writing assignment?

_____

_____

_____

_____

_____

_____

What have you done to correct those weaknesses in this assignment?

_____

_____

_____

_____

_____

_____

Evaluator's Name _____ Section _____ Date _____

PEER-EVALUATION SHEET: PEER-EVALUATOR #1

Writer's Name _____ Essay's Title _____

> **Directions:** (1) Remember not to write on another student's paper. Instead, use this form. (2) Offer concrete, specific comments using the terminology of writing (e.g., "The development in paragraph four might be improved by adding a brief example." or, "Check structure on page 3.")

What do you see as the strong points of this writing assignment: _____

_____

_____

_____

_____

What areas do you feel might need additional work: _____

_____

_____

_____

_____

Do you see any areas of grammar/mechanics (e.g. usage, spelling, fragments) that might need attention: _____

_____

_____

_____

_____

General comments: _____

_____

_____

_____

_____

Evaluator's Name _____ Section _____ Date _____

PEER-EVALUATION SHEET: PEER-EVALUATOR #2

Writer's Name _____ Essay's Title _____

> **Directions:** (1) Remember not to write on another student's paper. Instead, use this form. (2) Offer concrete, specific comments using the terminology of writing (e.g., "The development in paragraph four might be improved by adding a brief example." or, "Check structure on page 3.")

What do you see as the strong points of this writing assignment: _____

_____

_____

_____

_____

What areas do you feel might need additional work: _____

_____

_____

_____

_____

Do you see any areas of grammar/mechanics (e.g. usage, spelling, fragments) that might need attention: _____

_____

_____

_____

_____

General comments: _____

_____

_____

_____

_____

The Classification Paper

OVERVIEW

This chapter presents another very practical rhetorical form—classification. Students generally enjoy writing this paper, and their papers, as you will see when you read the examples in this chapter, usually are quite interesting and very often amusing. Classification is another unique rhetorical form that a writer should know how to use. It is yet another method of development, another way of communicating ideas and thoughts.

CLASSIFICATION

Classification—sometimes referred to as division, analytical division, or analysis—is a method of development which the writer uses to divide a group into subgroups by the consistent application of one or more principles of classification. Usually, each subgroup is then explained in depth. Classification is a process we use quite frequently. For example, when we go to a little league baseball game we begin to view the players as members of certain subgroups: the star, the bungler, the clown, the bench warmer, the coach's favorite, and the nice kid who just isn't a jock. Or, when we go to a restaurant and observe the people dining at the neighboring tables, we begin to recognize types of eaters we have seen before: the gobbler, the slow poke, the talker, the picker, the human garbage pail, etc. Classification, at least when practiced informally, is something that most of us do.

Formal classification is slightly more involved than casually studying the kids on the ball diamond in front of us or the diners at the table next to us.

 ## GUIDELINES FOR WRITING A CLASSIFICATION ESSAY

- **One,** formal classification requires dividing a large group into several smaller groups (called subgroups), usually three or more.

- **Two,** this division into subgroups must be done by the consistent and uniform application of classification principles. For example, the group known as laughers could be classified by using one or more of the following principles: what makes the person laugh, the effect of the laugh on other people, the volume of the laugh, the pitch of the laugh, the rhythm of the laugh, the physiological changes evident on the face of the laugher, etc. Not all of these principles would have to be used (although they all could be used), but there must be uniform application of the principle(s) to all subgroups. That is, what you say about **one** subgroup, say about **all** subgroups.

- **Three,** there should be no overlap between or among the subgroups; they should be exclusive.

- **Four,** there should be complete classification; that is, all of the subgroups added together should equal the group.

- **Five,** the essay should be structured and organized into unified and coherent paragraphs. To achieve this, many writers prefer to use a classification chart instead of a more-traditional type of outline. The chart usually lists the subgroups across the top; the principles of classification are listed vertically on the left side. (You will find examples elsewhere in the chapter; you will also find a blank form for you to use at the end of the chapter.)

- **Six,** use detail and example to develop the subgroups and the principles. This process begins when you fill in the classification chart.

Read and study the following example; I feel it illustrates all of the above-listed steps and suggestions.

First, the student did some brainstorming work:

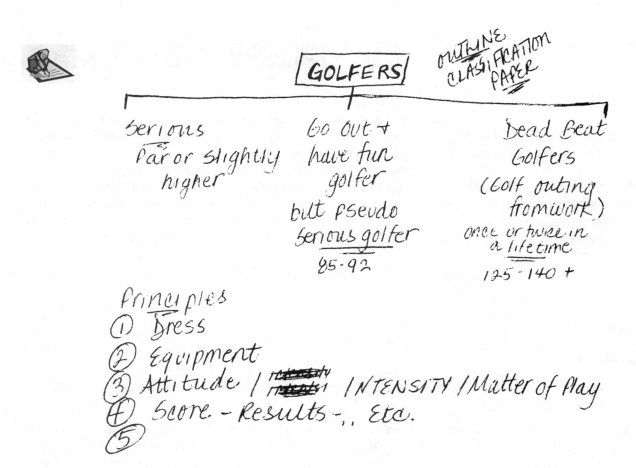

Next, the student did an outline/classification chart:

CLASSIFICATION PAPER - DUE 7/18   7/16

GOLFERS	Serious	Pseudo-serious golfer	Dead Beat Golfer
DRESS	Matching outfit green pants white shirt	Golf Shoes regular pants	Gym shoes cut-offs T-shirt
EQUIPMENT	Expensive clubs always rents cart very meticulous	Bought one set of clubs ↓ has used them forever	Borrowed clubs, one from several sets of clubs
ATTITUDE	Mental concentration is very good. must have silence/seriousness	has good attitude but doesn't have the proper mechanic	talking & laughing throws off others Shots More concerned with the beer
SCORES results	shoots in the area of par golf or slightly above	Average score 80-95 Glad he went out with the guys	shoots in the neighbor-hood of 130-150, if he can remember Has NO game itself usually too Sunburnt and hungover to remember.

Finally, the student drafted his essay:

A Wonderful Sport

1   Golf is a wonderful recreational sport. There is nothing like playing eighteen holes on a warm summer day. During the summer months and into early fall, the area golf courses are crowded with individuals who enjoy the challenge of sand traps, water hazards, and tree clusters.

2   Golfers fall into several categories. Once on the golf course, one can expect to observe any of the following types: the serious golfer, the pseudo-serious golfer, and the carefree golfer.

3   The serious golfer is the minority of the three categories. These individuals come prepared to wage combat with the golf course. Upon exiting their vehicles, their suit of armor includes the loud green trousers and the yellow golf shirt with an alligator on the pocket. To complement this ensemble, they wear the traditional white golf shoes with tassels. Everything is meticulously neat. Their weapons of battle are the golf clubs, the best that money can buy. Each club is individually covered with a fine leather case. The grips are hand crafted and the blades of the clubs are made of tungsten steel. The serious golfers are concerned with scores of 67 and below. Scoring low is the only excitement these individuals enjoy. When the game begins, concentration and silence are the prevailing strategies. Concentrate and the battle will be won.

4   The next category is what I call the pseudo-serious golfer. These golfers are the majority of all recreational golfers. To this category of golfer, the game is not a battle, but recreation. The pseudo-serious golfer usually dons the golf shirt minus the alligator and dons fashionable, knee-length shorts. Their golf shoes are several years old and have lost their luster. They still carry mud from the last outing. Their weapons of battle are the same clubs that they inherited from dad several years earlier. The grips are slightly worn and the clubs are pitted with rust. But most important to the pseudo-serious golfer, the clubs get the job done. The mind set of these golfers is, "Go out and shoot a good game, but enjoy the outdoors and the company of friends." Scores of 80 or 90 aren't unusual; these golfers simply know how to enjoy the game.

5   The final category of golfer is the carefree golfer. These golfers can be compared to the guy who sits behind you at the movies and talks the entire time. He is annoying. The carefree golfer comes dressed in an old Judas Priest t-shirt (that is later peeled off to "cop" some rays) and cut-off shorts. Golf shoes are unheard of. Converse gym shoes are the order of the day. Their weapons of battle are a bag of assorted clubs that they just purchased at a flea market. The clubs are bent and compiled from various brand-name sets. This golfer is loud and obnoxious. His idea of golf is driving around the golf course and performing donuts with the golf carts. His biggest priority is where the beer holes are located. Usually, these golfers are responsible for long back-ups between holes. Because the carefree golfers take having fun to the extreme, usually at the expense of the others, they are not concerned with their scores. This type of golfer would usually score in the area of 140 to 150. They are in a class all by themselves.

6   Golf is a wonderful sport. As you can see, golf is made up of all kinds. The next time you drive past a public golf course, see if you can identify any of these types of golfers.

Jim Myers

Jim's essay on golfers is quite good. It communicates, and it definitely entertains and interests its reader. In fact, this very week, as I was revising this chapter, I also happened to be vacationing at a golf resort in Mesa, Arizona. Although I am not a golfer (the resort was close to the home of my son and daughter-in-law and granddaughters—in case you were wondering), I was smart enough to sit on the balcony of our room which overlooked the golf course. As I sat in the January sun trying to forget what weather would await me back in Chicago, I became interested in watching the golfers parading before my eyes. I thought of Jim's classification paper and his subgroups as I watched the various golfers enjoying (usually) their games and the warm weather.

Jim's essay is structured and organized quite effectively. It has an introduction with a clear thesis/purpose. It has a good closing. In between, Jim has written his classification in unified and coherent paragraphs—clearly controlled by his chart (or outline). The paragraphs are also developed quite well; they are very concrete and specific. It is Jim's eye for detail which made me think about his paper as I sat watching the golfers. I remembered his comments about the shoes and the clubs, so I began to watch the various golfers for just those principles. Jim is quite accurate in his observations! The ability of a writer to observe life around him or her is what creates interest in a reader. This is how a reader identifies with the writer's thoughts and feelings.

CLASSIFICATION—A FEW MORE STUDENT EXAMPLES

Auto Shows

1   Well, spring is knocking on our back door again, and it is time for all of the hot rods and classic muscle cars to cruise our neighborhood streets. You know, the type of car that turns a head or two while sitting at a stoplight. It's also the best time of the year for local outdoor auto shows. Cars come together from all over Chicagoland to show off their rides. It can be quite interesting also, watching and observing the different kinds of cars and people behind the wheel entering the show. I have classified all the different kinds of people into four different categories: the young "wannabes," the beater who thinks otherwise, the average car nut and the all-out nut.

2   The young "wannabe" crowd is usually eighteen to twenty-two years old. They enter the auto show with a foreign car that has rust spots here and there. The car is sitting low to the ground because the tires and rims are unusually small. The windows are tinted and have the name of a car cub on the rear window with the letters so big it looks out of place. The car stereo is on full blast, deafening the crowd, which is a sure turn-off for most. These guys have about fifteen hundred to two thousand dollars invested in their cars, most of which is in the stereo. The usual wardrobe for "wannabes" consists of a tee-shirt three sizes too big and baggy, baggy pants. The attitude of these kids is loud and obnoxious. The "wannabes" don't know anything about a car either. One of them will open the hood of the car and six or seven of them will gather around it; none of them even know what they're seeing. The only thing I can say for the young "wannabe" crowd is, "Go show off your foreign junk car to the five-year old kids at the park."

3   The second category are the guys with the beater who think their cars are cool. This type is also young, twenty-two to twenty-five years old. They drive mid-eighties American cars; at least they're American cars like a Ford Granada or something. These cars are not as rusty as the "wannabes," but have a very dull paint job. The owners think these cars look nice because they usually have chrome rims with white lettering on the tires. (At least the tires and rims look good.) The car sounds very loud entering because the exhaust system is cut out, thinking it sounds tough. The cars are worth two to three thousand dollars, tops. The clothes this type will wear are an old Led Zeppelin tee-shirt and old, faded blue jeans. These people will try to get your attention by popping the hood of their beater. This technique is pretty effective; it makes people think the car is a sleeper. A sleeper is a car that looks like a "junker" but has a very fast engine. They should just leave the hood closed because ninety-nine percent of the time they only have a six cylinder, which is not very impressive. I feel bad for this type because they know their cars, but just can't afford a sweet ride.

4   Then there is the average car nut, which I favor the most. This group is thirty to fifty years old. Their cars are mostly late fifties, sixties and early seventies, American muscle cars. These cars have very nice and shiny paint jobs, hood scoops and chrome rims, and some are convertibles. Some of them also have "SS" stripes or flames painted on them. You can definitely tell when one of these pulls in; you hear the vicious rumble of the big block. Anyone who knows cars, even just a little, can tell a tough sounding motor on these "bad boys" when they hear one. Most of the muscle cars in this group range from ten thousand to twenty thousand dollars. The attire for this group is mostly a black tee-

shirt with a Chevy logo on it or something of that sort and blue jeans. They are also the most friendly type and are family oriented. Their group is very knowledgeable when it has anything to do with a car. The average car nut will do anything to help you out with a little glitch you might be having with your motor. Once again, this is my favorite group because I guess I fall into this category.

5　　I have one last group which I call the all-out car nut. This group is older; most of them are fifty to seventy years old. Their types of cars are mostly thirties, forties and early fifties American cars. These cars stand out the most because of the extensive modifications to them. Some examples are a chopped top, no hood and the motor is completely chromed out. You will not hear these cars running though; they enter on a trailer. (That's no fun!) These cars are very, very expensive, ranging from thirty-thousand dollars and up. You will see these guys wearing a pink or bright yellow polo shirt with cotton Docker slacks. These guys are so arrogant—that's an understatement! Sure, they have bad-ass rides, but if you don't have fifty thousand put into your car, they won't talk to you. They do know a lot about cars though, I'll give them that. I'd be willing to bet these guys don't even change their own oil. When I look at the all-out nut group, I will think to myself with a grin, I'm driving my baby home, ha, ha!

6　　My final thought is that auto shows are still fun and exciting to attend. To tell you the truth, it's fun taking time out and categorizing the cars and individuals. All in all, these types of people make attending a show that much more fun and exciting.

Steve Pratl

Memo to All "Road Jockeys" Entering This Office

Dear Road Jockeys:

1　　Most people know you simply as truck drivers. I know you by your self-proclaimed title of Road Jockeys. Once you step down out of your truck and cross this office threshold, you are entering my domain. Please check all bad attitudes at the door. There are some thoughts I want to share with a few of the different groups of drivers who enter here.

2　　First, to the Southern-born and bred drivers, I would like to say that you are the true gentlemen of the road. Your appearance is always impeccable. To you, using the words please and thank you is as natural as breathing. I love the "Yes, Ma'am, Thank you, Ma'am," that is part of your vocabulary. Your manner is so relaxed. The coffee is free, but you offer to pay for it anyway. You are courteous enough to pour a cup for me. Some of you have your wives with you. If you don't, I love to hear the calls home just to see how "mother" is doing. It is a pleasure to do business with you. You are all so sweet.

3　　Second, my thoughts are directed to the next group, the city drivers. You come in spotless and well-groomed. Some of you come in with snacks to go with the coffee. We see each other daily, and we have become good friends. We know about each other's spouses, children and jobs. I am always willing to take the time to catch up on your lives. There are times when you call home that I have had the opportunity to talk to your spouse or children. We have shared good and bad times together. Some of us have formed special bonds that I will always treasure. I will always be grateful for these times. You are the best group of people I have the pleasure to work with.

4   Third, my thoughts bring me to another group of drivers. When I see you, I think of mountains and cave-dwellers. Please feel free to use our plant sanitation process as you enter. Obviously, you didn't feel there was a need to visit a truck stop en route. Check them out! They have showers and these shiny objects called mirrors. If you don't like the reflected image, what makes you think I like the real object? Please use these services before you decide that you need to lean all over my desk as if you are about to impart the secret of financial success. You are not E.F. Hutton, and I am not listening. I like Halloween, but only on October 31st. I have to work the rest of the day. I don't have time for a hazmat team to come in and clean. Back off, furball!

5   At last, I come to those of you who consider yourselves Prince Charmings. You are definitely a group I want to address. When you walk through the door, I reach for my sunglasses. I didn't know so much gold existed outside of Fort Knox. With chains and earrings hanging from your neck, ears and wrists, it is a wonder you made it through the weigh scales. Here's an idea for you. Use some of those chains to make suspenders for another hanging item, your jeans. This would cut out the "moon" glare and certainly save my eyesight. I can deal with the long, permed hair and bulging biceps, but do you really think that an open shirt with chains reaching down to your protruding stomach is a good look? I don't think so, especially at lunch time. Please don't look from me to the coffeepot. I am not room service. If both of your arms are not in casts, it is a safe bet I am not pouring your coffee. Calling long-distance does not mean you need to shout into the phone. I don't need to know about the fight you are having with your wives or girlfriends. For some of you it happens to be both.

6   Now, here are some final words to all you Road Jockeys who come through my door. Your reputation as King of the Road has no meaning here. I am Queen of the Office. Take a tip from your southern counterparts. Please do not feel you can pull up a chair and become an office fixture. The better we get along, the faster I can get you on the road again. The Queen has spoken. Thanks for your attention.

Sincerely,
Queen Jane Hargus

The Customer Is Always Right?

1   Another day goes by at Acme Foods in Bridgeview, Illinois. Hundreds of customers walk through my line as I scan their groceries. These customers come from all walks of life. I get to know a lot about people from just scanning their groceries and conversing with them as I do.

2   There are many different types of customers I deal with daily at work. To simplify, I will categorize them under three different classifications, which would be the typical customer, the anal retentive customer, and the fussy customer.

3   First of all, I will begin by describing the typical customer. I would wager to say that the typical customer includes close to fifty percent of all the customers I see daily. This customer is generally friendly and courteous. He or she could be of any age and economic, social, or ethnic background. The typical customer doesn't complain at all, whether it be about the store, the prices, or a bad day at the office. These customers rarely argue the price of an item as atypical customers tend to do. The customer and I usually just

toss small talk back and forth, maybe exchange some recipes, and I send them on their merry way. Overall, an encounter with the typical customer is a pleasant experience.

4   The second type of customer, of the anal retentive variety, is a much larger challenge than the typical customer. Most of the time, these customers consist of the elderly and certain males with a hint of femininity. There are few exceptions to this rule. The easiest way to spot anal retentive customers, though, is when they first come into the lane. Do they fret about a wet spot on the belt? Furthermore, do they insist that I dry the wet spot with sanitizer before they even begin to unload their carts? Some other telltale signs of anal retentive customers are a calculator in hand to make sure that they aren't getting ripped off, and a neat little shopping list with checkmarks on it and carefully-cut coupons handily paperclipped to it. These customers' groceries are all arranged neatly on the belt, frozen foods first, then cans, meat, produce, and bread, respectively. None of the groceries have a scuff or even a scratch on them. There's no doubt in my mind that they were checked meticulously by the customer before purchase. Anal retentive customers are concerned mainly about how careful I am with their ripe tomatoes and if I remember their coupons. While I was scanning his order, one customer must have asked me fifteen times whether or not I had remembered the coupons. I kept telling him that I had to wait until the end of the order to add them on. Nevertheless, he kept asking me if I had remembered the coupons.

5   The final customer that I am mentioning is the fussy customer. These customers are mainly just annoying and disrespectful. From the time that they enter the line to the time that they storm out, they do nothing but complain. Most of the time they have complaints about the store. It's too cold, the floor is sticky, and the prices are too high. Those are somewhat valid complaints, but fussy customers just blow them out of proportion. They treat me as if it is my fault that watermelons are out of season and glare at me as if I'm to blame when their credit card doesn't come through. They're worse on busy days though, when the store is crowded and the lines are long. I actually had one customer yell at me from the end of the line to hurry up and, "get your little butt scannin'." These customers also rudely demand price checks because they insist that something was on sale and the price that came up was wrong. Usually the price was right in the first place. This causes them to grouch even more because they insist that they're right and I'm wrong. A similar situation occurs with the coupons that these customers use. Some of the coupons that they give me are for different brands than what they have purchased. When I tell them that I can't use the coupon, they insist that I can and make a big fuss over it. They usually end up making everyone else in line wait while they go back and get the correct product. Nearly everyone in line gets fussy when that happens.

6   In conclusion, I have observed three main types of grocery store customers: the typical, the anal retentive, and the fussy. Of course, I could have divided my customers into many different subgroups. The possibilities were endless, but I decided to sort them by something of importance to myself, which turned out to be how well they treated me.

Elizabeth Evans

Yeah . . . That's the Ticket!

1   As a police officer, I make traffic stops almost every single day. I make stops for speeding, violating stop signs, violating traffic signals, and just about every other statute in the Illinois vehicle code. No matter what the violation, the driver will always fall into one of three categories: the honest violator, the completely innocent driver, and the driver who knows that he's guilty, but gives a totally lame excuse for his actions.

2   I have an easy way of identifying which type of driver I've stopped. I ask, "Do you know why I've stopped you?" The driver's response will immediately tell me which of the three categories he fits into.

3   The honest violator will respond, "Yes. I was speeding." He won't even attempt to justify his actions. If anyone has a chance of getting off with a warning, it's this guy. He doesn't want to argue. He knows that he screwed up and that I'm only doing my job. This driver is a pleasure to deal with. Unfortunately, they're very rare.

4   The exact opposite of the honest driver is the completely innocent driver. I have to admit that I have never figured out if the completely innocent driver is trying to pull a fast one, is completely insane, or if he actually believes that he is innocent. Perhaps it's a combination of all three.

5   This is the driver whose response to "Do you know why I've stopped you?" will be a look of total and complete annoyance, followed by the statement, "I have no idea." I think that these types of drivers have meetings and newsletters to keep in contact with one another, because they all do exactly the same thing when I tell then that they were speeding. First, he asks to see the radar. Then, once he sees the radar, he says, "How do I know that's me?" I feel certain that if I were to show him the video tape of his car speeding, he would say, "How do I know that you didn't speed up the tape?"

6   Not only does this driver have no chance in hell of getting off the hook, he will often talk himself into a second or third ticket. I once had a driver say to me, "Haven't you got anything better to do?" I took a step back and said, "Let me show you how little I have to do." I proceeded to walk slowly around his car. As I came upon a new violation, I would call out to him, "I see you have a cracked windshield." I continued, "How long has this headlight been out?" By the time I got to the lack of a muffler, he had five tickets. NASA could use a genius like this guy.

7   The last driver is the most entertaining of all. This is the driver who knows that he is guilty, but tries to justify his actions by the lamest excuse possible. I love this guy. This is the guy who, when he is stopped for speeding, will say, "I'm not from around here. I'm from Crestwood." I'll say, "Do they have speed limit signs in Crestwood?" He'll say, "Yes." I'll close the conversation by saying, "They're the same here. We try not to change them, for fear of confusing people." Ultimately, I will explain to him that all we are required to do is post the speed limit signs. We can't force people to read them.

8   One of my favorite excuses from this driver is, "I know I was speeding, but I was going downhill." I'll shine my flashlight down on the floorboard, near the driver's feet. When he asks what I'm looking for I say, "I was just checking to see if this model came equipped with the brake option."

9   Equally entertaining is the guy who claims, "I know that I was speeding, but I'm lost." Maybe I'm crazy, but when I'm lost, I usually slow down in order to look for familiar streets and landmarks. They're much more difficult to spot at 55 mph than they are at 35 mph.

10   Who could forget the ever-popular, "I was speeding because I was running out of gas." The classics die hard. Without even attempting to get into the physics of fuel consumption, I usually take the easy way out by simply pointing out, "Well, if you hadn't been speeding, you'd probably have spotted the gas station that you just passed up."

11   People will do just about anything to void getting a ticket, short of simply obeying the law. It never ceases to amaze me when I see drivers pull up to an intersection alongside of my squad car, and they reach over and casually put on their seatbelt. They'll put on a seatbelt to avoid a ticket, but they won't put it on to save their lives.

12   Whatever category you happen to fit into, please know that calling a policeman a liar will get you nowhere that you care to be. We've been listening to excuses far longer than you've been making them up. There is no conspiracy to get you. There is no second radar gun up on the grassy knoll, and there was no bloody glove planted at O.J.'s house. If you screw up, admit it. It's far easier to overlook a mistake than a lie.

Scott Sodaro

All Aboard!

1   Of all the possible subjects that a potential hobbyist might choose, one that continues to soar in popularity is model railroading. At one time or another, everyone is fascinated with model railroading; its participants range in age from one to one-hundred and one. The versatile talents of those who participate in this hobby result in many new and exciting "places" that fellow hobbyists, and non-hobbyists alike, can explore for hours at a time. Having been a model railroad enthusiast for approximately fifteen years, I have found that all hobbyists are not alike. Most fit into the following four groups: the "Once-a-Year" railroader, the "Good Father" railroader, the "4 x 8 Sheet of Plywood" railroader, and the "Empire Builder" railroader.

2   The "Once-a-Year" railroaders become active a few weeks before Christmas. Their inexpensive train set is usually found "on sale" at the local Walgreen's. It consists of a plastic, battery operated locomotive, accessories decorated in the current seasonal motif, and a basic oval track. When the track is placed beneath the holiday tree, the scenery falls into place immediately: one large tree, hundreds of pretty lights, and a multitude of gift packages strategically placed to simulate a tunnel or two. As the train travels the track, the grinding of plastic gears, an annoying clickity-clack, and the incessant ringing of a bell can be heard until, thankfully, the batteries go dead or the baby breaks the off/on switch. Usually after one day of operation, the train will become neglected until it is disassembled and put away with all the other holiday decorations. One note to the inexperienced: remove the batteries before storing for the next season. If this is not done, there is a possibility that the batteries may leak and cause irreparable damage . . . darn!

3   The next type is the "Good Father" railroader. The "good fathers" are the most-patient and understanding of all model railroaders. This is because they are forced to deal with adverse, external factors not directly related to the hobby: screaming and whining children, limited space to work, and an endless variety of other chores that need to be done at the same time. The train set that they work with is a moderately priced, midsize HO scale variety found at Toys "R" Us. Its parts are big enough so that the children won't swallow them, but too small for their uncoordinated fingers to work with. An electric trans-

former eliminates the need for batteries and allows just enough power to operate a single locomotive. The figure-eight track is usually set up on the children's bedroom carpeting, and it has a rather crude trestle where they cross in the middle. The scenery is more creative: buildings made of Lego blocks, metal Hot Wheels or Matchbox vehicles, and small stuffed animals or action figures. If all goes well, the train can negotiate most of the track until it gets to the top of the trestle. At that point, the inadequate track connectors will come apart under the weight of the locomotive causing a severe derailment. At this point, the children and the "good dad" become disinterested and take an extended break. This break can last for hours, days, or months during which the train and track get stepped on, kicked, or used for other things. It will eventually end up at the bottom of the kids' toy box.

4　　　If the "Good Father" railroader experiences any success, he may graduate into the next group: the "4 x 8 Sheet of Plywood" railroader. These railroaders should be given a great deal of credit for all their accomplishments. They take the same HO scale railroad set that ended up at the bottom of the kids' toy box, repair or replace any damaged parts, and find a private location where they make improvements to the original concept without "help" from the rest of the family. They patiently research the intricacies of the hobby by looking at track plans found in the "Guide to Model Railroad" primer sold at the local hobby shop. These track plans will suggest to the "hobbyist" (at this point, the title takes on meaning) ways to get the most track in the smallest area that will hopefully result in acceptable performance. The track is nailed together on a sheet of plywood measuring 4 foot wide by 8 foot long, hence the classification of this group. The plywood is painted green or covered with indoor/outdoor carpeting to simulate "greenery" and a road is also painted on later. The Lego blocks and Hot Wheel cars are replaced by plastic buildings, trees, rocks, and vehicles that are "in scale" with the actual railroad components, giving the layout a realistic look. Eventually, additional track is added, buildings are arranged to make better use of the limited real estate, and a more powerful transformer is added so two locomotives can be run at the same time. This type of modeler runs out of ambition around the same time he discovers that his layout can no longer accommodate any more modifications, or golf season begins. The layout is then stood up against a basement or garage wall (hidden) until the kids discover it. At this point, the railroader will have no choice but to relinquish all his hard work back to them.

5　　　The last group of railroaders is by far the most ambitious. They start as "Once-a-Year" modelers, survive the "Good Father" phase, and pay their dues as a "4 x 8 Sheet of Plywood" experimenter. They ignore their family, take control of the check book, and disappear to become the "Empire Builder" railroader. The scale of their layout doesn't matter because space is of no concern; this modeler takes over the entire basement in order to fulfill his dream of building the most elaborate train layout known to man. His components, only those considered top-of-the line by the National Model Railroad Association (NMRA), are purchased in bulk to help save a dollar or two. A grid-type benchwork twists and turns around the furnace, water heater, washer and dryer; any usable space is fair game. Tunnels, valleys with simulated water, and trestles are designed into the track plan. Numerous turnouts, sidings, and spurs are found along the double-mainline track. Anything that simulates a prototypical railroad operation is included. The buildings are handmade from wood and plastic parts. They are painted and weathered to match the "theme" of the layout. Miniature trees and bushes, rocks from the driveway, and earth-colored scenery are used to make this type of layout come "alive." And don't forget its most impressive feature: computer control! Money is no object if this modeler wishes to control everything from the "control room." The "control room" is a special location where the computer and monitor, a television for watching the football game, and a small beer cooler are located. If all the track is laid perfectly, the "Empire Builder" will be able to run multiple trains around the layout without having to do anything more than call for help if the beer runs out.

6   As you can see, model railroaders follow a defined path of development. In the end, they will drive their spouses crazy with all the "train" talk, their lack of concern when caught at train crossings while groceries spoil in the trunk of the car, and their inability to check the savings account balance before heading off to the local hobby shop. Friends and relatives will notice these changes and offer their sincere condolences to the "train widow." This behavior continues until text and pictures describing the "Empire Builder's" layout are published in the September issue of *Model Railroader* magazine. Soon after, the layout is carefully disassembled by professional movers, set up at the Railroad Historical Museum, and a check for $15,000 is presented to the modeler on national television. His friends and relatives think he is awesome. They call him day and night asking for advice on how to build their own model railroad.

Richard Donnellan, Sr.

Prague's Restaurants and Pubs

March 28, 1996

Hi Randy,

1   Perhaps one day you will decide to go to Europe and see some different countries. And if you have enough time, you shouldn't forget to visit one of the most beautiful places in the world, the architectural jewel—Prague, the capital of the Czech Republic. You won't find just the indescribable spirit of the town and the finest crystal, but you'll also get an opportunity to try the great liquid which we Bohemians are very proud of—the Czech beer, incomparable with your American stuff. Before you stop for several beers and some food after tiring sightseeing, here are three basic groups of restaurants which you can easily find: the luxurious restaurants, the middle class restaurants, and the pubs. I think that it is good to know some primary facts about each of these.

2   First, the luxurious restaurants are usually located in the most attractive areas in the centre of the town, and it is often obvious at first glance of the menu that you will have to spend an amount large enough for several other days of your visit. They are usually very nice places with quiet music, and the professional staff always speaks at least some basic German and English. Their cuisine is international, and they serve the best beers such as Pilsner Urqell or Czech Budweiser, who sold the name to the U.S. after WW II, in 0.3 liter bottles. The 0.3 liter bottles are quite rare, and they are usually determined only for export. The common bottles are 0.5 liter, and beer in the other restaurants is served in 0.5 liter heavy glasses, too. These luxurious restaurants are mostly visited by the rich and by snobs or are used for official business meetings and more significant celebrations. I definitely wouldn't suggest these spots to go in for dinner and beer!

3   The second group are the ordinary restaurants. They are located everywhere from the centre to the edge of the town. These places are clean, often stylish. Sometimes part of the restaurant is a little garden with huge, old trees, so people can enjoy their tasty lunches outside during nice days or just drink and have fun under a sky full of stars in the warm evenings. If you are lucky, the staff will speak a little English, but don't worry if they won't! They have menus in English and German, so it is all right to just point with your finger and say "PIVO" which is a simple Czech word that means beer. They serve many so-called finished foods, which are already cooked and kept warm, or you can order food such as steak, etc., which takes longer. The food is usually very appetizing. These restaurants offer beer from some of Prague's breweries or breweries somewhere near Prague, always on tap, and the choices are 10, 11, or 12 degree beer. The degrees tell you how strong the beer is. You can also get some other beers in bottles and a wide selection of soft drinks. The price of beer is kept a little higher to discourage the alcoholics, and you would pay between 10 and 30 Kc (Czech Crowns), which is roughly $0.40 to $1.20 for half a liter of great beer. The food ranges from 25 to 100 Kc ($1–4). These places are frequently visited by businessmen and working people during lunch breaks, people who don't want to cook, and groups of friends. It can be an appropriate place for a business meeting or a party, too. I would highly recommend a place of this type for its wonderful food and beer, clean environment, and especially very favorable prices.

4   The third group, pubs, can be found everywhere outside the downtown area, but you will probably not find them anywhere else in the world. These pubs, often pretentiously called restaurants, are old, ugly, and without unnecessary decorations. The smoke inside is often so thick that it is hard to breathe. They serve some simple food such as beef stew, warm or cold meatloaf, sausage, etc. The 10 or 12 degree beer is always on tap, and it is extremely cheap but good. The price of a half a liter beer is around 6 Kc for 10 or 12 Kc for 12 degree beer which is 25 or 50 cents. The servers usually can hardly speak Czech correctly, but you don't have to say anything, and your beer will be put in front of you without any questions. Don't be surprised if another glass full of cold beer with huge white foam on the top will hit the table after just about one inch of beer is left in your beer glass! The pubs are noisy, and nobody really cares what you are doing if you don't care about them. Drunks are often discussing politics or singing nasty songs. Eighty to ninety percent of customers are heavy alcoholics and workers who spend their free time there after, or sometimes also before, their shift. The rest of the people whom you can meet there are youths, artists, or accidental visitors who just come for a beer as would be you. I believe that it is a necessary experience in Prague to visit not just the great popular tourist attractions, but also places such as these pubs which belong inseparably to the culture. And isn't it gorgeous to get completely drunk just for $ 2.50 or less!?

5   Now, it is up to you to decide what you are going to do in Prague during your prospective visit, but don't forget that every beer you will drink will help the Czechs stay first in beer consumption in the world!

Bye,
William B.
William Bohutinsky

POSSIBLE TOPICS

The possible topics for a classification paper are virtually unlimited. My students seem to enjoy classifying people, but any objects, ideas, or places can be classified.

Here is a list of topics that might inspire you. Most of these come from papers my students have written.

> ministers, students, teachers, drinkers, partygoers, eaters, smokers, gum chewers, girl watchers, TV weathermen, talk shows, soap operas, movie heroes, plane and train passengers, laughs, kisses, kissers, lovers, parents, children, rock singers, rock groups, people in the bathroom, salesmen, customers, attics, basements, garages, backyards, suburban neighborhoods, politicians, accountants, lawyers, TV police shows, librarians, blind dates, first dates, philosophies, religions, governments, puddle jumpers, gas station attendants, d.j.'s, waiters, dancers, swearers, obscene phone calls. . . .

I hope this list gives you some ideas. If you still don't have an idea for your classification paper, go to a shopping center, sit down, sip on a cola, and watch the people. See any possible topics? If not, classify people who cannot think of topics for writing assignments!

THE CLASSIFICATION PAPER: YOUR TURN

1 Choose the topic or group.

2 Break the group into subgroups and select those principles of classification you wish to incorporate into the essay.

3 Make a classification chart and fill in some of the details you will use when you write the paper.

4 Review the chart you have just completed. Make certain that the subgroups are thorough and are free of overlap. Also be certain that you will have adequate detail to develop each subgroup. Next, tentatively decide how you are going to paragraph the subgroups.

5 Write the rough draft of your paper.

CLASSIFICATION PAPER PLAN SHEET

Part One: Choose a topic for a classification paper.

Topic (group): _____

Next, list the subgroups.

1. _____

2. _____

3. _____

4. _____

5. _____

Next, list the principles of classification.

1. _____

2. _____

3. _____

4. _____

Finally, construct a thesis statement for the essay. _____

_____

_____

If you wish, go ahead and write the introduction at this time.

_____

_____

_____

_____

_____

_____

Subgroups: → Principles: →			

SELF-EVALUATION SHEET: PART ONE

Assignment: _____

Strong points of this assignment:

_____

_____

_____

_____

_____

_____

_____

Weak points of this assignment:

_____

_____

_____

_____

_____

_____

_____

General comments:

_____

_____

_____

_____

_____

_____

_____

(over)

SELF-EVALUATION SHEET: PART TWO

What were the strong points of your last writing assignment?

_____

_____

_____

_____

_____

_____

What were the weak points of your last writing assignment?

_____

_____

_____

_____

_____

_____

What have you done to correct those weaknesses in this assignment?

_____

_____

_____

_____

_____

_____

Evaluator's Name _____ Section _____ Date _____

PEER-EVALUATION SHEET: PEER-EVALUATOR #1

Writer's Name _____ Essay's Title _____

> **Directions:** (1) Remember not to write on another student's paper. Instead, use this form. (2) Offer concrete, specific comments using the terminology of writing (e.g., "The development in paragraph four might be improved by adding a brief example." or, "Check structure on page 3.")

What do you see as the strong points of this writing assignment: _____

_____

_____

_____

_____

What areas do you feel might need additional work: _____

_____

_____

_____

_____

Do you see any areas of grammar/mechanics (e.g. usage, spelling, fragments) that might need attention: _____

_____

_____

_____

_____

General comments: _____

_____

_____

_____

_____

PEER-EVALUATION SHEET: PEER-EVALUATOR #2

Writer's Name _____ Essay's Title _____

Directions: (1) Remember not to write on another student's paper. Instead, use this form. (2) Offer concrete, specific comments using the terminology of writing (e.g., "The development in paragraph four might be improved by adding a brief example." or, "Check structure on page 3.")

What do you see as the strong points of this writing assignment: _____

_____

_____

_____

_____

What areas do you feel might need additional work: _____

_____

_____

_____

_____

Do you see any areas of grammar/mechanics (e.g. usage, spelling, fragments) that might need attention: _____

_____

_____

_____

_____

General comments: _____

_____

_____

_____

_____

The Definition Paper

OVERVIEW

Definition, sometimes referred to as extended definition, is a method of development in which the writer explains a word, a phrase, or a term. Extended definition is the method of development we use to answer a child's question such as, "What is school?" or to answer an old person's question such as, "What is aging with dignity?". We also use definition when we explain words that have strong emotional ties: a definition of life when we are arguing abortion, a definition of freedom when we are discussing gun control or censorship, or a definition of love when we are planning a marriage or a divorce. Anytime we find ourselves explaining a word, a phrase, or a term, we are using the expository method of development known as definition.

DEFINITION

When people hear the word *definition,* they may also think of the word *dictionary,* and this is a good association. The **dictionary definition** is the most common approach to defining a word, a term, or a short phrase. A dictionary definition includes a brief history of a word, a pronunciation guide, and several brief and objective meanings. Dictionary definitions are written by lexicographers whose primary purpose is to describe the most common meanings of words in a language.

For example, if you were to look up the word *lexicographer* in the dictionary, you would probably find the following entry:

lexicographer: an author or compiler of a dictionary

This definition describes the meaning most-commonly ascribed the word. One cannot disagree, for this definition is fairly standard. It is objective.

Although few people realize it, there is another way to define a word, with a **formal definition.** In a formal definition, the term is defined by placing it in a class (genus) and by describing or explaining the qualities that differentiate it from other members of its class.

This is the general formula for a formal definition:

term to be defined = class + differentiating characteristics

To formally define a word, simply "plug" it into this formula. For example, let's define the words *heartburn* and *mumps.*

TERM	CLASS	DIFFERENTIATING CHARACTERISTICS
Heartburn	Disease	A burning discomfort behind the sternum.
Mumps	Disease	An acute disease, characterized by a fever and by swelling of the parotid gland.

Both mumps and heartburn are diseases, but the differentiating characteristics readily define the two terms. As you can see from the above examples, the formal definition is brief, precise, impersonal, and objective. It usually is not longer than a sentence, and its main purpose is to inform.

EXTENDED DEFINITION

Extended definition contrasts with the two previous methods of definition we have discussed. While dictionary definitions and formal definitions are precise, logical, concise, and objective, extended definitions are lengthy, personal, and highly subjective. Extended definitions vary in length from sentences to paragraphs to essays to entire books. Extended definition, as a form of expository writing, is usually written to explain the writer's view of an abstract term. Or perhaps the writer wishes to disagree with the formal or dictionary definition of a term. A great many extended definitions actually begin with the dictionary or formal definition of the word being defined. Other writers use extended definition to clarify their view of a term or to explain their interpretation of a current fad or slang term. Whatever his or her reason, the writer of extended definition writes with a purpose.

 ## GUIDELINES FOR WRITING AN EXTENDED DEFINITION ESSAY

- **One,** an extended definition is usually longer than a dictionary definition; thus, the name: *extended*. This is a relative statement, obviously; extended definitions can be as short as a paragraph or two or as long as several hundred pages (such as a legal definition of *obscene,* for example, or a legal definition of words such as *sanity* or *life*).

- **Two,** an extended definition is a personal (or subjective) explanation of a word, a term, or a phrase. Whether the reader agrees or disagrees with the writer's definition is irrelevant. What is relevant is that the reader knows and understands what the word means to the person who wrote the definition.

  This subjective quality of extended definition is best illustrated by an example. What, for example, is a good teacher? Ask this question and you will likely get a variety of answers. A lot of people might not even make a connection between the words teacher and school. Some people might say a good teacher is a person who leads an exemplary life. Others might say a good teacher is a minister or a guru or a home computer. If the word is linked with school, the definition will still reflect differences of opinion. Some students might think a good teacher is one who gives everyone A's or makes tests and assignments so easy that everyone "earns" high grades. Still other students might define a good teacher as a person who works students past their abilities and then demands even more. Other students might define a good teacher as an instructor who is a friend as much as a teacher, an individual who gets involved both personally and academically with his or her students. Obviously, extended definition allows the personal expression of ideas. As long as each person expresses his ideas clearly and fully, the definition should be clear. This is the basic principle that you must keep in mind when writing an extended definition essay.

■ **Three,** when choosing a topic for an extended definition essay, choose a word which is abstract or which is of interest to you. Although this is a suggestion and not a requirement, it does make the task easier. Most students find it easier to define a challenging abstract word, such as *fear* or *boredom* or *education,* than to define a very concrete word, such as *pencil, wine glass,* or *cigar.* Generally, the more-challenging topic also proves to be more-interesting to both writer and reader.

■ **Four,** provide the essay with structure and organization. This requires that the writer accept total responsibility for shaping the essay; there is no certain way to write an extended definition. The structure and the organization (and the method or methods of development) must be determined by the writer. This is one of the reasons that extended definition is taught after other methods of writing papers and paragraphs. One writer, for example, might define *neighbor* by describing the person living next to her. Another writer might define *neighbor* by comparing-contrasting two people he has lived next to. A third writer might define *neighbor* by classifying the various people who live on her block. In short, a writer might wish to define by classifying, by describing, by using example(s), by comparing-contrasting, by analyzing cause-effect situations, or by a combination of these or other methods. By now you have learned a lot of writing theories about narration, description, and exposition; use that knowledge to write an extended definition.

■ **Five,** use detail and example to develop each paragraph. Since your topic is most-likely an abstract word, it is your responsibility to make it concrete and meaningful to your reader. As this text has shown, the best way to create images in a reader's mind is to use specific detail and example.

Before we continue our discussion of extended definition, let's look at a student example.

War

1   <u>Webster's New World Dictionary</u> defines war as, "open conflict between countries or between factions within the same country. Any active hostility, contention or struggle; conflict."

2   What this definition lacks is the emotion connected to war. People can read about war, or they can watch war movies on television. The only true way to define war is to experience it. I know; I served in Vietnam from 1970 through 1971. I will define war from a personal view.

3   The first effect war has on a person is that of fear. You arrive in the combat zone scared to death. You realize that people will be trying to kill you every second, minute, and hour of each day that you are there. This killing is sanctioned and legal. You question yourself everyday, "Will I get 'zapped' today or tomorrow?". The thing about war is you never know when you're going to get it. The thought of dying is constant; it's always on your mind. You can't eat, sleep, think, or relax for a minute. War has a profound effect on the senses.

4   In war, you see death in its most violent form. You see it up close. Killing another human being from a distance of twenty feet or most times closer than that is a horrible sight. When you fire your weapon or toss a grenade, you see the results first hand. You literally see people being ripped apart. Blood, body parts, and clothing are thrown everywhere.

5   The sounds of gunfire and shelling are heard daily. These are the sounds of war. As a result of the shellings, men, women, and children are all casualties of war. You can hear people screaming in pain, their bodies ravaged by bullets or shrapnel. They cry out

for their mothers or someone to come to their aid. Some are so badly wounded that they literally beg you to put them out of their misery. As you try to aid the wounded, you can still hear the bombs falling, the gunfire, the jets and the choppers all around you.

6   Caring for the wounded requires a good sense of touch. Here, you can touch the effects of war as you frantically attempt to save the casualties. You administer morphine, bandages, or anything that will stop the bleeding in order to save a life. You hold a fellow soldier in your arms to comfort him. You stroke his hair and tell him that he'll make it, even though he knows that both of his legs have been blown off. You have to keep telling him that he's going to make it.

7   In war, many people don't make it. This is when your sense of smell is affected. You can smell death all around you. The smell of bodies lying in the hot jungles decaying. The bodies eventually explode from the gases that build up in them. Imagine the carcass of a dead deer on hot asphalt after five days, only ten times worse. Or, the excrement from the bowels of the soldier that is dying or has died in your arms. You can smell the gunpowder after a fire fight and the kerosene in the jet fuel if they fly low enough after a bombing raid.

8   Lastly, you can taste war. As you walk through the jungles fully equipped, you sweat profusely. The sweat pours down your face into your mouth; you can taste the salt. All of a sudden, the artillery and the rockets begin to fall. In order to survive, you have to hit the ground. You taste the dirt and dust as the bombs fall all around you. If you're really lucky, you'll survive.

9   War is a horribly tragic event. There isn't much to laugh about, but there is plenty to cry about. War is not for the weak, but for the fittest. War is emotional. When your best friend dies in your arms or you see a child's body that is turned inside out, you have to question the validity of war or "open conflicts between countries."

10   In the last several months of the war in the Persian Gulf, Americans had been tying yellow ribbons around trees and proclaiming how great the war went. I wonder if most of these Americans were to see the real outcome of the war, particularly the 150,000 civilian deaths, would they think that war was so wonderful? Is killing 150,000 people over oil worth it? Or, is death on a massive scale condoned in order to justify how wonderful one's country is over another's? Someone once said, "War is hell." I don't agree. At least in hell you know you're dead. The pain of seeing, hearing, touching, smelling, and tasting war is over. Hell would be a vacation from war.

Jim Myers

Now that you have finished reading Jim's essay, I think you know what the word war means to him. You might not agree, nor might Mr. Webster, but you do understand what the term means to Jim. He has succeeded in defining the word. This is the purpose of extended definition. However, he has not just defined the word war; he has also used his essay to make definite and strong statements about war. In paragraph nine, for example, he really communicates his feelings about war: "When your best friend dies in your arms or you see a child's body that is turned inside out, you have to question the validity of war or 'open conflicts between countries.'" This statement's strength comes not only from its concreteness—that is, Jim's ability to use concrete and specific detail—but also from the conviction of its writer. The entire essay is clearly well-developed. The essay communicates like a strong, brisk punch to the gut.

The essay is well-structured and well-organized. Paragraphs are unified and coherent. Jim's outline reflects his control over his writing; in this instance, he opted to use—primarily—the senses to order his ideas:

OUTLINE

WAR: Definition

definition: lacks emotion, the confrontation

Describe war from ~
1. The mind: fear
2. How it affects the senses.
   A. sight - see destruction, killing
   B. hearing - bombs, rockets, people crying because they've been hit or crying because they want to go home. you also hear the people.
   C. Smell - To smell death, finding the remains of the dead after weeks in the hot jungle.
   D. Touch - Frantic attempt to render first aid to your buddies who have been hit or ripped apart by booby traps.
   E. Taste - sweat pouring off your face from the heat and fear. Eating dust and dirt as the choppers land or as you fall to the ground from rocket attacks.

The next example is based upon a job description, a subject that many of my students write about. As you read her definition of her job, notice the many methods of development she used to define medical transcriptionist.

More Than Typists

1   I am often asked, "What do you do on your job?". I reply, "I'm a medical transcriptionist." This reply is processed, interpreted, and relayed back to me as, "Oh, you're a typist." At that point, the hairs on the back of my neck bristle, my jaw tightens, and my teeth clench. I will endeavor to explain how my job as a medical transcriptionist is comprised of much more than being a "typist."

2   The literal definitions of transcribe (which transcriptionist is a derivative of) are: "1. To make a full written or typewritten copy of (dictated material, for example). 2. To transfer (information) from one recording and storing system to another. 3. To translate or transliterate." The American Association for Medical Transcriptionists (AAMT), a professional organization for medical transcriptionists, describes a medical transcriptionist as a "medical language specialist," an expert in patient care documentation.

3   As a medical transcriptionist in a community hospital, a teaching university, or even as a home-based independent contractor, I must be able to transcribe the basic four documents: 1) Histories and Physicals, 2) Consultations, 3) Operative Summaries, 4) Discharge Summaries. Since I am employed in a local community hospital, my job as a transcriptionist requires that I transcribe X-ray reports, pathology reports which includes both the gross and microscopic descriptions, psychology evaluations, electroencephalograms (EEG), cardiac catheterization reports, Do Not Resuscitate orders, patient progress notes, some insurance correspondence, and committee-based doctor correspondence.

4   But, before I was able to transcribe the above reports, correspondence, etc., my keyboarding skills (typing speed) had to be tested. A minimum of 65 wpm was required. A course in Medical Terminology was a prerequisite. Most hospitals also require "previous experience" as a medical transcriptionist. Since I was fortunate enough to be hired by a hospital, it meant I had the tenacity to overcome the "Catch 22" implied in that phrase "previous experience." How do you get "previous experience" if the hospital you're applying to won't hire someone who needs to be trained? Working for a medical transcription service, being paid by the lines you produce, and literally, "learning on the job," while you have no benefits at all, is how I overcame the "Catch 22."

5   Computer skills are required also. The basics of being able to find my way around a computer keyboard were essential. Knowing what the function keys do in the particular program I am working in certainly helps. I had to learn the word processing program I would be working with daily. Most word processing programs for transcriptionists also have an abbreviation program. This means an abbreviation can be typed instead of the words, phrases, whole paragraphs, and "normals" that are repeatedly used in medical transcription. Then, that abbreviation is instantly replaced by whatever it represents. For example, typing the letters pa, then hitting F7, would replace those letters with the word patient. Sounds like a time saver doesn't it? As of the last reprinting of our abbreviation list, we have 17 pages (yes 17), of just abbreviations. To try to remember what the abbreviation is for certain phrases, words, etc., as I listen to a foreign-born, heavily-accented, English-as-a-second-language doctor has been quite a challenge.

6   All of the above—knowledge of the "basic 4" reports, keyboarding and computer skills, education and experience, certainly help define what a medical transcriptionist is, but beyond the basics there are some "value added" qualities which should be incorporated in that definition.

7   When English is a second language for those who are dictating, I must interpret the effect of their accent on their dictation, and sometimes sentence structure as well, which

may be based on their native language. Regional accents among U.S.-born natives also presents a challenge. Since most people speak differently than they write, most dictation cannot be transcribed verbatim. Since it is my job to translate the spoken word to the written word, I must interpret and edit, <u>never</u> changing the meaning of the dictation or the style of the dictator.

8   Dictation is often done while the doctor is doing other things. Often times there are background noises of ringing phones, dogs barking, children crying, the dictator eating or chewing, burping (my personal favorite), or traffic noises if he is dictating in his car. Any sounds other than the dictation itself obscures the dictation. Sometimes background noise is so loud, the dictation cannot be separated from it. The dictator may dictate excessively slow or fast. He may mumble or be loud. All these factors influence the degree to which the dictation can be understood. I have developed an "ear" for transcribing. All background noises are filtered out. I have learned to pick up that dropped syllable at the end of the word. The lab results that are "chewed through," while the dictator is eating a snack or lunch must be transcribed, and transcribed accurately.

9   Internal inconsistencies in a report are recognized when I have typed a previous report on a particular patient. Perhaps a consultant is dictating on a patient whose History and Physical I have typed for the patient's attending doctor, and he indicates that he does not have the records in front of him and that the history is being taken from an unreliable patient (i.e., a nursing home resident). If something is dictated that sets off my "internal bell," such as incorrect lab values, inconsistencies in a patient's history, etc., I will flag this report for the dictator's attention. This type of monitoring sets the stage for a consistent medical record for the patient.

10   Sometimes dictation includes new words, new procedure, new equipment, slang, or difficult-to-document terminology. I remember the first time a doctor dictated that a patient had had a cabbage. Until I was able to verify this to mean the patient had had a CABG (coronary artery bypass graft), I had no idea what to document in this patient's records. I must be current on new terminology, new procedures, and new equipment. To do this I subscribe to several trade and professional magazines. Reference books must be kept current. Besides the reference books that are provided by my employer, I have a whole library of books I purchased to research new, unfamiliar, or difficult-to-find terminology. No, I am not reimbursed for this expenditure by my employer. It is something I do because I take pride in being a medical transcriptionist.

11   Transcription is the process of translating the spoken word to the printed word (paper-based or computer-based). I edit for grammar and syntax, reorganize content, research new or unfamiliar terminology, make obvious corrections and translate abbreviations when their meaning can be determined. I do this in a work environment which is sometimes less than ideal. I may have inadequate or out-dated references. I don't have access to the patient's medical record or the dictator, which would be my best source for clarification and accuracy of what I am documenting. I sometimes work with unqualified medical transcriptionists. And, I do this under the constant pressure where "quantity," not "quality," is stressed.

12   The next time you have access to your hospital medical records, think about the definition of a medical transcriptionist (as you have known it up until now). Until I became one, I never knew they existed either. Nor did I know how the record of my hospitalization reflected the transcriptionist that typed it. Medical transcriptionists are more than "typists." Tell a friend.

Bea Paller

EXTENDED DEFINITION—AN ALTERNATIVE APPROACH

Have you or your group of friends or your family ever taken a word which is common to most people and given it a new meaning? Or have you ever created a new word? If you have, you have no doubt used this altered or new word in front of someone unfamiliar with your definition and received a look of shock, bewilderment, surprise, or amusement. When you tell that person what the word means and when you explain how to use the word, you are making use of extended definition. If you explained your word to enough people and they began to use it and explain it to other people, your word might eventually appear in a dictionary.

Every year, the English language adds many new words and phrases (or "new" definitions to "old" words) that someone (it might as well be you) created. When I wrote the very first edition of this book back at Cave Man University, for example, my vocabulary did not contain words such as robotics, modem, gigabyte, couch potato, internet, fax, and teleconferencing. And although I might have used them, the following words have an entirely new meaning to me today: mouse, web, toolbar, chat room, gopher, hardware, virus, and disk. It's obvious that our language is alive—and hopefully well.

It isn't just the world of technology that creates new words; we all do. Within our groups of friends and/or families, we tend to "speak the same language." That is, we create words—or create new and/or different meanings for existing words. In the day-to-day communication within our household, for example, it is not uncommon to hear the phrase, "Augie Fagel did it!" This means the invisible man who lives with us has struck again, usually in the middle of the night. Augie has been known to devour the last piece of French Silk which was being closely coveted by a sleeping family member, the last piece of deep-dish pizza left from the previous night's dinner, or the last few scoops of chocolate ripple just waiting for their rightful owner to claim them. Augie isn't just into food, however. He loves to drive but is not knowledgeable about pumping gas, he loves to wear whatever someone else has had cleaned and bagged, and he is adept at borrowing anything from a hairbrush to a twenty to a favorite CD—all of which are never returned. And since no one under our roof ever admits to any of these deeds, we know that it is Augie who is at fault. We even use his last name as a verb; this morning, for example, when I discovered my new sweatshirt was missing, I stared at the empty space in my dresser and exclaimed, "Damn. I've been Fageled!" Once, a visitor in our household overheard these carryings-on and inquired as to the origin of Augie's name. I had always suspected that this invisible man lived with us, but I never knew his name. Until. . . . To make a long story short, my son Eric came home from preschool one day after rehearsing for the Christmas program. As he walked into my home office, he was still singing the last song they had rehearsed. Smiling, he belted out—majestically, I must add with paternal pride—"Oh come, Augie Fagel. . . ." Don't tell me that Augie Fagel isn't a "real word," that it isn't in the dictionary. To me and others in my family, it communicates thoughts and feelings. Like all words/phrases, Augie Fagel is a symbol of meaning. It is real.

What "real" words do you know that the rest of us don't know? Why not share them? Doing so could make writing extended definition a lot easier—and as one of my students once said—much funner. When writing about a word of your own creation, you are still using the basic approach outlined earlier in this chapter. You are still taking a grouping of letters and explaining what thoughts, ideas, and/or feelings are represented by those letters. Your definition is still precise, subjective, organized, structured, and developed. Sure sounds like writing an extended definition paper, doesn't it!

Let's take a look at an example:

Dawn-flection
or
Dawn's Reflection on My Life

1   Dark clouds are edged with muted violet and silver; faint streaks of crimson glow behind them. Dim outlines of trees take shape as their leaves flutter with the passing breeze. The balmy wind is sweet with the fragrance of hollyhocks and roses, wet with dew. A symphony of sounds plays upon my ears, as crickets and birds broadcast their tunes for all who will listen. Occasionally, their melodies are drowned by the rumblings of an impending pre-dawn storm. With beauty filling my senses, I do nothing but sit and contemplate the past experiences of my life.

2   This is better known as **dawn-flection**. Dawn-flection is the act of reflecting upon past or future events in the early morning hours before the sun breaks the horizon.

3   As I sit, images of my life permeate my mind. I think back to the first time I met my wife. A smile spreads across my face when I think back to our lengthy conversations. Her seductive brown eyes would dance when we spoke of music, history or other subjects that challenged our intellect. Love spreads itself over my heart when I look upon her in my mind's eye. Her long, brown hair, shapely lips and almond-shaped eyes are enchanting. I close my eyes for a moment in an attempt to savor this picture as my brain shifts to a different thought.

4   My mind races to another time of my life. This one involves my family and the night my mother died. My eyes fill with tears as grief pours out from my heart's core. Instantly I'm there, watching her piercing blue eyes making a final sweep over those who had gathered around her bed, sharing her last moments on earth. Her eyes closed as she took her final, heaving breath. The look of pain on their faces and the appearance of peace blanketing my mother's face are boldly contrasted as I relive the moment of her agonizing—yet—beautiful death. I still see my hand reaching out for hers at the precise moment she died, attempting to show my love for her. Comprehending that she is no longer here, regret and guilt make their way to the pit of my stomach; these feelings violate my conscience for not being a good son. Nearly ten years have passed, and yet, it still seems like yesterday.

5   My thoughts focus upon my relationship with my father. He has grown so old in the last few years. It is hard to imagine that he ruled our family with cruelty and ignorance. My face begins to pulse hot with anger when I think back to the love he neglected us. Did he think he would be a lesser man if he showed any love or compassion toward his wife and children? Quickly I move to the next image, not wanting to contemplate this question or his actions any further.

6   I conjure thoughts of joy when I flash upon the humorous times I've shared with my wife and step-daughter. Times we've spent Christmas shopping, midnight drives in the country, camping and the funny stories we would tell each other over dinner . . . I still hear our laughter echoing inside my head. A tinge of sadness strikes my heart as I realize that my step-daughter is married and lives far away.

7   My train of thought jumps ahead toward the future. I imagine fame favoring me and dream of seeing myself becoming a novelist. I envision conversations with the best known writers of the world and guest appearances on late night talk shows. Reality settles in as I realize that I am still a student, but maybe someday I'll be accomplished enough to have my writing published. I shouldn't quit my day job, I think to myself.

8   Suddenly, my eyes become fixed on the turmoil of thunderclouds overhead. Thunder and lightning snap my senses to attention. Erratic sounds of raindrops fill my ears as the rain falls upon the trees and strikes the ground. A feeling of serenity is sent through my being, witnessing the splattering rainfall as it increases in volume. Tree branches and flower stalks sway in the gusts of wind. Rain reaches my nose, and a mist sprinkles my face, as the storm unleashes itself around me.

9   Finally, the act of dawn-flecting draws to a close. Peace and tranquility fill my soul; I leave the patio and take my place next to my slumbering wife and fall into a restful sleep.

Gerry Home

Gerry's essay clearly defines his word dawn-flection. He has provided his essay with solid structure, organization, and development. Gerry's essay clearly shows that he understands the concept of how to write extended definition; moreover, he has used the means of extended definition to a definite end: he had something important he wanted to say to himself and to his readers. Since there was no word that represented what he wanted to say, Gerry simply created his own word. And I like the word dawn-flection. Like Gerry, I value and celebrate early morning. I, too, like to walk onto our back deck and collect my thoughts and memories and dreams before I begin to face the day. Gerry's word communicates with me and to me.

Many times in our lives—perhaps daily—we find that we have an idea or an emotion for which we cannot think of an appropriate word or "we can't find the right word." Have you ever felt that the English language has such inadequacies, that there are "things" that exist which no word accurately describes? I think we all feel this way at times. Here is one student's solution to such a situation. I think you will enjoy reading this extended definition.

Mada

Mada (mä dä) n., 1. a person that is a cross between a Mother and Father,
2. a hybrid creature created from need and lack of responsibility . . .

1   It is almost inescapable to me in my life, at least once a day, to be referred to as a "single mother." Whether I'm at the grocery store, talking to one of my children's teachers or meeting someone for the first time, it never fails that sooner or later that term crosses my path. I've come to the realization over the years that the term leaves too many open doors for explanation and doesn't really describe me for what I truly am. So, either by coincidence or bad grammar, my children have given me the name that truly explains me to the world—Mada.

2   To me, a Mada is a person who has every responsibility in the maintenance and care of all in her domain. All of it falls in line like a grocery list: holidays, schooling, potty-training, football, dreams and nightmares, Matchbox Cars and nail polish and everything else in between. It is easier to say what a Mada doesn't take care of than what she actually does (although a man can be a Mada—would you then call him a Dama?). But, all of that is superficial responsibilities that every parent, single or not, deals with on a day-to-day basis. A Mada deals with the "blood and guts" of parenting.

3   Feat, guilt, loneliness and unanswerable questions are the core emotions of a Mada. A mother's number one responsibility to her child is to nurture him/her into a spectacular human being. The man "on high" created both a mother and a father to care for and

protect, as well as nurture, their children, as well as each other. So, what happens when the equation is diminished by one? For one to nurture, one also has to be nurtured, or all strength is lost, because strength begets strength. How do you teach your children to be sure of themselves when you, yourself, are constantly unsure of what you are doing? How do you teach them pride, when every day guilt ebbs from every pore on your body? What does the way people "look" at you do to the way you "look" at you.? The answer, believe it or not, is really quite simple. You make yourself. You get up each day, brush the guilt off your sleeve, and you make the most of it all. It doesn't matter how you do it. Lie, cry, get scared . . . who cares? The point is, to take those emotions, ball them into one, and use it as the fuel to make you go. If you can do that, and believe me you can, although it might take you some time, not only can you do just about anything you set your mind to after that, but you then can have some fun with what's really important—your kids.

4   Grab the "fun" out of being a female father. Learn how to rough-house with your boys. All it takes is a couple of Buffy the Vampire Slayer episodes and you're a pro. Hell—even the neighborhood boys your kids play with will have some fun. Take a few minutes and put all of those Hot Wheels race tracks together and get them to fly through those loops and turns with those really awesome looking cars you trip over and step on at 3 am.

5   Remember to enjoy being a mother to your daughters. Be warm to their friends; they might even let you borrow their lime-green fluorescent nail polish, and if you're really lucky, they might even let you into their private thoughts and you'll remember (if for just a few precious minutes) what it's like to be eleven again. And if you're even luckier, you'll get to know why your daughters are friends with these girls, and why these girls are friends with yours. Play Barbies with your youngest—she'll think your choice of accessories is "the bomb," a great ego booster.

6   Most importantly, don't waste your time playing "Good Cop—Bad Cop"; you can't play that game 'cuz there's only one cop. Don't lose sleep over not having anyone to bounce ideas off of; it all works itself out in the end. Above all, never pay attention to how other people critique how good or bad of a job it is you are doing and feel that they need to correct you; they only criticize you because what you and your children are going through is something everyone is terrified of happening to them. You'll most likely feel that people are looking at you almost as if to say, "How dare you!?!" They're not aimed at you; they're scared of you.

7   A Mada is every marriage's nightmare. You are concrete, walking, talking evidence of a good dream gone bad. The "critical masses" might look at you like a bug under a microscope (you think), but after you leave the parent-teacher open house or tee-ball game they met you at, guarantee that later, under the covers in their nice warm bed, they'll be putting themselves under that microscope as well.

8   And, last but not least, remember the two most important rules of all: don't sweat the small stuff; EVERYTHING is small stuff.

Beth Stokes

As you can see, there are many people who find inadequacies in our language. If you find that there are such inadequacies or if you'd just like to make this assignment a little more fun, why not create your own word and define it?

DEFINITION—A SUMMING UP

Whether you choose to write an extended definition of a word which is used in a variety of ways or to create your own word, you will be writing what I consider the most challenging assignment up to this point. As a teacher, I have been able to explain extended definition to you, but as a writer, you are on your own in many ways, especially with structure, organization, and development.

I have confidence that you will do just fine if you have understood all of the information about writing presented in the earlier chapters. Just remember that definition, like comparison-contrast, process, classification, description, and narration, is a method of communicating your thoughts and your feelings. If you truly have something to share with a reader, and if you think before you begin to write, you should find that extended definition is just one more way you have of reaching your audience.

DEFINITION—MORE STUDENT EXAMPLES

Here are some more examples of students' extended definitions. The words defined, the methods of composition, the styles, and the writers themselves reveal the variety of ways this assignment can be approached.

Ramadan

1   All over the world there are many religions. Each has its own aspects and requirements. Islam is one of these religions which is known to many people. Islam is built on five pillars, which are: (1) believing that there is no God except Allah and that Mohammed is his messenger, (2) praying, (3) fasting during Ramadan, (4) alms-giving, and (5) making a pilgrimage to Mecca.

2   Ramadan is one of the most-confusing phrases for people of different religions. Ramadan is a month out of the year in which Muslims fast. Muslim countries have two kinds of dates, one of which is called the Meladi date, and the other is the Hejra date. The Meladi date started the day Jesus was born and continues up until the present day. The Hejra date refers to the date of Mohammed's immigration from Mecca to Medina. Ramadan is the ninth month of the Hejra year, as September is the ninth month of the Meladi year. Muslims know the first day of Ramadan by the shape of the moon. Astrologists announce the first day of Ramadan when the moon has the shape of a crescent.

3   Ramadan's formal meaning is the month in which the Koran, the Holy Book of Islam, was sent down as a guide for all human beings. Fasting during Ramadan means that people are not allowed to eat or drink from sunrise to sunset. During the fast days, Muslims continue their day without even a drink of water, an ounce of food, or a cigarette. When the sun sets, which is between five and six o'clock in the evening, Muslims are allowed to break their fast and start to eat and drink. The meal they break their fasting by is called the breakfast because it is the first meal of the day.

4   The reason that Muslims can tolerate a long time without eating or drinking is the meal they eat between midnight and sunrise, which is called El-Suhor. The El-Suhor meal contains melons, jam, honey, and proteins to supply the body with energy for the whole day ahead.

5   The Muslim fast is not meant for self-torture; therefore, if anybody is ill or on a journey, the prescribed period should be made up later. Although it is more-strict than other kinds of fast, it provides exceptions for special circumstances. Fasting is for any Muslim who is able. For example, children who are between five and seven do not have

to fast because they are still young and cannot distinguish between right and wrong. Muslim families start to teach their children fasting when they are ten. Ten is an age when children can understand and recognize the importance of their worship. Fasting is also for free people. Free people are those who can control and manage themselves. For instance, in former times, slaves could not do what they wanted because they were under the control of someone else. Also, fasting is for healthy people. Mentally ill people have a valid reason for not fasting. These exceptions are made because Allah is lenient and because people may hurt themselves.

6 The spiritual meaning of Ramadan is that Muslims stick together creating the spirit of cooperation. Ramadan teaches people patience by tolerating hunger and thirst. Furthermore, the method of fasting cleanses the body and the soul by providing Muslims with a feeling for the poor. Also, the distance between God and his creatures becomes closer through worship. By understanding the spiritual significance of the fast, people will not say that Ramadan is a husk without a kernel. If we realize this, we shall look upon Ramadan not as a burden, but as a blessing.

7 Fasting during Ramadan is both a physical and spiritual form of worship for Muslims. True Muslims prove that they are firm believers in God and his prophet by obeying the five pillars and following the Koran. Ramadan is one of the many requirements that Allah asks Muslims for.

Amal Al-Dadah

The Oldest Profession

Dear Mr. Wonderful,

1 In my world, I am often met with people who view the job of a "full time mother" in a condescending way. While I usually let the opinions of complete strangers roll off my shoulders, I will no longer continue to allow you to treat me as someone who is mindless and worthless, someone whose main purpose in life is to scrub toilets and pick up dirty socks. I have carefully chosen my profession. I do realize that your job, as a police officer, is both physically and mentally demanding. From the way you make snide remarks about my job, it is apparent that you have no clue as what I do every day. You say that I spend my days watching the lives of imaginary people evolve on soap operas. You claim I do this soap opera viewing with the telephone in one hand and a bag of Hershey Kisses in the other. You claim if I am a "stay at home mom" then I should be scrubbing toilets, washing floors and feeding my husband a four course dinner the minute he walks in the door from work. I say you misread my job title. I never took on the job of "stay at home mom!" Just as you proudly wear your badge to work each morning, I proudly wear the title "full time mother." I challenge you to come and spend some time in my world. Are you brave enough? Are you strong enough? Somehow, I doubt it.

2 I begin my day at 5:30 a.m. I get up with the birds and my husband, David. I send David off to work with a freshly packed lunch. Please note, the reason I get up to make David, my husband and your brother, his lunch is because he is my cheerleader in life. He is the one person who truly supports and understands my job! (Unlike some other people.) Once David has left for work, I usually do some laundry. I read the morning paper. I exercise and shower. I plan the school day for the children. I wake the children. It is only 7:00 a.m.

3   Once the children are dressed and fed, the most important part of my "full time mother" position begins. Teacher. Since David and I have chosen to home school the children, the "teacher" part of my position is the single most important part. I sort through four different levels of math, grammar, history, science and reading. It is sometimes difficult to keep all of their subjects straight. It is also the most awesome experience to see them loving to learn. I take pride in the fact that they love to learn because of the time I am investing in them. You say I should get a "real" job, one that pays cold hard cash. I say you need to realize our children are the future. I want to play a big part in the kind of people they become. I want them raised with my values. I do not ever lose sight of the fact that my small investment of time in the children now will provide incredible returns in their future. I can see their dividends building day after day.

4   The rest of my duties as "full time mother" revolve around my teaching duties. The children usually finish their written work and reading assignments by 11:30 a.m. Then it is off to whatever club is on the calendar for that day. Our family is involved in Cub Scouts, 4-H Club, Grassroots Homeschoolers and the South Suburban Homeschool Gym Group. I also teach religion classes at our church. I chauffeur the children to all of these programs. Our children participate in all of these programs. I am an active leader in all of them. Since David is the Cub Master, I am the one who coordinates most of the activities for the Cub Scout Pack. I am also the treasurer and religious coordinator for the Cub Scout Pack. I am an assistant leader in the 4-H Club. In addition to being the librarian for Grassroots Homeschoolers, I am also the one who created a website to represent the organization on the internet. I am a team leader in the gym group. I participate as a leader in all of these programs because I believe they are important for the children. I am also living what I teach the children everyday. I am giving back to our community what is being given to our children. I hope that some day they will do the same with their children.

5   Regardless of where I am or what I am doing, I am always on call, twenty-four hours a day, seven days a week. There is no vacation pay. There are no paid sick days. I am the nurse in our family; I help mend scraped knees and broken hearts. I do all of the grocery shopping. I do most of the cooking. I do some of the household cleaning; I am not a maid. Everyone pitches in to do their share of chores. (David helps clean the house; he does not plop in front of the television each night like some men I know. I sometimes cannot believe the two of you are brothers!) I also keep track of all of the household and family expenses and bills.

6   You see, Mr. Wonderful, most people appreciate the experience I have. They also realize I am not some mindless twit who overdoses on chocolate while watching imaginary people have torrid love affairs on a soap opera! Respected community leaders, parents, and my husband value my opinions and my contributions to my family and my community. I am investing my time in my children. I am raising them to be strong, capable people. I would hope that as a police officer you would be able to recognize the benefits of providing young, growing minds with a stable family life where both parents take an active role in raising their children. I will not go to work for any amount of money if it means leaving my children with a baby-sitter or on their own. A baby-sitter could not do a better job than I am doing! I am the best qualified candidate as "full time mother" for my children. I love what I do! The pay off is not financial, but it is definitely satisfying to me.

7   I realize your job as a police officer is physically and mentally demanding. It is stressful. It is important. However, I think you need to realize that my job is equally important. I am raising and teaching a piece of the future. You need to stop spewing negative remarks towards me that put down my chosen profession. I have chosen one of the oldest professions. I am a "full time mother." I do not seek your approval or your blessing. I do demand your respect.

Sincerely,
Karen Z. Hoogland

Spanglish

1   Not to say that Orland Park is not a good city, but when my family first moved out here seven years ago, I didn't enjoy it too much. I honestly felt out of place. I was a Latino in a white world. It was such an awkward time and feeling, but now, it's kind of neat.

2   Our family is bilingual, and living in a community that doesn't speak Spanish is quite fun. We're able to speak without having others understand us and speak about people without them knowing. My generation is the second here in the states, which diminishes the native language. The entire family isn't fluent, so to make up for that we use another language, "Spanglish."

3   Spanglish is a common language used among bilingual families in the U.S. It starts with the first generation in the states who have kids. The parents most often only speak the native language, but the kids grow up learning two languages at once. Even though the best time to learn another language is when you're young, it does get confusing. You know what you wish to say, you're just not sure on how to say it. In such a case, Spanglish is used. And as the older generation starts to learn English, they tend to speak Spanglish instead.

4   Spanglish is a combination between Spanish and English. It's not a formal language, but it's widely used. Just go to any Latino gathering and you'll hear Spanglish. When you first hear this language, it may sound weird, but it's actually very interesting. To a person who happens to speak both languages, it's completely understandable. But to someone who doesn't, it'll kind of sound like people are skipping necessary words in a sentence.

5   Since it's not a formal language there are no written rules, but there is structure. The rules from Spanish and English structure Spanglish. This language is only spoken, which makes it all the more interesting. When someone speaks, they can either begin in Spanish or English, whichever they prefer. But then somewhere mid-sentence, they'll either switch over to the other language completely or just add a few words.

6   After some honest thought about this language, I realize how weird it is. It's just because people communicate without thinking of what they are going to say. They say the first words that come to mind, words that express what they mean, no matter what language it is. It just makes me laugh thinking how common this is to everyone in our family, but to an outsider this would be weird. But I'll give you a little taste. . . .

7   English: The other day, a friend and I were going out to a restaurant to eat dinner. On the way there he realized he had left his money back at his house. I didn't have enough to pay for us both, so we went back to his house. Once we got there, we both went in and decided we didn't want to go out to eat, so we just stayed home and ordered pizza.

8   Spanish: El otro dia, mi amigo y yo ibamos a salir a un restaurante a desayunar. Por el camino, se dio de cuenta que dejo su dinero en la casa. Yo no tenia suficiente para pagar por los dos, pues fuimos para tras a su casa. Cuando ilegamos, decidimos que no querianos salir a comer, y nos quedemos en casa y ordenamos una pizza.

9   Spanglish: The other day, un amigo y yo ibamos a salir a un restaurante to eat dinner. On the way there, se dio de cuenta that he left su dinero en la casa. Yo no tenia enough a pagar por los dos, so we went back to his house. Once we got there, nosotros dos entremos y decidimos que no querianos salir a comer, so we stayed home and ordered pizza.

10   To me, all three languages sound normal, but it's the way I was raised. So I guess in some way I'm trilingual, if you want to go that far. Now I just appreciate more being Latino and bilingual, because not everyone gets to experience other languages.

Gabriel Almodovar

Simple Word!?

1   STOP! POLICE! There has been a crime committed. An injustice has been done. Someone must call the "word police." You know of no such force? Then let's sign petitions, call the media, picket the Library of Congress. We must take action now. We must stop this unfair treatment. How many more are out there suffering under this type of discrimination? Why should such a simple word suffer so—never given the respect that it deserves. This word has such vast meaning. How can such a word be denied its place? This little word has so much feeling behind it. It has a well-rounded form. It deserves an award for its outstanding usage. It should be placed among the greats, given special honorable mentions.

2   What for, you say? How could such a simple looking word hold so much power? What could such a word mean that we must sit back and take notice of it? Well, please give me the honor of your attention to explain it to you. Mr. Webster put it ever so eloquently when he said, **"An exclamation expressing surprise; used to attract attention; exultation."** Let us start by carefully examining Webster's definition. Then look beyond the text for a vast meaning.

3   **Exclamation expressing surprise.** This can occur in a few forms, as when shocked over an unbelievable situation that has been brought to your attention. It could be along the lines of hearing about your sweet angelic niece, who has just pierced her tongue. Possibly it could hit closer to home, such as your two-year-old running a double roll of toilet paper through the whole house, while you are signing for a delivery. As you take a minute to take in the shock of what you have heard or seen, most likely the term "Ho-kay" comes to mind. This gives you a chance to take a deep breath. Now, you can attempt to accept what has happened without killing someone. You want to save that for a more deserving time.

4   **Attract attention.** This is commonly known as "how to get someone's attention." In the case of a parent who has been informed that the child she bore believes, that he, "THE CHILD," is now in charge of HIS own life, her calm, cool parental reaction is "Ho! I don't think so! You are NOT going anywhere, young man!" Then there is the opposite side when the big, macho, man's man gets a big head. His caveman mentality takes over when he sees a beautiful girl. He shows his ten-percent IQ. He begins to speak in a deep, loud groan "Ho, ba . . . bay." At this time, you can guarantee that there will be physical punishment forthcoming.

5   **Exultation** in itself means **"to be jubilant; to rejoice greatly."** Well, doesn't this happen often in the presence of male bonding moments? The basketball kisses the rim and falls in, or the player has the ball in hand and fumbles just ten yards short of the end zone. There is an echo from the T.V. room "Ho . . . ow!" Now depending on the call of the referee, a few choice words may be tastefully expressed, as the sense of disappointment or furious rage fills the house. There is also the pre-game hype when the players are geared up to perform in the game. This is done to build up the adrenalin levels. While in a huddled mass with deep grunts roaring from the middle "HO . . . wO, HO . . . wO, HO . . . wO, HO . . . wO, HO . . . wO!" Completely hyped, they rush out onto the field.

6   It does not stop there. This level of excitement is even in the celebrations at church. This word is being used to praise and worship a Ho . . . ho . . . ly God. The children are joining in the jubilation. They are singing the song called "Ho . . . ho . . . ho . . . sanna." Let's get an AMEN and a HALLELUJAH from the congregation.

7   This brewing of excitement can be seen in the presence of a woman, who is overcome with excitement by a bundle of preciousness. She will squeal "HO . . . O . . . OH . . . WAH, what an adorable baby!" This catches on in the same way a virus would spread. A room full of females' hormones being dragged out in a chorus of oohing and ahhing over a tiny new life. This is the form of female bonding.

8   Then there comes that moment in time when total upset is brewing, when frustration is unable to be vented. This upset is usually expressed by children, who are trying to get their feelings out, without hurting someone. This is their way of controlling the swearing that they are not allowed to verbalize. At the moment of explosion, something may come out sounding similar to a wind storm hitting the house. It goes something like this, "HO . . . Owa, you just don't understand!," which a parent can interpret easily as "No! You don't understand. You are still not getting it!"

9   Then there is that one person who has a limited vocabulary. Yet, who is so warmly received, and who expresses one phrase over and over again "Ho, Ho, Ho, Merry Christmas." It works for him, so I say go for it. It brings people a lot of joy to hear those words said for a month every year. The man has been around since the 1800's. He is like Elvis; he has never left the building. (Yet, I think we should start questioning the ones passing that information along!)

10   Now, you can try locking it up behind closed doors, but our wondrous word cannot stop its dynamic power. This word can be used for pure pleasure. "How?" you say. Well, in the midst of an intense sexual moment, "ho . . . o . . . o, ho . . . o . . . o" being said in a deep, sweet female whisper, could bring both of you to a climax. Since this is done in a hushed tone, you will not be hearing the voices of your children, or have them knocking at the door afraid that you're hurting mommy, while destroying the mood at the same time.

11   With this kind of rhythm flowing through your bones, you can begin to come into the understanding of this word. Feel the music surrounding you. You've got it! Let it seep into your bones. You are be-bopping to the core beat. Don't fight it; let it flow. Make it smooth; let go. That's it! Say it now, "Ho . . . owo, Ho . . . owo." You got the soul ridin' through you.

12   Now you are ready to look at the ethnic side to this word. It is possible this word could have been enslaved, then freed to be all that we have seen here today. It is hard to know the true root of such a complicated word. Yet one term stands out from the Dark Age. However, to truly grasp the full meaning of this term, you must use your soul rhythm. Now, with true ethnicity in your voice, "She be a ho."

13   We can only imagine the emotional depth such a word can reach. We cannot fathom to what extreme this little word has been taken—the abuse it must have endured along the way. So, no longer should we be so insensitive. We must hold this word up with the respect that it deserves. We must deny this word no longer. Hold your head high and salute with me in honor of this glorious word, "Ho." Then when you're done, look around, because the joke is on you, "Ho-ho!!"

Luanne Lemme

Grandmother

1   *Webster's Random House School and Office Dictionary* defines grandmother as "The mother of one's father or mother." It is an interesting description, but it doesn't tell the reader a thing about what or how a grandmother interacts with her grandchildren.

2   When my son called to tell me I was going to be a grandmother, several thoughts ran through my mind. Of course, the first one was am I old enough to be a grandmother? Once I got past that question, I started asking myself what kind of a role model did I want to be for this child? This started me thinking of my childhood, and the influence my grand-mothers had had on my life.

3   Granny Fickle, my father's mother, had lived in Mulberry, Indiana. It was a small, friendly town where everybody knew each other. She lived in a white two-story house with flower beds and blooming trees around the property. I could hear the whippoorwills singing early in the morning, and I always think of Granny when the lilacs are blooming. She always had a cookie jar full of homemade sugar cookies when I came to visit, and I knew she would read me stories every night before I went to sleep. There were lots of children in the neighborhood with whom to play kick the can and hide-and-seek. It was always a treat to go visit Granny.

4   Grandma Killin, my mother's mother, lived on a large working farm, and both of my grandparents were active on the farm. There were uncles, cousins, and a plethora of farm hands that worked the farm. They would meet for lunch (a large meal) in Grandma's kitchen every day. I would go to the barn with my uncles early in the morning to milk the cows. I confess I was miserable at this task, and it wouldn't be long before I would join my Grandmother in the hen house, collecting fresh eggs. We would feed the hens, pigs, and sheep. We would give the kittens some fresh milk; then Grandma would head to the kitchen to start the noon meal. I would join my cousins Bob and Dave in the soybean field or cornfield to dig out the thistles. After the noon lunch, I would help do the dishes and then work in Grandma's vegetable and flower garden. This big week for me was the

week they would bale the hay. I was allowed to ride on the flatbed wagon out on the hayfields, and Grandpa would drive the tractor. I would stay out of the way and fill cups with cold water at break time while the help would stack the rectangle bales of hay high on the wagon. When the flatbed was full, I would climb up on top of the bales of hay with my cousins, and we would ride back to the barn where the help would stack the hay in the top floor of the barn. It was a great place to play hide-and-seek on the weekends. Oh, how I looked forward to visiting the farm every summer!

5   Well, these were great memories, but I didn't live on a farm, or in a small town where everybody knew each other. When my grandson Morgan arrived, I was living in Stamford, Connecticut, and we were living a fast paced city life. I lived a long way from Indiana, so our time together was limited. By the time Morgan was four, I had moved back to the Midwest just outside of Chicago. Morgan's life had also taken some twists and turns. His mother and father who were no longer together, and he had a new stepfather and a little brother. Davina, his mother, assured me I could have him anytime I wanted. I took her up on that offer, and I began to decide how we would spend our time together.

6   Morgan was an easy child to deal with; he had good manners and an easy disposition. I decided to make reading a daily routine when he was visiting, so Borders Bookstore became our hangout rather than Toys R Us. After lots of searching, I would let him choose the book he liked best, and then I would choose one for him too. We would also pick out a CD of rhyming songs to sing to each other as we negotiated the two-hour drive back and forth to Lafayette, where Morgan lives. We spent many an hour looking for treasures in the *I Spy* books, and bedtime was always a treat with our many books to read.

7   Little boys aren't crazy about baths, brushing teeth, combing hair, and putting on clean clothes. This is the time to introduce new, fun words. Believe me, there will be plenty of time for them to learn words that we don't really want to hear come out of their mouths. When it came to getting cleaned up so we could go on an adventure, my approach was it was time to get "Spiffy!"

8   After we were both cleaned up and dressed, we would meet in front of a long mirror, we would check ourselves out, and then we must both agree that the other looked spiffy enough to start our adventure. Every once in a while Morgan would get a gleam in his eye and say, "Grandma I don't like that shirt you have on." I would say, "Fair enough," and go change it. If I pointed out that his face still had toothpaste on it or he had put a dirty shirt back on, he would always go give it one more try to look spiffy. It took him several tries before he could say the word just right; we would get a big chuckle over the other sounds that came out of his mouth.

9   On our first visit to downtown Chicago, Morgan was far more interested in the tall buildings than he was in the Christmas decorations. We started with the John Hancock Building. This was his favorite building, so he told me. However, after our visit there, he suddenly decided that wasn't his favorite building after all; he was sure it was the Sears Tower. I agreed we would add it to our next visit, and chuckled. This child was really working Grandma . . .

10   Morgan is now eight, and we have spent a lot of time in the museums and the Art Institute. We have had days when I was the child and he was the adult. He would go purchase the tickets for the train to the city and ask a guard where we would find the Vincent Van Gogh exhibits. I'm amazed at how adept he has become.

11   We have also had special moments at home. When he was six, we were snowed in over New Years Eve. We got dressed up, I fixed a special dinner, and we watched a movie till it was time to watch the ball being dropped at Times Square in New York City. I got out the champagne glasses and a cold bottle of ginger ale: the bubbly stuff. We poured, we toasted, and oh how we giggled. We have also graduated to the Harry Potter books. Now, however, Morgan is reading the adventures to me.

12   When Morgan is preparing to visit, I'm told he tells his friends he is going to go have, "Adventures with Grandma." I have also heard him tell people that I am the best Grandma in the whole world. These words are music to my ears. I hope when he grows up and is off in the busy world, he will remember and cherish his adventures with Grandma.

Carol Pearson

The Vapor Mist Culture

1   Bombing, burner, dope, fade, and throwup are a few of the many terms used in the culture known as Graffiti. According to the *Graffiti Dictionary,* the term "graffiti" is derived from the Greek term "to write," meaning a drawing or scribbling on a flat surface, originally referred to those marks found on ancient Roman architecture. Today, graffiti is more than a marking on a wall. To some, graffiti is a way of life. Graffiti writers can be analyzed into three different perspectives. First, there is the graffiti bomber. Next, are the writers who burn. The most technical are the writers who choose to do murals. Usually, the most psychotic writer is often known as a graffiti bomber. A bomb is done with ink or paint. Bombs are not very complex and usually are performed with two or three colors. Bombers put their tags or throwups on spots that are very noticeable. A tag is the artist's signature, a throwup is a name painted very quickly with one layer of spray paint and an outline. The choices of canvas for a bomber vary. Graffiti removal service vehicles are popular, as well as sides of very populated buildings, any public transportation vehicles, truck trailers, train cars, and just about anything else that will absorb paint or marker. Bombers are all about becoming all city. All city implies that the artist is up all over the city. This is done for fame and respect from other graffiti writers. Graffiti bombers are really just specialized to vandalize. A tagbanger could also be listed with graffiti bombers. Tagbangers are a new subculture that developed in southern California. Tagbangers do not write or throwup; they just tag. They are gangbangers with guns and spray paint. Tagbangers are really a negative influence on the whole graffiti culture.

2   "Burn" to beat the competition with style. Burn refers to a really good piece, as in one that "burns." A piece is a graffiti painting, short for masterpiece. There must be at least three colors involved for a painting to be recognized as a piece. This is where the skills of a writer will be challenged. If the writer displays a piece that is wack, the piece will be lined, and the writer will be labeled as a "toy." A toy is an unexperienced writer who uses stock spray can tips, has a sloppy style, and is just downright wack. If the writer displays a piece that is "dope," meaning cool, he or she will receive mad "props," respect from the graffiti community. Graffiti writers who do pieces that burn usually have to choose a spot that is concealed. A good piece usually takes five to ten hours, and sometimes the piece is done in two late night sessions. Today, piecing is becoming more respected and is being used in the commercial art field. Some companies are hiring graffiti artists to design and paint their logos on the side walls of their buildings. Worthy graffiti artists are given designated walls throughout the city to express their fine art. For example, two

world renowned graffiti artists, How and Nosm, who write for R.A.L. Crew, are given walls throughout New York's Bronx to legally express their burning graffiti pieces. The company Coca-Cola also uses How and Nosm's artistic abilities to design new artwork for their cans and logos. A good piece is a trophy to a graffiti artist; most of the time the average person can't figure out what the hell it says, but it looks good. The bright colors, 3D lettering, and the wildstyle flow always catches the human eye.

3   The most technical and respected level of the graffiti culture is the all out mural production walls. A production is usually when three or more writers go and roll out an entire wall from the top to the bottom. The production is usually done with the best writers in the "crew." A crew is a group of writers who all represent the same clique that they formed. Crews use three to four letters to represent their crew's name, for example T.K.C., Total Kaos Crew. The production always has a background. A theme or color scheme is used to create a tight background. Once the background has been established, the crew has an order and a certain amount of space that the writer can use. This stops the people in the crew from running their artwork into each other's. The graffiti artists try to keep their pieces all the same size. This makes everything proportionate, so the whole wall flows together. To make the murals more technical, the writers demonstrate their true talent by putting cartoon characters, real life drawings, and many other environmental topics blending in with their pieces. Mostly all production walls are done legally. The time it takes and the amount of spray paint needed would be very difficult to hide from the police. Murals take up 100 to 300 cans of spray paint and about 5 gallons of background paint. The time it takes to complete a full production can range from 10 hours to weeks of hard work. In the culture of graffiti, the production is the highest level of skill that a graffiti artist can express. The Chicago Transit Authority sponsors graffiti crews throughout the city once a year to compete and see who has the dopest production. The winning crew is ranked and titled the best in the city by the C.T.A. and given the respect from writers throughout the world.

4   Graffiti started back in the day of the Egyptians to put markings on great monuments and to depict great stories of life. Today graffiti is expressed through different levels of art. There is the all out street bomber, who is specialized to vandalize. Then there is the graffiti artist, who expresses his or her tag name through piecing. The most respected form of the culture is the all out wall production. Today, graffiti is one of the most controversial forms of art there is. People need to realize that there are these levels of graffiti. Graffiti is just not some punk kid with a can of spray paint. It is a culture with roots dating back to 54–68 AD. So enjoy—this culture is here to stay.

Steve McClintock

DEFINITION—POSSIBLE TOPICS

This is one paper where the topics and possibilities are truly limitless. Your topic for the paper is also dependent upon the approach you use in writing your extended definition.

If you decide to create your own word or to define a word which you have created, think back to its origin. Try to think of the contexts in which you use it and which, if described, would help your reader understand your word and make it a part of his vocabulary.

If, on the other hand, you decide to use the more-traditional approach to definition, I would advise you to choose a word that has significance to you. The more abstract the word, the easier I think you will find the assignment.

WORDS TO INSPIRE YOU OR GIVE YOU A TOPIC			
love	war	death	life
hate	peace	security	courage
cowardice	deceit	bravery	hero
woman	man	person	dedication
stupidity	intelligence	hypocrisy	frustration
fulfillment	satisfaction	good	evil
knowledge	god	friend	boredom
excitement	prejudice	conflict	old
young	freedom	slavery	justice
success	warmth	humane	loneliness
democracy	radical	conservative	enemy
student	teacher	lover	parent
poverty	wealth	America	injustice
fear	joy	sorrow	disgust
crude	dumb	communication	learning
beauty	pride	vanity	wild
rowdy	marriage	ecstatic	guilt
obscene	art	literature	music

DEFINITION—YOUR TURN

1 Decide upon subject matter. What do you want to communicate to a reader? What thoughts, feelings, and ideas do you want to share? What word or phrase "goes with" these thoughts, feelings, and ideas?

2 Decide upon the method or methods of structure, organization, and development.

3 Jot down some of your ideas and shape them into an outline. Include some of the detail and example that you would use to define the term.

4 Write the rough draft of your extended definition.

DEFINITION PAPER PLAN SHEET

Part One: First, choose a topic (word) for an extended definition paper.

Topic (word): _____

Next, write the dictionary definition of the word (should you wish to begin with it or include it).

_____

_____

_____

_____

Now, write a thesis statement. _____

_____

_____

List the methods of organization/development you might use. (Try to include a brief mention of how each might contribute to the paper.)

    1. _____

    2. _____

    3. _____

    4. _____

    5. _____

    6. _____

If you wish, go ahead and write the introduction at this time.

_____

_____

_____

_____

Outline: Body

_____

_____

_____

_____

_____

_____

_____

_____

_____

_____

_____

_____

_____

_____

_____

_____

_____

_____

_____

_____

_____

Name _____ Section _____ Date _____

SELF-EVALUATION SHEET: PART ONE

Assignment: _____

Strong points of this assignment:

_____

_____

_____

_____

_____

_____

_____

Weak points of this assignment:

_____

_____

_____

_____

_____

_____

_____

General comments:

_____

_____

_____

_____

_____

_____

_____

(over)

SELF-EVALUATION SHEET: PART TWO

What were the strong points of your last writing assignment?

_____

_____

_____

_____

_____

_____

What were the weak points of your last writing assignment?

_____

_____

_____

_____

_____

_____

What have you done to correct those weaknesses in this assignment?

_____

_____

_____

_____

_____

_____

Evaluator's Name _____ Section _____ Date _____

PEER-EVALUATION SHEET: PEER-EVALUATOR #1

Writer's Name _____ Essay's Title _____

> **Directions:** (1) Remember not to write on another student's paper. Instead, use this form. (2) Offer concrete, specific comments using the terminology of writing (e.g., "The development in paragraph four might be improved by adding a brief example." or, "Check structure on page 3.")

What do you see as the strong points of this writing assignment: _____

_____

_____

_____

_____

What areas do you feel might need additional work: _____

_____

_____

_____

_____

Do you see any areas of grammar/mechanics (e.g. usage, spelling, fragments) that might need attention: _____

_____

_____

_____

_____

General comments: _____

_____

_____

_____

_____

PEER-EVALUATION SHEET: PEER-EVALUATOR #2

Writer's Name _____ Essay's Title _____

Directions: (1) Remember not to write on another student's paper. Instead, use this form. (2) Offer concrete, specific comments using the terminology of writing (e.g., "The development in paragraph four might be improved by adding a brief example." or, "Check structure on page 3.")

What do you see as the strong points of this writing assignment: _____

_____

_____

_____

_____

What areas do you feel might need additional work: _____

_____

_____

_____

_____

Do you see any areas of grammar/mechanics (e.g. usage, spelling, fragments) that might need attention: _____

_____

_____

_____

_____

General comments: _____

_____

_____

_____

_____

The Cause-Effect Paper

OVERVIEW

The cause and effect relationship between events is frequently a part of our daily thinking. We find ourselves asking why we bet fifty dollars on the wrong team, why we bought a new television when we didn't really have the money for it, or why we decided to order prime rib when we really wanted Dover sole. When we pursue this line of thinking, we are asking ourselves about causes. We are trying to answer the questions, "Why?" or, "What caused this to occur?" Sometimes we find ourselves pondering other types of questions, questions such as, "I wonder what will happen if I do this?" or, "I wonder what results this action will produce?" When we pursue this line of thinking, we are asking ourselves about effects.

This type of thinking is the basic premise behind the cause-effect essay, sometimes referred to as a **causal analysis essay**. When a writer develops an idea from a cause-effect perspective, he or she is trying to establish why some event has occurred or what effects an event will produce. A cause paper examines a single cause or a series of related causes that brought a situation into existence. An effect paper examines a single effect or a series of related effects that a situation is likely to produce. A cause-and-effect paper examines both the cause (or causes) and the effect (or effects) of a situation. This chapter will explain each of these three types of essays.

THE CAUSE PAPER

Let's begin with what I call a "given situation." That's a fancy term for anything which exists. (I know my philosophy professor friend would want to argue whether anything exists, but let's not tell him we are making this leap of faith.) A given situation could be anything. Here are a few examples: the Chicago Bulls have become the Chicago Bores, you are leaving your main squeeze, your mother has become addicted to gambling, your grandmother has taken up rollerblading, your brother has decided to change his major from pre-med to running the Tilt-a-Whirl at the county fair, and your life is more thrilling since you adopted a stray puppy.

What brought all of these given situations into existence? Your answer to that question would be based upon causes. It could be one significant cause, a series of causes, or a combination of causes. If you explained, in an essay, what brought that given situation into existence, you would be writing a cause paper. You would explain—in detail—what caused your brother to give up on pre-med, what caused Granny to buy a set of blades for herself, what caused your mother to become addicted to the slots on the riverboat, and what caused you to adopt the black Lab puppy that wandered into your life.

If you follow a few simple, common-sense guidelines, writing a cause paper should not put a major dent into your free time (which you'll soon be sacrificing to take that new puppy to obedience school).

 # GUIDELINES FOR WRITING A CAUSE PAPER

- **One,** choose a topic/given situation which interests you. Try to examine what all of the contributing causes were that brought it into existence. Focus on those which seem most-important and most-significant. Try to focus on **immediate causes** rather than **remote causes**. Immediate causes are those causes which occur closest in time to a given situation. Remote causes are those which are more-distant in time. For example, let's say you decide to write about the traffic accident you had while on your way to campus last week. The immediate causes might have been any of the following: packed snow and ice on the streets, road construction which obstructed your vision, your tendency to drive fifteen miles over the posted speed limit, and the fact that you and your main squeeze were fighting World War Three in the front seat. Remote causes might have been: the intersection was poorly planned twenty years earlier, the mechanic who fixed your brakes last year might not have adjusted them properly, and Henry Ford invented the automobile which is why you weren't riding a horse.

- **Two,** organize and structure your causes. If it helps, make an outline. Some students like to write in traditional essay format: introduction, body, conclusion. The body is generally structured and organized with one cause per paragraph. For example, perhaps you decide to write the paper about the traffic accident mentioned in the last paragraph. You could list five contributing causes and discuss each cause in a separate paragraph. You might also want to break away from such a traditional approach. If you feel that narration and description are some of your strengths as a writer, begin your paper with the story of the accident. Narrate and describe it and place your reader in the driver's seat with you. Then, once you have the reader's attention, delve into an explanation of the causes.

- **Three,** develop your causes with detail and example. Be specific and concrete. An in-depth explanation of the causes is the surest way to communicate.

I think we are ready to read and analyze an example of a cause paper:

A Career in Nursing

1   Ever since I was a young girl, I have always been interested in the medical profession. I had grown up playing doctor, nurse, surgeon, and patient. Finally, at the age of twenty-four, I decided to pursue a career in nursing. I registered for my first class, and I was on my way to fulfilling a lifelong dream. There are three main reasons why I chose to enroll in college in pursuit of a career as a registered nurse: to accomplish a lifelong goal, to achieve financial security, and to set a good example for my children. I would like to share these reasons with you.

2   My interest in the field of medicine began when I was quite young. My father used to wear a white lab coat to work, and it really impressed me. It accentuated his features and gave the eminence of intelligence, yet it commanded respect. At that particular time, he was the Director of Pharmacy at Northwestern Memorial Hospital in Chicago. He would

bring home notepads, pens, and magnets that all bore the names of various pharmaceuticals. I was curious about these names, so I consulted my father's PDR (<u>Physician's Desk Reference</u>). I was interested in finding out about the diseases that these drugs were intended to treat. All the medical terminology and information I read simply left me intrigued and with a passion for more.

3   Then, years later, I was given an opportunity to explore my dreams in a more-concrete way. As a senior in high school, I enrolled in the Health Careers Program. This was a one-year course designed for high school students with an interest in the medical profession. After completing two semesters of class work, students were required to complete a clinical rotation at an assigned hospital or other medical facility. The clinical experience helped to master the students' skills, such as bed-making, taking vital signs, implementing aseptic techniques, and providing many types of essential patient care. Upon successful completion of this program, students were certified as CNA's (Certified Nurse Assistant).

4   After receiving straight A's in the Health Careers Program and thoroughly enjoying the classes, I knew that someday I would continue my education to become a registered nurse.

5   This decision was a critical one and a financial one. Not only did I want to experience the personal satisfaction of succeeding in my field, but I desired the financial rewards as well. The Chicago Hospital Council published the results of their July, 1989, survey which stated that the average salary for the south suburban nurse was $28,600 per year.

6   To some people, this salary may not seem to be very large at all. However, to me, the salary is a fairly respectable one. In fact, it is more than three times the salary I earn as a part-time cashier at a union grocery store.

7   Registered Nurses have been in demand for the last few years and the problematic situation seems to be getting increasingly worse. Subsequently, pay has been driven upward, and bonuses have become more common.

8   For example, in the spring of 1991, Rush Presbyterian-St. Luke Medical Center announced a $10,000 sign-on bonus in the hopes of recruiting more nurses. Interested nurses were required to sign a two-year contract to work nights in exchange for the monetary incentive. Rush's bonus program, along with their highly competitive hourly rates, can help solve the nursing crisis at that institution while, at the same time, allowing the nurses they employ to make a comfortable living. I would definitely work midnights for two years for a $10,000 cash reward. This sum of money could buy a new car, pay off a lot of outstanding bills, or take the family on a well-deserved vacation.

9   My husband and I realize that both of us must work to support our family. It is difficult, at times, to afford all the bills, two cars, and mortgage on a middle-class income. When the time comes when I can say that my name is Shelley Mayer, R.N., I will be in a position to help alleviate some of my family's financial difficulties. It is a sacrifice that I feel I must make for my family. I would like to see my children attend the college of their choice. I dream of giving my daughters big, beautiful weddings (if they so choose) when they are ready to marry. In short, I want them to have more than I did, and a career in nursing will be a definite asset to help me to achieve the financial security my family needs.

10   The third and final reason why I chose to continue my education is perhaps the most important one of all: to set a good example for my children. Before I started taking college courses, I always felt ashamed and embarrassed that I was "just a cashier."

11   I regretted the fact that I didn't have the opportunity to go to college right after high school like all my friends did. By the time I was twenty-four, many of my old classmates were successful stock brokers, accountants, and teachers, while I was still working at Eagle ringing up their groceries on Saturday afternoons. That really hurt. I had always felt like there was something "bigger and better out there" for me, and I decided to go find it.

12   I enrolled in college classes, and I am now in my fourth semester and preparing to start the Nursing Program. My teenaged and 3½ year old daughters are so proud of me. What better way to demonstrate the importance of a college education to your children than to enroll yourself.

13   I try to share with them the subjects and books I am studying, and I tell them all about *my* day in school after they tell me about theirs. My 3½ year old, Shannon, is already preparing for a life of academics. She is saving all her pennies and nickels so that she can go to college when she gets "big," "just like mommy." Nothing makes me prouder than to see her heart swell with pride when she says something like that. She gets out her Snoopy construction paper and crayons and "does homework" with me at the kitchen table. When my husband, Don, makes out the bills at the desk in our bedroom, Shannon tells me to, "Be quiet, Mommy; Daddy is trying to study." She is already learning a lot just by being exposed to college and all it entails, and I am proud of it.

14   The other reason the children need my positive example is due to the present "information age" and the increased education required just to keep abreast of new changes. Our society is so technically advanced that our children will need secondary education to be competitive in the job market when they are ready to enter the workforce. For now and the future generations, college education is a basic necessity for success in life. In a way, I am giving my children the best gift I can: a future.

15   I am looking forward to fulfilling my lifelong dream, achieving financial stability, and setting a good example for my children. It is so wonderful that I have the potential to achieve so much simply through the pursuit of just one goal in life.

16   After reviewing my reasons for pursuing a career in nursing, I have finally come to realize that, yes, I made the right decision.

Shelley R. Mayer

Shelley's essay is a good example of a cause paper. After reading "A Career in Nursing," the reader knows the three primary causes of Shelley's decision to attend college and pursue a career in nursing. Shelley has clearly stated the causes (both in the introduction and the body), and she has explained them concretely and specifically. Had Shelley prepared a scratch outline before writing her first draft, the outline might have looked like this:

Introduction and Statement of Thesis: There are three main reasons why I chose to enroll in college in pursuit of a career as a registered nurse.

Body:
    Cause One: to accomplish a lifelong goal
        Childhood games
        Observing my father and what he did
        Investigating the PDR
        High school Health Careers Program & clinical experience

Cause Two: to achieve financial security
    Investigating salary potentials
    Availability of positions & signing bonuses & differentials
    Desire to contribute more to the family income
Cause Three: to set a good example for my children
    My embarrassment about my level of education & work
    Compared myself to the classmates of my past
    Desire to look for something "bigger & better"
    Role modeling importance of study habits & learning
    Wanted to give my children "a future" in this world
Closing: Fulfilling my dream
          Reaching my goals
          I did make the right choice to pursue nursing

THE EFFECT PAPER

Remember that anything which exists is a given situation (if you skipped the last section—tsk, tsk; shame, shame—go back and read it). If you examine the results or the ramifications or the repercussions of that given situation, you are looking at its effects.

As with causes, the effects of any given situation could be one or two major ones, a series of them, or a combination of them. If you explained, in an essay, what effects a given situation has brought about or will bring about, then you would be writing an effect paper. You would explain—in detail—the effects of your brother's decision to switch majors from pre-med to Tilt-a-Whirl, the effects of your Granny's rollerblading hobby, the effects of your mother's addiction to riverboat slot machines, and the effects of adopting your new Lab puppy.

 ## GUIDELINES FOR WRITING AN EFFECT PAPER

■ **One,** write about a topic/given situation which interests you. Try to examine the most-important and most-significant effects. Also try to focus on **immediate effects** rather than **remote effects**. Immediate effects are those which occur closest in time to a given situation. Remote effects are more-distant in time. For example, what were the immediate effects of that traffic accident you had last week on your way to campus? Perhaps some of the following sound familiar: although you were only bumped and bruised, your health and well-being were affected. So was your mental health; stress and anxiety levels probably escalated. You might now be facing transportation problems for school and work, and your social life might get put on hold. You might have some legal matters to tend to, such as filling out accident report forms and insurance forms, going to court, and talking to your insurance agent about the possibility of increased rates next billing period. A remote effect would be your tendency to worry—twenty years from now—about your own children being in an accident while driving to classes.

■ **Two,** organize and structure your effects. Outlining might, as usual, be helpful. The same principles apply here as in the cause paper. Sometimes the one-effect-per-paragraph rule will guide you. If the paragraphs become "too lengthy," however, use another method. Or, if you wish, write the paper inductively. Or combine some narration and/or description. Don't hesitate to use the many skills you have acquired.

■ **Three,** develop your effects with detail and example. Be specific and concrete.

Here is an example of an effect paper:

Your Absence from My Life
(A Letter to My Estranged Father)

Dear Estranged Father,

1   I had a dream when I was about four years old. It was twenty-two years ago when I had this dream, yet the images are as clear as if I had the dream last night.

2   In the dream, I'm following you to a screen door that looks exactly like the one to our back door. You are yards ahead of me; my little legs cannot keep up to your strides. As I follow I ask, "Daddy, where are you going?". You do not answer. Without turning around you continue to walk out the door.

3   With a desperate heart, I run to the door to catch it from shutting. I was too late. I cover my ears with my hands; the sound of the door slamming is piercing to my ears. I slowly remove my hands from my ears and try to open the door. "Daddy, don't go!" I plead. The door will not open. A rush of panic fills my heart as I yell for you, "Daddy! Daddy!" Behind the door there is nothing but a strange red mist. The mist frightens me. I don't want you to go into the mist but you keep walking further into it. I think to myself, "He can't hear me." My pleas become louder: "Daddy, Daddy, come back! Don't go! Daddy, turn around! Look at me!"

4   At this point, more panic enters my heart as I begin to try to go around the door. There is nothing but red mist at each side of the door, yet some invisible wall is stopping me from getting to you. I begin to scream as tears stream down my face, "Daddy no! Daddy, I love you! Don't leave, Daddy! Come back!" You continue to walk away as you slowly fade into the red mist.

5   I continue to scream, shout and tear at the door. I am now on my knees pounding as you disappear. I can only see the red mist. You are gone. With what strength I have left, I scream one final desperate plea, "Daddy, come back! Please . . . Daddy!"

6   Within a flash of a second I wake up and quickly sit up in my bed. I'm still crying as hard as I was in my dream. I try to catch my breath. My tummy hurts, my body is shaking, and my heart feels it is about to explode with grief. I hold my chest to try to get rid of the heavy feeling in my heart. My tummy quivers with each breath I take. After a while, I am finally able to calm myself down but my heart feels empty. A part of me is gone.

7   I believe this dream was a premonition of what was to pass. You haven't been in my life since I was ten years old. I feel you should know about some of the effects this has had on my life.

8   The guilt of feeling as if I have done something to turn you away from me made me feel ugly on the inside and out. I developed a very low self esteem that led to my having a co-dependent personality toward men. An example of this is how I would spend hours at the mirror to get ready to go anywhere. I didn't dare let anyone see me without makeup, and I became obsessed with how I looked. Another example is how I would spend a lot of time and energy to become the person my boyfriend wanted me to be. I often compromised myself to fulfill his desires. I would do almost anything to keep him in my life. My boyfriend thought that I was too needy and broke up with me. I thought it was because I did something wrong or he discovered that I was ugly.

9   The insecurity of not having the protection and guidance of a father made me feel weak. As a child, I would fall and if no one was around, I would cry more than the wound

hurt. I would sit there and cry like a baby because the reality of you not being there to cleanse, bandage and kiss my "boo-boo to make it better," hurt more than the "boo-boo" itself. You being a paramedic, you used to take pride in showing me how to take care of my "boo-boos" myself. I miss that kind of fatherly guidance. I spent my life learning about life's "boo-boo's" the hard way—by trial and error. I have learned to cleanse, bandage, and even avoid life's "boo-boo's," but I still have no daddy to kiss and hug me and tell me that everything will be okay.

10   My co-dependency and insecurities caused me to be vulnerable to deceivers and abusers. I was always looking for someone to see value in me. Therefore, anyone who gave me compliments and/or acted as if he/she cared about me, I would instantly attach myself to that person. I would put all my faith and trust in that person without knowing I was being manipulated. A prime example is my soon to be ex-husband. I fell in love with him because he resembles you in many ways. He has the same coloring and a similar personality as you. In the beginning, he was humorous, charming and helpful. He always wanted to be around me and complimented me on my appearance. Later I found him to be abusive, like you. After three years of domestic violence, I left my husband for the last time.

11   This is where my anger for you plays a major role in my life. I spent the next three years male bashing and blaming men for all the wrong in the world. I began to see men as dead beat dads who beat their girlfriends and wives. My anger caused me to withdraw and live in isolation. I didn't take care of myself and concentrated only on taking care of my two children. Whenever my girlfriends and I discussed men, I would make the comment, "Men are all the same! They're nothing but lazy, violent, subhuman-beings without a conscience! Their only purpose in life is to satisfy their own desires!" I would add, "Look at my husband and my dad! What are they doing?"

12   Don't worry, Father, I have gotten over my anger and most of my insecurities in spite of your lack of presence, but I still have some deep emotional scars. I still find myself crying some nights thinking of how I have not had the security, guidance and protection of a daddy. I think of my children and how hard it is to explain to them why they don't have a grandpa, and I cry. I still mourn the years past and the fact that you were not there to share the good times and my victories with me. As in the dream, you walked out the back door, into the mist, and a part of me is gone, forever.

Your estranged daughter,

Laureen
Laureen Arnold Parker

Laureen's essay is a good example of an effect paper. After reading the essay, a reader is very much aware of how the absence of Laureen's father in her life has affected her. Laureen had a definite purpose in writing her essay, and she had a definite audience: primarily her estranged father (and secondarily, I would guess, herself). Because she is writing from the heart, her paper is exceptionally well-developed. The opening dream flashback in the extended, narrative introduction is quite powerful; by the time I get to her statement of thesis in paragraph seven, I am hooked; I want to continue reading. This feeling continues until I get to the closing, which she has nicely tied back to the introduction by mentioning the dream itself as well as the mist and the back door. These closing "dream images" give the essay a very professional style and leave the reader with a strong emotional response to what Laureen has written.

Laureen's essay is also well-structured and well-organized. Had she written a scratch outline of her essay, it might resemble the one printed below:

intro: flashback of childhood dream
    statement of thesis

body:
    effect one: feelings of low self esteem & co-dependence
    effect two: feelings of weakness
    effect three: became vulnerable to deceivers and abusers
    effect four: feelings of anger

closing

THE CAUSE-AND-EFFECT PAPER

Sometimes a writer wants to address both cause and effect in the same essay. This next example illustrates an effective and efficient way of doing this. As you read and study the example, pay particular attention to structure and organization; note where the causes appear and where the effects appear.

Splish . . . Splash

1   This summer my wife and I decided that instead of taking a vacation we should take the amount of money we would have spent and instead spend it on an above-ground swimming pool for our backyard. We carried through with this idea. There were several causes for this decision, and there have likewise been several effects.

2   My wife and I both love to swim; this was the primary reason for our decision to invest in a pool. Our children also love the water, and we have always encouraged them not to fear it, but rather to have fun in it. With the largest of possible pools, we knew that we would be able to enjoy ourselves in the comfort and privacy of our home.

3   A second reason for our decision was our health. My wife and I both have heart disease histories within our families. Swimming is one of the best exercises there is for total body conditioning, including the cardiovascular system. Buying a pool and using it daily in the spring and summer and late fall meant that we could invest in our own longevity.

4   A third reason was convenience. We had previously belonged to a club and court that had a pool. Although the fee for membership was not expensive at seven-hundred dollars per year, the distance of fifteen miles from our home proved to be prohibitive to our swimming with any frequency or regularity. We averaged maybe once a week as a family; the kids maybe attended twice a week at most. It was not convenient for the expense. Having a pool in our own backyard seemed a remedy for this situation.

5   After the pool had been in for only a brief time, we began to notice that it had an assortment of effects on our lives.

6   One effect was expense. We bought a good pool and all the accessories that were made for it. This meant that the pool and the deck and all the other manufactured goodies to accompany it—plus professional installation—came to several thousand dollars. The endless supply of chemicals and water filters and water additives seem to eat a hole in the family budget. So, too, do the electricity and water utilities.

7   A second effect was the drastic increase in our popularity with the neighbors, especially the children. Neighbors that we had not seen for some time suddenly wrote us on their social calendars again. So did people in the neighborhood who previously had not even waved at me or my family members. This was ever so noticeable in the children. I discovered, too, that there was a correlation between the temperature and the degree of friendliness of neighbors; the hotter the day, the more the phone and the door bells rang!

8   The biggest effect, of course, was the desired one. Our pool, when it is devoid of neighbors and stray children, is a haven of relaxation. My wife and I enjoy our evening and weekend swims. The kids can swim in our backyard and we no longer have to worry about them biking or finding a ride to the club pool. It is convenient, relaxing, and, I suppose, healthful.

9   Next year if you and your family cannot agree on or decide upon a vacation spot, consider your own backyard. I suppose that owning a pool is not for everyone, but for my family it proved to be a good decision.

Edward Bridges

Edward's essay deals first with causes and then with effects. Most writers who examine both cause and effect in the same essay generally keep the two major areas of the paper separate and examine the causes in the first part of the essay and examine the effects in the second part of the essay. In between is a good spot to practice your skills with transitional paragraphs. Had Edward scratched out an outline before drafting his essay, it might have resembled this one:

 Introduction and Statement of Thesis: There were several causes for our decision to install a pool, and there have likewise been several effects.

Body:
    Cause One: Our family loves to swim
    Cause Two: We wanted the exercise and the health benefits
    Cause Three: We wanted the convenience of our own pool

    Transitional Paragraph

    Effect One: Expenses
    Effect Two: Impact on social life
    Effect Three: The benefits of owning a pool

    Closing Paragraph

THE CAUSE-EFFECT PAPER: AN ALTERNATE APPROACH

It is possible—and sometimes necessary—to examine a given situation in a way that makes it impossible to structure and organize by using the one-cause-per-paragraph or one-effect-per-paragraph guideline. Sometimes, the subject matter just doesn't lend itself to that kind of "neat" dissection. However, the writer can still use causal analysis to communicate his or her thoughts; the writer can still say something by examining the causes, the effects, or the causes and effects of a given situation. This is when the writer's skills with narration and description prove valuable.

The following essay illustrates this type of approach. It is a causal analysis essay; it examines some causes and many effects of a given situation. Like the previous examples in this chapter, this essay is well-structured and well-organized. You'll also find that its writer had much to communicate—and her use of cause-effect allowed her to do so—quite effectively.

Sanctuary

1   There is nothing more tranquil and pleasurable than living in the country and being surrounded by nature three hundred and sixty-five days a year. For my husband and me, it was our lifelong dream. Loving nature, my husband and I often drove out to the suburbs on Sunday to walk in the forest preserves; each week we would go to a different area. On one particular Sunday, we took a different route, and we found ourselves in a residential area on the outskirts of Palos Park, an area which was surrounded by forest preserves. There, to our surprise, was our dream house.

2   It was a California-style, brick, raised ranch nestled on the top of a hill, on a picturesque, tree-bordered, 1.3 acre wooded lot; it had a wrap-around, wooden sun deck from which we could enjoy the beautiful scenery. Best of all, there was a For Sale sign in front of the house, and it was open for inspection.

3   We fell in love with the house immediately and pulled in the long driveway to look in the backyard. A view of the backyard revealed that the property was undulating and seemed to go on forever. We got out of the car and walked toward the back of the property, one area of which was overgrown with weeds and tall grass. There were stately trees such as willow, honey locust, pin oak, maple, elm, catalpa, flowering crabapple, apple, and plum to name a few. There were also many varieties of evergreens, both large and small, that divided a portion of the backyard in half and were adjacent to a small creek. The creek ran through the backyard, disappeared underground, and reappeared at the side of the driveway, subsequently draining out to the culvert by the street. There were also flowering shrubs such as Rose of Sharon, Snowball, Forsythia, Hibiscus, Korean Lilacs, Viburnum and so many others I couldn't even begin to name them all.

4   We then decided to view the inside of the house. We walked down a small hill and up an incline toward the patio which was fenced in. In the center of the patio, which was adjacent to the breakfast room, there was a huge black locust tree that shaded the kitchen and the breakfast room as well as the surrounding patio area. Adjacent to the patio and directly outside the master bedroom was a beautiful crabapple tree in full bloom. We entered the breakfast room through the sliding glass doors, which were part of a glass window wall, and we toured the inside of the house.

5   The inside of the house had all the amenities we wanted, including a gorgeous view. The living room and two of the bedrooms overlooked the forest preserves across the street, and the backyard could be viewed from the master bedroom, dining room, kitchen, and breakfast room. The view was absolutely magnificent. I closed my eyes and imagined a winding path leading from the patio to a woodland garden; I imagined it being filled with bluebells, primroses, ferns, and wildflowers. I envisioned another area of the yard with rhododendrons, azaleas, and giant hostas, and still another area with yucca plants and groundcover.

6   Part of the backyard was undulating, and there, at the base of the sloping hillside, I envisioned a rock garden with a small grotto which would be lined with flagstone and edged with river rock. There would also be water coursing through the rock garden to a small waterfall; the water would be dripping from the top of the grotto into an oval-shaped pool below. The pool would be encircled with periwinkle, groundcover, roses, tulips, daffodils, crocus, hostas, and ferns. Underneath the pin oak, next to the grotto, I would place a bench; this area would be my secret garden. This is where I would meditate.

7   I opened my eyes, looked at my husband, and we both nodded our heads in affirmation. This would be our new home. This was surely nature at its best! We made an offer to buy the house, which was accepted. We subsequently sold our house and moved in during the month of December.

8   The first morning after we had moved, we were having breakfast in the breakfast room overlooking the patio. It was a cold day, the wind was sharp, and there were heavy, wet snow flakes falling. We looked out through the glass doors, and there, groundfeeding, in all of its splendor, was a beautiful red male cardinal. Shortly thereafter, he was joined by a female cardinal. The male hopped over to the female, and she tilted her head slightly to the left and opened her beak. He tilted his head slightly to the right and put food from his beak into her beak. It was a beautiful sight. We sat in wonderment at seeing such beauty, hesitating to move because we didn't want to frighten them away. We stayed until they flew away and realized we had boxes to unpack. Periodically, we ambled over to the breakfast room to see if we could see any more birds. There were a few that would come and go.

9   Snow continued throughout the day. The view was spectacular; each branch of the evergreens, trees, and shrubs was tipped with glistening snow flakes. We had our private winter wonderland. Soon the grounds were covered with snow and it began to get dark.

10   We sat in the living room in the dark and looked out across the expanse of front lawn to view the forest preserves. Soon, two deer emerged from the forest preserves and came across the street onto our lawn. It was easy to see them with all of the snow on the ground. We were amazed at their grace and beauty. The deer continued to move closer. We sat down on some boxes in the living room and watched them approach the hill in front of our picture window. They stopped, not more than fifteen feet from us, and began to graze. They were absolutely magnificent. Watching them was so restful, it seemed like all the tightness from our day of unpacking left our bodies. Here we were, right in the middle of all this beauty. We were overjoyed at the thought of the deer visiting our property. We decided after seeing such beauty that day that we would feed the birds and the deer that visited our home.

11   The next day, my husband Bob went to get a bag of bird seed and a couple of salt blocks for the deer. He placed the salt blocks in the front of the house for the deer, and he also made it a regular practice to throw bird seed on the patio for our fine, feathered friends. We enjoyed the antics of the birds and the deer all winter.

12   Soon, spring came, and we began the slow process of making our fantasies come true in the backyard. We cleared the backyard area of weeds; we raked, hauled dirt, bought plants, and made our woodland garden. We dug dirt, hauled rocks, and soon we had our rock garden, complete with grotto and waterfall. I planted many varieties of roses, hostas, and ferns. The bulbs would be planted in the fall. We also made a secluded, mini-meadow in one area of the backyard, which we surrounded with flowering shrubs. In that area, we left the grass longer and planted numerous wildflowers which attracted the butterflies. Also, we put platform feeders and hanging feeders throughout the property. We did not consider any of this hard work. Rather, it was an enjoyment to see our dreams come true.

13   We purchased several books on wildlife habitats and also wrote to the National Wildlife Federation and requested information on how to create our own wildlife "sanctuary." The information we received from the National Wildlife Federation was helpful in getting our "sanctuary" started.

14   Some of the food was provided by nature, such as berries, nectar, nuts, buds, and seeds. We also purchased bird seed and suet which we placed in the feeders throughout our property. Bird seed was also thrown on our patio for the ground-feeding birds. As it turned out, in addition to the birds feeding on seeds, nuts, and suet, we found that the squirrels and raccoons also helped themselves to a daily meal. Our vegetable garden of herbs and fresh vegetables, planted that first spring, not only provided food for us, but also fed many rabbits. For the deer, we provided corn, alfalfa, and salt blocks which were

placed in several areas in the front and in the back of our property, all placed where we could easily observe the deer during their feeding hours in the late evening.

15   The water in the grotto not only added an exciting dimension to our property, but it was an added attraction for the birds. Since we had the grotto at the base of a sloping hillside adjacent to a pin oak tree, it was a natural place for the birds to bathe and drink. Sometimes there would be four or five birds in the grotto at a time, and they would energetically splash water all about. They were a joy to observe. The creek and bird baths also provided water for the wildlife visiting our property.

16   Cover or shelter was provided by the many trees, evergreens, and large shrubs on the property. We also had several different styles and sizes of birdhouses, where many different varieties of birds took shelter. Grass was left longer at the base of the shrubs where birds and other wildlife could forage and hide. The trees and dense shrubbery also protected the wildlife from the elements.

17   Reproduction areas, or nesting sites as they are sometimes called, were also provided by birdhouses of various shapes and dimensions. Also, the trees and long grasses at the base of the shrubs proved to be good nesting areas. Nesting materials, such as dried twigs, twine, and straw were placed in conspicuous areas throughout the garden and were easily obtained by the birds and other wildlife.

18   We now had all the essentials. There were trees, shrubs, flowers, berries, nuts, seeds, feeders, water, cover, nesting areas, and most important, the desire to help our wildlife friends. We furnished a sketch of the property to the National Wildlife Federation, listing the many varieties of trees, shrubs, and flowers. We also had to indicate on the sketch the areas where food, water, shelter, and nesting sites were located. We told them what kinds of visitors we had, which now included birds, deer, rabbits, ducks, raccoons, butterflies, and occasionally, a possum or two. We were subsequently approved by the National Wildlife Federation and given a certificate to show that we were part of their program to furnish food, water, cover, and reproduction areas for wildlife.

19   Our home in the country was, for us, a private outdoor world, a green oasis. It proved to be a constant source of excitement and enjoyment, a place where we could forget our troubles and be in tune with nature. It was a "sanctuary" for us and also for our wildlife friends.

Loretta Shicotte

CAUSAL ANALYSIS—MORE EXAMPLES

Here are several more student examples for you to study.

What Is the Cause of Iridescent Colors?

1   Have you ever wondered what causes the extraordinary brilliant and beautiful coloration of many birds, butterflies, fishes, and insects? Or, more specifically, have you ever wondered how it is possible for these spectacular colors to change, for example, from a metallic-green to a deep violet, simply by changing the angle of view? If so, you will be interested in knowing about the two causes of iridescent colors.

2   The first cause of iridescent colors is due to the interference of light waves from the front and back surfaces of a thin, clear membrane (dragonfly wings and oil-slicks work well). If the two reflected light waves return in step, they will add together to cause a bright reflection. If the two reflected waves are out of step, however, they will cancel each other and cause a dim reflection. Thus, the brightness of reflection depends on whether the two waves are in step or not in step. Also, since white light is composed of a collection of all colors of the rainbow, the thickness of the membrane causes one color to reflect in step and the others to reflect out of step. Therefore, the thickness of the membrane "tunes in" to a particular color of light wave much as a radio "tunes in" to a particular radio wave within a broad spectrum of radio waves. This "tuning effect" is what causes such pure colors in iridescence. Also, a change in viewing angle causes an "apparent" change in the membrane thickness, thus changing the "tuning" or the color.

3   The second cause of iridescent colors is due to diffraction of light waves. Diffraction of light is very similar to interference; their end effects are exactly the same, but they are caused by different means. Diffraction of light is caused by the reflection of light from a large number of microscopically small opaque surfaces (such as the scales of butterfly wings). The minute size of the reflecting surfaces tends to have a "tuning" effect on the incident white light which produces iridescent colors. Diffraction of light, for instance, is what causes the intensely vivid metallic-green color of Milkweed Beetles and Tiger Beetles. The striking colors of Peacock and Humming Bird feathers are also produced by diffraction.

4   In conclusion, iridescent colors are produced either by the interference of two light waves when reflected from the two surfaces of a clear membrane, or by the reflection of light from multiple, microscopic, opaque reflectors. The end result of the two causes of iridescent colors is the same: to produce brilliant, pure colors which change color depending on the viewing angle.

George Tarpanoff

How Working Has Affected Me

Dear Former High School Teacher,

1   As a teacher of high school students, your job was to encourage. Well, I guess you did what you felt was best. I just thought I would drop you a note telling you how having a part-time job has really affected me. You felt that it would cause many problems and that I should quit. You felt it was much more important to focus only on school, nothing else. Well, I believe the outcome of working through school did not have these ill effects.

2   The first lesson I have learned is how to balance my time wisely. I have learned to keep a schedule, so that I have time to do everything I want to. I no longer procrastinate over projects; I just get them done right away. I learned that being early counts in the real world. It didn't matter if I attended school all the time. At work, by coming in early and never missing a day, it only proved to my bosses that I was able to handle just about anything they threw my way. I also found that by not waiting to the last minute to get things done, it alleviated a lot of unnecessary stress.

3   The second lesson I learned was responsibility. At work, I am now responsible for making sure invoices are correctly set up for payment in a timely and efficient manner. If

the work is not done properly, management comes down on me to pick up the pace and be more careful. As a cashier, I took care of hundreds of dollars at a time. If any drawer did not balance, I would be written up. The thought of being held responsible for that money loomed over my head, and I paid close attention to what went on. I also learned that the more responsible I am, the more I am trusted to take care of. It is a good feeling to know that I am trusted.

4   I also learned that hard work does pay off. By doing my work and making sure it was done efficiently and quickly, I moved up the ranks. I started as a cashier, then I moved to the customer service desk, and now I am in accounts payable. In high school, it never really mattered how well you did your homework or even if you did it at all. Many of my teachers would assign homework but never collected it, or if they did, they always gave students an extension. At work, you are expected to have done what is given to you before you go home. When that time comes and you don't have it done, then you must stay until it is. If that isn't an incentive to work hard and fast, I don't know what is.

5   I found that working makes a person become more social and friendly. I always was the person who could go a whole day without speaking. When I first started work, I was forced to talk to customers and associates. Now talking comes pretty easily for me. I am sure that you can remember how I never spoke up in class and found keeping my head down was a great escape for me. After dealing with all types of customers, I can safely say conversation is starting to come easier for me.

6   I don't believe that high school prepared me for college as much as my job has. With the help of my job, I learned why attendance and being on time is just as important as getting the work done. College professors don't give extensions on work, and if you miss a class you are totally lost. High school was too easy on us. Those that behaved could get by with no problem. Here it takes work and time. My job showed me that.

7   I hope my letter showed you that a part-time job doesn't hinder students; it helps them. I may not be at Harvard, but I am doing all right. In fact, I am doing great. I don't have to worry about paying off a loan for school, and I don't have to always depend on my parents for support. So, please, instead of discouraging your students who work, encourage them. It would do a lot for their self esteem and education.

Sincerely,
Emily Fleming

I'll Finish It Later: Confessions of a Procrastinator

October 30, 1998

Dear Liz,

1   What in the world do you think you're doing? It's already eleven o'clock in the evening, a mere twelve hours before this very paper is to be handed in. And you've barely gotten started! Do you remember how school used to be? When we were younger, all of your homework was finished days before it was even due. We got to relax and enjoy our spare time after the work was finished. Life isn't like that anymore, though. You spend time running from place to place, finding only enough time to procrastinate on your homework. The problem is not entirely with a lack of time. Albeit our free time is consid- erably limited, there are plenty of hours in the day for you to study. You don't just pro-

crastinate on homework, though. Have you seen our room lately? No one in their right mind would want to set foot in the pigsty without a pair of heavy duty galoshes! There is also another point of concern. When was the last time you called Cathy to ask how she was doing or wrote a letter to Kristina who is away at college? We promised to keep in touch with our old friends from high school. Instead, they are sadly becoming easier to forget. I'm beginning to wonder how destructive your procrastination is becoming.

2   First of all, putting off homework is a serious offense, but even more severe is not doing it at all. Remember geometry class in high school? You loved that class, and you were good at memorizing theorems and solving problems. But you couldn't focus on anything but Neal, who sat next to you in class and shared your book with you when he forgot his. I think he was the biggest crush you ever had during sophomore year. Of course, he did worse than you when it came to geometry. You didn't want him to feel bad, so you pretended not to care about the class or your grade. And every night, when you'd pull your geometry book out on the kitchen table, you'd start to think about Neal and your future children, not about geometry and your future test.

3   This is when I believe that you became fixed in your procrastinating ways. It became so much easier to study boys than it was to study parallel lines or congruent triangles. Just a few years before, you would have finished all of your homework with time left over to study for next week's test. Those were the days in which worry was never a problem. We would get home from school, and you would go straight for the table and blanket it with the contents of your backpack. Once sitting, you would not get up until the work was done. Then after supper, you were free to be young and have fun. Sometimes you even used that time to go over your homework, to make sure that it was just perfect. I can't bring myself to understand how one person could be able to change so much in the process of growing up.

4   Another problem that I must confront you with concerns our room and the fact that it is nearly unlivable. There may very well be various health hazards presented by its un-kempt nature. Simply an action like entering the room could be dangerous due to the possibility of tripping over something and landing on something else. For example, just yesterday we tripped over a shoe and landed on a hammer and the toolbox. Who even knew the toolbox was in our room? That brings up yet another quandary caused by our filthy and cluttered room. Some of our most precious belongings have been lost in our room and have never been found. Remember that time a couple weeks ago, when you lost our one-hundred-and-seventy-dollar paycheck somewhere in the depths of our room? You were so upset that you searched everywhere for it. You ended up having to tell our boss, have her issue a stop payment on the check, and wait for her to get us a new one. There was also a ten dollar service charge for issuing another check. Needless to say, that was ten dollars wasted on something that could have been avoided. Another problem is that just the thought of a dirty room depresses us. It brings to our hearts the thoughts of disorder and chaos. God did not make us someone to function well under all of that stress. It caused us to want to curl into a ball and procrastinate some more.

5   Can't you remember how clean our room was before, though? Everything had its own place. There was a toy box over by the wall under the shelves, the neatly stacked shoe boxes contained our precious collections of Legos, and our drawers were filled with nicely folded clean clothes. When we brought something out to play with, such as the Legos, we would put them neatly away when we were done. I could always find our favorite yellow T-shirt. Our room must have been spotless back then. We were always much happier when our room was clean. It was definitely more enjoyable, and since everything was easy to find, it was much less frustrating.

6   The last point that I need to deal with right now is your problem with procrastinating about keeping in touch with old friends. Not many people decide to keep in touch, but for you that isn't an honorable excuse. At the end of the school year, when we graduated, I watched you promise to each of our friends to "keep in touch." Since then, you've only sent one lonely letter to a friend at the University of Illinois, and that was only because she sent you one first. Why don't you try to be the first of our friends to send everyone a letter or give them a phone call? It's one of the easiest things to do, but at the same time one of the hardest things to get around to doing.

7   Didn't you feel good about yourself in junior high when you wrote back and forth to your friends from summer camp? We must have kept in touch with them for at least three years after last seeing each other. We felt pretty special receiving a letter from them just as you anticipated. Think of how your old buddies will feel when they unexpectedly find a note in their mailbox from you.

8   Ultimately, it would be extremely beneficial to us and our life if you would take the time to reconsider your habits of procrastination. We would definitely feel more self ful-filled by finishing what needs to be done on time. Procrastination can affect our grades, our emotional well being, and even our social life. I ask you to please think of what I have said here and reconsider your actions the next time you feel tempted to procrastinate.

Sincerely,
Elizabeth Ann Evans

That Monday

Dear Laura,

1   Now that you are a mother of two sons, you have truly entered the "real world." I know this world can be a frustrating place at times. Despite this fact, I would like to remind you to take the time to really appreciate everyone and everything in your life today. Right now. Do not wait. I cannot believe what was discovered during three min-utes of my life on a sunny fall afternoon has changed me so very much. I woke up on that Monday, just as I have every morning for the last few years, going through the motions of my wife and mother duties. By late afternoon, however, my once-predictable life had been turned upside down. I now see life so very differently.

2   Prior to that Monday, my life was humming along. Each morning I would get up with David. I would send him off to work and get on with my day. I exercised. I ate breakfast and read the newspaper. I would become incredibly annoyed if a child or canine inter-rupted my morning routine. Every day had been filled with teaching the children. Reading stories, helping with math work and doing science experiments were just a regular part of my every day world. The children kept me so busy that I barely noticed the days on the calendar being crossed off! If we did not complete something one day, it was not a big deal. If we did not get to go for that walk in the afternoon, it did not matter. After all, sunny days are a dime a dozen. Right? Before that Monday, there was always plenty of time to do all those missed things "tomorrow."

3   Prior to that Monday, I felt like I had been a teacher forever; I felt like I had been a mother even longer. In a moment of frustration, with the four children battling over whose turn it was to use the computer, I vividly remember thinking that they will be little kids forever. Would they ever grow up? It seemed like I was always a referee. The children

always seemed to nag at one another about the silliest things. Does it really matter if Timothy looked at Jeffrey *that* way? Why is it such a big deal if Douglas gets to drink out of the yellow cup? Why does Victoria pout if we do not have ham for lunch? On and on the days went by with me settling all of their little life problems.

4   Prior to that Monday, I raced from task to task throughout the days and nights. Teaching in the mornings. Field trips in the afternoons. Cub Scouts on Monday evenings. 4-H Club on Wednesday afternoons. My classes at Moraine Valley on Tuesday and Thursday nights. Date nights with David on Tuesdays and Saturdays. Religion classes to teach on Saturday mornings. Don't forget all the laundry and the grocery shopping. I did it all with the energy of the Tasmanian Devil.

5   On Monday, October 25, 1999, everything changed. I had made that appointment weeks ago. The annual checkup. It is one I will never forget. You see, something completely unexpected happened during that appointment. I never in a million years thought the doctor would find a lump on my right breast. One little hard lump and my once whirlwind life had come to a screeching halt. The brakes of my fast paced life have locked up. I have been forced to take a step backward to reassess everyone and everything in my life. Suddenly, things that were trivial have become important. Other things that used to be a big deal are now swept into the back of my mind.

6   Four days have passed since that Monday. I had so many tasks on my "to do" list for today, yet I could barely get out of bed this morning. The only things racing today are the thoughts in my brain. All I can do is think about the "what-ifs." What if it is cancer? What if I die from this? What will David do with three little boys to raise? Did I mail that life insurance premium? I am obsessing. I tell myself to snap out of it. Get up, get a grip. Take the kids outside and play in the sunshine. I do it.

7   Although it has only been four days since the lump was found, I feel like I am one hundred years older. I lost track of what day it is several times today. I took the garbage outside, and I noticed the sun was shining. One little lump and all of a sudden the chore of taking out the trash is pleasant because the sun is shining? Not really, I suppose. This little lump does make me wonder how many more sunny days I will really see. It also makes me realize I need to enjoy each and every sunny day, rather than letting it pass on by.

8   Only four days have passed since that Monday, and I cannot stop looking at the children, watching them play and talk. Their voices do not bicker today. Or maybe they are bickering, but I choose not to hear them that way? Today, I heard them giggling in the kitchen. Timothy was telling disgusting jokes about various bodily functions. Jeffrey, Douglas and Victoria were laughing so hard! Today, disgusting jokes told by my firstborn are funny. I stayed on the other side of the wall, eavesdropping on their silly talk. I wonder if I will be here next year to listen to their silly talk. I want to stay here forever.

9   You see, Laura, three minutes in my doctor's office have forever changed my life. She said simply, "Can you feel this?" Four little words to describe one little lump. I feel like that lump is a potential time bomb, ticking away at the minutes of my life. I feel like it is a wake up call. I now realize that I have been so caught up in the business of living that I was missing some opportunities to treasure every day. Our dad has always said to take time and smell the roses. Perhaps this little lump is a sign for me to really become aware of how fortunate I am to have a wonderful husband, terrific children and a really beautiful life. Maybe this little lump is God's big way of telling me to slow down and appreciate life. And maybe, just maybe, this is a message I am meant to share with my sister.

Love,
Karen Hoogland

Making a Statement Without Saying a Word

1   "Why do Muslim women have to cover their heads?" This is a common question I'm asked periodically. The answer is simple—because it is instructed in my religion, Islam, to do so. By wearing hijab, the covering of the head and body, I am making a strong statement about my identity. It is my assertion that judgement of my physical appearance bears no role on social interaction. Therefore, I can only be judged by my character. While society depicts hijab as a form of suppression, it is actually a form of liberation. While society sees it as a form of oppression, it is really a form of protection. While society views it as a form of religious fundamentalism, in essence, it is a form of modesty.

2   A common assumption made by society is that I am suppressed by my parents or husband to wear hijab (even though I am not even married). Yet in actuality, it is my personal choice. I wear hijab to attain liberation from a corrupt society. It is a form of liberation in the sense that my body is my own business. I am not pressured to comply with society's fashion demands to look like the next Cindy Crawford. Hijab is a means of freeing myself from bondage of all the difficulties that stem from sexism in our society. When I speak to men, I want them to ignore my appearance and be attentive to my personality and mind. I have a higher level of self-esteem because I don't need men to tell me that I look good. That is, my inner beauty tends to shine through when I consider myself a strong individual.

3   Another common assumption made by society is that hijab is a form of oppression or weakness. I see it from a different perspective. I see it as a form of protection. I wish to protect my society and stop the existence of immorality. I do not wish to be demoralized, as so many females of America are considered to be. A maturing American girl learns little by little to accept the dictum of society that her body is for display and that sexual interest and admiration on the part of boys is a compliment to her—and the lack of it, at this age, is often felt as one of life's greatest tragedies. However, I, as a Muslim woman, value my chastity like a bright jewel. The idea of exposing myself for the admiration of men is completely abhorrent and can never under any circumstances be considered flattering. In fact, I consider it grossly insulting and regard it as the degradation of the woman into a sex object.

4   My hijab is often looked upon as a form of religious fundamentalism or radical militancy. Yet I'd like to consider it as a form of modesty. Most non-muslim women I see are the slaves of appearance and the puppets of a male chauvinistic society. Every magazine from <u>Seventeen</u> to <u>Cosmopolitan</u> dictates how women should look and behave around men and amongst themselves. Most advertisements pressure them into wearing glamorous yet revealing enough clothing for strange men to gaze and gloat over. As if being a slave to fashion and the latest trends are not enough, hours are spent on the hair and face so as to resemble, as close as possible, the air brushed, plastic models they once saw in <u>Mademoiselle</u>. The majority of women in our society spend big bucks and time in order to transform themselves into nothing but sexual objects to satisfy the desires of males. Caught up in trying to prove themselves to men, they forget that they have a personality and a spiritual side to their lives. This very side of the personality is what I feel hijab nourishes. Through the implementation of the hijab, I am able to guard my modesty so that men do not approach and take advantage of me. I believe that a woman that covers herself is concealing her sexuality, but allowing her femininity to be brought out.

5   Many people wonder why religion should have anything to say about dress, as this appears to them to belong to the realm of personal taste. I think religion requires us to do things that are for our own good. I see hijab as forms of protection, modesty, and liberation. No one will ever know if I "Look like I just stepped out of a salon" or if I've "Got legs and know how to use them." I have no desire to expose my body and display my sexuality to the best advantage in order to attract and arouse males. Hijab gives me complete confidence in my own self-respect and integrity and allows me to make a statement without saying a word.

Ibtihal Rahima

CAUSAL ANALYSIS—POSSIBLE TOPICS

The topics available for this assignment are numerous, depending upon you and your interests. Below are some topics my students have used. Maybe one of these topics will be suitable for you or at least give you an idea for a paper. Most of these topics can be approached either from cause or from effect. Explore the causes and/or effects of . . .

- attending the particular college you attend
- taking a certain course
- having a specific teacher
- going to a play, movie, concert, sports event
- buying a new car, TV, stereo, house, pet, DVD, CD, book, camera, suit, etc.
- getting lost
- losing something
- taking a vacation
- moving when you were younger
- getting married, divorced, separated, engaged
- living together
- finding something
- going to garage and rummage sales
- having the TV, stereo, car, radio, etc., in the repair shop
- having your plans "fall through"
- going on a blind date, a double date, a first date, a bad date, a good date, a cheap date, an expensive date

- not dating
- having to write an English paper every week and a half of the semester
- smoking, drinking, swearing
- abstaining from smoking, drinking, swearing
- dying your hair, cutting your hair, growing a beard, having a face lift, losing twenty pounds, gaining twenty pounds
- working the job you work
- shopping for Christmas in August
- being a smoker in a nonsmoking society
- handing in assigned homework on time
- being a procrastinator, a b.s.'er, a never-on-timer, a full-time worker and a student
- going to school and raising a family
- being a square peg in a round hole
- getting a tattoo
- getting a piercing

CAUSAL ANALYSIS—YOUR TURN

1 Think of a topic, a given situation.

2 Decide whether you want to examine causes, effects, or causes and effects.

3 Formulate a thesis.

4 Jot down some ideas in an outline.

5 Write the first draft.

The last time I confided in her, she spelled the beans.

CAUSAL ANALYSIS PAPER PLAN SHEET

Part One: First, choose a topic (given situation) for a causal analysis paper.

Topic (existing condition): _____

Next, write a thesis statement for a *cause* paper. _____

_____

_____

Now, outline the body of the paper, including some detail/example.

Cause One: _____

_____

_____

_____

Cause Two: _____

_____

_____

_____

Cause Three: _____

_____

_____

_____

Cause Four: _____

_____

_____

_____

_____

_____

_____

_____

Outline the body of the effect paper, including some detail/example.

Effect One: _____

_____

_____

_____

_____

Effect Two: _____

_____

_____

_____

_____

Effect Three: _____

_____

_____

_____

_____

Effect Four: _____

_____

_____

_____

_____

Name _____ Section _____ Date _____

SELF-EVALUATION SHEET: PART ONE

Assignment: _____

Strong points of this assignment:

_____

_____

_____

_____

_____

_____

_____

Weak points of this assignment:

_____

_____

_____

_____

_____

_____

_____

General comments:

_____

_____

_____

_____

_____

_____

_____

(over)

SELF-EVALUATION SHEET: PART TWO

What were the strong points of your last writing assignment?

_____

_____

_____

_____

_____

_____

What were the weak points of your last writing assignment?

_____

_____

_____

_____

_____

_____

What have you done to correct those weaknesses in this assignment?

_____

_____

_____

_____

_____

_____

Evaluator's Name _____ Section _____ Date _____

PEER-EVALUATION SHEET: PEER-EVALUATOR #1

Writer's Name _____ Essay's Title _____

> **Directions:** (1) Remember not to write on another student's paper. Instead, use this form. (2) Offer concrete, specific comments using the terminology of writing (e.g., "The development in paragraph four might be improved by adding a brief example." or, "Check structure on page 3.")

What do you see as the strong points of this writing assignment: _____

_____

_____

_____

_____

What areas do you feel might need additional work: _____

_____

_____

_____

_____

Do you see any areas of grammar/mechanics (e.g. usage, spelling, fragments) that might need attention: _____

_____

_____

_____

_____

General comments: _____

_____

_____

_____

_____

Evaluator's Name _____ Section _____ Date _____

PEER-EVALUATION SHEET: PEER-EVALUATOR #2

Writer's Name _____ Essay's Title _____

> **Directions:** (1) Remember not to write on another student's paper. Instead, use this form. (2) Offer concrete, specific comments using the terminology of writing (e.g., "The development in paragraph four might be improved by adding a brief example." or, "Check structure on page 3.")

What do you see as the strong points of this writing assignment: _____

_____

_____

_____

_____

What areas do you feel might need additional work: _____

_____

_____

_____

_____

Do you see any areas of grammar/mechanics (e.g. usage, spelling, fragments) that might need attention: _____

_____

_____

_____

_____

General comments: _____

_____

_____

_____

_____

The Persuasion Paper

OVERVIEW

Persuasion is one of the four basic types of writing. The purpose of persuasion is to convince the reader to accept, to adopt, or to act upon the ideas of the writer. This is a clear distinction from the purpose of exposition, which is for the reader to understand the writer's ideas. Persuasion is more-forceful. The writer of persuasion—either in a very subtle or very blatant fashion—says to the reader, "Here are my ideas. I will present them so clearly, I will explain them so thoroughly, and I will develop them so logically that I will convince you to accept my ideas and perhaps even to act upon them." This distinction between understanding ideas and accepting ideas is the primary distinction between exposition and persuasion.

An expository essay on exercise might explain to the reader the benefits of a regular exercise program. This does not mean that the reader will get up out of his chair and begin exercising; nor does it mean that the reader will consult his physician about an exercise program, or that the reader will join a health club. The expository essay explains the benefits to the reader. On the other hand, a persuasion essay on exercise would attempt to persuade the reader to begin an exercise program or to join a health club. If the writer of the persuasion essay is successful, the reader will no longer simply understand the benefits of exercise; he or she will accept the writer's statement that all individuals should have an exercise program. The reader accepts the ideas and acts upon them. He will begin a program of exercise, or she will join a health club.

Persuasion is not a rhetorical method of organization, structure, or development; it is a type of writing. This means that persuasion is very dependent upon other types of writing for its structure, its organization, and its development. Persuasive writing, in fact, relies heavily upon expository, narrative, and descriptive writing. I'd be willing to bet that you make some use of persuasion almost every day of your life. Your use of persuasion might be over such a slight matter as trying to persuade a teacher to postpone a test, trying to convince someone to drink his coffee black instead of with cream or sugar, or trying to persuade someone to do a job for you such as washing the dishes, taking out the trash, or shoveling the snow. On the other hand, your use of persuasion might be more-serious in nature. Perhaps you try to persuade someone to loan you $2,000 or his new car. Or maybe you try to persuade someone that she should give up smoking or drinking. Whether the subject is of personal significance or of world-shaking importance, persuasion is a method of conveying your thoughts. Being able to write persuasion is very important, and this chapter should make you a better writer of persuasion.

THE PROPOSITION

As you know, the very heart of an expository essay is the thesis statement. In a persuasion essay, however, the thesis statement appears in a slightly different form—the proposition.

A **proposition** is a type of thesis statement and, as such, functions in the same way as does any thesis statement. The proposition, however, is written in a slightly different form. The proposition is a statement which the reader can accept or reject. As the writer of a persuasive essay, your responsibility is to persuade the reader to accept your proposition.

Before you try to write a persuasive essay, it is important that you understand the difference between a thesis statement and a proposition.

SETS OF THESIS STATEMENTS AND PROPOSITIONS	
Thesis Statement:	I have learned my lesson; as long as I live in the city, I will never own another large dog.
Proposition:	Cities should pass ordinances prohibiting ownership of large dogs.
Thesis Statement:	In the following paragraphs, I would like to examine the advantages of a couple living together at least six months before they get married.
Proposition:	All couples considering marriage should live together at least six months before they get married.
Thesis Statement:	There are several problems you are liable to encounter if you do your own home wiring; knowing about them ahead of time can prevent problems later.
Proposition:	Homeowners should never attempt to work on wiring in their homes; this job should be left to professionals.
Thesis Statement:	Heavy cigarette smokers, such as my mother, risk several serious side effects to their health.
Proposition:	Mother, you should stop smoking; you are seriously risking your health.

At the end of this chapter are some plan sheets to help you distinguish between writing thesis statements and writing propositions, between setting up an expository essay and setting up a persuasive essay.

THE PERSUASION PAPER

In this section I would like to present some "steps" or guidelines to assist you in writing persuasion essays. Some of these steps are simple; others are more-complex and will require some concentration to understand and some practice to implement.

 ## GUIDELINES FOR WRITING A PERSUASION ESSAY

- **One,** as you learned in the last section of this chapter, is to begin with a focused proposition. Because this step is so important, it was presented in a section all to itself. (If you skipped the previous section, I would persuade you to backtrack and read it!) The proposition is the central and dominating idea which all other ideas support and develop; if the proposition is missing, is weak, is poorly focused, or is somehow not done correctly, the essay itself—no matter how brilliantly written—is most-likely not going to be very persuasive.

■ **Two,** good persuasive writing is organized. Most people are impressed by writing which is organized; most people are not impressed by writing which lacks organization. The writer who thinks through his ideas and presents them in an orderly and logical fashion is much more likely to convince the reader than is the writer who wanders, repeats, and jumps from one thought to another. Although there is not a certain way that persuasion must be organized, the writer should have a way, such as progressing from the least important argument to the most important; classifying in one paragraph, comparing in another, and defining in a third; or examining an issue in terms of chronology. If the writer appears to have control of the organization of the writing, he will also appear to have control of his thoughts, and that is very persuasive.

■ **Three,** structure is also important. Write paragraphs that are unified and coherent so that there is a logical progression from one thought to another. This polish will also add to the overall persuasiveness of the essay. Also control the length of paragraphs to avoid extremes. Choppy paragraphs can be unsettling and confusing; lengthy paragraphs can be boring.

■ **Four,** develop your ideas so that they are explained fully and clearly; achieve this through the use of detail and example. Avoid being general. No one is persuaded by generalizations. Which of the following statements is more persuasive?

> General Statement: I urge all of you to attend class. A lot of students who miss classes do not do well in this course.

> Specific Statement: I urge all of you to attend class. Sixty-five per cent of the students who miss six or more class sessions earn a grade of D or lower in this course.

The second statement obviously has more persuasive impact. Don't think, however, that development of persuasion means the non-stop quoting of facts, figures, and statistics. Here are two more statements; notice how persuasive the second is:

> General Statement: If you think that colleges offer courses in nothing besides academic subjects, you are wrong. Colleges offer a lot of courses that appeal to people's interest and curiosity.

> Specific Statement: If you think that colleges offer courses in nothing but English, chemistry, and probability and statistics, you are misinformed. Colleges offer courses in subjects as diverse as the art of clowning, cake decorating, planning a retirement lifestyle, and self-awareness through dreams.

■ **Five,** be aware of the relationship that exists between writer and reader. The term **stance** is used to describe this relationship. The most-effective persuasive stance is to assume that the reader and the writer are equals. There are two stance extremes to avoid. One, avoid an **apologetic stance**. Don't assume that your reader is more knowledgeable than you; this causes a lack of confidence and a tone in which the writer apologizes for not being an expert on the subject. Two, avoid a **condescending stance**. Don't assume that you are an expert on the subject and that your reader lacks intelligence; this causes an overabundance of confidence and a tone in which the writer insults the reader. Readers are not persuaded when the writer lacks confidence in himself, his topic, or his ability to write. Similarly, readers are not persuaded when they are insulted. The following example opening paragraphs illustrate the three stances:

Apologetic Stance:
Although I don't know a lot about poetry or poets, I would like to try to convince you that Carl Sandburg is a really good poet. He is sometimes criticized for having written in language that was common—the way you and I talk—and thereby having written poetry that was too shallow. I don't know how you feel, but I feel that that is not a very fair criticism. From my limited knowledge on the subject, I might be able to convince you that this charge is unjust.

Condescending Stance:
Anyone with any sense or formal education realizes that there are, obviously, various modes of expression and levels of vocabulary. After years of dedicated research and study of the poet Carl Sandburg, I find it perfectly inane to say that the man was not an exceptional poet simply because he was a practitioner of ordinary language in verse form. How anyone can disagree with this position baffles me, but just in case someone is misinformed on the topic, I would like to correct their error in judgment. Sandburg is a gifted poet who wrote in the common vernacular.

Appropriate Stance:
The poet Carl Sandburg has always been popular with readers, but he has suffered at the hands of some critics who find his use of everyday language to be a flaw in his verse. I believe that Sandburg's use of language that is identifiable to the common man is, in fact, his real strength as a poet. I have several reasons for taking this position, and I will make them clear in the following paragraphs.

Clearly, the appropriate stance encourages the reader to follow the writer's arguments; an inappropriate stance discourages the reader from reading.

■ **Six,** try to use a blend of appeals. Persuasion works most-effectively when the writer appeals to both the intellect and the emotions of the reader. Facts, figures, and statistics appeal to a reader's intellect. Information which deals with the senses appeals to a reader's emotions. Examples and details that are likely to cause reactions such as fear, joy, sorrow, anger, or frustration also appeal to a reader's emotions. Although this blending of intellectual and emotional appeals might seem difficult to achieve, we do it daily. Assume you need to borrow money from someone. Perhaps you begin by appealing to the person's intellect. You point out that you are a good credit risk, that you have had the same job for fourteen years, that you have a stock portfolio which will pay dividends shortly and allow you to repay the loan with interest, that you have a mortgage-free home to use as collateral, and that you have borrowed from this person once before and repaid the note before it came due. Although these arguments are somewhat emotional, their appeal is mainly to the person's reason or intelligence. To make certain that your proposition for the loan is accepted, however, you also appeal to the person's emotions. Perhaps you remind the person that you support your parents, your wife, your five children, and your kennel of cute beagles. You also mention that you have had medical bills lately, and you have also had to pay tuition for the children's school. Mention that there might not be enough money to buy birthday gifts for the twins or to buy grandmother an airline ticket to her fiftieth class reunion. Neither appeal—emotional or intellectual—is very effective by itself. Too much intellectual appeal becomes dry and boring; too much emotional appeal makes the reader feel like he is invading someone's privacy or listening to a sob story. Try for a blend of appeals.

■ **Seven,** when appealing to your reader's intellect, you want to be certain that your thoughts are logically sound. There are several errors in logic—commonly referred to as **logical fallacies**—that you want to avoid.

1. The **hasty generalization:** this logical fallacy means that the writer has drawn a conclusion too quickly or without adequate support; the writer has formed a general opinion based upon an inadequate sampling:

   > Men are no good at art. There are more men than women in our art class, but all of the really spectacular art projects and the high test grades are achieved by women.

   > (Explanation: A class, regardless of size, does not provide an adequate sampling to label all men as "no good at art.")

2. **Attacking the person/poisoning the well:** This logical fallacy means that the writer has attacked another person instead of attacking the person's ideas. It is name-calling:

> How could you possibly reject my suggestion for restructuring the Church's budget? Who are you? You're not an accountant, are you?

> (Explanation: Rather than explaining how the budget should be restructured, or rather than countering the opponent's plan, the writer prefers to attack the person.)

3. **After this; therefore, because of this:** Sometimes called the **cause-effect fallacy**, this logical fallacy means that the writer assumes that because one event precedes or follows another event, that there is a cause-and-effect relationship between them:

> Every time I wash my car it rains. I want it to rain on my newly planted garden, so I am going to wash my car.

> (Explanation: The writer assumes that because it rains every time he washes his car that there is a cause-effect relationship between the two events. Even though one event (washing the car) precedes the other (rainfall) in time, there is not a cause-effect relationship between the two.

4. **Begging the question:** This logical fallacy means that the writer assumes the truth of a statement which has not been proven, a statement which the reader might not agree with or accept:

> Don't worry about loaning me your new car tonight. I won't wreck it. Before I drive it back to you in the morning, I'll fill it with gas just to show you my appreciation.

> (Explanation: The writer assumes that he or she will not be in a car wreck. That is an unjustifiable assumption.)

5. **The non-sequitur** (Latin for **"it does not follow"**): This logical fallacy means that the writer makes a statement which appears to be based on a previous statement (either stated or implied); upon examination, however, the logical relationship between the statements is shown to be invalid or nonexistent:

> Henry must not like nature. He prefers staying in a motel to camping out.

> (Explanation: The writer's statement that Henry must not like nature is based upon a series of previous, implied statements: people who like nature camp out; people who stay in motels do not like camping out—or nature; therefore, Henry does not like nature. There is no logical relationship within or between any of these statements.)

6. **The false-disjunction:** Sometimes called the **either-or-fallacy**, this logical fallacy means that the writer takes what is a very complex issue and reduces its solution to one of two options or choices. Usually, the choices are stated so that the one which the writer favors is made the most acceptable; the other choice is often absurd:

> The local community college is going to have to resolve its financial problems. The Board of Trustees is either going to have to raise tuition or cut programs and staff.

> (Explanation: the writer reduces the solution of a problem (the financial problems of the community college) to one of two choices: (1) raise tuition, or (2) cut programs and staff. There are other logical choices, such as cut expenses, raise taxes, recruit more students, or increase efficiency.)

7. **False Analogy:** (An analogy is a brief comparison between two subjects.) This logical fallacy means that the writer has drawn an illogical comparison between the proposition or subject he is arguing for and a second proposition or subject which the reader already accepts. By linking his proposition to one which the reader already finds favorable, the writer hopes to gain accep-

tance. For the analogy to be valid, however, there must be a logical and parallel relationship between the two subjects. If this relationship does not exist, the analogy is said to be false:

> Professional writers are free to use an outline when they write a book; dentists use an X-ray when they are working on teeth. Students should, therefore, be allowed to use notes whenever they have to take an exam.

> (Explanation: The writer draws an analogy between: (1) professional writers and dentists, and (2) students. The analogy is false, however; the professional writer and the dentist are not in a test situation, and the student is. There is not a logical relationship between the subjects in the analogy.)

Avoiding these seven common logical fallacies should help you persuade your reader logically—and honestly. Most writers of persuasion try to gain acceptance by being honest. They present their arguments in such clear, organized, structured, and developed fashion that their readers are certain to accept the proposition. Propaganda writers intentionally misuse logic and intentionally try to gain acceptance of a proposition by using any type of persuasive technique—ethical or unethical. Strong persuasion is honest; it might be subjective or selective in its presentation of facts or its use of logic, but it does not attempt to conceal or to distort. Propaganda does. When you construct the arguments for your proposition, remember that you are writing persuasion, not propaganda. (When reading an essay or an article or a brochure, study its logic. Is someone misusing logic to control your mind?)

■ **Eight,** anticipate how your reader will respond to your best arguments. In persuasion, as in all writing, it is important to analyze audience. You are obviously not writing to someone who shares your opinion. Your audience could be a reader who has no opinion, which means that he is relatively uninformed or uninterested; this is the most-difficult reader to reach. At best, your reader is informed on the topic, but is opposite you in viewpoint. Try to imagine what this reader will say to negate your argument. What is your reader's counter-argument? You can address that counter-argument and refute it in your persuasion, and thereby accomplish two tasks: (1) you "steal" the reader's best argument, and (2) you use it against the reader. That makes your argument and your proposition much-more-difficult to reject. This process is called refutation, and refutation of counter-argument is one of the most effective persuasive devices that a writer can use.

Here is how refutation works. First, since you are writing a persuasion paper and not having a discussion or a debate with someone, you must "assume" that person's/audience's position on the issue. You must consider the argument from the other side's perspective. "Second guess" your reader. Assume, for example, that you are trying to persuade your friend to give up his weekly gambling trips to the riverboat. You have many good arguments that you can use to support this proposition. Before you complete your essay, however, ask yourself, "Why will this reader say no to my proposition? What arguments will my friend use to counter (or argue against) my arguments?". Then, incorporate these counter arguments into your essay—and refute them. Show how his counter arguments are not valid reasons for rejecting your original proposition; by refuting his counter arguments, you are more likely to gain acceptance for your proposition. If your friend, for example, counter argues by saying that he is under stress at home and work, that he finds gambling to be relaxing, he has made a good point about his gambling habit. You can refute it, though. Point out that there are many other cheaper methods of managing stress, such as an exercise program, a hobby, or even smoking! Or if he counter argues that he limits his losses to a set amount each week, you can refute that by reminding him that his credit cards are maxed out, the interest is killing him, and that he still owes you the hundred bucks you loaned him last summer when his car was towed; his set limit on the boat each week is money he really doesn't have. You can also remind him he's stressed because he is working a part-time job in addition to his full-time job so he can have extra pocket money. . . . Just plan ahead, look at the issue from the reader's perspective, and turn your reader's "No!" into a "Yes."

THE PERSUASION PAPER—A STUDENT EXAMPLE

A Different Kind of Vacation

1   Are you tired of fighting long lines at the baggage and ticket counters every time you get ready to leave or return from vacation? Have you had it with airlines that lose luggage, trains that lose time, and hotels that lose your reservation confirmation? Each and every summer, thousands and thousands of American families subject themselves to this kind of headache and frustration, all in the name of fun. My suggestion is that anyone who lives in the Midwest and wants to consider a summer vacation next year should go to Michigan and live in a cottage for a week.

2   The biggest advantage to this type of vacation is the travel expense. Most Midwesterners can drive to Michigan in one day or so. This means that there are no hundreds of dollars to spend on airline tickets, motel rooms, and expensive restaurants. Gasoline, although not cheap, is still relatively inexpensive when compared to other ways of travelling. Vacationers from places such as Cincinnati, Indianapolis, Saint Paul, Chicago, or Milwaukee can reach a nice Michigan vacation spot for well under one-hundred-fifty dollars. That is far less than what it would cost a single family member to travel any distance by air. And since the family will be travelling by its own car and its own time schedule, this means that the family can stop at its favorite fast-food restaurants along the way and save a considerable amount of money on travel expenses.

3   Besides the economic advantage of travelling, there is the added economic advantage of room and board. Hotel and motel rooms—as well as rooms at lodges and resorts—can cost anywhere from fifty to two-hundred dollars a day. And that price does not include meals. A family of four could easily spend at least four-hundred dollars or more for a place to sleep for a week. Meals can add another several hundred dollars, depending, of course, upon the size of the family, the tastes, and the type of restaurant. Renting a cottage, however, is comparatively cheap. A nice three bedroom cottage can cost no more than one-hundred-fifty to two-hundred-fifty dollars for a week. Almost all cottages include a kitchen with complete cooking facilities. Thus, the week in the cottage costs the family no more to eat than it would normally spend for a week.

4   Michigan is especially nice for families who enjoy outside life. There is fishing, for example. Michigan has Lake Michigan to its west and Lakes Huron and Erie on its east. The interior of Michigan is dotted with lakes, ponds, rivers, and streams all teeming with fish. The many lakes also mean boating, skiing, and swimming. Even a late-evening stroll along a lake is very relaxing. So, too, is building a fire at lakeside and watching the sun go down and the moon and stars come up, all while sipping on your favorite beverage. Hiking, sailing, biking, rock collecting—whatever it is you like to do, Michigan has it.

5   Michigan, because of its diversity, offers the vacationer much more than the natural beauty it is known for. For example, Michigan has a lot of wineries. All of them provide tours and samples. There is also a lot of industry in Michigan, and many of the industries offer tours: the cereal industry in Battle Creek, the auto industry in Detroit, and the wooden shoe factories in Holland. Michigan has other attractions for families: The Gerald R. Ford Presidential Museum in Grand Rapids, The Henry Ford Museum and Greenfield Village in Dearborn, the Grand Hotel on car-less Mackinac Island, and the Cherry Festival in Traverse City. Lighthouses, sand dunes, sandy beaches, orchards, golf courses, tulips in Holland, and friendly people . . . all these and more combine to make a week in Michigan very interesting and relaxing.

6 One of the objections that people voice about a vacation in a cottage is that it means that there is still work to be done and work detracts from the fun of a vacation. It's true that there is still cooking to be done, which also means groceries to buy and dishes to wash. Even this disadvantage, however, is easily surmountable. The entire family can pitch in with chores such as dishwashing and shopping. If everyone helps, the family can get out and enjoy the area faster and in the process can save enough money to stay an extra few days. This is usually enticement enough to get even the laziest of family members up to their elbows in dishwater. Even junior becomes interested in cooking when the family is about to eat the fish that he caught that morning. Work doesn't always seem like work when a person stands looking out a kitchen window and sees towering pines and rippling lake water reflecting a setting sun. That's a different view than one sees doing dishes in a suburban neighborhood.

7 Next summer when you come back from vacation, you might find yourself with a lot of good vacation stories if you visit Michigan. You can show pictures of the fish, the light-houses, and the gang sitting around the campfire at night. Or, you could fly West again. Then you can return home with more stories about lost luggage, lost time, and—while shaking your head from side to side—utter, "Next year I'm going to Michigan."

                        Paul Randall

  Paul's essay on vacationing in Michigan is a good example of a persuasive essay. At the heart of the essay is a clear proposition: . . . anyone who lives in the Midwest and wants to consider a summer vacation next year should go to Michigan and live in a cottage for a week.

  The essay also exhibits excellent structure and organization. An outline of just the topic sentences reflects the writer's control:

   I. Introduction and Statement of Proposition
   II. Economic advantages of vacationing in Michigan (commuting expenses)
   III. Economic advantages of vacationing in Michigan (room & board expenses)
   IV. Outdoor activities available in Michigan
   V. Other activities and points of interest available in Michigan
   VI. How to keep housekeeping chores from ruining a cabin vacation
   VII. Conclusion

  Any of the essay's body paragraphs could be studied to determine the effectiveness of detail and example in building a persuasive argument. Paragraph four, for example, is quite thorough in its explanation of outside life/activities. It mentions specific activities: fishing, boating, skiing, and swimming. It mentions specific places to do these activities: Lake Huron, Lake Erie, Lake Michigan, and the interior lakes, ponds, rivers, and streams. These are just a few of the details and examples from the paragraph.

  Another effective aspect of the essay's development is that the essay tries to anticipate the objections that someone might offer to counter the essay's proposition, for instance, renting a cottage means work, just like home. Paul then answers (or refutes) this counter-argument. He does this in paragraph six; all of paragraph six, in fact, is devoted to refuting the counter-argument. When the writer of persuasion develops the proposition to this extent, he or she is doing almost everything possible to guarantee acceptance of the proposition.

Another effective technique used in this essay is a range of appeals. Paul's paper is sound logically. He does not make broad, sweeping generalizations that cannot be supported or explained in a brief essay. He is certain to appeal to his reader's brain, to his intelligence. For example, in paragraphs two and three, he speaks about the economic issues involved, particularly how much money can be saved. Other paragraphs appeal more to the reader's heart, to his or her emotions. Paragraphs four and five are especially strong in emotional appeal, such as the suggestions to take a stroll in the moonlight, build a fire at lakeside and watch the sunset, and sip on your favorite beverage at lakeside.

For these—and other—reasons, Paul has written a solid persuasive essay.

THE PERSUASION PAPER—STUDENT EXAMPLES

Here are more student examples of persuasion for you to read and study. I think you will find quite a variety of approaches, styles, and topics. I also think you will find yourself agreeing with some of the writers.

Take a Hike

1   When I was a child growing up, I had two means of transportation: my feet and my bike. Now, as an adult, I have added several more: a van, a sports car, a motorcycle, a canoe—even a pogo stick if I can get to it before the children do. Recently, however, I have rediscovered my love of my earlier means of transportation: my feet. As a result of some minor health problems (and some major scares), I have taken up daily walking, so much so, in fact, that I prefer walking to driving. I have had so many exhilarating experiences on my feet that I am convinced that all adults should walk whenever and wherever possible.

2   Although it should be obvious, let's belabor the point anyway: walking is good for your health. I'm not going to bore you with a repetition of all the statistics and studies that I am sure you have seen or read or heard in the past few years. You and I both know that walking stimulates circulation, respiration, etc. What I have discovered, however, is the tremendous stress reduction that walking provides. I have learned that the muscles in my legs give me a feeling of groundedness when I use them, stretch them, and warm them up. I feel like I am back in touch with the earth when I walk across it. (I don't get that feeling when I drive over asphalt at forty or fifty miles per hour.) I also notice that I often hum or whistle; these activities replace the talking to myself that often accompanies my drives to and from work or school or the countless thousands of errands I find myself running (no pun intended).

3   Walking also relaxes me in other ways. I find that I often take the time to notice and observe what otherwise I might have missed. Last fall, for example, I heard, really heard, the crunch of autumn leaves under my feet. I smelled—perhaps for the first time since childhood—the real smells, the real essence of autumn. It was crisp, cool, slightly musty, and always there—waiting for me right outside my door (just as it will await you outside your door this fall . . .). And don't tell me that you drive through the woods every fall—slowly—with the car windows down. It isn't the same. I have also found that I stop to enjoy wildlife. Yes. Wildlife. Right in my suburban neighborhood. There are small snakes, there are birds of hundreds of kinds and sounds and colors, and there are even man and woman's domesticated friends: wandering dogs and cats and assorted other creatures (if you're wondering what other assorted creatures, walk around and see for yourself). Leave your TV and car behind and see what is waiting for you down the block and around the corner.

4   One of the real benefits of walking is the improved social life. I can't begin to count the number of friendly smiles and faces and greetings that I have experienced in the myriads of blocks that I have meandered. The world is filled with nice, warm people; don't believe—totally—what the news would have you believe. Not every bush hides a mugger; not every corner presents a criminal. Sure. You might encounter these types in some areas. But I have not had a single incident that was negative. I have encountered many other walkers who smile, say a greeting, smile, and keep on walking. That smile, by the way, is almost like a secret greeting of sorts. It's a certain smile that walkers flash to others of their species. Ahh! You don't believe me, do you? Well, go on. Go experience it for yourself. You'll see. And you will even get to meet some of the people who live very close to you. Those people that you wave to as you drive by. . . . Just think. You can actually see what they look like up close and you can talk to them.

5   One of the biggest advantages that walking offers is solitude. Between the seconds of conversations and greetings, beyond the studying of nature and other people's landscaping and decorating—there is solitude. Walking is mostly you alone with your own mind. You can take the time away from friends, family, phones, TV's, pagers, doorbells, barking dogs . . . whatever distractions that exist in your own life. And you can walk along with your own thoughts. Doing this while driving is dangerous. Doing this while walking is wonderful (just be careful of sidewalk bumps and busy intersections). Or, if you want to walk with someone close to you, it is an excellent way of growing even closer. I have walked with my wife when we just wanted to "get away" and be together. I have walked with my children to discuss the smallest of trivia and the largest of traumas, from why did I drop the pop foul behind third base to why haven't I got a prom date yet. Somehow, when you are walking and talking, life seems to have ways of being managed.

6   Many times, people tell me that they don't have time to walk. I find that hard to believe. Most of us have all kinds of time we waste in one form or another. If we want to walk, we will find time. If walking is a priority, there *will* be time. Other folks say that there is no where to walk where they would feel safe or find something of interest to view. Well, in that case, drive. Drive somewhere safe and interesting, park the car, and—yes!—walk! Others raise objections about routine and weather. Well, drive to a mall (if one isn't within walking distance) and walk around the main concourse or lobby areas. Some shopping centers even encourage such practices. Before you give up, call around and see what does exist in your own neighborhood. Again: if the desire is there, you will get your feet moving under you.

7   Well, there are a lot of other reasons, but you probably could figure them out for yourself. You know, that walking will make your legs more shapely and muscular, that you will probably sleep better, that you will find yourself feeling more relaxed and peaceful, that you will be saving all that wear and tear on your nerves that comes from driving, that you will be saving money at the gas pump, that . . . well, you get the message. And just think. I haven't spoken—yet—about the second method of childhood transportation that I have rediscovered: my bike. But that's another paper. Right now, I'll shut up. In fact, I think I'll go for a walk. Care to join me? C'mon. . . .

Brad Doyle

Dear Mom

Dear Mom,

1   As you know I am planning on going away to college next year. I know you would rather I stay home and continue attending a community college, which is fine for some people, but I would like to experience being away from home. In this letter I am going to try to convince you that my going away to school can be beneficial and rewarding.

2   One of the things I would gain by going away to college is more responsibility, which I know you'll love. You always complain that I should start doing things on my own, for example, the laundry or the cooking. No matter how much you complain, or how long I put it off, you usually end up doing these things, for me anyway. If I went away to school you wouldn't be there to do all these things, and I would be forced to do them on my own. I would have the responsibility of looking after myself, making sure I eat, get enough sleep, keep my grades up, and manage my money. I neglect to do these things while I'm home because you're always here to help me, which is great, but won't prepare me for the future.

3   Meeting new friends has always been important to me, and if I went away I would have the opportunity to meet new and interesting people. One thing that I have noticed in going to a community college is that you go to class, the teacher lectures, and then you leave without barely saying a word to any of your classmates. I tend to only talk to my high school friends and meet very few new friends. I feel that going away to school almost forces me to make new friends. There are people from all over the country who don't know many people on campus either and are looking to meet new faces. Someone once said that college is where you meet your friends for life.

4   Another advantage of going away to school is that I would be less dependent on you. You won't be there to loan me money, ask me if I finished my homework, or make sure I'm not late for class in the morning. It's nice to have someone to make sure I do these things, but you won't always be there for me in the future, and I need to learn to be dependent on myself. Going away to college will help me become better prepared for the future.

5   As much as I love my home town, I feel it is time for me to move on to a new environment. I have lived here all my life and have never experienced living anywhere else. What is good about going away to school is that I can come home on certain weekends and summers. This way I would never have to leave my home town permanently and still experience living somewhere else. This would give me a chance to know what it feels like to move out of the house and would prepare me for when I leave home for good. I know you hate the thought of me leaving, but the time has come that I move on and look to the future.

6   The one advantage of staying home is the price. Staying home and going to a community college is cheaper, but I feel going away is more rewarding and worth the money. I know you hate the idea of me paying off the loans for the rest of my life, but it is my decision and money. I know this is a big decision to make, but I feel that I am old enough to know what is right for me.

7   Going away to school will bring on more responsibility, dependence, and new experiences that will help better prepare me for the future. Staying home this year has helped me to realize that it is not for me, and I'm geared for a new adventure. I feel that I am ready to take on more responsibility, and I'm looking forward to the challenge of living on my own. I know you'll miss me, but think of all that I will gain from this experience. Going away to school will bring new memories and friends that I will never forget.

Love always,
Beth (Pawlicki)

A Good Employee

Dear Boss,

1   Yesterday, as I am sure you recall, you and I met for my six-month review. As usual, you told me I was doing a good job and I was a good employee. You remarked that you were glad that I had decided to attend the local college instead of going away to school after I graduated from high school so that I could continue to work for you for a while longer. Then we shook hands and went separate ways. After work, as I was driving home, I thought back to our meeting and your comments, and I have come to a few conclusions that we need to discuss.

2   First, let me say that I have come to the conclusion that you are correct: I am a good employee. Let's define some terms.

3   To me, a good employee would be one who would be dependable and punctual. I definitely meet these requirements. I have only called in unable to work because of illness or an emergency five times in three years. That includes part-time work after school, weekends, and full-time work in the summers and over long vacations (such as Christmas and spring break). If I know that I have a conflict between work and something important, such as college orientation, the dentist, or a family function (such as my parents' 25th anniversary party), I let you know well in advance so you can arrange to have the floor and the stock room covered. I don't spring any last minute surprises on you and leave you short-handed. When you find yourself short-handed because someone else has taken advantage of you and your scheduling policies, I am the one you almost always call. And I almost always show up, even if it means canceling my plans for a night or a weekend. Remember? I am the one who canceled a weekend camping trip because Bill was in an accident and you had no one to cover the floor while he was out. So I was there for you.

4   A good employee would seem to be a person who positively represents the place of employment and the employer. That means that when I am working on the floor, let's say the plumbing section for example, I should know what I am talking about when a customer has questions about products and procedures. I am always honest in my answers. If I don't know an answer, I take the time to look it up or to consult you or someone else with more experience. Unlike some of my co-workers, I don't make up answers, figuring that by the time the customer learns the truth I'll be gone or no longer working here. I also control my temper and my mouth when customers become irate or nasty or angry. I don't say anything insulting in return; if the problem seems really out of control, I try to find you or one of the managers. If you heard how some of the floor people talk to some of the customers, you wouldn't wonder about the drop off rate of return customers. Some customers can be really rude. It takes a lot of self control to deal with these people. A good employee exhibits that kind of self control. In the end, that benefits you, your business and your profits.

5   A good employee is one who learns about his work. I have tried my best to learn what I don't know. When I first started, I was pretty ignorant about the electrical part of our business. So I made it a point to try to work with the managers who knew a lot about that area. I asked them questions as we worked, and I took home books, manuals, training brochures, and even a few video tapes to try to increase my knowledge.

6   A good employee is honest. I really do what I am assigned to do, even if it is part of the job that I don't especially like, such as cleaning out the stock room, the returns room, or even worse: the bathrooms. If I work the register, it balances. I don't walk out the door with small items in my pocket or my lunch box. I don't switch price tags from cheap items to high-ticket items. I don't ring up discounts to friends who come in the store. If you tell me to face shelves in the housewares or hardware section, I really face all the shelves and not just the ones you are known to check. When I do inventory I really do count items. I mention all of these areas because as you know, there have been problems like these from some of my co-workers during the time I have worked here. You don't have to worry about my honesty.

7   I am certain that there are other attributes to a good employee, but these would seem to be some of the important ones. As I have tried to point out, I seem to fit all of these requirements. So your comment yesterday was correct: I am a good employee for you. What do I get in return? I get an automatic raise (which honestly is pocket change) every six months. I feel like I deserve more. There are several other reasons why I deserve a real pay raise, reasons beyond those I've mentioned.

8   You know and I know that I am a better employee than the other part-time people I work with. You know that I probably help to bring in or keep more business than they do. Some of that business I help generate could help pay for a true pay increase for me. If you had to train someone to replace me (and I could remain here for another year and a half to two years), think of how much of your valuable time that would require. (I would also remind you that I currently do a lot of the training of the new part-time workers.)

9   We are not a union store. I understand that you want to treat everyone the same, so everyone gets the same pay raise. But we are not the same. Isn't that why we do these six-month employee reviews? Reward those who do well; give those who don't do as well reasons why they need to improve to receive a raise. My wages are my business. I don't broadcast my hourly pay rate.

10   As a part-time worker and part-time student, I have a lot of expenses. I have tuition, car payments, car insurance, and the usual personal and entertainment expenses. Luckily, I live at home and my parents provide me with room and board, although I do try to contribute. I know that my bills are my responsibility and not yours, but I want you to know that I need a job that will pay me a fair wage for my sweat and my ability. Although much of the world probably sees me as a young person, I have adult responsibilities when it comes to finances. I know I could be earning more money for what I have to offer. I hope that I can get that increase from you so I don't have to look elsewhere for employment.

11   I like my job and I like working for you. I like what I do. I don't want to leave and work somewhere else. I also want to be rewarded for the extra effort I give, for the skills that I have, and for the values that I try to bring to work with me. I really hope that you can review my performance and reward me with the kind of pay increase that I have truly earned. In all honesty, I don't feel that I am asking for anything that I haven't earned. I await your reply.

Sincerely,
Rob Morgan

PERSUASION—POSSIBLE TOPICS

Persuade someone to . . .

- get a _____
- see a _____
- read a _____
- attend a _____
- withdraw from _____
- mail _____
- buy a _____
- sell a _____
- rent a _____
- loan a _____
- arrange a _____
- invent a _____
- write a _____
- dictate a _____
- make a _____
- bake a _____
- eat a _____

- drink a _____
- join a _____
- lose a _____
- steal a _____
- quit a _____
- begin a _____
- try a _____
- break a _____
- repair a _____
- decorate a _____
- fly a _____
- sail a _____
- drive a _____
- invest in a _____
- go to a _____
- boycott a _____
- strike against a _____

- vote in favor of a _____
- assemble a _____
- employ a _____
- accompany a _____
- travel to _____
- speak to _____
- install a _____
- learn to _____
- plant a _____
- organize a _____
- think _____
- collect _____
- save a _____
- commit a _____
- keep a _____
- go on a _____
- join you in a _____

PERSUASION—YOUR TURN

1 Choose a topic.

2 Focus on audience and purpose.

3 Construct a proposition.

4 Make a list of arguments for acceptance of the proposition.

5 Jot down supporting details for each argument.

6 Assume the role of your audience: ask yourself why the reader might say no to your proposition, why the reader might reject rather than accept your proposition. How can you refute those counter arguments? Build that refutation into your essay.

7 Decide upon methods of structure and organization.

8 Rough out an outline.

9 Write the first draft.

THESIS STATEMENT AND PROPOSITION PLAN SHEET

Part One: These exercises are designed to help you practice constructing thesis statements and propositions. Choose a topic and write a thesis statement and a proposition based on that topic.

Topic: _____

Thesis Statement: _____

_____

_____

_____

_____

Proposition: _____

_____

_____

_____

_____

Topic: _____

Thesis Statement: _____

_____

_____

_____

_____

Proposition: _____

_____

_____

_____

_____

Topic: _____

Thesis Statement: _____

_____

_____

_____

_____

Proposition: _____

_____

_____

_____

_____

_____

Topic: _____

Thesis Statement: _____

_____

_____

_____

_____

Proposition: _____

_____

_____

_____

_____

PERSUASION PAPER PLAN SHEET

Part One: Pre-Planning the Persuasion Paper.

First, choose a topic for a persuasion paper.

Topic: _____

Next, write the proposition: _____

_____

_____

List the methods of organization/development you might use. (Try to include a brief mention of how each might contribute to the paper.)

1. _____

2. _____

3. _____

4. _____

5. _____

Now, consider some of the arguments of someone opposing your views. What are your counter arguments?

Opposing view: _____

_____

My response: _____

_____

Opposing view: _____

_____

My response: _____

_____

Part Two: Using the information from Part One, write the outline for the persuasion paper.

Body Outline:

_____

_____

_____

_____

_____

_____

_____

_____

_____

_____

_____

_____

_____

_____

_____

_____

_____

_____

_____

_____

_____

_____

_____

SELF-EVALUATION SHEET: PART ONE

Assignment: _____

Strong points of this assignment:

_____

_____

_____

_____

_____

_____

Weak points of this assignment:

_____

_____

_____

_____

_____

_____

_____

General comments:

_____

_____

_____

_____

_____

_____

(over)

SELF-EVALUATION SHEET: PART TWO

What were the strong points of your last writing assignment?

_____

_____

_____

_____

_____

What were the weak points of your last writing assignment?

_____

_____

_____

_____

_____

What have you done to correct those weaknesses in this assignment?

_____

_____

_____

_____

_____

Evaluator's Name _____ Section _____ Date _____

PEER-EVALUATION SHEET: PEER-EVALUATOR #1

Writer's Name _____ Essay's Title _____

> **Directions:** (1) Remember not to write on another student's paper. Instead, use this form. (2) Offer concrete, specific comments using the terminology of writing (e.g., "The development in paragraph four might be improved by adding a brief example." or, "Check structure on page 3.")

What do you see as the strong points of this writing assignment: _____

_____

_____

_____

_____

What areas do you feel might need additional work: _____

_____

_____

_____

_____

Do you see any areas of grammar/mechanics (e.g. usage, spelling, fragments) that might need attention: _____

_____

_____

_____

_____

General comments: _____

_____

_____

_____

_____

PEER-EVALUATION SHEET: PEER-EVALUATOR #2

Writer's Name _____ Essay's Title _____

> **Directions:** (1) Remember not to write on another student's paper. Instead, use this form. (2) Offer concrete, specific comments using the terminology of writing (e.g., "The development in paragraph four might be improved by adding a brief example." or, "Check structure on page 3.")

What do you see as the strong points of this writing assignment: _____

_____

_____

_____

_____

What areas do you feel might need additional work: _____

_____

_____

_____

_____

Do you see any areas of grammar/mechanics (e.g. usage, spelling, fragments) that might need attention: _____

_____

_____

_____

_____

General comments: _____

_____

_____

_____

_____

Research Documentation

When writing, sometimes it becomes necessary to go beyond our own voice. To add depth or meaning or variety to our writing, we incorporate the voice or voices of others. Our reasons for incorporating these other voices are most-likely varied. Perhaps we simply lack the knowledge to write in-depth upon a subject or one aspect of a subject. Perhaps someone else just had a better way of saying something. Perhaps the mere mention of another person's name will add depth or credibility. Maybe it's just something our instructor told us we had to do. Whatever the reason, when we turn to others, we are incorporating the results of research into our writing. That is, we are documenting our research. Doing research is a matter of library skills, interviewing skills, data-gathering skills, etc. Documenting research is a matter of writing skills.

Although Section Five provides some information on conducting research, most of Section Five deals with the writing aspect of documenting (in writing) the information which your research has produced. You will learn how to work with the three primary components in the research documentation process: the citation, the note, and the list. If you become competent in working with each of these components, you should find research documentation a lot-less frustrating and time-consuming. That being true, you ought to have a lot more time to spend in the library doing your research (or in the apartment upstairs helping to drain the keg without spilling on your toga). However you choose to spend your time, aren't you pleased to know that less of it will go to struggling with research writing?!

Caveat: As you will learn in this section, most college research writing is now based upon the MLA and APA formats which require the use of textnotes (or parenthetical notes) instead of the older methods of footnotes and endnotes. (If all of this seems like a foreign language, relax; that's why there is a chapter beneath this page.) This chapter conforms to presenting current MLA documentation standards.

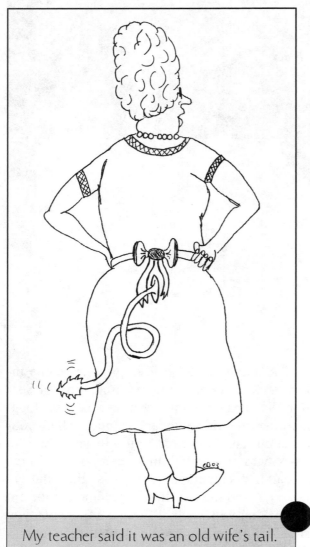

My teacher said it was an old wife's tail.

She is my own flushing blood

The Research Paper

OVERVIEW

Research paper, library paper, documentation paper, term paper . . . regardless of the name applied, nothing seems to strike more dread, fear, and anxiety into a student's heart than to be given this assignment. As a student, I reacted the same way. As a teacher, I am aware that the reaction hasn't changed much since I moved to the other side of the desk. I have also learned—and would like to share with you—that being able to research and document research in a paper is a very vital skill which all students (and many more career people than I used to realize) must be able to do well and do with confidence. And, if you can stretch your imagination enough to believe this, writing a research paper isn't really all that time-consuming or difficult. It's another type of writing; you need to know what you're doing and why you're doing it, and then acquire a little practice. This chapter should take care of all three of these areas. Just think, this could mean the end to those days of dreading a "term" paper for three-fourths of the semester, of camping-out in the library the last week of school, of late-night typing marathons when even the dog has gone to bed, and of holding your breath as you look for the grade on the last page of the returned paper. Sound better? Read on. . . .

RESEARCH PAPERS—WHY?

The reason for writing a research paper is rarely explained to the student. If you are assigned a research paper, ask the teacher what you are to learn from it, why you are expected to write it, and what is expected of you. Most times, of course, it depends upon the teacher, the class, and the course level. For example, I ask my writing students to write a research paper so that I can make sure they really do know how to write one. If the papers reveal confusion, we can correct problems before they reappear and possibly affect grades in other courses. When I teach literature courses, I ask students to write research papers so they can deepen their knowledge about a particular aspect of the course content. Similar to an examination, a lab, a field trip, or a movie, a research paper is a learning device.

College classes in a student's major, especially at the junior and senior level, often require each student to provide each class member with a copy of any research that has been submitted for the course. This permits each student to collect a lot of information in a field in which he or she intends to become a professional. This collected research will prove to be beneficial, for it reveals what people are respected in a field, what their theories and ideas are, what they have written and published, and where it can be found. Such information is invaluable to the person who is "getting started" in a college major or in a career.

Graduate degrees, required in many careers and professions, are essentially research degrees. The coursework itself relies heavily upon conducting, summarizing, and reporting research; the master's and doctoral degrees generally are based upon extensive research which is presented in a thesis and/or a dissertation.

Many careers—especially those based upon a college degree—require writing which makes use of research and research documentation. Although the end result might differ from the type of research paper you hand your statistics, natural science, or humanities teachers, the **process** you use to research and document for your employer will likely be similar. Allow me to illustrate (and brag) within our own family. Brian, for example, has a graduate degree and works in the field of human factors/ergonomics, specifically in aviation. He frequently publishes articles (as lead author, no less) and makes presentations about his work, particularly the relationships between pilots and aircraft. And Valerie has finished a graduate degree in clinical psychology; her research has been in two areas: eating disorders and human sexuality. (Every time she walks by me with the *DSM IV*, I try to act normal!) My wife, a psychotherapist, is well-known for her workshops and presentations on Jungian dream interpretation and analysis; although she is an expert in this field, she is constantly researching to expand her knowledge on a subject she is passionate about. (Mike & Eric, I'll brag on you guys in the next edition—promise!) So, if you think you are finished with research when you walk across the stage and grab your diploma, think again.

Research, in fact, is an on-going life skill totally removed from school and/or career. Yesterday, while on the Internet, I did research on some matters of pressing importance in my life. As I type this, I anticipate the arrival of spring in Chicago. For me, spring means bass fishing! So I visited some of my favorite bookmarked Web sites on bass fishing to refresh my aging memory about nesting and feeding patterns, water depth and temperature variances, etc. Lately, my wife and I have been building a log home (just what every bass master needs). As I cruised the WWW, I found myself doing a lot of reading, bookmarking, and note scribbling about log homes. . . . There are many other interesting topics to learn about, such as no-load mutual funds, biographies of blues artists, and the true value of items being auctioned at e-Bay. I can find all kinds of interesting topics to research rather than sit in front of my computer and revise this chapter, but I think you get my point: research isn't something you do just for a teacher, a grade, and/or a credit hour. It is sometimes something you do for yourself. Last summer, a middle-aged man in my class showed so much enthusiasm for doing research, especially on the Health Reference Center database, I teased him that I would have to buy gold stars to affix to his returned essay. He took me to the side and explained that he wanted in his hands all the research information he could get, especially on breast cancer. His wife had been diagnosed the week before. He was on a mission of many purposes, the least of which was a paper for our class.

Obviously, research and research documentation are important skills in our lives. I'm not suggesting that being the best in your class at research papers will guarantee you an A, a better job than your sibling, or even a longer life. But knowing how to do research efficiently and knowing how to document it correctly might give you less frustration and more free time away from your computer and library—time to spend doing what you'd rather be doing, such as bass fishing. . . .

A Few Words About an Important Word: Plagiarism

Bluntly, plagiarism is cheating; it can be intentional or unintentional, but it is always serious. In fact, it is illegal. **Plagiarism is using the words and/or ideas of others and not giving credit for those words and/or ideas.** If you turn in a paper and all the words and ideas in the paper are yours, then only you deserve credit; your name goes on the title page as author. If you "borrow" ideas (either word for word or "summarized"), you must document the source of those words and/or ideas. (This chapter teaches you how to document.) If you do borrow and fail to document, you have plagiarized.

There are many ways to cheat in a writing class, such as buying a paper from a Web site, having someone else extensively write or "proofread" your essay, typing an essay from a magazine and turning it in as a piece you have written, etc. In this chapter, however, we are specifically addressing not documenting work which you have researched and incorporated into your writing. Here are some excuses I have heard recently when I confronted students with plagiarism problems:

- "I couldn't think of a good topic, and this sounded like something you would like, so I copied it. I did it for you."

- "You said I needed to improve my detailing. Since I didn't know a lot about this subject and wanted a good grade, I had no choice but to copy this stuff out of a book."

- "I copied this from an e-mail from a friend. It's definition which is what you assigned. Besides, my friend isn't famous. It wasn't published in a book or anything."

and my personal favorite:

- "This can't be plagiarized. You didn't assign a research paper. It comes later in the class. How can this be plagiarized if you didn't assign a research paper?"

Each of these speakers incorporated into their own writing—without acknowledgment or documentation—the words and/or ideas of others (the nature of the source is irrelevant, be it book, Internet document, e-mail correspondence, newspaper article, MTV interview, or a letter from the Pope). I repeat: using the words and/or ideas of others without documentation is plagiarism.

The penalties for plagiarism vary. Most colleges have outlawed tarring and feathering and beheading; they were effective deterrents but hard to enforce in a zero-tolerance environment. Some colleges/universities and faculty have penalties almost as harsh. Failing grades for specific assignments or courses are not uncommon; neither is expulsion. Plagiarism, as I stated earlier, is indeed serious. When in doubt (or experiencing an anxiety/panic attack), talk to your instructor.

 ## GUIDELINES FOR WRITING A RESEARCH PAPER

The remaining text in this chapter divides into two basic skill areas: conducting research and documenting research. What follows in this particular section, as in the preceding chapters, is an overview of a process (steps) that might make research paper writing a little easier. Research papers, perhaps more than any other type of college writing, dictate each writer find the most-expedient and most-efficient method.

- **One,** if given the opportunity, choose a topic which is important to you or which interests you. Because most research papers are written to fulfill course requirements, they usually examine specific areas related to course content. A few teachers assign topics. (To be honest, I have never understood why I would want to read several dozen papers on the rain forest, but I know some teachers do. . . .) Frequently, teachers distribute lists of possible topics; if your teacher doesn't, request one or ask for a brainstorming session. If possible, try to connect the subject matter of the course to areas of your own curiosity or interest.

   For example, once a student in a literature course told me she had no interest in anything except textile design and fashion. How could she possibly write a research paper for a lit. course? She had fears of failing American Literature I. After we did some brainstorming, she decided to trace the way different illustrators had portrayed the character of Hester Prynne in *The Scarlet Letter*. The student researched book covers, interior illustrations, and film versions. The variety of interpretations and suggestions about guilt, punishment, and human sexuality was fascinating. The student definitely did not fail; she wrote a very informative and very interesting essay.

■ **Two,** at this point, with the topic issue settled, most students would head to the library to conduct research. Although many teachers would disagree, I would not recommend it. I want my students' research papers to be papers written by them, papers supported with and illustrated with researched information. I want my students' voices to dominate the researched information, not be obliterated by researched information. I don't want to read research papers that "feel" like a "greatest hits album of quoted passages" on a particular topic.

Write a first draft which communicates your feelings and ideas on your subject—a draft containing no researched information. Concentrate on the areas of writing which always require concentration: audience and purpose, organization, structure, development, coherence, unity, etc. Researched or not, writing is still writing. Don't abandon the strengths of your writing which you have developed, including narration and description. Just because you need to include research, you don't have to totally alter the way you express yourself. You are simply going to add researched information.

Once you have committed a quality rough draft to paper or disk, you are in a better position to focus your research efforts.

■ **Three,** finally, let's go visit our librarians. We can visit them in person. Or, using the modem on our home computers, we can "visit" them and the library's databases; we don't even have to get dressed or brush our teeth! Being social, however, I prefer to visit in person. In the library, we have at our fingertips all of the holdings of our campus library, as well as countless terminals for the Internet and abundant databases (magazine/periodical indexes). It is a wealth of information—which is exactly why I suggested getting focused in a rough draft before conducting research.

Let's say you want to write about cancer. Lots of students do. If you had walked in the library knowing nothing except, "I am writing about cancer," you probably would have found a zillion magazine articles and Web sites, plus a gazillion books, pamphlets, videotapes, newspaper articles, etc. Overload!! But thanks to your rough draft, you have a very focused perspective, audience, and purpose. You are not going to write another one of those endless, boring, just-like-all-the-other cancer papers. No. You are going to persuade your main squeeze Biff to give up smokeless tobacco.

Now that you are focused, you can limit your searches in several ways. You are researching cancer in males only, specifically males in a certain age group. You are not interested in smokers; you are focusing on smokeless tobacco users. At this time, read your draft. Analyze some of the areas where incorporating case studies, statistics, warning signs, long-term and short-term effects, etc. could really beef up the development and get old Biff's attention. If you really love the old Biffster, you will want to write a solid paper which truly focuses on him. Perhaps you have offered a few suggestions (translation: nagged) about this habit of his in the past. Or maybe the two of you have had a few conversations (translation: major fights) about this, which means you are aware of the issues where he is inflexible (translation: pig-headed), and you will need to really turn to your research to communicate. As you skim through available research materials and documents, choose those which best "fit" your purpose. After you've made your selections, dropped a mint's worth of dimes in the copy machine or bruised big-time your debit/print card, you are out the door with your sources and your draft adding to the weight in your book bag. Now really, that wasn't so bad, was it. . . .

■ **Four,** you're home now (unless you opted to sacrifice personal hygiene and conducted your research from home via the modem). Your next step: blending the researched information with your own draft. The key word here is blend. Not cram in. Not put in at the beginning or end or one big hunk in the middle. Blend. This is where, honestly, it gets tricky.

Most teachers will tell you this is when you need index cards. You read your researched material and highlight most of it (often rendering the text almost illegible). Next, you copy (transcribe might make it sound more academic) huge hunks of this highlighted information onto index cards;

then you even highlight some of the transcribed notes. Once this is done, somehow, magically I suppose, you shuffle these cards into a coherent essay which provides your instructor with an intense intellectual orgasm.

Most students will tell you this process doesn't work. I agree; it never worked for me as a student. And although I tried for years to get my students to have it work for them, it honestly did not work. Now, I save index cards for recipes. I do all my writing—researched or non-researched— at the keyboard. Since my students tell me the index card method doesn't work for them (and I've read lots of supporting evidence in thirty years), I suggest they also try the blending-without-index-cards approach at the keyboard.

Sit at the keyboard and read your draft. Have nearby the sources you chose and have read several times (hint hint). Think back to when school was good because you worked on puzzles and got milk and cookies. Use those same puzzle-piecing skills here. Your puzzle pieces are the draft you've written and the researched information you've gathered. Now, how can you piece together the puzzle pieces?

For example, in paragraph four of your draft, you are talking to Biff about his smokeless tobacco habit, particularly focusing on his belief (as he has often told you) that nothing is going to happen to him, that he won't get cancer. Looking through your sources, you notice one of the magazine articles contains a case study of someone just a little older than Biff who had the same attitude—until he got his diagnosis. Citing some of that case study in this section of your essay should be very effective in breaking through Biff's denial and reshaping his attitude toward his mortality. Use your insert key and begin to type in some of the information from the case study. You want to concentrate—for now—on including the information. Transitions can always be added or adjusted later on. For now, simply concentrate on incorporating the information, on putting together the puzzle pieces. (Some of the citations from the sources will be quoted and some will be paraphrased. There is a section in this chapter to help you understand these concepts.)

Like anything attempted the first time, this blending process might feel a little awkward; with time, practice, and patience, however, the awkwardness should disappear. You will master the art of using sticky notes, paper clips and paper weights to keep all of your information close to the keyboard, balanced in a pile, and juggled in order of how you think you intend to use it. As with most activities in college, it is a learning experience.

■ **Five,** now that you have added your research to your draft, it is documentation time: textnotes and works cited page. An entire section of this chapter is dedicated to helping you document, including a fairly extensive section on troubleshooting the pesky problems that always seem to pop up.

■ **Six,** your research paper is now like any other paper at this stage of the writing process: revision to add more development of main points, smoothing transitions, running spell check, editing, proof-reading, etc. Maybe, just maybe, we have tamed the beast. . . .

CONDUCTING RESEARCH: A FEW BASICS

RESEARCH BASICS: THE USE OF PAPER INDEXES

Even in this age of the cybercollege, many libraries provide paper indexes (that is, they are printed on paper) instead of or in addition to computerized indexes (databases). Some small colleges and some public libraries don't have the funding to support computerized indexes. Even if your college library has highly computerized facilities, sometimes the systems crash or the electricity goes off. It's a good idea to know many ways to retrieve information. Paper indexes list information found in three types of sources: (1) books, (2) periodicals (a generic term for literature published periodically—magazines and journals, for example), and (3) newspapers.

The following is a partial list of commonly used indexes to books:

- *Books in Print*
- *Paperbound Books in Print*
- *Cumulative Book Index*
- *Publishers Weekly*

- *Books in Print: An Author-Title-Series Index*
- *The National Union Catalog*
- *The Library of Congress Catalog of Books*

You might also find *The Book Review Digest, The Book Review Index,* and *The Index to Book Reviews in the Humanities* to be helpful research tools. As the titles indicate, these sources provide information about the content of books.

The following is a list of the most-commonly used indexes to periodicals. The first one on the list indexes general popular magazines such as *Time* and *Newsweek;* the others index more-specialized journals:

- *Readers Guide to Periodical Literature*
- *Social Science Index*
- *Humanities Index*
- *Popular Periodicals Index*
- *General Science Index*
- *Poole's Index to Periodical Literature*
- *Social Sciences and Humanities Index*
- *Art Index*
- *Business Periodicals Index*
- *Current Abstracts of Chemistry & Index Chemicus*
- *Education Index*
- *Engineering Index Monthly*
- *Index to Legal Periodicals*

- *Applied Science & Technology Index*
- *Index of Economic Articles*
- *Music Article Guide*
- *Physical Education Index*
- *Accountant's Index*
- *Computer Literature Index*
- *Mathematical Reviews*
- *Music Index*
- *Sociological Index*
- *Bibliography and Index of Geology*
- *Index to U. S. Government Periodicals*
- *Biological and Agricultural Index*
- *Cumulative Index to Nursing and Allied Health Literature*

The following is a list of the most-commonly used indexes to newspapers:

- *New York Times Index*
- *Index to the London Times*
- *Newspaper Index*
- *The Wall Street Journal Index*
- *The Chicago Tribune Index*

- *The Los Angeles Times Index*
- *The Christian Science Monitor Index*
- *The Washington Post Index*
- *The National Newspaper Index*

Most of these indexes are organized and coded in similar fashion. Once you have learned to use one index, you will have little difficulty in using any of the others.

RESEARCH BASICS: THE CARD FILE

Known to most students as the card catalogue, the card file is an alphabetically arranged list of all books held by a library. Some card files also include all holdings of records, slides, films, videotapes and video cassettes, audio tapes and audio cassettes, maps, charts, and computer hardware and software. Although many libraries are computerizing their card files, many of them still have the long drawers filled with index cards. The card file is most-often located in a central area of the library, usually in the proximity of the circulatlon desk. The card file is composed of cabinets containing drawers of cards. On the front of each drawer is an indication of the alphabetical holdings of the drawer.

There are three basic types of cards found in those drawers—although the card types are rarely mixed: (1) author card, (2) title card, and (3) subject card. Although different libraries have different ways of filing these cards, most libraries follow one pattern: author and title cards are interfiled in one set of cabinets, subject cards are isolated in another set of cabinets. All cards, however, are prepared identically by all libraries; they all contain the same basic information. Become familiar with the systems used in your college library and your city library.

Each of the three types of cards has a specific purpose and function. If you are looking for a specific work, such as a book, and you know only the writer's name, you would be able to locate the book by looking in the card file under the author's name. If you know the title of a book, but not the author, you should be able to locate it by looking in the title card file. If you are beginning to investigate an area of knowledge where you know neither names of writers nor titles of books, the subject card file would have a list of the library's holdings on that subject.

Here are examples of the three types of cards in the card file:

Author Card (sometimes called Main Entry Card)

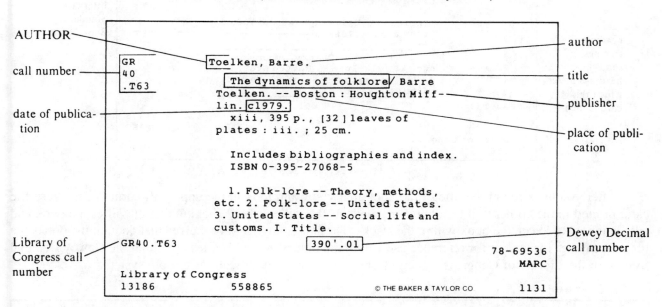

Title Card

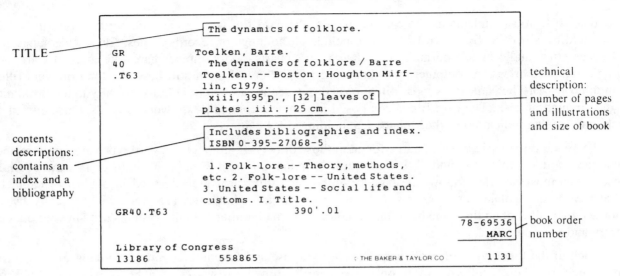

TITLE

technical description: number of pages and illustrations and size of book

contents descriptions: contains an index and a bibliography

book order number

Subject Card

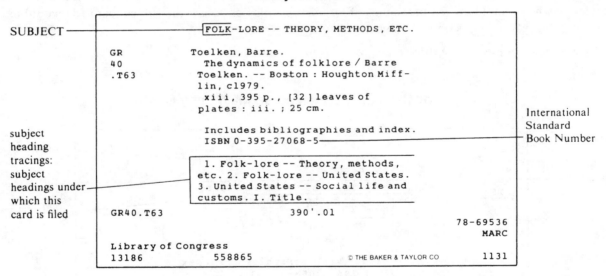

SUBJECT

International Standard Book Number

subject heading tracings: subject headings under which this card is filed

After you have found the title of the book that you want, look in the upper left corner of the card file card; printed in the corner will be a number known as the *call number*. That number classifies the book and tells you how to locate the book within the stacks. The *stacks* are the bookshelves that contain the books the library provides for loan or for reference use within the library. Most libraries use either the Dewey Decimal System or the Library of Congress System. Here are the main classifications of both systems:

THE DEWEY DECIMAL SYSTEM					
000–099	General Works	400–499	Language	700–799	The Arts
100–199	Philosophy	500–599	Pure Science	800–899	Literature
200–299	Religion	600–699	Technology (Applied Sciences)	900–999	General Geography and History
300–399	Social Sciences				

	THE LIBRARY OF CONGRESS SYSTEM		
A	General Works	M	Music
B	Philosophy, Psychology, Religion	N	Fine Arts: Architecture, Painting, Sculpture
C	History and Auxiliary Sciences		
D	History and Topography (except North and South America)	P	Language and Literature
		Q	Science
E–F	History: North and South America	R	Medicine
G	Geography and Anthropology	S	Agriculture
H	Social Sciences: Economics, Sociology, Statistics	T	Technology
		U	Military Science
J	Political Science	V	Naval Science
K	Law	Z	Bibliography and Library Science
L	Education		

RESEARCH BASICS: THE COMPUTERIZED CATALOG/PAC

As the world becomes increasingly high-tech, most libraries have begun to replace their card files with computerized catalogs, sometimes referred to as on-line catalogs. Instead of going to the multiple sets of drawers that house the card catalog, you type the appropriate information into a computer terminal keyboard. Then, the information that you are seeking is displayed on the screen, and in many cases, can be printed out so that you can have a copy of the information. The computerized system contains the same information and functions in the same way as the three types of cards discussed earlier in this chapter: author, subject, title.

For example, if you were to open the card file drawer to see how many books by Ernest Hemingway were in the library, once you had located the correct section of the drawer, all of Hemingway's books that the library owned would be listed and catalogued—each one represented by a card. If you were using the on-line catalog, you would type the name Hemingway into the system and it would access (or tell you) a listing of all Hemingway books housed in the library. You can also access information by typing in titles (or partial titles) or subjects.

Needless to say, because of variations and expenses of the many on-line systems, you will have to do some exploring at your college or public library. However, the on-line system is an extremely valuable tool for the researcher, either novice or seasoned. If the on-line system is available, you should find that you are doing research more effectively and efficiently.

Recently, I was in our campus library doing research for one of my favorite courses to teach, a class on horror films and horror literature. I decided to check our library's holdings in this area. When I went to the on-line catalog terminal, the screen was lit and informed me that I could access the library's holdings in three ways: I could type A for author, S for subject, or T for title. Since I was interested in the subject of horror, I typed S (for subject). The screen quickly changed and gave me directions to type the subject that I wanted to search for. After I typed the word *horror,* the screen changed again:

```
You searched for the SUBJECT: horror
12 SUBJECTS found, with 28 entries; SUBJECTS 1-8 are:

  1     Horror  → See Also FEAR .......................... 1 entry
  2     Horror Fiction ................................... 1 entry
  3     Horror Films ..................................... 3 entries
  4     Horror Films History And Criticism ............... 3 entries
  5     Horror Tales →  See Also GHOST STORIES ........... 1 entry
  6     Horror Tales ..................................... 6 entries
  7     Horror Tales American ............................ 3 entries
  8     Horror Tales American History And Criticism ...... 1 entry
```

Notice that the catalog informed me that there were 12 subjects found under the heading of horror, but only the first eight appeared on the screen. This is simply because only eight entries at a time will fit the size of the screen. So, I hit the forward or continue key, and the catalog provided the remaining entries (note that there is some overlap):

```
You searched for the SUBJECT: horror
12 SUBJECTS found, with 28 entries; SUBJECTS 5-12 are:

  5     Horror Tales → See Also GHOST STORIES ............ 1 entry
  6     Horror Tales ..................................... 6 entries
  7     Horror Tales American ............................ 3 entries
  8     Horror Tales American History And Criticism ...... 1 entry
  9     Horror Tales English ............................. 5 entries
 10     Horror Tales English History And Criticism ....... 2 entries
 11     Horror Tales Fiction ............................. 1 entry
 12     Horror Tales History And Criticism ............... 1 entry
```

The next step was for me to select which of the twelve sub-headings or areas of horror I wanted to examine in more depth. Since I was primarily interested in the criticism of horror fiction, I typed in 12; that is, I told the catalog that I wanted to know what item #12 was. After typing the 12 and hitting ENTER, I found myself looking at the following screen:

```
TITLE          Horror fiction [filmstrip]
PUBL INFO      Peoria, Ill.; Thomas S. Klise, © 1981.
DESCRIPT       1 filmstrip (80 fr.); col.; 35 mm. + 1 sound
               cassette (17 min.) + reading script.
NOTE           Sound accompaniment compatible for manual and
               automatic operation.
               Writer, Barbara Christie; art. David Seay.
SUBJECT        Horror tales --History and criticism.
               Literary form.
ADD            Thomas S. Klise Company.
AUTHOR
    LOCATION         CALL #                      STATUS
  1 > Listen/View    PN3448.S45 H6 FILM STRIP CASSETTE
                                                 CHECK SHELVES
```

This screen provided the same kind of information that I would have found on the cards in the drawers of the card catalog. There are differences in the kinds of provided information, however, most notably the entry of STATUS. STATUS told me to CHECK SHELVES, meaning that the item was not checked out, that it was available. Note, too, that the screen told me the location of the item within the library (LOCATION): the Listening/Viewing area. Had I wanted to check out the item, all I would have had to do was hit PRINT. Then, the catalog would have provided me a printed slip with the call number. (I am still waiting for the day that a card catalog drawer hands me a written call number and sends me in the correct direction to find materials. Long live technology!)

At this point, I decided that I would go check out those few items that interested me and then go to class. By this time, I had spent under five minutes at the terminal. As I wrote earlier, the on-line catalog is an efficient and effective way to do research. (When the system is down, however, the good-old-fashioned card catalog still proves very useful. I think the smart college student knows how to "operate" both systems.)

RESEARCH BASICS: THE COMPUTER SEARCH/THE DATABASE SEARCH

In years past, conducting research was often a tedious, time-consuming task. Although the paper indexes and the card files made the job manageable, it was still a job. Thanks to the computer (and those wizard software writers), however, the researcher's job has been made easier. Almost all libraries now provide computer searches (of databases/databanks) which generate lists of articles on a specific subject. Each item listed provides complete bibliographical information (author, name and date of original publication, length, etc.). Usually, each entry will also have an abstract (a summary) of the article. Many databases, in fact, are called **full-text**; they not only provide a list of articles plus their abstracts, but the computer (if politely asked) will even print the complete text of the article (thus, the label full-text).

Like most college and public libraries, our campus library offers several databases for doing computerized periodical searches: Academic Index, Expanded Academic Index, InfoTrac, Health Reference Center, Pro-Quest, etc. Although there are differences in how the software operates in each system, the basic process is the same (and they all usually offer simple, on-screen prompts): type in the topic or subject you are researching, if possible narrow or restrict it, and let the computer provide you a list (including sub-topics), perhaps a cross reference, and—if you are lucky—the full-text of several articles listed in the search.

These databases usually store information from hundreds of magazines and journals, major newspapers, and even some reference books and pamphlets (again, depending upon the nature of the database). And as we all know nowadays, technology changes often, so don't be surprised when you walk into the library to a database you have grown comfortable with and discover the commands menu might have been changed or the menu screens seem different. Check the screen for directions, or ask the person using the terminal next to you, or ask the librarian at the information kiosk. Because there will be updates and changes in software, just be prepared for change. These frequent changes also make it difficult for me to give you specific directions for doing a computer search (especially for each database). What I can do, however, is provide an example of the basic process.

The other day, for example, I visited our campus library (camouflaged as a Learning Resources Center, but those tricky librarians can't fool me at my age). I wanted to do some research about gambling, so I approached the terminal of the Expanded Academic Index and simply typed in **gambling**. The first entry to appear on the screen was a listing of item availability—by subtopics; here is part of that listing:

- **Gambling**
  View 126 articles or Narrow by subdivision
  See also related subjects

- **Gambling Casinos**
  See Casinos

- **Gambling Clubs**
  See Casinos

- **Gambling Equipment Industry**
  See Gambling Industry

- **Gambling Industry**
  View 206 articles or Narrow by subdivision
  See also related subjects

- **Gambling Information Act**
  See Wagering Information Act

- **Gambling Problem (Mathematics)**
  See Games of Chance (Mathematics)

- **Gambling Systems**
  View 4 articles

- **Gambling, Compulsive**
  See Compulsive Gambling

- **Compulsive Gambling**
  View 16 articles

I brought onto the screen some of the articles, a few of which are printed below:

- High stakes: a fantasy theme analysis of the selling of riverboat gambling in Iowa. Margaret Duffy. The Southern Communication Journal, Winter 1997 v62 n2 p117 (16). Elec. Coll. A19682675.
  -- Text Available --

- Deleting cybercrooks: prosecutors want tough laws to put Internet hackers, scam artists and pedophiles on permanent log off. (includes related articles) Jon Jefferson. ABA Journal, Oct 1997 83 p68(6).
  -- Abstract Available --

- This week's sign that the apocalypse is upon us. (New Hampshire Pari-Mutuel Commission approves program to give gamblers a rebate if they put the money into new wagers) (Scorecard) (Brief Article) Sports Illustrated, Sep 8, 1997 v87 n10 p22(1). Elec. Coll.: A19722842.
  -- Text Available --

- World wide wagering. (gambling on the Internet) (includes related article on possible class action lawsuits against the gambling industry) (Cover Story) Sandra Rosenzweig and Dirk Olin. Mother Jones, July–August 1997 v22 n4 p42(2). Elec. Coll.: A19550475.
  -- Abstract and Text Available --

- Cyberspace crapshoot. (Internet gambling) Michael Krantz. Time, June 2, 1997 v149 n22 p61(2). Elec. Coll.: A19444600.
  -- Abstract and Text Available --

If you take a few minutes to study the entries in the list, you'll probably find interpreting most information pretty self-evident, especially which entries offer an abstract and/or full-text. Author, article title, name of publication, volume and issue number, etc. are pretty clearly indicated. The long number, such as A19444600 in the last entry (Krantz: "Cyberspace crapshoot"), is the access number. (Sometimes, if you have the access number for an article, you can type it into a database and "pull up" the article.) The only "tricky" part is pagination. In the first entry listed (Duffy: "High Stakes . . ."), for example, the pagination is listed as p117(16). Translated, the article began on page 117 and was a sixteen page article. Without the original article (not the text typed/loaded into a database), you cannot be sure what sixteen pages they were. Don't assume consecutive pages beginning with page 117. Pagination for the last entry (Krantz: "Cyberspace crapshoot") is listed as p61(2). It began on page 61 and was a two page article, but not necessarily pages 61 and 62.

Finally, some entries provide information about the subjects covered in a particular article; this is usually when there is neither an abstract nor full-text available, so you at least have some idea as to whether this is or is not the one killer article you need to write that A paper your prof. is expecting. Although the database cannot provide you the text of the article, there are other ways to obtain it. You might locate it on another database. You might find the actual magazine or journal shelved in the library's stacks; you are more likely to find it reproduced on a reel in the microfilm cabinets. If you cannot locate it in any of these other formats, politely ask one of the librarians to have it faxed from another library. (Impolite requests are usually met with a statement that you can just drive to the other library and find it for yourself.) The fax machine is another of those handy gizmos to assist researchers. (If all this technology had been available when I was in college, I probably would have graduated. . . .)

RESEARCH BASICS: INTERNET SOURCES/THE WORLD WIDE WEB

To explain to you how to use the Internet/WWW requires a book, a workshop, a class—or you could do what I did and just surf by trial and error until you feel pretty comfortable working your way through the incredible and unbelievable amount of information awaiting the marriage of your fingertips and mouse clicks. The Internet is not, obviously, the savior of higher education, nor is it the damnation thereof. It is just another incredible research tool, a fascinating way to lose track of time (and your phone bill), and a great way to confront how vast is the knowledge all of us have collectively and how little each of us knows individually.

Exploring the Internet is basically the same as exploring one of the databases such as InfoTrac or the Academic Index (see last section). You can use a **search engine** (think of it as someone you hire to search what seems like all the printed material in the world) to assemble a list of sources (or Web sites) which you can then "go to" or "visit" to gather information. This is very similar to finding a full-text article on a database, except you are using Yahoo, Lycos, Alta Vista, Webcrawler, Excite, Infoseek, Google or any other search engine to do your looking for you. Last semester, for example, one of my students was doing research on shark cartilage as an alternative therapy for cancer treatment. When she typed in the words **shark cartilage**, the search engine gave her a list of dozens of "hits" or connections to her topic. Some of those "hits" were articles reprinted from magazines and journals. Some were testimonials posted on the Internet from people who had experience with shark cartilage. Some were commercial postings from people selling shark cartilage products. Her "surfing" led her to lots of quality information which she used in her paper.

Sometimes, instead of typing in a topic or subject to explore, you can type in the Web address for a specific Web site which you want to visit. All information posted on the Internet/WWW has a specific address. This address is really known as an **URL** (Uniform/Universal Resource Locator). It is difficult to exist in today's culture and not be bombarded by URLs; they are in the daily newspapers, in the credits and announcements for talk shows, in beer and sporting goods ads, in concert promotions, etc. An URL is that weird-looking combination of letters, numbers, and/ or punctuation marks, all of which must be transcribed perfectly and exactly in order to access the correct site. The following is the URL for my college (Moraine Valley Community College): http://www.moraine.cc.il.us

Most Common URL Domains

com: commercial/business
edu: educational institution
gov: government
mil: military
net: networking/Internet service provider
org: organization which is noncommercial

When you analyze an URL, especially from the perspective of a person conducting research, you want to pay attention to the part of the address which is known as the **domain.** The domain is an abbreviation (suffix) for where the document originated or is stored.

Sometimes, the domain is important when you are determining whether or not to use a source. For example, last semester I had a student whose wife had served in the military during the Gulf War/Desert Storm. He was doing research on medical conditions allegedly caused by the war. He would not use any source that had an URL with either a gov or a mil domain. When I asked why not, he explained. He felt that his father (a Vietnam veteran) and other veterans had been misinformed about the effects of Agent Orange during the Vietnam War; he was therefore skeptical of any information coming from either the government or the military about the use of chemical warfare during Operation Desert Storm. He wanted to use information from other domains.

RESEARCH BASICS: ELECTRONIC SOURCES: A FEW FINAL THOUGHTS

InfoTrac, Academic Index, and ProQuest are only three of the many computerized indexes that are available today. With the advent of and common access to Internet and the World Wide Web (WWW), the researcher will have an almost overwhelming amount of information at his or her finger-tips. This is going to make necessary several adjustments in how academia reacts to research and research documentation.

For one, none of us can ever be satisfied with our skills involving technology. Although we probably range in desire and ability from doubters to hackers, we must all learn to use what technology exists at our fingertips. Libraries are beginning to cut budgets for renewals of journals and magazines (and books); their funding is now going into databases and electronic sources. What we once found in the stacks (if it hadn't been misplaced or trashed), we will now find a mouse click (or two) away from the computer screen before our eyes. A revolving cart of CD Roms can house as much information as a grocery cart filled with microfilm and paper copies of magazines. Playing soon at a home near you will be a computer which is linked (via a modem) to your college and/or public library; you will be able to sit at home and conduct a lot of your research. This isn't going to happen overnight, but it is here, and all of us need to make the adjustments.

Adjustments require patience, both from the teacher and the student. Most of us are new to this. For example, in the past two years, almost every writer of and publisher of college English textbooks has revised chapters such as this one because only a few short years ago, not a lot was needed about electronic documentation (documentation of print sources involving technology). You will now find a more-thorough section covering this information in this edition. There is much confusion and disagreement among faculty about how some forms of electronic sources should be documented. In due time, all this will settle down, but for now, we are all dealing with the after-effects of the technology explosion. All of us are going through a learning process together, and it requires some patience, some brainstorming, and some creativity.

I would like to offer a few common sense suggestions:

One, start early on any given project. Don't assume that the research process will be very quick and efficient because you are going to use Internet or some other electronic source. Yesterday, for example, between two of my classes, I thought I would drop by the library and do a little "surfing" to gather information for some research projects I was working on. First, I had to wait in line a few minutes to get a free terminal. Then there was a problem with the network accepting my password. Next, there was a systems problem connecting with the host server. The final problem was with the printer. When I left an hour later, I was feeling frustrated. Later, after my last class, I tried again. I found what I needed, but it took some time. As I know you have heard, there is a lot of "interesting-but-not-totally-useful" (albeit fascinating) information on the Internet. (I am trying to make this point politely.) You will probably find what you are looking for, but it will take you a while to find it, in part because you will have to "wade through" a lot of junk, and in part because you will become "sidetracked" by all of the totally-useless-but-totally-fascinating junk.

Two, technology is only as effective as the person using it. I know you know this, but don't let yourself be one of those students who sometimes forgets this. You will have more information at your fingertips, but you still have to know what to do with it, have something to say about it, and know how to incorporate it with your own ideas. You can be your class' best master of electronic sources, but that doesn't guarantee you an A on your research paper. In some ways, all this technology is going to provide us with more information, but it isn't necessarily going to increase our intelligence.

Three, learn to trust and use your librarian, your campus media guru, and your writing teacher. Collectively, these folks should be able to help you navigate technology. That doesn't mean they know everything there is to know; it means that like the rest of us, they are eager explorers of this new world.

You will find more information on electronic documentation in the Works Cited section of this chapter. Good luck and happy surfing.

Research Basics: Style Sheets/Style Manuals/Handbooks

A style sheet, style handbook, or style manual is a book with which all serious students should become acquainted. Basically, it provides information on how documentation should be handled in a paper. For example, some style sheets dictate that new paragraphs should be indented five spaces; some style sheets require eight spaces; others require ten. Some style manuals require that notes in a paper must appear at the bottom of the page on which the citation itself appears, and furthermore, that the notes be numbered consecutively throughout the paper. Other style handbooks recommend that the notes appear at the bottom of the pages of text, but that with each new page, the numbering of notes begins with number one. Other style manuals recommend that all notes appear as endnotes at the end of the text and be numbered consecutively; still others specify parenthetically inserting the information in the text and omitting numbers.

As you can see, style manuals can differ considerably. It is the wise student who, when assigned a research paper, asks the instructor which style manual to follow. Oftentimes, instructors don't care as long as the student is consistent. Other instructors care a great deal. Some departments and some colleges "adopt" a style manual for campus-wide use. This is really for the students' benefit. Imagine the hassled student who has papers to write for English, statistics, and political science courses and each instructor requires the use of a different style manual. Style manuals are quite valuable and extensive. They specify for the writer of the research paper, be it a two-page English 101 paper or a doctoral dissertation, how the cover sheet should be prepared, how and where to place documentation, the margins to be used, the kind of paper, typing or writing guidelines, the requirements for documentation, the forms of documentation, etc.

Most of the information presented in the remainder of this chapter is based upon the *MLA Handbook,* the style sheet published by the Modern Language Association. It is used here because the majority of teachers surveyed who use this book requested it. There are many other style manuals. **If you use this book as a model for documentation, be aware that you are indirectly following the *MLA Handbook.***

The extended title is the *Modern Language Association (of America) Handbook For Writers of Research Papers (5th ed., 1999),* authored by Joseph Gibaldi. And, as was mentioned, this is only one of many handbooks or style manuals that is commonly used in higher education. At some point in your education/career, you might want or need to consult other style manuals. The following are only a few of the other standard, recognized style manuals:

CBE Style Manual: A Guide for Authors, Editors, and Publishers in the Biological Sciences

The Chicago Manual of Style (University of Chicago)

Handbook for Authors of Papers in American Chemical Society Publications

A Manual for Authors of Mathematical Papers

Publication Manual of the American Psychological Association (APA)

Electronic Style: A Guide to Citing Electronic Information (APA-based)

Columbia Online Style (COS)

These are only a very few of the many style manuals. Many of them are very specialized. **The Chicago Manual of Style**, for example, is mainly used by publishers who are concerned with typesetting manuscripts (and it is also used by authors whose books are converted from word-processed manuscripts to typeset books . . .). **The Publication Manual of the American Psychological Association (APA)** is a very common and important one used quite extensively in the social sciences. **The Columbia Online Style (COS)** is a new guide used to supplement most other style sheets listed here, its specialty being electronic documentation (or the documentation of electronic sources, such as databases and the Internet).

DOCUMENTING RESEARCH: A FEW BASICS

DOCUMENTATION: THE THREE BASIC PARTS
THE CITATION, THE NOTE, THE WORKS CITED

⬛ Part One: The Citation

To cite material is to borrow material; that is, you incorporate the ideas and/or the words of someone else into your research paper. There are two types of citations, both of which must be acknowledged: (1) **quotations** and (2) **paraphrases**. Quotations (or quotes) are "copied" word-for-word. The ideas and the words are taken from the source. Paraphrased material is material which is put into your own words, totally or partially. The ideas come from the source; possibly, so do some of the words. Regardless, paraphrased material must be acknowledged/documented. Each citation which appears in the text of your paper will be assigned a note to explain where the citation appeared originally. (The next section explains notes in more depth.)

Quotes appear in your research paper exactly as they were written in their original context; there are no changes in grammar, sentence structure, spelling, or anything else (unless properly indicated). Quotation marks are used at the beginning of the quote to announce that the voice in the paper is no longer that of the writer, but of another person who is being quoted. At the end of the quoted passage are quotation marks which alert the reader to the return of the voice of the writer of the paper. Following the quote is the note.

For the sake of illustration, let's pretend that you are preparing a paper on writing anxiety, particularly that felt by students on the first day of a writing class. As a source, you use the *To the Student* section of this textbook (page xiii). As you write the paper, you decide it might be effective to show that someone who is now a writing teacher also experienced (and still does!) writing anxiety. This is the passage of your paper where you quote:

> . . . that writing anxiety is very common among college students of all ages and abilities. My writing teacher, himself a published writer, admits that he, too, as a student suffered nervousness when he took his first college writing course. He related his experiences in one of his writing textbooks. "Although it was over thirty years ago, I remember vividly my first day as a student in a college writing class. . . . I felt vulnerable; I felt like I was going to be judged . . ." (DeVillez xiii). So, as you can see, even people who feel like they are fairly good writers can experience . . .

By comparing this passage from a "student's" paper to the original passage on page xiii, you will see that the material in the passage is an exact reproduction of the original. That is, the material is quoted.

Let's assume that you want to cite this passage, but you would prefer to paraphrase rather than quote. The process is similar. You still borrow the ideas, perhaps a few words, and you acknowledge the citation. The quote marks, however, are omitted. The note follows the citation to acknowledge that the preceding material is cited. Here is the passage altered to paraphrase:

> . . . that writing anxiety is very common among college students of all ages and abilities. My writing teacher, himself a published writer, admits that he, too, as a student suffered nervousness when he

took his first college writing course. He related his experiences in one of his writing textbooks. He explained how even after three decades he had a clear memory of his first day in a college writing course. He remembers feeling vulnerable and feeling like he was going to be judged on everything from his expertise with grammar to his very feelings (DeVillez xiii). As this illustrates, even people who feel like they are fairly good writers can experience . . .

By comparing the paraphrased passage with the original on page xiii, you can tell that the ideas are taken from the source; even a few of the words are borrowed. The student has correctly acknowledged (by placing the note following the citation) that he/she has cited a source.

 ## SUGGESTIONS FOR CITATIONS

- **One:** When citing, don't interrupt the flow of your own writing. You want your paper to read clearly and smoothly. The most-common way to disrupt the coherence of your own paper is to "introduce" citations. Many writers think it is necessary to always introduce a citation, especially quotes, by writing phrases such as, "Dr. Smith says that . . ." or, "According to Sally Brown, noted expert in the field. . . ." While these introductions are not necessarily incorrect, they are not required. If the reader of your paper wants to know whom you are citing, the reader will find that information in the note for the citation (which is why notes exist).

- **Two:** Be certain that you provide each citation with its own note. Although notes will be explained in the next section, it is important at this time that you recognize that each citation has an accompanying note to provide the reader with bibliographic information.

- **Three:** Don't make yourself a human photo-copying machine. Or, when citing, particularly quoting, don't quote any material that is not necessary. Be selective. Many students do not realize it, but they have a certain amount of freedom to edit or slightly alter a quotation when they use it in their own writing. These changes are made to adapt the style of the quotation to the style of the writer of the paper. (These changes should not in any way change the content or the meaning of the quoted material; such a change would be unethical and possibly illegal. The changes are made for more-cosmetic reasons.)

  Frequently, for example, quotations are too long and the writer wants to cut them or eliminate passages of unnecessary or irrelevant information. This is done by the use of the *ellipsis* (. . .). The three dots indicate that material has been omitted. The omitted material might be a single word or a sentence or even more. Examine the following example of how one student decided to "cut" material and make use of ellipsis.

  ❑ original passage from which quote is taken:

  > Cruises tend to appeal to a surprising number of young people. Gone are the days when only gray-haired couples danced in these spacious floating ballrooms; today, as many young people book two-week cruises as do people 55 and over. Last year, 30% of all two-week cruises were booked by persons under 24 years of age.

  ❑ the student's adaptation:

  > And finally, don't let the fact that you're a college student dissuade you from talking to your travel agent about that cruise. "Cruises tend to appeal to a surprising number of young people. . . . Last year, 30% of all . . . cruises were booked by persons under 24 years of age" (Smith 23). As you can see, you won't be stuck on ship with . . .

- Another method of altering a quote to adapt it to the writer's style is to use square brackets (not rounded parentheses) to show that the writer is making slight changes to either clarify a passage, to make it consistent with grammatical aspects of his own paper, to correct or update an error or antiquated spelling, or to make more-compatible the two writing styles. Here is an example:

❑ original passage from which quote is taken:

> At this particular point in American history, the news tabloid was as much a political device as it was a means of informing the public. Most tabloids were owned by political powerhouses or controlled by political parties who tried to influence the reading public.

❑ the student's adaptation:

> "At this particular point in American history, the [newspaper] was as much a political device as it was a means of informing the public. Most [newspapers] were owned by political powerhouses or controlled by political parties who tried to influence [their readers]."

■ **Four:** When you are working with several sources, be selective when quoting and paraphrasing. If you have a choice, make your writing more-smooth, more-polished, more-coherent. Do this by quoting from sources that are written in a style that is more-compatible with your own. Paraphrase those which are more-distinctive.

■ **Five:** Although some teachers disagree with this particular practice, if a quotation is more than four typed lines, set it off. Do this by beginning a new line, indenting ten spaces, typing single spaced, and omitting quotation marks. Generally, a quotation of this type and length is introduced by a colon.

You are now familiar with some of the basic concepts of citing. Should you need additional information or more-specific information, consult the most-current edition of the *MLA Handbook*.

■ Part Two: The Note

The note is the component in the documentation process that identifies the source (and sometimes the type of source) from which a citation was taken. As stated previously, each citation has a corresponding note.

Textnotes, sometimes referred to as parenthetical documentation, are the type of notes commonly used today in research writing. Textnotes appear in the text (thus their name) within parentheses immediately following the citation. Textnotes are clear and simple, generally containing only the name and pagination. Textnotes refer the reader to the more-complete bibliographic information which appears in the list of works cited (or bibliography) at the end of the paper. Because textnotes appear next to the citation they identify, they use no numbering system.

The following example illustrates the use of textnotes:

> . . . in fact, several American writers have seen this connection between the arts and the sciences. "Poe [equated] the poetic imagination with the scientific imagination. Already he has stated that the imaginative mind worked by the perception of analogies; now he assumed that it also had the power of extrapolation" (Jacobs 416). Poe seems to be suggesting that the artist . . .

In the works cited at the end of the paper, the entry would appear as follows:

> Jacobs, Robert D. <u>Poe: Journalist and Critic</u>. Baton Rouge: Louisiana University Press, 1969.

As you can see, textnotes are brief. They do not interrupt the flow of the prose. Also keep in mind that their purpose is to refer the reader to complete bibliographic information in the list of works cited at the end of the paper. Therefore, there is a connection between what appears in the text and what has to appear in the textnote. For example, if the text itself clearly identifies an author's name, there is no need for the name to appear in the textnote. For example:

. . . in fact, several American writers have seen this connection between the arts and the sciences. Commenting upon Edgar Allan Poe, Robert Jacobs observed that "Poe [equated] the poetic imagination with the scientific imagination. Already he had stated that the imaginative mind worked by the perception of analogies; now he assumed that it also had the power of extrapolation" (416). Poe seems to be suggesting that the artist . . .

In the works cited at the end of the paper, the entry would appear as:

Jacobs, Robert D. <u>Poe: Journalist and Critic</u>. Baton Rouge: Louisiana University Press, 1969.

If there is more than one citation per paragraph, insert the parenthetical acknowledgment after each citation (quote and/or paraphrase). The following is an example:

. . . audience involvement in the horror movie was the next logical step for Hollywood. Even though many people think they are too good to look at horror, we all have within us what horror writer Stephen King calls the auto-accident syndrome. ". . . Very few of us can forgo an uneasy peek at the wreckage bracketed by police cars and road flares on the turnpike at night" (xv). This latent desire we have to view the horror was really brought into play in the horror movies of the early Nineteen Fifties with the advent of 3-d movies. "The very fact that three-dimensional films had concentrated on horror rather than on other less violent genres pointed the way to the next step: an increased audience participation was in order if the horror film was to survive. The producers organized a campaign of gimmicks that stopped short of nothing but actual frontal aggression on the public" (Clarens 138).

In the works cited, the following complete entry for each work used in the preceding paragraph would appear as follows:

Clarens, Carlos. <u>An Illustrated History of the Horror Film</u>. New York: Capricorn Books, 1967.

King, Stephen. <u>Night Shift</u>. New York: Doubleday & Co., 1976.

Keep in mind that if the student had used other sources, they too would be listed in the works cited.

Textnotes: Problem Solving

Actually, the use of textnotes keeps problem solving to a minimum. Most of the time you simply need to remember where to place the quotation marks (if you are quoting) and where to place the period. Write the last name of the person cited and the page number (if the source was a print source). Period. That's it. Your problems are solved. Every once in a while, however, a textnote might require a little-more thought and a little-more problem solving.

SUGGESTIONS FOR TEXTNOTES

- **One:** If the source you are citing is only one page in length, then there is no need to cite pagination in the textnote; the page number will be identified in the works cited entry at the paper's end.

- **Two:** If you are using a source which is not written or printed (such as an interview, a lecture, a film, or a television program), then there obviously will not be any pagination indicated in the textnote. The note would contain only the name of the person(s) cited. The following example is from a student's paper on cremation:

Obviously, people's preferences are changing. This is due in part to the Catholic church's liberalization of its directives regarding cremation. After Vatican II, Catholics began to celebrate death AND life everlasting. They no longer wear black but wear white vestments, and they do not sing funeral dirges but they sing alleluias. "A funeral is a celebration of a life that has been lived" (Anderzunas). But, seeing your loved one's body placed in the cold, dark ground is a depressing sight and not a cause for celebration. Cremation helps us to honor a person's life because it is easier to remember someone as vitally alive when you do not witness the actual burial.

Melodie French

The presence of quotation marks alerts the reader to the cited material and informs the reader that the information is a quotation (not a paraphrase). The reader also knows that the source is someone named Anderzunas, and we know that the source was not a printed source (because there is no pagination present in the note). To gain more information, the reader consults the works cited section, where the following entry is listed with all the other sources:

Anderzunas, Raymond. Personal interview. 30 Nov. 1987.

Sometimes, it is acceptable and informative to add a title or descriptor to the works cited entry:

Anderzunas, Raymond. Mortician. Personal interview. 30 Nov. 1987.

- **Three:** If you are citing authors (or sources) who have the same last name, include a first initial to clarify which person is being cited in each instance. The example which follows is from a student's research paper which dealt with an analysis of the autobiographical approach to literature (that is, to understand and appreciate a work of literature, a reader should also have some knowledge of the writer's life):

It was in the Nineteenth Century that this trend really gained wide acceptance. Many of the popular anthologies of literature had prefaces which espoused the autobiographical approach. In a very popular anthology about prose writers, one editor very clearly expressed his views on the importance of knowing about each writer in his collection: "It seems necessary to a due understanding of an author's mind, that some of the circumstances of his education and general experience should be known to us. To be able to think with him and feel with him, we must live with him . . ." (R. Griswold 5). This same philosophy is present in the preface to another similar anthology some thirty three years later: "These sketches are for those busy people who wish to know something of the private life and personal history of their favorite authors. These sketches are devoted . . . chiefly to the home life of the various authors . . ." (H. Griswold 5). Since both anthologies took the same autobiographical approach and since both sold quite well, we can assume that there truly was . . .

Edgar Montresor

Since both writers have the same last name—Griswold—it was necessary to include a first initial to clarify which source was being cited. For more-complete bibliographical (or publishing) information, the reader needs to look at the works cited at the end of the essay. On that page, among the other cited sources, would be the following two entries:

Griswold, Hattie. <u>Home Life of Great Authors</u>. Chicago: A. C. McClurg and Company, 1888.

Griswold, Rufus. <u>Prose Writers of America</u>. Philadelphia: Parry and McMillan, 1855.

■ **Four:** If you are citing more than one work by the same author, include in the textnote the title or an abbreviation of the title. That way, you have identified not only the author but the exact source by that author. The following example is from a student's paper on writer Anne Rice. When writing her paper, the student turned to one of the definitive sources on Anne Rice, Rutgers University professor Katherine Ramsland. As frequently happens, Ms. Ramsland has written extensively on Rice, so it was inevitable that the student would be using several sources written by Ramsland:

> This twin theme occurs in horror literature quite often, from Roderick and Madeline Usher in "The Fall of the House of Usher," the "two" sides of Henry Jekyll and Edward Hyde, Thad Beaumont and George Stark in Stephen King's <u>The Dark Half</u>, and the twin brothers in the novel <u>Twins</u> (the film <u>Dead Ringers</u>). So, when Anne Rice incorporates twins into her book, she is following well-established tradition. "Symbolically, twins are the synthesis of dual aspects of one person, or the wholeness of the psyche. Not only do they portray a pull in contrary directions, but they depict apparent symmetry, and also paradox, for two are as one" (Ramsland, <u>The Vampire Companion . . .</u> 438). The twins in the vampire chronicles are examples of this concept of duality, of the "twin" sides of human nature. "The use of twins emphasizes the theme of duality that occurs in the novel, a symbol of ambiguity as well as of the repeated image of two sides of a single entity" (Ramsland, <u>Prism . . .</u> 304). One scene in the novel, in particular, illustrates . . .
>
> Louis Florescu

Note that in the above textnotes, the name is followed with an abbreviated title (underlined) and there is a comma between the name and the title, but there is no comma between the title and the page number. When both works are listed in the works cited at the end of the essay, complete titles (and other publishing information) are provided:

Ramsland, Katherine. <u>Prism of the Night: A Biography of Anne Rice</u>. New York: Dutton, 1991.

–––. <u>The Vampire Companion: The Official Guide to Anne Rice's The Vampire Chronicles</u>. New York: Ballantine Books, 1993.

(For an explanation of the three hyphens and a dot substituted for the name in the second works cited entry, see page 416.)

Note: These abbreviated titles are underlined because they are book titles; had they been the titles of articles, for example, they would have been placed within quote marks. However the title is punctuated in the works cited entry is how you should punctuate the title in the textnote. Again, be certain to use ellipsis (three dots) to show abbreviated titles.

■ **Five:** If you are working with a source that has several authors, the rule/guideline you follow depends upon the number of authors. If the work has more than one author but not more than three, list the last name of each person. The following example illustrates:

> . . . and it surprises many fans of the film and the book to learn that there was a real Dracula. "The real Dracula, who ruled the territories that now constitute Romania, was born in 1431. . . . He died in 1476. . . . He was very much the by-product of the Europe of his day—the Renaissance, essentially a period of transition" (Florescu and McNally 13). This exposure to transition is very apparent in . . .

The above example shows the use of the word *and* to join the two names; note the absence of punctuation between the names and the page number. Complete publishing information would be included in the works cited entry:

> Florescu, Radu R., and Raymond T. McNally. <u>Dracula: Prince of Many Faces</u>. Boston: Little, Brown and Company, 1989.

If the work you are citing has more than three authors, list the first author's last name followed by et al. The following is an example:

> . . . classify this type of woman as silent. "The inability of the silent women to find meaning in the words of others is reflected also in their relations with authorities. While they feel passive, reactive, and dependent, they see authorities as being all-powerful, if not overpowering" (Belenky et al. 27). In the novel . . .

Study the textnote in the above example. One name is listed, followed by et al. (Note the lack of a period after *et,* the space, the *al* followed by a period.) There is also a space between et al. and the page number. In the works cited entry, complete publishing information is provided:

> Belenky, Mary Field, Blythe McVicker Clinchy, Nancy Rule Goldberger, and Jill Mattuck Tarule. <u>Women's Ways of Knowing: The Development of Self, Voice, and Mind</u>. New York: Basic Books, 1986.

It would also be acceptable to use the abbreviation for *and others* (et al.) in the works cited entry after the first author's name. (As a person who has co-authored books, however, my ego always enjoys seeing my name listed for the work I've done. I have many nicknames; et al. is not one of my favorites.)

■ **Six:** If you write a research paper, sooner or later you will encounter what one of my students referred to as a quote within a quote. That is, you cite a source that cites another source. Technically, a citation of this type is called an **indirect citation**. A **direct citation** is one taken from the original source; it is better to use direct citations when possible. Sometimes, however, indirect citation is unavoidable.

Keep in mind one basic guideline: give credit to the original source you are citing, and give credit to the secondary source where you "found" the information. Give credit to both sources.

Let's assume that you are a student in my Literature 220 course: The Literature of Horror and Jung's Concept of the Shadow. You are writing a research paper on why horror writers write horror (as opposed to, say, fantasy, romance, or detective stories). For one of your sources, you use Douglas Winter's book on Stephen King: *Stephen King: The Art of Darkness*. In the section of your paper which deals with various writers' childhood stage, you decide to quote from Winter's book; however, the section you are quoting is not from Winter, but is from King cited by Winter. If you clearly identify in the text of your paper that you are quoting (or paraphrasing) Stephen King, then his name does not appear in the textnote:

> . . . King doubts that his genesis as a horror writer can be attributed to childhood events: "People always want to know what happened in your childhood. . . . In truth, the urge to make up unreality seems inborn, innate, something that was sunk into the creative part of my mind like a great big meteor full of metallic alloys, large enough to cause a compass needle to swing away from true north . . ." (qtd. in Winter 15). In King's memory, the first time that the needle swung toward . . .

If the text of the paper does not identify the source as King, then the note has to clarify the source:

> . . . More than one modern horror writer has negated the sentiment that the genesis of a horror writer begins with a childhood event or trauma. "People always want to know what happened in your childhood. . . . In truth, the urge to make up unreality seems inborn, innate, something that was sunk into the creative part of my mind like a great big meteor full of metallic alloys, large enough to cause a compass needle to swing away from true north . . ." (King qtd. in Winter 15). In King's memory . . .

The works cited entry for this indirect citation would simply be the one for Winter's book:

Winter, Douglas. <u>Stephen King: The Art of Darkness</u>. New York: New American Library, 1984.

- **Seven:** Just in case you skipped the section on using electronic databases (I hope you are appropriately embarrassed about this), I'll remind you to pay attention to the pagination as indicated in the computer printout. Here's a sample entry from the Expanded Academic Index:

❏ High stakes: a fantasy theme analysis of the selling of riverboat gambling in Iowa. (Social Influence in Changing Times) Margaret Duffy. The Southern Communication Journal, Winter 1997 v62 n2 p117(16).

The pagination for this article is listed as p117(16). This means the article began on page 117 of *The Southern Communication Journal* and was a sixteen page article. Without looking at the original article, however, you don't know which sixteen pages. Don't assume that the article began on page 117 and was printed on consecutive pages. In a textnote for this source, use the beginning page number followed by a plus sign:

> . . . blah blah blah" (Duffy 117+).

It's that simple. Unfortunately, some teachers use other methods. Some tell their students to "guess" pagination based upon the number of printout pages in ratio to the number of original typeset pages. Other teachers (I have witnessed this procedure in the library or I wouldn't have believed it) have their students use a ruler to measure the printout, divide the total length of the printout by the number of pages, draw lines across the paper to "make" pages, and then number them. (The number you get after dividing could be the IQ of the instructor. . . .) I don't know how the Modern Language Association feels about either of these methods, but I wouldn't recommend you use them. Remember: beginning page number and a plus sign.

- **Eight:** What do you do when there is no author? Unsigned (or anonymous) articles are fairly common. Whether you are using a "paper" copy or a database copy, the solution to the problem is the same. Let's look at an example:

❏ Filter ventilation levels in selected U.S. cigarettes, 1997. Morbidity and Mortality Weekly Report, Nov 7, 1997 v46 n44 p1043(5) -- Abstract Available --

You have two choices for the textnote when there is no listed author.
Method One: you can use the title of the magazine or the journal:

> . . . blah blah blah" (<u>Morbidity and Mortality Weekly Report</u> 1043+).

This method works well, unless you have used more than one issue of the same publication—and—none of the articles have an author; in that case, add either a date or an abbreviated title of the article to the note to clarify which specific issue you are documenting:

> . . . blah blah blah" (<u>Morbidity and Mortality Weekly Report</u>, "Filter ventilation levels
> . . ." 1043+).

or:

> . . . blah blah blah" (<u>Morbidity and Mortality Weekly Report</u>, 7 Nov. 1997 1043+).

Method Two: you can use the title or an abbreviated title of the article:

> . . . blah blah blah blah blah" ("Filter ventilation levels . . ." 1043+).

Notice that magazine/journal titles are underlined, article titles appear in quotation marks, and ellipsis can be used to show abbreviation.

- **Nine:** It is sometimes difficult to write textnotes for Internet sources. Some information which comes off the Internet lists author, title, page numbers, etc. and some information is missing some or all of these bibliographic tidbits. If you find an article which has been published previously in another format, then you are using the Internet in the same way that you would use a database such as InfoTrac or The Expanded Academic Index. The textnote would list author, or title (in the case of an unsigned article), and page number. The works cited entry would provide your reader with the "trail" of how to find that article posted on the Internet.

  It's when information gets posted on the Internet without a previous publishing history that writing textnotes can get a little more complex. Most legitimate postings have a title as well as an author and/or an organization. There are usually page numbers on the documents when they leave the printer (such as page 1 of 6). And if you look closely enough, you will usually find a date when the information was posted and/or last updated. Most importantly, there will be the Uniform Resource Locator (URL). Usually, you will locate enough bibliographic information to work with. If you have an author, it is author and page number in the textnote, as usual. If there is no author, use a title (or abbreviated title) and a page number. It is also acceptable (**as a last resort**) to use an abbreviated URL and a page number.

  If you have found information which contains little or no bibliographic information, I would suggest not using that source and its information. There is abundant material on databases and on the Internet; why use sources (and maybe, why trust sources) which don't follow some of the basic principles of scholarship?

  The following illustrate Internet source textnotes:

> . . . blah blah blah" (The Natural Death Center 4)
> . . . blah blah blah" (Dow Jones & Co. 8).
> . . . blah blah blah" (Bunday 5).
> . . . blah blah blah" (http://www.raptor 22).'

Note: If you use an abbreviated URL (as above), do not use ellipsis (three dots) to show that it is abbreviated.

> . . . blah blah blah" ("Choosing a Browser . . ." 4).
> . . . blah blah" ("HPV [Human Papilloma Virus]" 13).

■ **Ten:** There will always be a textnote or two to write for a source that just doesn't conform to any guidelines. Don't get so caught up in the trivial pursuit of textnote perfectionism that you forget the purpose of a textnote: to indicate which source has been cited. After looking at a textnote, the reader of your paper should be able to turn to your works cited page and know exactly which source that particular textnote refers to. When in doubt, remember this basic textnote function and also this advice: **generally, whatever appears first in the works cited entry (such as a person's name, a title, the name of an organization, the name of a Web site, etc.) appears first in the textnote.**

■ Part Three: The Works Cited/Bibliography

The list of *works cited* appears at the end of the paper. It is a complete listing, alphabetically arranged, of all the works which were cited in the paper—thus works cited. Other terms for this list are *bibliography* and *works consulted*. The *MLA Handbook* now prefers the works cited label. Your teacher, however, might have different requirements. For example, works cited means that all the works listed were cited in the paper. A list labeled *bibliography* or *works consulted* would include all works which were cited in the paper, but could also include other works which were consulted but were not cited. The list of works cited appears at the end of the paper, beginning on a new page (continue the pagination of your paper throughout the list of works cited pages). On the first page of this section, type the words *Works Cited* centered one inch from the top of the page. Double space between this title and the first entry. Each work listed in the works cited begins at the left hand margin; if a second line is needed, it is indented five spaces from the left margin.

Double space the entire works cited page, including within and between entries.

Write each works cited entry correctly, following the MLA guidelines, paying close attention to content, punctuation, underlining, spacing, etc. List each source once in the works cited. Alphabetize the entries according to the first word in each entry (except for **a, an,** and **the**); usually—but not always—the first word is an author's last name.

THE WORKS CITED: PREPARING EACH ENTRY

The following are common-source examples of entries for a works cited list. The manner in which each entry presents bibliographic information is very important. As you study the examples, pay particular attention to indenting, content, punctuation, capitalization, abbreviation, etc. These are examples for you to use as models, substituting the information you have into the proper "formula." **Remember: double space within and between entries.**

Works cited entry for a book with one author:

Jacobs, Robert D. <u>Poe: Journalist and Critic</u>. Baton Rouge: Louisiana University Press, 1969.

Works cited entry for a book with an editor:

Hartwell, David G., ed. <u>The Dark Descent: The Evolution of Horror</u>. New York: Tor Books, 1987.

Works cited entry for a book by multiple authors:

Nash, Constance, and Virginia Oakey. <u>The Screenwriter's Handbook: Writing for the Movies</u>. New York: Harper and Row Publishers, 1974.

Works cited entry for a book with more than three authors:

Dorenkamp, Angela G., et al. <u>Images of Women in American Popular Culture</u>. New York: Harcourt Brace Jovanovich, 1985.

Works cited entry for a book with a group or a corporate author:

The Edgar Allan Poe Society. <u>Myths and Reality: The Mysterious Mr. Poe</u>. Baltimore: The Edgar Allan Poe Society Press, 1987.

Works cited entry for a book with an author and an editor:

Wolf, Leonard. <u>The Essential Frankenstein: The Definitive, Annotated Edition</u>. By Mary Shelley. New York: Plume, 1993.

Shelley, Mary. <u>The Essential Frankenstein: The Definitive, Annotated Edition</u>. Ed. Leonard Wolf. New York: Plume, 1993.

 In the text of your paper, if you have cited the work of the author—Shelley—begin your textnote with the author's name. If you have cited the work of the editor, begin your textnote with the editor's name.

Works cited entry for a selection from an anthology or an edited book:

Ramsland, Katherine. "Angel Heart: The Journey to Self as the Ultimate Horror." <u>Cut!: Horror Writers on Horror Film</u>. Ed. Christopher Golden. New York: Berkley, 1992. 189–197.

Works cited entry for an introduction, preface, foreword, or afterword in a book:

King, Stephen. Foreword. <u>Scars</u>. By Richard Christian Matheson. 1987. Los Angeles: Scream Press, 1987.

Van Herk, Aritha. Afterword. <u>Bear</u>. By Marian Engel. 1976. Toronto: McClelland & Stewart, 1990.

 In the first example, the date of the novel is the same as the date for the foreword. Both were published for the first time at the same time. In the second example, the novel was originally published in 1976; the afterword was published in a later edition in 1990.

Works cited entry for an article in an encyclopedia:

"Santa Claus." <u>The World Book Encyclopedia</u>. 1987 ed.

Works cited entry for a pamphlet:

<u>Breast Self Examination</u>. Chicago: American Cancer Society, 1988.

Works cited entry for an article from a newspaper:

Quinlan, Jim. "Coast Guard Cutback Plan Here Assailed." <u>Chicago Sun-Times</u> 13 Jan. 1988, Metro Final ed.: 6.

Hubbard, Jan. "Are Soviets Ready To Invade the NBA?" <u>The Sporting News</u> 7 Mar. 1988: 36.

Works cited entry for an editorial:

"Israel Punishes The Messenger." Editorial. <u>Chicago Tribune</u> 12 Jan. 1988, Sports Final ed., sec. 1: 12.

Beck, Joan. "Innocent till Proven Guilty Competes with the Olympic Ideals." Editorial. <u>Chicago Tribune</u> 3 Feb. 1994, Southwest ed., sec. 1: 21.

Works cited entry for a review in a newspaper:

Bommer, Lawrence. Rev. of <u>The Fantasticks</u>. Touchstone Theatre, Chicago. <u>Chicago Tribune</u> 1 Feb. 1994, Southwest ed., sec. 1: 18.

Chatain, Robert. "The Strange, Impossible Worlds of Horror Fiction's Modern Masters." Rev. of <u>The Weird Tale</u>, by S. T. Joshi. <u>Chicago Tribune</u> 20 May 1990, Southwest ed., sec. 14: 6.

Works cited entry for a letter to the editor published in a newspaper:

DeVillez, Randy. "Matheson's Time." Letter to the editor. <u>Chicago Tribune</u> 21 Nov. 1992, Southwest ed., sec. 1: 24.

Works cited entry for an article from a magazine:

Greenfield, Meg. "When Right Isn't Right." <u>Newsweek</u> 4 May 1987: 88.

Ornstein, Robert, and David Sobel. "The Healing Brain." <u>Psychology Today</u> Mar. 1987: 48–52.

 If it is a one-page article, list the single page number. If the article is printed on consecutive pages, list them as inclusive: 48–52. If the article is not printed on consecutive pages, write only the first page number and a plus sign.

Works cited entry for an anonymous article:

"A Most Unusual Olympics." <u>Newsweek</u> 15 July 1985: 10.

Works cited entry for an interview published in a magazine:

Matheson, Richard. Interview. By Paul Sammon. <u>Midnight Graffiti</u> Fall 1992: 18–49.

Works cited entry for a personal letter:

King, Stephen. Letter to the author. 5 Nov 1980.

Matheson, Richard. Letter to the author. 5 Sept 1992.

 The word *author* in these entries refers to the writer—author—of the research paper.

Works cited entry for a published letter:

Sandburg, Carl. "To Robert Frost." 28 March 1938. Letter 394 of <u>The Letters of Carl Sandburg</u>. Ed. Herbert Mitgang. New York: Harcourt, 1968. 361.

Works cited entry for a cartoon:

Schulz, Charles. "Peanuts." Cartoon. <u>Chicago Tribune</u> [Chicago, IL] 12 Jan. 1988: sec. 5: 6.

Works cited entry for a lecture:

Dukinfield, William Claude. "The Child and Family Dog as Social Nemesis." Alcoholics Anonymous Convention. Philadelphia. 25 Dec. 1946.

Schreiber-DeVillez, Susan. "Dreams Insight to Yourself." Address. Northern Illinois University Lecture Series. DeKalb, IL. 8 Apr. 1992.

Works cited entry for an interview:

Devon, Gary. Personal interview. 6 Aug. 1988.

Devon, Gary. Telephone interview. 6 Aug. 1988.

Devon, Gary. E-mail interview. 6 Aug. 1988.

King, Stephen. Interview. Interview With Stephen King by Mat Schaffer. WBCN-FM Radio's Boston Sunday Review. WBCN, Boston. 31 Oct. 1983.

 If adding a descriptor or a title would clarify or identify the expertise of the source, or if adding a descriptor or a title would add credibility to a source, place it after the name.

Devon, Gary. Writer. Personal interview. 6 Aug. 1988.

Potter, Jessie. Psychotherapist. Personal interview. 21 Oct. 1993.

Mulcahy, Edward. Certified Public Accountant. Telephone interview. 15, Apr. 1994.

Harker, Jonathan. President, Transylvania University. Telephone interview. 6 Nov 1994.

Works cited entry for a television/radio program:

"Moyers: Joseph Campbell And The Power of Myth." Narr. Bill Moyers. Prod. Catherine Tatge. Dir. Bill Moyers. Exec. prod. Joan Konner and Alvin H. Perlmutter. PBS. WTTW, Chicago. 23 May 1988.

Works cited entry for a video recording:

Communicating: With Dr. Jessie Potter. Videocassette. Sterling Productions, 1987.

The Hitcher. Dir. Robert Harmon. Perf. Rutger Hauer. Videocassette. HBO Video/Silver Screen Partners, 1986.

Forrest Gump. Dir. Robert Zemeckis. Perf. Tom Hanks, Gary Sinise, and Sally Field. Videocassette. Paramount, 1994.

Never Give a Sucker an Even Break. Dir. Edward Cline. Perf. W.C. Fields, Gloria Jean, and Margaret Dumont. 1941. Videocassette. MCA, 1988.

 In the preceding example, the first date (1941) is the original release date; the second date (1988) is the videocassette copyright date.

Grand Illusion. Dr. Jean Renoir. Perf. Erich Von Stroheim and Jean Gabin. 1938. Videodisc. Voyager, 1987.

Works cited entry for a film:

You Can't Cheat An Honest Man. Dir. George Marshall. With W.C. Fields, Edgar Bergen, Charlie McCarthy, and Mortimer Snerd. Universal, 1939.

Dr. Jekyll and Mr. Hyde. Dir. Victor Fleming. Perf. Spencer Tracy, Ingrid Bergman, Lana Turner. MGM, 1941.

Works cited entry for a recording:

Frost, Robert. "The Road Not Taken." <u>Robert Frost Reads His Poetry</u>. Caedmon, TC 1060, 1956.

Clapton, Eric. "Tears in Heaven." <u>Unplugged</u>. Reprise Records, Reprise 945024-2, 1992.

Morrison, Jim. "Break on Through." <u>The Best of the Doors</u>. Elektra/Asylum, Elektra 60345-2, 1985.

Works cited entry for an album jacket note:

Russ, Patrick. Jacket notes. <u>Christopher Parkening: Simple Gifts</u>. EMI-Angel, DS-37335, 1982.

Iglauer, Bruce. Jacket notes. <u>The Alligator Records 20th Anniversary Blues Collection</u>. Alligator Records, ALCD 105/6, 1991.

 GUIDELINES FOR ELECTRONIC DOCUMENTATION

As stated earlier in this chapter, the documentation of electronic sources is one of the newest areas in research writing. Because of the amount of information on databases, computer networks, computer disks, CD Roms, etc., you can expect to have to document information from these types of sources. Although there is some disagreement among academics, the following guidelines are those most generally accepted.

For the most part, cite these sources in the same way as you would a book; however, add information about the medium (disk, CD Rom, computer network, etc.), the name of the vendor and/or computer service (if known), the date of electronic publication, and/or the date of access (when you obtained the information from the source). In some cases, such as computer software, you might also provide information which helps to clarify and/or identify the software: the computer the software is made for, the number of bytes and/or memory, the program form, and the operating system.

The following sample entries should help you with most of the electronic documentation you will be required to do:

Works cited entry for computer software:

<u>Harvard Graphics</u>. Vers. 3.0. Diskette. Software Publishing Corporation, 1991.

 If you know the name of the author, place it first, as in the following examples.

Ann Arbor Software. <u>Norton Textra Writer</u>. Vers. 2.5. One diskette and manual. New York: W.W. Norton & Company, 1992.

Tuman, Myron C., and Ann Arbor Software. <u>Norton Textra Connect For Word For Windows</u>. Two diskettes and manual. New York: W.W. Norton & Company, 1995.

 If you wish, you can add information which helps to clarify and/or identify the software: the computer the software is made for, the number of bytes and/or memory, the program form, and the operating system. The following examples illustrate.

<u>Harvard Graphics</u>. Vers. 3.0. Diskette. Software Publishing Corporation, 1991. IBM PC. DOS 3.1 or higher. 640KB.

Tuman, Myron C., and Ann Arbor Software. <u>Norton Textra Connect For Word For Windows</u>. Two diskettes and manual. New York: W.W. Norton & Company, 1995. Requires Windows 3.1 and Microsoft Word 6.0 for Windows. 8MB Ram.

Works cited entry for information from a computer information service (such as ERIC):

Schomer, Howard. "South Africa: Beyond Fair Employment." <u>Harvard Business Review</u> May–June 1983: 145+. Dialog file 122, item 119425 833160.

 If the material in the database was previously published, provide the previous publishing information before the database number. The following example illustrates.

Frary, Robert B. <u>Statistical Detection of Multiple-Choice Answer Copying</u>. <u>Applied Measurement in Education</u> 6 (1993): 153–65. ERIC EJ468017.

Works cited entry for a CD-ROM source:

Brown, Lloyd W. "Baraka as Poet." <u>Amiri Baraka</u> 1980: 104. <u>DiscLit American Authors</u>. CD-ROM. OCLC and G.K. Hall. Feb. 1996.

Books by Richard Matheson. 1996. <u>Books in Print</u>. CD-ROM. Online Computer Systems and R.R. Bowker. Mar. 1996.

Meyer, Dorothy J., et al. "The Medical Evaluation in Cases of Fetal Demise." <u>The Indian Health Service Primary Care Provider</u> April 1993: 61–64. <u>SIRS Government Reporter</u>. CD-ROM. SIRS, Inc. Access HE 20.9423:18/4. March 1996.

Cohn, Ruby. "Edward Albee: A Survey of His Early Work." <u>Edward Albee</u> 1969: 48+. <u>DiscAuthors</u>. Gale Research, Inc. 1996.

Dillon, John F., and Glenn R. Tanner. "Dimensions of Career Burnout Among Educators." <u>Journalism and Mass Communication Educator</u> 50:2 Summer 1995: 4–13. <u>Compact Disclosure.</u> CD-ROM. Digital Library Systems, Inc. Access CIJDEC95. 1995.

Andrews, Jennifer, et al. "Accessing Transgenerational Themes Through Dreamwork." <u>Journal of Marital and Family Therapy</u> 14:1 Jan. 1988: 15–27. <u>Compact Disclosure</u>. CD-ROM. Digital Library Systems, Inc. Access CIJAUG88. 1995.

"The Beatles." <u>Compton's Interactive Encyclopedia</u>. CD-ROM. Compton's NewMedia, Inc. 1995.

Day, Kathleen. "Genetics Research Begets Questions." <u>The Washington Post</u> 8 May 1996: A1+. <u>CD NewsBank</u>. CD-ROM. NewsBank, Inc. Access 00867*19960508*01234.

Dillow, Gordon. "Toward a More-Perfect Human?" <u>The Orange County Register</u> 2 July 1995: EO1+. <u>CD NewsBank</u>. CD-ROM. NewsBank, Inc. Access 00844*19950702*01022.

 Some of the above examples contain two dates. The first date is the date of original publication; the second date is when the information was posted electronically. Some instructors also want students to provide—at the very end of the entry—an access date—the date the researcher accessed the information.

Works cited entry for information from a database/CD-ROM database:

 The general format is last name and first name of author (if available), article title (in quotation marks), magazine/journal title (underlined), volume and issue numbers (if available), original publication date (if available), pagination, name of the database, and access number.

Grudin, Michaela Paasche. "Discourse and the Problem of Closure in the Canterbury Tales." <u>Publications of the Modern Language Association</u> 107-5 (Oct. 1992): 1157–1167. <u>ProQuest</u>. Access 01175539.

Centers for Disease Control and Prevention. "Cigarette Smoking Among Adults." <u>JAMA: The Journal of the American Medical Association</u> 273 (1 Feb. 1995): 369+. <u>InfoTrac Health Reference Center</u>. Access 77M3570.

Corman, Roger, and Joe Dante. "Memories of Vincent Price." <u>Sight and Sound</u> 3-12 (Dec. 1993): 14–15. <u>ProQuest</u>. Access 01803732.

Office of Technology Assessment/U.S. Congress. "What Problems Do Literacy Programs and Providers Face?" <u>Adult Literacy and New Technologies: Tools for a Lifetime</u> (July 1993): 9–11. <u>SIRS Government Reporter</u>. Access Y 3.T 22/2:2 AD 9/2.

Cosgrove, Cindy. "Dreamlight Diary." <u>Whole Earth Review</u> (Fall 1991): 13+. <u>InfoTrac Magazine Index Plus</u>. Access 61D4715. 1994.

Hajek, Peter, and Michael Belcher. "Dream of Absent-Minded Transgression: An Empirical Study of a Cognitive Withdrawal Symptom." <u>Journal of Abnormal Psychology</u> 100-4 (Nov. 1991): 487+. <u>InfoTrac EP Academic Index</u>. Access 11602373. 1994.

"Delight in Disorder." <u>Homemaker's Journal</u> 116-42 (4 July 1996): 33+. <u>Expanded Academic ASAP</u>. Access B182736477.

"Designing Your Retirement Home." <u>The Modern Retiree</u> 26-4 (15 April 1998): 132+. <u>Expanded Academic ASAP</u>. Access B19283746.

 See the note at the end of the previous section for information about multiple dates and/or access dates.

Works cited entry for an on-line computer service/Internet source:

 The general format is: last name and first name of author (if available), title of the work (if available), previous publication information (if available), title of the electronic site (underlined), a version or volume number (if available), date of electronic posting or most-recent update, name of the institution or organization sponsoring the site (if available), the date you accessed the information, and the URL/electronic address (if available, within angle brackets < >).

 Not all instructors agree with posting the URL within angle brackets; they feel it adds confusion to an already confusing mixture of letters, numbers, and punctuation marks.

 MLA and COS do not recommend using page numbers for Internet sources. Some instructors, however, require page numbers. Most printouts from an Internet site will have page numbers (such as 3 of 6, 4 of 6, etc.), or you can number them. Use the printout page number in the textnote and show the pagination in the works cited entry, placing it before the access date.

 As stated earlier, writing works cited entries for electronic sources, especially Internet sources, is difficult. Follow the guidelines to the best of your ability—and ask your instructor for help.

The following examples illustrate:

The Natural Death Center. <u>A Bibliography of Available Publications</u>. 8 April 1999 <rhino@dial.pipex.com>.

Redig, P. T. A published bibliography from <u>The Effect and Value of Raptor Rehabilitation in North America</u> by P. T. Redig. 1995. 6 Mar. 1999 <http://www.raptor.cvm.umn.edu/>.

Mitchell, Shay. <u>Commotion Strange: Anne Rice's Newsletter to Her Fans</u>. 11 Jan. 1996 <jsm8f@ecosys. drdr.virginia.edu>.

"Jackson Hole, Wyoming." <u>CyberWest Magazine</u> 21 Oct. 1996 33pp. 23 Jan. 1998 <http://www.cyberwest. com/10jack1.html>.

Bond, Jeff. "Echoes of Matheson." <u>Writer Richard Matheson Holds Forth on His Influential Career in an Exclusive Eon Interview About the Film "A Stir of Echoes."</u> <u>Eon Magazine</u> Issue 26.0 3 March 2000. 13 March 2000 <http://www.eonmagazine.com/archive/9910/features/features_frameset_movies.htm>.

Mitchell, Mary. "Hands of a Village Help Family Turn Teen Around." <u>Chicago Sun-Times</u> 27 February 2000. 12 March 2000 <http://www.chicagosuntimes.com/output/mitchell/mitch27.html>.

Kass, John. "When a Miss is as Good as a Miracle." <u>Chicago Tribune</u> 22 February 2000. 8 March 2000 <http://www.chicagotribune.com/news/columnists/kass/0,1122,SAV-0002220274,00.html>.

"Dynamite and Boats Don't Mix: 1998 Darwin Awards Nominee." <u>WWW.DarwinAwards.Com: The Official Darwin Awards</u>. 12 March 2000 <http://www.darwinawards.com/darwin1998-07.html>.

 Caveat: As I wrote earlier, there is some disagreement among English faculty about the nitty gritty of documenting electronic sources. The preceding examples and guidelines adhere to the basic guidelines of the *MLA Handbook*. Most disagreement exists about the ordering of information and about minor punctuation. For example, placing a period after an electronic address (or path/protocol) would make the address incorrect, although older MLA guidelines would have required a period at the end of a works cited entry.

   Some English faculty who belong to the MLA also belong to the Alliance for Computers and Writing, a national organization working to bring standards and consistency to this area of research. Until that standardization has been brought about, your best bet—when in doubt—is to ask your own classroom instructor.

THE WORKS CITED: FINAL ADVICE

   Keep in mind that the preceding are the common kinds of sources used by college students. If you cannot find here what you are looking for, consult the *MLA Handbook*.

   One final suggestion about preparing the list of works cited: how to handle listing several works by the same author. When citing two or more sources by the same author, list the name in the first entry only. In the following entries, do not repeat the name, but rather replace the name with three hyphens and a period. Then, skip two spaces and type the title. Because the entries are all listed under the same author's name, alphabetize the entries by the first word in the title (excepting **a, an** and **the**). Here is an example from a student's research paper:

Atwood, Margaret. <u>Bluebeard's Egg And Other Stories</u>. New York: Fawcett Crest, 1983.

---. <u>The Handmaid's Tale</u>. New York: Fawcett Crest, 1985.

---. <u>Lady Oracle</u>. New York: Fawcett Crest, 1976.

---. <u>Life Before Man</u>. New York: Fawcett Crest, 1979.

---. <u>Surfacing</u>. New York: Fawcett Crest, 1972.

THE RESEARCH PAPER: STUDENT EXAMPLES

In addition to their work with documentation and research, the following student examples differ from the others published in this text in one other significant way. These examples—including the works cited—are typeset to appear as typewritten (except they are **single-spaced rather than double-spaced** to save paper and money). This has been done in order to give you "the feel" for genuine student-authored and student-typed research writing.

I grew up in a neutering environment.

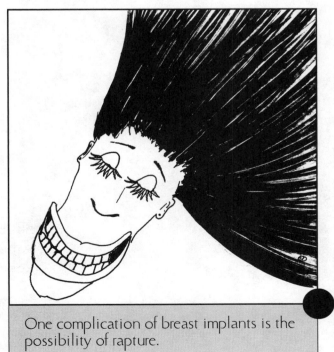

One complication of breast implants is the possibility of rapture.

FLEXTIME OR NO TIME!

Betty Shapiro
Paper #5
Research/Persuasion

PROPOSAL

DATE: December 4, 1997

TO: Jim Rice, Executive Director
               Park Center for Children and Adults with
               Developmental Disabilities

FROM: Betty Shapiro, Operations Manager
               Vocational Services Division

SUBJECT: Flextime working hours vs. standard working hours

1   Jim, I have worked for this agency for three and a half years, and not once in that time have I worked the standard 35-hour workweek. Though I have tried to keep the 8:30 a.m. to 4:00 p.m. schedule, it simply is not enough time to perform all the aspects of my position competently. Therefore, I have always worked additional hours to meet customer deadlines, complete projects, get organized, or prepare for the following day or week. Routinely I work the hours of 8:30 a.m. to 5:30 or 6:00 p.m. (and sometimes even later) five days per week. I also work an additional two to three hours on Saturday afternoons. Additional responsibilities have been assigned to me over the course of these three years that prohibit me from ever hoping to work a regular workday. A normal day at the workshop is very chaotic, a point I don't think I need to stress to you because you experienced it yourself when you held my position several years ago. Interruptions are just the nature of the beast. Behavior and discipline problems with the participants, staff absenteeism forcing management personnel like myself onto the floor to run production, handling multiple customer accounts that require several phone calls and meetings on a daily basis -- all of these contribute to the interruptions of the day. I welcome those few additional hours of peace and quiet when everyone else goes home to collect my thoughts and do my paperwork. That "quiet time" is often disrupted by after-hour customers calling for information about our services or parents calling about their (adult) children being returned home five minutes late. These are important phone calls, and they should be addressed; however, the departments that handle these issues are not available, so I frequently become the

"Park Center Answer Lady" after normal working hours. I get farther behind with my own work, thus creating the need to work even later. It is becoming increasingly more difficult to balance this heavy workload with other aspects of my life such as family, school, volunteer work and social life. There just simply is not enough time.

2   I know there are other dedicated people in this agency who also work the extra hours to get the job done. This is not a new phenomenon. In fact, statistics say that "[in] the United States, one employed person in four puts in 49 hours or more at work each week; one in eight works 60 hours or more" (Dolnik 52+).

3   I'm not complaining, Jim, nor requesting an increase in salary. I realize funding from the federal and local governments to social service agencies such as ours is at an all-time low. Because of this, salary increases are not available every year. Therefore, I believe it is important for employers such as Park Center to offer other benefits and incentives to compensate for the lack of salary increases. According to U.S. Representative John Linder, "Successful businesses and smart proprietors value their employees and provide benefits that entice workers to stay on board. Such benefits foster loyalty, good morale and a healthy work environment" (1). Representative Linder supports the Family Friendly Workplace Act. This act "offers flexible scheduling options to private sector employees, which has been widely available to federal employees since the 1970's" ("Ashcroft Flextime . . ." 1). President Clinton feels "broad use of flexible work arrangements to enable . . . employees to better balance their work and family responsibilities can increase employee effectiveness and job satisfaction, while decreasing turnover rates and absenteeism" (qtd. in Linder 1). Leslie de Pietro, Coordinator of the Family Care Resource Program at the University of Michigan, also agrees. A flexible workplace can reduce employee stress, improve morale and increase employee loyalty to the organization, which may then be better able to recruit competent staff members. In addition, varied schedules may allow the organization to provide extended hours of service. Productivity may increase when employees are allowed to work at off-peak times with fewer interruptions. Flexible scheduling also can allow for more

–3–

efficient use of limited office equipment (qtd. in <u>The University Record</u> 1). I'm sure you agree, Jim, these are attractive alternatives to overcoming the low morale and high turnover rate at Park Center plus enabling the workshop to increase its hours of operation.

4   All of this has prompted me to research the benefits this agency can experience with flextime scheduling. I believe it is a great incentive to offer the employees of Park Center. Flextime can benefit departments, not just selected groups. Here are some popular flextime plans that I believe could work successfully at Park Center:

> *The Flexitour Plan* -- This allows employees to select arrival and departure times within a flexible band. Once selected, those become the employee's regular hours. All employees have to work a standard amount of hours per week.
>
> *The Gliding Schedule* -- Similar to the Flexitour plan, this schedule allows employees to select arrival and departure times. However, employees are also allowed to vary their hours day to day and week to week, as long as they fulfill the basic requirements for hours worked.
>
> *The Four-Day Workweek* -- Employees work four ten-hour days per week, with one day off (<u>Flextime . . . productivity</u> 1).

5   Compensatory time is also listed as an alternative flextime plan. I chose not to include it in this list because it is already practiced at Park Center, although somewhat ineffectively. Comp time is now offered to any salaried employee who works over 35 hours per week. I, for one, take very little comp time, mainly because it puts me farther behind with my work. Others in the agency feel the same way. Some supervisors tend to frown when an employee asks them for approval to take comp time. There is a general consensus that "no time is a good time" to take it because there is no such thing as a "slow" period or "down" season. Although it is a well-deserved break from a stressful workload, comp time does not increase productivity -- flextime <u>does</u>.

6   I'd like to point out some instances where I think a flextime schedule could benefit the workshop. Let me start with Frank Smith, the Coordinator of the Vocational Services Division. Frank starts every day at 7:00 a.m. He opens the building and does a complete check of all production and warehouse areas. His most productive hours are between 7:30 and 8:30 a.m. The rest of the staff arrives around 8:15 a.m., and the participants arrive at 9:00. When the workshop closes at 4:00 p.m., Frank leaves for his second job where he starts at 5:00 p.m. His travel time between jobs is approximately 40 minutes. He very seldom takes comp time and has a low absentee rate. He is, however, stressed to the limit from trying to balance both jobs. In today's economy, two jobs are almost essential. If Frank's hours were 7:00 a.m. to 2:30 p.m. or even 3:00 p.m., he would still be able to perform all job functions, including opening the building. Frank's presence is also not as imperative after 3:00 p.m. since that is when the participants leave for the day. Flextime would certainly benefit Frank.

7   I'd like to continue with Angie Lopez. Angie is just one of many Park Center employees who drive several miles to work. She is also one of the many "working moms" in the agency. Because of the distance between work and home, Angie cannot spare any additional time at the workshop. She does, however, take the entire participant payroll home on weekends to calculate. She occasionally uses comp time to take her son to the doctor or to attend school meetings. Balancing work and family is a big concern for Angie. In fact, in 1994, the U.S. Department of Labor reported that the number one concern for 66 percent of working women with children is the difficulty of balancing work and family (qtd. in Kerrigan 1). Jim, approximately 66 percent of Park Center's employees are women with children. Flextime would definitely help Angie and the rest of the working moms. First of all, if Angie were to work 4 nine-hour days instead of 5 seven-and-a-half, she would reduce the usage of her car roughly 20 percent (Catlin 12+). Think of the wear and tear saved on the roads and automobiles if ten people worked a four-day flex schedule. Second, Angie would have the time to complete the client payroll at the office and still have one extra day to spend with her family.

-5-

8   JoAnne Sherman, the receptionist, could also benefit from working a 4-day flex schedule. She has a two-year-old son in day care and also lives about 30 miles from work. JoAnne could cut costs at the day care center and save on the usage of her car. She could also have time to juggle those doctor appointments, school appointments with her older daughter, etc. Her husband is a police officer. If JoAnne worked flextime, she and her husband could balance their hours and even spend some precious time together with their family. Her schedule would also help Park Center. JoAnne turns the night service line on every day at 4:00 p.m. If she worked 8:00 a.m. to 5:30 or 6:00p.m. four days a week, the switchboard could remain open, and she could personally answer those calls that come in after 4:00 p.m. On the fifth day, a part-time contingency worker could answer the switchboard by working the same hours of 8:00 to 5:30 p.m.

9   The Transportation Department at the workshop would also greatly benefit from working a flex schedule. Many of the calls to the workshop after 4:00 p.m. are transportation related. Worried parents call if their son or daughter is even five minutes late. Traffic difficulties could make the delay much longer than five minutes, and van or bus breakdowns are always a possibility. In the past, there has even been an accident involving agency vehicles with participants on board. Parents have a right to know about these kinds of delays. Keep in mind, Jim, our participants are up in age, making their parents <u>way</u> up in age. They can't help but worry and deserve proper attention, which in my mind (and I think in yours, too), means personal handling of their calls by the transportation department.

10   I personally would also benefit by working a flex schedule. My most productive hours are between 4:00 and 6:00 p.m. The clients have gone home, the workshop and warehouse are closed, there are no deliveries being made, and there are a lot less interruptions (except for the phone calls on night service!). It is easier to do inventory adjustments on the computer, finish shipping and receiving documentation, give vendors details regarding the day's production, and catch up on faxes and correspondence during these hours. I also supervise the janitorial services in the building. It just makes more sense for the janitor to clean the building during "off-peak" hours

rather than during the day when the participants are in and out of the bathrooms and lunchroom. If I worked 10:00 a.m. to 5:30 p.m. everyday, I could get just as much accomplished as I do working 8:30 a.m. to 6:00 p.m.

11 Just this fall, I started attending school three nights a week. Along with school, comes homework. There is not much time to do homework when I work late and go straight to school. If I worked 4 nine-hour days, I would still accomplish all I need to, plus have time to do homework, register for school and juggle other family matters. My son is nineteen and away at college. He does not need my attention as much as he did when he was younger. My elderly parents, though, live close by and do need my attention and assistance to get them to doctor appointments. Four nine-hour days or a flexible schedule five days a week -- either plan would help me, Jim.

12 How would all of this flex scheduling work, you ask? First, everyone needs to understand that "flexibility is privi-lege, not a 'right.' There has to be some reciprocal flexibil-ity on the part of employees such as a willingness to come in for meetings, to check in with supervisors and to document hours worked" (The University Record 1). "In addition, flexible scheduling works best when staff members function as a team, negotiating schedule changes with one another and participating in cross-training so that colleagues are available to cover for each other when needed" (The University Record 2). Diane Newhouse, a manager with Eastman Kodak, sums it up very well, "Flextime employees don't do less work, they just do it in a different way" (qtd. in Costello 19+).

13 Jim, for a long time you have wanted the workshop's hours extended, thus having more exposure and accessibility. Introduc-ing flex scheduling will allow this to become a reality plus help the employees of Park Center.

Works Cited

"Ashcroft Flextime Bill Wins Support of Labor Committee."
    News Release. 18 March 1997. 1p. 13 Nov. 1997 <http://
    www.senate.gov/~ashcroft/3-18-97.htm>.

Catlin, Charles S. "Four-Day Work Week Improves Environment."
    Journal of Environmental Health (March 1997): 12+.
    Expanded Academic ASAP. Access A19280161.

"Communication, Teamwork Keys to Making Flextime Work." The
    University Record. 9 April 1996. 2pp. 13 Nov. 1997
    <http://wwwumich.edu/~newsinfo/U_Record/Issues96/Apr09_96/
    artc114.htm>.

Costello, Martine. "Dealing With Downshifters." Working Woman
    (Dec. 1995): 19+. Expanded Academic ASAP. Access A17770880.

Dolnick, Edward. "Is Your Job Taking Over Your Life? Trade
    Money for Time." Health (Oct. 1994): 52+. Expanded
    Academic ASAP. Access A15805761.

"Flextime Can Increase Productivity." 1p. 13 Nov. 1997
    <http://www.ragan.com/manage/flextime.html>.

Kerrigan, Karen. "Bill Mixes Flextime, Comp Time, Overtime."
    Atlanta Business Chronicle archive. 16 Sept. 1996. 3pp.
    13 Nov. 1997 <http://cgi.amcity.com/atlanta/stories/091696/
    smallb2.html>.

Linder, John. U.S. Representative. Comp Time: Flexible and
    Family Friendly. 2pp. 13 Nov. 1997 <http://www.house.gov/
    linder/comptime.htm>.

SO, AMANDA . . .

Melissa Ervanian
November 22, 1999
Communications 101-33

SO, AMANDA . . .

1   "I'm going to be a model someday." I cringed as I over-heard you mention this to your friend. I turned to look at you as you applied your make-up, stopping to see if the boys walking past looked at you. My first instinct was to slap you across the face, but I realized that I could be arrested for that. I figured that getting a record for hitting a girl because she wanted to be a model wouldn't go over too well at the Ervanian household. Needless to say, I declined. It wasn't anger toward you that was triggered in me; it was anger toward society. I dedicate this essay to you: the girl in the mall whose life revolves around being beautiful. I will call you Amanda. Please, do not fall into the trap that society has set for you. All I ask is that you listen; sometimes beauty can make you ugly.

2   I know that you probably think that modeling is easy and makes you desired by millions of guys around the world, but do you know anything about the models themselves? Most of the time, the pictures you see aren't even *them*. All the make-up and lighting portrays them as beautiful and flawless, but in reality they are just like you and I. Plus, computers are used to "trim up" models' legs, arms, waists and even faces if they are "too fat." The beautiful women you see on the cover of *Cosmo* don't actually exist; you are chasing an unattainable goal. According to Peggy Claude-Pierre, this supermodel syndrome is a trigger of anorexia (67). Nobody will admit it, but carrots and water don't actually count as a meal. Supermodels are all slightly anorexic, but young girls refuse to see this. All that is on their minds is being beautiful and popular. Sound familiar, Amanda? You didn't know that ". . . anorexia is in part caused by a culture that values appearance over substance and prizes women only when they are thin," did you (Claude-Pierre 66)? You are falling into a trap, and you are a perfect target.

3   First, let me explain what anorexia really is, because it is more than just not eating.

> Anorexia nervosa is a disorder of self-starvation
> which manifests itself in an extreme aversion to food
> and can cause psychological, endocrine and gynecologi-

cal problems. It almost exclusively affects adolescent
white girls, with symptoms involving a refusal to eat,
large weight loss, a bizarre preoccupation with food,
hyperactivity, a distorted body image, and cessation
of menstruation . . . and about 10-15 percent of anorexia nervosa patients die, usually after losing at
least half their normal body weight ("Facts About Anorexia Nervosa" 1+).

Sounds a little bit worse than just "not eating," doesn't
it? The scary part is that you fall into the same category as
most anorexic patients, and I saw signs that could lead to
the disease. "Anorexia nervosa patients typically come from
white, middle to upper-middle class families that place heavy
emphasis on high achievement, perfection, eating patterns and
physical appearance" ("Facts About Anorexia Nervosa" 1+). You
were wearing an Abercrombie shirt, your hair and make-up were
perfect, if I had offered you a candy bar you would have refused and you were concerned with one thing: your looks. This
incredible preoccupation with body image and beauty branches
out of the negative perceptions that anorexics have of
themselves.

4   When victims of anorexia look into the mirror, they do
not see reality ("Distorted Perceptions" 1). Comparisons are
constantly made between themselves and others. ". . . They
cannot see their own good traits . . . because of the low
self-esteem they have of themselves" (Distorted Perceptions
1). Modeling is a cause of these perceptions and lack of
self-esteem. The unattainable perfection of these women lead
children to believe at an early age that they can achieve a
perfect figure. Children are dying because they try to attain
that perfection (Claude-Pierre 67). What starts out as an
attempt to lose a few pounds before a school dance turns into
an obsession. Low self-esteem causes young girls to hear
voices that ". . . come from that place within [them] plagued
with negativity and self-hate, encouraging [them] to continue
with [their] eating disorder, and convincing [them] that
[they] do not deserve recovery, that [they] deserve a life
of pain" (Helping to Stop the Voices 1).

5   These voices lead them to believe that they really are worthless and that nobody will love them until they become thin. The voices never cease; they criticize young victims every time they look in the mirror. At a body weight of 75 pounds, the girls still believe that they are fat, hating themselves even more because they can't lose the weight. This is the point when anorexia has taken so much that recovery is doubtful. The voices are hard to overcome and sometimes can't be. The victim's weight can't decline fast enough, according to the inner voice, and hope is lost. The hypothalamus in the brain can no longer maintain water balance or regulate body temperature, the secretion of the endocrine glands or the sugar and fat metabolism ("Facts About Anorexia Nervosa" 1+). Anorexics believe that to live any longer would place a burden on the world; the voices have won. Recovery is no longer an option and the girls become statistics: the 10-15 percent who die.

6   Do you still want to be a model, Amanda? Even if you do not become anorexic, you could cause another young girl to. Children are very impressionable, and "[the] seeds of anorexia [can be] planted at a much earlier age than the one at which individuals become body-conscious" (Claude-Pierre 67). If a little girl sees you in a magazine, she will want to be you. She has been brought up in a society that respects only beautiful women. Without hesitation, she will do anything to look like you. The voices in her head will tell her that she is stupid, worthless, deserving to be unhappy and not to eat (Helping to Stop the Voices 1). She sees herself as fat, even if she weighs 10 pounds less than you. She could become a statistic, but would it bother you? Could you cope with the knowledge that you caused a young girl to give up her life to be like you? I hope not. Society has caused so many problems by telling women how they should look and act; we don't need anymore.

7   Amanda, there is so much more to life than just being beautiful. It only lasts for so long. When it starts to fade, women try desperately to get it back. This is one of the wonderful gifts that society has bestowed upon us: women are worthless unless they are thin and beautiful. You don't need to listen to that; you don't need to agree with that. I chal-

lenge you to stand up against what society has told you all your life; do not become a model. You can be a beautiful person without flaunting yourself all over a magazine. Make-up only shows how insecure you really are. You must feel that there is something wrong with the way you look if you have to wear make-up. You will tell me that you just like the way it makes you look, but deep down you are trying to cover something up. If you are a strong person and believe in yourself, you can fight the voices that tell you you're not. Beauty comes from the inside. If you are a good person, people will like you for that. You don't need to be beautiful to be loved. If that is what love is based on, you will only set yourself up for disappointment. I know you are smarter than to fall into that. Beauty radiates from the inside. If it comes only through physical appearance, what is the purpose of a heart, mind and soul?

Works Cited

Claude-Pierre, Peggy. <u>The Secret Language of Eating Disorders</u>.
    New York: Times Books, 1997.
<u>Distorted Perceptions</u> 1996 3pp. 20 Nov. 1999
    <http://www.somethingfishy.org/perception.htm>.
"Facts About Anorexia Nervosa." National Institute of Child
    Health and Human Development. (Nov. 1990): 1+. <u>Info Trac</u>
    <u>Health Reference Center</u>. Access A9080504.
<u>Helping to Stop the Voices</u> 1996 2pp. 20 Nov. 1999
    <http://www.somethingfishy.org/ed-net.htm>.

Aggressive Driving

Richard Donnellan
July 27, 1999
Communications 101-82

-1-

AGGRESSIVE DRIVING

1   All of us take for granted our daily lives. As we become
lost in our busy schedules, we forget that the rest of the
world is moving at the same frantic pace. In our attempt to
cope with our daily routine, we find it necessary to interact
with others. This is done in many different ways: while talking on the phone, in the grocery store checkout lane, or at
work or school. We also experience another form of contact
with others: driving our cars. For most, this is a very
stressful activity.

2   How many of us find ourselves "talking" to other drivers
at stop lights? How about trying to get the driver in front of
you to move faster by tailgating? Do you curse at, or berate
your fellow driver when they make a move that threatens your
space? At times I find myself wishing that other people "would
learn how to drive." I find it very hard to believe that some
of them actually passed their driver's test! Honestly, does
this sound like appropriate driving behavior to you? Would you
really want me driving behind you after I have had a particularly bad day at work? Most of us might not see the harm in
these actions; we are just driving "defensively." But believe
it or not, when we act that way, we are taking
on the role of aggressor. Studies have confirmed that nearly
every driver on the road has felt angered by another driver's
actions and has wanted to retaliate in some way (James 1).
We must learn to recognize the symptoms of this behavior and
modify our driving habits accordingly; we are risking the
lives of ourselves and others.

3   What is aggressive driving? Sometimes referred to as
"road rage," it is generally defined as "any display of aggression by a driver" (Joint 13). At first, we envision the
angry motorist who tracks down and kills another driver because he felt wronged during a particular driving incident.
Actually, this is only a specific outcome of the most-extreme
act of driver aggression: physical assault occurring as a result of a disagreement between drivers. It is predicted that
this type of behavior will increase as each new generation
takes its turn behind the wheel.

4   "Road rage" can be broken down into groups based on separate acts of individual aggression. First is the "unfriendly driver" who shows mental or verbal unkindness towards another driver. Second is the "hostile driver" who visibly communicates displeasure or resentment, and often displays a desire to punish. The "violent driver" carries out acts of hostility, such as making obscene gestures, or honking and yelling at someone through a closed window. The next driver is capable of "lesser mayhem." He exhibits road rage within his own personal limits, sometimes going as far as getting out of the car and engaging in a verbal confrontation, or by actually trying to run another car off the road as punishment. The last, and most-dangerous, is the driver who will perform acts of "major mayhem." He will get out of his car and beat or batter someone as a result of a driving incident, try to run down someone whose actions have angered him, shoot at another car, or kill someone (James 8-9). Regardless of how good a driver we think we are, we probably display symptoms of one or more of these groups at any given time. Which group do you fall in?

5   Road rage is not a new problem. In 1817, Lord Byron wrote of a "row on the road . . . with a fellow in a carriage, who was impudent to my horse. I gave him a swinging box on the ear, which sent him to the police" (qtd. in Bowles and Overberg 17A). Since the early decades of this century, the numbers of vehicles on our roadways have doubled. The inhabitants of our planet are "the most technologically pampered, the richest, the freest things on two legs the world has ever seen" (Ferguson 2). Because of this, we are incognizant to the fact that we drive aggressively and provide little or no courtesies towards our fellow drivers. It is common occurrence to see, hear, or personally be involved in a driving altercation; many of us accept it as daily life. But because of this constant exposure, we become immune to the symptoms that cause such acts of aggression.

6   Aggressive driving has caused a great impact on society. First, injury and death take their toll on all who they involve. Many men, women, and children are injured or killed each year by other angry motorists. Additionally, many driving altercations prove fatal to innocent people who find them-

selves caught in the wrong place at the wrong time. These victims are someone's son or daughter, husband or wife, usually someone who is expected home for dinner. Secondly, treating those who are injured in such situations places strain on an already overwhelmed health care industry. Ultimately, we will see a gradual increase in our automobile and health insurance premiums, the inability of our judicial system to manage all the legal aspects, and an increase in tax revenues to provide for those who can no longer work.

7   Many studies have been conducted in an attempt to identify the physical causes of aggressive driving behavior. These studies have been trying to determine if road rage is the result of biological or psychological force, or are we seeing a trend that suggests it is the result of learned behavior? It has been proven that all animals learn survival through their biological and evolutionary instinct. But it is "unclear to what extent a firm biological basis for aggression can be assumed, as opposed to being a learned response developed through imitation of others and reinforced by the experience of its results" (Connell and Joint 10). If the biological hypothesis is supported, then any anger, not just that expressed on the highways, would diminish as soon as our expressions of emotion were complete; instead we continue to pursue additional confrontation. If the reasons are mainly psychological, then that might explain our inability to act rationally when finding ourselves angered by specific driving instances. It has also been theorized that, as children, we may have inherited our aggressive behavior by watching our parents and other adults drive, or by seeing bad driving habits depicted at the movies or on television (James 6).

8   Many researchers have tried to categorize aggressive driving behavior based on confirmed demographic criteria: sex, age, ethnic origin, and physical location. Because local databases do not always distinguish between aggressive driving altercations and other types of traffic occurrences, the results are mostly speculative. From what is known, women who engage in aggressive driving behavior are as dangerous as men. Age plays a role only because a younger driver is less-experienced behind the wheel and unable to deal emotionally when involved in a driving mishap. Race plays no significant role

when singling out a potential driving group. Of course, there are exceptions, but they are unique and isolated incidents. One environmental condition that seems conducive to aggressive driving is overcrowding. Certain studies have found that direct measures of population density or available space can cause aggressive behavior, but only when that density is perceived by a subject as an invasion of his or her space (Connell and Joint 8).

9   What does all this data mean? Clearly, it points to the fact that everyone of us is capable of being an aggressive driver. You might refuse to accept this idea and will offer arguments that might seem valid, but try spending a day or two driving around town and observing other drivers; you might begin to see things differently.

10   One of the first things that drivers must do is "pay more attention to their own level of emotion" (Connell and Joint 9). We also need to understand our fellow drivers better. What causes them to act the way they do while sitting behind the wheel of their car? One likely answer is that they may have had a bad day or troubles at work; these problems often infiltrate their driving experience and could eventually take over. Another reason is that many of us are territorial, and our car is an extension of our territory (Joint 13). We don't like people "invading" our space. If threatened, we retaliate by allowing our emotions to take over. This can cloud our judgement and make us susceptible to further acts of aggression. We also fail to understand that momentary errors in judgment by other drivers should not be perceived as aggression (Joint 13).

11   Each time we attempt to drive, I suggest that we all evaluate our stress level. If we are having a particularly bad day, we should try to eliminate our stress before turning on the ignition: don't drive when you are angry or tired, concentrate on being relaxed, listen to music that might help reduce any anxiety, and alter your route to avoid congestion (Mizell 12). Make sure that you allow enough time to get where you are going and double check to make sure that you have everything you need before leaving.

12   If you become involved in a traffic dispute, stay calm. Even if you are right, don't become part of the problem by

provoking the other driver. Be courteous, avoid condescending remarks, and call the police immediately. Above all, be a smart driver. "Smart drivers have acquired emotionally intelligent skills that allow them to accommodate rather than oppose the diversity of drivers" (James 10).

13   Many times I see another driver do something that I feel is a direct violation of state law. This is where the "why don't you learn to drive?" idiom comes into play. Remember, we are not perfect individuals and, at times, we make bad decisions. I would encourage everyone, especially those who have been driving for twenty years or more, to review the "Rules of the Road" for your state. Most of the laws are not different from when we first learned to drive, but through years of "experience" and our cavalier attitude, we fail to abide by many of the rules involving speed, right-of-way, passing, lane usage, and signaling and turning. Many of our shortcomings can lead to serious, and often fatal, accidents.

14   We also need to set a better example for all "new" drivers; we don't want our sons and daughters developing this type of driving behavior. Most schools and law enforcement agencies are now emphasizing the value of maintaining a good and proper attitude while driving. "The road-rage habit can be unlearned, but it takes more than conventional driver's ed." (qtd. in Ferguson 4). Teaching ourselves to deal with the hostility of other drivers is the key to suppressing our own driving aggression.

15   Law enforcement officials have been called upon to "beef up" the security of our roads. "One of the reasons many drivers are aggressive is because they can get away with it" (qtd. in Incantalupo A5). But punishing this type of offender is difficult because the current laws are not adequately written for this specific type of crime. Some states have defined aggressive driving as speeding, and committing two or three other infractions—erratic lane changes, tailgating, and failure to yield (Bowles and Overberg 17A). Police will not hesitate to write a citation to a driver guilty of these offenses, and along with new government legislation, they hope to send a message to the public that this kind of behavior will not be tolerated.

16   Most of us will argue that we do not go around driving like maniacs: chasing people down or shooting them because they did us some injustice. But what about all the other symptoms that contribute to the overall problem? Do you ever curse at other drivers? Do you wish bad things against them? Do you find yourself taking a "superior" attitude when you take to the road? These are all signs of aggressive behavior that, if a situation presents itself, might provoke another driver into causing you or another harm.

17   Of course we would like to think that we are infallible on the roads. We don't go out of our way to provoke another driver, do we? Again, many incidents of road rage are sparked by a momentary loss of good judgment. Most of us are good and considerate drivers under the right conditions. But we still are capable of error. And that error can lead to a serious, maybe deadly, altercation if we say or do the wrong thing. We are not all psychologists; we cannot predict whether another driver is carrying a gun and has the courage to use it.

18   My advice is that we "analyze" our driving behavior the next time we get in our car and drive somewhere. Do we act rational? Or are there moments when we lose our self control? After reading reports and applying their opinions to my own driving situations, I can honestly say that I have a new understanding of how I should act every time I get behind the wheel of my car. I now find it easier to accept the fact that others might see situations from a different point-of-view, even if they are not always positive. I also agree that by not being in such a big hurry, taking on a positive attitude, and being comfortable and relaxed do make a big difference in how I view my driving experience.

19   The next time you get in your car, please make sure you get where you are going safely. If possible, try planning a "safer" route. Try avoiding contact as much as possible: "No one gets angry when they see an empty stretch of highway" (qtd. in Bowles and Overberg 17A). Your driving experience will be more enjoyable and all the negative energy will be replaced by clear constructive thinking. And most importantly, your loved ones will appreciate your safe arrival.

Works Cited

Bowles, Scott, and Paul Overberg. "Aggressive Driving: A Road Well-Traveled." USA Today (23 Nov. 1998): 17A. SIRS Researcher. Access 093679.

Connell, Dominic, and Matthew Joint. "Aggressive Driving: Three Studies." AAA Foundation for Traffic Safety March 1997 10pp. 9 July 1999 <http://www.aaafts.org/text/research/agdrtext.htm>.

Ferguson, Andrew. "Road Rage." Time 12 Jan. 1998. 9 July 1999. <http://cgi.pathfinder.com/time/magazine/1998/dom/980112/society.road_rage_html>.

Incantalupo, Tom. "Rage on the Road." Newsday (4 July 1997): A5+. SIRS Researcher. Access 019026.

James, Leon. "Aggressive Driving and Road Rage: Dealing with Emotionally Impaired Drivers." The Subcommittee on Surface Transportation Hearing March 1997 11pp. 9 July 1999 <http://www.house.gov/transportation/surface/sthearin/ist717/james.htm>.

Joint, Matthew. "Aggressive Driving: Three Studies." AAA Foundation for Traffic Safety March 1997 17pp. 9 July 1999 <http://www.aaafts.org/text/research/agdrtext.htm>.

Mizell, Louis. "Aggressive Driving: Three Studies." AAA Foundation for Traffic Safety March 1997 12pp. 9 July 1999 <http://www.aaafts.org/text/research/agdrtext.htm>.

One for the Road

Scott Sodaro
Com101-40

1   As the weekend approaches, are you making plans to go out with your friends? Are you thinking of going to a bar, listening to some music, and knocking back a few cold ones with your significant other? Are you hoping to meet someone new and after a few drinks, maybe take that someone home for some hot and steamy sex? Are you planning on killing yourself, your friends, and a couple of strangers for good measure? No? Nobody does, but every day, it happens to people just like you and I. How? By drinking and driving. If you are planning to drink, call a taxi, or have a designated driver.

2   Very few people who get behind the wheel after having a few drinks are even aware that their ability to drive has been impaired. The first thing that alcohol affects is judgement. That's the beauty of this beast. It makes you feel like you're still in control when you are not. Not only is judgement affected by alcohol, but your motor skills are affected as well. "It affects every system in the body . . . just about every major organ" (Litten qtd. in Eaton 2).

3   It is true that alcohol in moderation can be beneficial to your health. A glass of wine with dinner can actually help to prevent certain forms of heart disease. No one will deny you your glass of wine. It's when that glass of wine becomes a bottle that you may get yourself into trouble (Eaton 1).

4   Have you ever gotten up in the morning and wondered how you got home from the bar last night? Have you ever gone to the garage after a night of drinking and actually walked around your car, searching for dents? Have you ever woken up with a complete stranger and thought, "Who the hell is this, and how did she get so fat since just last night?" Does this sound like someone who is in control? Yet at the time, it seemed so natural.

5   On the subject of the morning after, how do you usually feel after an all-nighter? Have you ever woken up the next day (I would have said morning, but we both know that it's well into the afternoon), and you just can't seem to focus mentally? For some reason, last night seems like it was last week. Sometimes, things don't seem too clear for several days. "Memory loss and impaired cognitive functions can also last long after a bender has ended" (Eaton 2).

6   This being the case, if you were to get into an accident the next day, it could be successfully argued that it was alcohol-related. Although most people would probably never see the connection.

7   In October of 2000, President Clinton signed a bill which set 0.08 BAC as the legal limit for drivers. The bill makes that limit a national standard. Any state which does not comply with the standard by 2004 will lose millions of dollars in federal highway construction money. Illinois is one of 19 states which now define drunken driving as having a BAC of 0.08. The remaining 31 states still go by the old limit of 0.10, or they don't set a specific standard (Hunt 1).

8   BAC means blood-alcohol content. Each drink is equivalent to 0.015 BAC. "Don't be fooled. The contents of the typical bottle or can of beer, glass of wine, or liquor drink (mixed drink or straight liquor) each contain virtually identical amounts of pure alcohol" (Carrol qtd. in <u>Drinking and Driving</u> 7). Do the math yourself. That means that six drinks puts a person at 0.09 BAC. Some people are unfit to drive after just one drink, depending on their size, weight, metabolism, and how often they drink. The National Highway Traffic Safety Administration warns that lack of sleep and food consumption could also affect an individual's BAC (Hunt 1).

9   As a police officer, I arrest people all the time for driving under the influence. Sometimes I find them before they find something or someone to crash into. Sometimes I don't. In either case, they usually have one thing in common: they don't believe that they are intoxicated. Yet alcohol use has been a factor in almost 40 percent of all fatal traffic accidents in recent years (Hilkevitch 1).

10   How do you know if you're too impaired to drive? You don't. "Alcohol researchers are still trying to figure out how exactly alcohol interacts with the body and the brain" (Eaton 2). If the experts aren't certain, how can you be? You can count the drinks that you've had, and figure out mathematically if you're over the legal limit, but this is not about the legality of your actions. It's about your willingness to live the rest of your life without having to wonder how things might have turned out had you not had that "one for the road."

11   Allow me to paint a scenario for you. It's Sunday in the early part of September, and you've just been at your buddy's house to watch the Bears lose their first game of the season. You've only had four beers. At the very worst, your BAC is 0.06. You are not legally intoxicated. In fact, you feel perfectly normal.

12   You're driving home, and the speed limit is 35 MPH. Your speed is 42 MPH. Again, you're within a reasonable range of the speed limit where most police officers won't give you a second glance. About 100 feet ahead of you, a football has just landed in the roadway, and a seven-year-old boy just ran after it.

13   The process of evaluating a hazard after it has been perceived and then deciding which course of action to take is called a complex reaction. Depending on how complicated the situation is, these can require anywhere from 0.3 seconds to 1.3 seconds. For a person who has had four beers, it can actually take a little longer. At 42 MPH, 1.3 seconds will take you 80.26 feet further down the road. That leaves you slightly less than 20 feet away from the boy.

14   You've now perceived the hazard and have decided to slam on the brakes. At 42 MPH, you are travelling at 61.74 feet per second. You have approximately 1/3 of a second to move your foot onto the brake pedal and bring the car to a complete halt. Do you think you can make it? Do you think that those four beers might affect this scenario? There's no doubt in my mind that the next sound that you would hear would be the sickening thud of that seven-year-old's body being hit by your car.

15   Could you live with that? Would you be able to convince yourself that those four beers had no effect on the accident and that it was just one of those unavoidable disasters? Would you be able to convince that seven-year-old's parents of the same? How about a jury? Is it really worth it?

16   According to Dr. Ray Litten at the National Institute on Alcohol Abuse and Alcoholism, drugs like cocaine, opiates, and psychedelics have focused effects on specific neurotransmitters within the brain. Alcohol affects ALL neurotransmitters across the brain (Eaton 2).

—4—

17   "In 1999, 15,726 Americans were killed in alcohol-related crashes, including over 2,200 children" (Hunt 2). That's just one year. If you play the lottery, figure it out for yourself. You have a greater chance of being one of those people, than you do of winning the lottery. You play the lottery every week, hoping you'll beat the odds, and you play Russian roulette every weekend, hoping that you won't.

18   If you've never had a DUI in your life, I implore you to talk to someone who has. If you have had a DUI, you already know what I'm talking about. Unless, of course, you're one of those fools who believes that you were screwed by the police, and you're still carrying on as usual. You don't get it. That police officer who arrested you was trying to save your life. To you, I say our paths will cross. You may not know my face, but you will know my car. It's black and white with pretty red and blue lights on top. You won't be happy to meet me, but I can hardly wait to meet you.

19   In case you were wondering, to bring a car to a complete stop on an asphalt road with all four wheels locked at a speed of 42 MPH takes 3.2 seconds. You wouldn't have made it. In fact, at 42 MPH with instantaneous braking, you would need 98.65 feet to bring the car to a complete stop. This being the case, if you took any longer than .007 seconds to perceive the hazard and react, you would strike the child. You made two mistakes. First, you drove after those four beers, which may have led to your second mistake of feeling confident enough to drive above the speed limit. Your reflexes were impaired, and there was no way that you could react in 7/100ths of a second.

20   At 35 MPH, you would have had 1.8 seconds of reaction time. These are not guesses or suppositions. These are facts, and they're indisputable. You can't change the laws of physics, but you can change the way that you think about drinking and driving. The choice is yours.

Works Cited

<u>Drinking and Driving</u> Alcohol: Problems & Solutions Site (24 Mar. 2001) 11pp. <http://www2.potsdam.edu/alcohol-info/ DrinkDrive?DrinkingDriving.html>.

Eaton, Tim. "<u>Drink Much</u>." (21 Feb. 2000) 3pp. 24 Mar. 2001 <http://health.aol.drkoop.com/news/stories/feb/drunk.html>.

Hilkevich, Jon. "Drunken Drivers Get Hard-core Attention" <u>Chicago Tribune</u> (03 Jul. 2000) 1. 24 March 2001. Access CTR0007030206.

Hunt, Terence. "Clinton signs Drunken Driving Bill." <u>The Associated Press New Service</u> (23 Oct. 2000) 2pp. 24 March 2001. Access 001023ASP04144271.

THE RESEARCH PAPER: SOME FINAL COMMENTS

I hope this chapter has eased your anxieties and given you suggestions about writing research papers. Regardless of your attitude, you will probably continue to encounter research and documentation with increasing frequency as you continue your education and, possibly, as you go on into a career. I doubt that you'll ever include writing a research paper on a list of your ten favorite pastimes; however, knowing how to research and document properly should give you enough confidence so that you would never place it on your list of ten most-dreaded activities. Having the proper skills and attitude will make the task a lot easier.

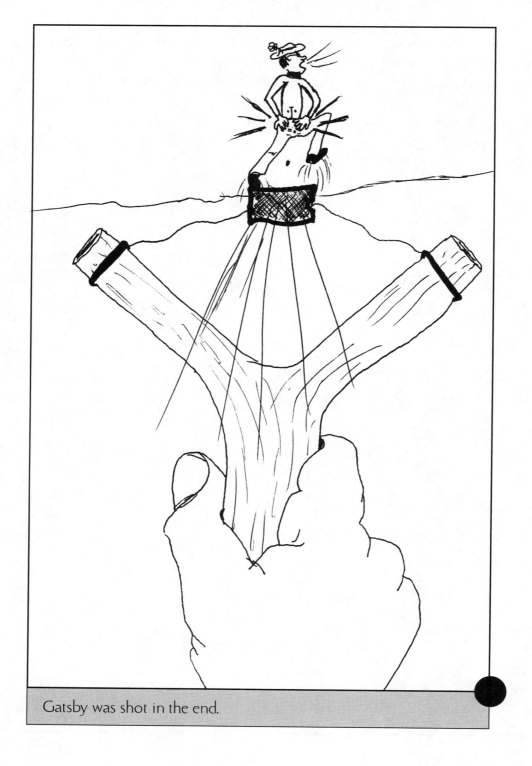

Gatsby was shot in the end.

Name _____ Section _____ Date _____

SELF-EVALUATION SHEET: PART ONE

Assignment: _____

Strong points of this assignment:

_____

_____

_____

_____

_____

_____

Weak points of this assignment:

_____

_____

_____

_____

_____

_____

General comments:

_____

_____

_____

_____

_____

_____

(over)

SELF-EVALUATION SHEET: PART TWO

What were the strong points of your last writing assignment?

_____

_____

_____

_____

_____

_____

What were the weak points of your last writing assignment?

_____

_____

_____

_____

_____

_____

What have you done to correct those weaknesses in this assignment?

_____

_____

_____

_____

_____

_____

Evaluator's Name _____ Section _____ Date _____

PEER-EVALUATION SHEET: PEER-EVALUATOR #1

Writer's Name _____ Essay's Title _____

> **Directions:** (1) Remember not to write on another student's paper. Instead, use this form. (2) Offer concrete, specific comments using the terminology of writing (e.g., "The development in paragraph four might be improved by adding a brief example." or, "Check structure on page 3.")

What do you see as the strong points of this writing assignment: _____

_____

_____

_____

_____

What areas do you feel might need additional work: _____

_____

_____

_____

_____

Do you see any areas of grammar/mechanics (e.g. usage, spelling, fragments) that might need attention: _____

_____

_____

_____

_____

General comments: _____

_____

_____

_____

_____

PEER-EVALUATION SHEET: PEER-EVALUATOR #2

Writer's Name _____ Essay's Title _____

> **Directions:** (1) Remember not to write on another student's paper. Instead, use this form. (2) Offer concrete, specific comments using the terminology of writing (e.g., "The development in paragraph four might be improved by adding a brief example." or, "Check structure on page 3.")

What do you see as the strong points of this writing assignment: _____

_____

_____

_____

_____

What areas do you feel might need additional work: _____

_____

_____

_____

_____

Do you see any areas of grammar/mechanics (e.g. usage, spelling, fragments) that might need attention: _____

_____

_____

_____

_____

General comments: _____

_____

_____

_____

_____

Conclusion

This chapter has the echo of a commencement speech—the old cliche of, "This isn't the end but the beginning." I hope this final chapter *is* a beginning for you.

I feel that teachers who write textbooks about writing and teachers who teach writing have two responsibilities. One, of course, is to teach the concepts of writing. The other responsibility is to help each student to become a good, confident writer, independent of texts and teachers. I hope this is where you are now—a good writer, a confident writer, an independent writer.

As you have worked your way through this text, you have learned through theory and practice the basic concepts and techniques used by writers. If you find yourself facing a writing assignment now—personal, educational, or professional—you should know how to approach it. In fact, you should be able to select from a variety of ways to approach it.

A good point to keep in mind is that writing is a skill, and like any other skill, writing requires practice, attention, and discipline. If you have worked hard at improving your skills in this writing course, don't let them slip. Good writing skills will be useful to you all of your life, whether in school or on the job.

(continued on next page)

Santa, of course, had that tinkle in his eyes.

I hope, however, your experiences and growth in writing skills this semester transcend usefulness. I hope they have given you good feelings about yourself and your communication. I hope you have come to appreciate once again that writing can be a source of feeling good about yourself, your thoughts, your ideas, and your feelings. I hope that we—together—have recaptured some of the magic that walls and crayons once offered you! By the time you reach this chapter, you are about to part company with your writing teacher and with me. But you and your writing are going to continue.

Thanks for using my textbook. When you hold it in your hands, you are also holding thousands of hours of my life which I have dedicated to writing and rewriting in hopes of helping you. Every once in a while, a student of mine will say something positive about the book—and then the student follows up that comment with one like, "but you probably knew that," or, "but I bet you don't really need to hear that from a student." Wrong! When a student takes the time to say I made a positive difference in another person's life, I enjoy it. When a student on campus—a student I don't know but whose teacher uses my book—makes an effort to go out of his or her way to find me and say something positive about this book, I love it! Students also make positive suggestions about what they wished the book had, didn't have, or did differently. When I rewrite, I try to address some of the suggestions and comments. Like all writers, I, too, learn from the comments of others.

I hope this book has helped you learn about writing and about yourself. If you have comments about the book, especially how to make it better, I would appreciate hearing from you. You can write to me via the publisher.

Good luck with your writing in the future.

One of my favorite pieces of music is Swine Lake.

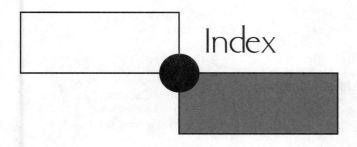

Index